1968 and Global Cinema

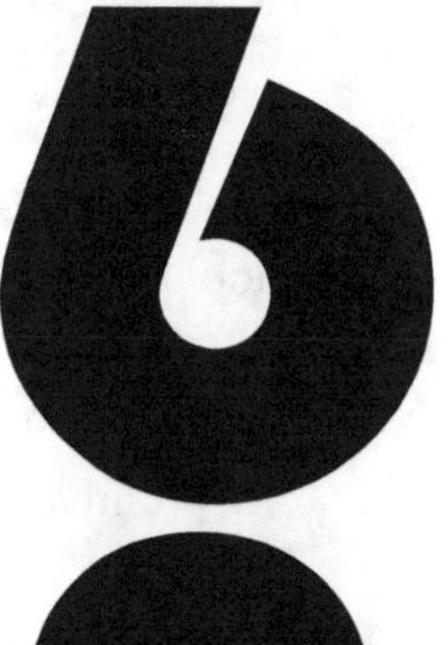

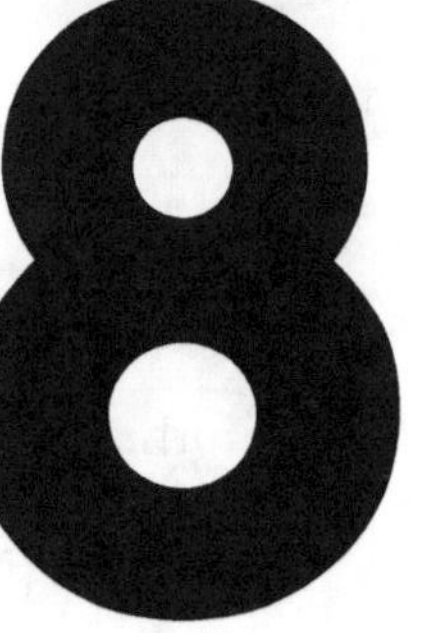

Contemporary Approaches to Film and Media Series

A complete listing of the books in this series can be found online at wsupress.wayne.edu

1968 and Global Cinema

Edited by
Christina Gerhardt and
Sara Saljoughi

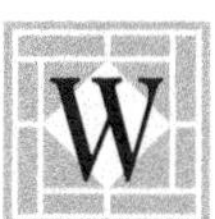

Wayne State University Press
Detroit

Library of Congress Cataloging Number: 9780814342930

ISBN 978-0-8143-4293-0 (paperback)

ISBN 978-0-8143-4542-9 (printed case)

ISBN 978-0-8143-4294-7 (ebook)

Wayne State University Press

Leonard N. Simons Building

4809 Woodward Avenue

Detroit, Michigan 48201–1309

Visit us online at wsupress.wayne.edu

Contents

Acknowledgments vi

Introduction. Looking Back: Global Cinema and the Legacy of New Waves around 1968 1
Christina Gerhardt and Sara Saljoughi

I. The Long Sixties: Cinematic New Waves

1. The "Long 1968" and Radical Film Aesthetics 23
Robert Stam

2. "What Am I Doing in the Middle of the Revolution?": Ennio Morricone and *The Battle of Algiers* 43
Lily Saint

3. Before the Revolution: The Radical Anxiety of Paulo Rocha's Cinema 61
Rocco Giansante

4. The Czechoslovak New Wave Revisited 77
Peter Hames

5. Internationalism and the Early Student Films of the German Film and Television Academy Berlin (dffb) 95
Christina Gerhardt

6. *The Hour of the Furnaces*: A Film "Happening" 117
Rita de Grandis

7. Toward a New Mode of Study: The New Student Left and the Occupation of Cinema in *Columbia Revolt* and *The Battlefront for the Liberation of Japan—Summer in Sanrizuka* 145
Morgan Adamson

8. Oshima, Korea, and 1968: *Death by Hanging* and *Three Resurrected Drunkards* 165
David Desser

9. The Hypothetical and the Experimental: Reading Lindsay Anderson's *If . . .* Alongside Pier Paolo Pasolini's *Teorema* 183
Graeme Stout

10. Obscurity, Anthologized: Non-Relation and Enjoyment in *Love and Anger* (1969) 199
Mauro Resmini

II. Aftershocks

11. Re-presenting the "Just Image": Godard-Gorin's *Vent d'est* and the Radical Thwartedness of Maoist Solidarity after May 1968 219
Man-tat Terence Leung

12. Medium UnCool: Women Shoot Back; Feminism, Film, and 1968—A Curious Documentary 241
Paula Rabinowitz

13. Third Cinema in the First World: L.A. Rebellion and the Aesthetics of Confrontation 273
Allyson Nadia Field

14. The Politics of (In)Action: Humanism, Violence, and Revolution in Satyajit Ray's *Pratidwandi/The Adversary* 289
Sarah Hamblin

15. Maysles Films: Some Paradoxes of Direct Cinema in the 1960s and 1970s 311
J. M. Tyree

16. The Rhetoric of Parapraxis: The 1967 Riots and Hong Kong Film Theory 329
Victor Fan

17. Cultural Revolution Models on Film: The Third World Politics of Self-Reflexivity in *On the Docks* (1972) 345

Laurence Coderre

18. Workers Interrupting the Factory: Helena Lumbreras's Militant Factory Films between Italy and Spain (1968–78) 363

Pablo La Parra-Pérez

19. Political Cinema, Revolution, and Failure: The Iranian New Wave, 1962–79 385

Sara Saljoughi

List of Contributors 405

Index 409

Acknowledgments

Annie Martin, our editor at Wayne State University Press, understood the importance of the book from our first conversation. We thank her for her vision, support, and flexibility as the book grew from idea to a fully realized manuscript.

We thank Barry Keith Grant, editor of the Contemporary Approaches to Film and Media Series, for his enthusiasm and support for the project. We would like to thank the anonymous readers for their generous feedback, which helped shape the volume into the book it is today. We thank Dawn Hall, copy-editor, for working so diligently and precisely. Many thanks to Rachel Ross, the designer of the book, for understanding our vision and exceeding our expectations. We thank the promotions, marketing, and advertising team for their stellar work: Kristina Stonehill, Emily Nowak, and Jamie Jones. Last but not least, we thank Kristin Harpster, Editorial, Design, and Production Manager, for her excellent work.

The book benefited from several conference panels devoted to the topic of 1968 and global cinema at the 2016 and 2017 meetings of SCMS, the 2016 and 2017 ACLA conference, and the 2017 MLA. We thank the MLA executive committee on Screen Arts and Culture for sponsoring the panel on this topic. The papers and audiences at these conferences confirmed our suspicion that there is much, much more to say about the long 1968.

Our deepest gratitude goes to our contributors, whose work has shaped the book into something far beyond what we initially imagined. As *1968 and Global Cinema* developed, we were fortunate to have the involvement of existing friends and colleagues, as well as the formation of new intellectual communities, some of which have already produced new collaborations. We look forward to future conversations and projects generated by this volume.

Introduction

Looking Back

Global Cinema and the Legacy of New Waves around 1968

Christina Gerhardt and Sara Saljoughi

The year 1968 was a watershed that brought about radical political and social changes internationally. These changes are both reflected in and constitutive of new cinemas around 1968. Throughout the 1950s and 1960s, anticolonial wars of self-liberation and self-determination were being waged throughout Africa, Southeast Asia, and Latin America. A vibrant discourse critical of imperialism formed a key node of the social and student movements of the 1960s, with particular attention paid to the transition from the Indochina Wars to the US-Vietnam War. The conditions that these movements sought to change varied from country to country, but their lasting impact and their dialogue is undeniable.

On its fiftieth anniversary, the year 1968 continues to signify predominantly the massive demonstrations by students in France and in the United States. In cinema, too, 1968 is primarily associated with the French or US traditions. The aesthetics and politics of the cinemas of 1968 intersect with new waves, national cinema traditions, political cinemas, debates on realism and modernism, and significant changes in the study of film. *1968 and Global Cinema* takes the occasion of the anniversary of May 1968 to explore the interplay of political and aesthetic affiliations that make up this historical moment, to examine lesser known film cultures engaged in the politics of 1968, and to provide new readings of canonical film texts of what, following Fredric Jameson, we will call the long sixties and the long 1968.[1] As Jameson put it: "Here . . . the 'period' in question is understood not as some omnipresent and uniform shared style or way of thinking and acting, but rather as the sharing of a common objective situation, to which a whole range of varied responses and creative innovations is then possible, but always within that situation's structural limits."[2] The notion of a long 1968 opens the cipher of "1968" to consider how the politics and aesthetics preceding and following this date inform 1968. In order to think of 1968 as "long," a longer, more processual periodization and one that emphasizes a wide-ranging set of artistic, political, social, and economic practices and forces must be taken into consideration.

The influence of both anticolonial discourse and international solidarity movements on film cultures around 1968 forms a key focus of the book. This volume reexamines the complex ways in which the politics and the image of the 1960s were undertaken differently in varied national, linguistic, cultural, and political contexts. As we move into a new century of political cinema, it is ever more vital to write new genealogies and histories of radical cinema. In part, this attempt to write new histories of 1968 and of global, political cinemas attends to the rather belated discussion of the global and non-Western in the disciplines of film, media, and visual studies. In writing this new history of 1968, our emphasis in this volume is on the political and aesthetic affinities across film cultures, the influence of anticolonial discourse, of international solidarity, of discourses of modernism and realism, and of radical documentary traditions. Following Sylvia Harvey, we are analyzing this crucial historical moment "moved by the need to view it and review it in the hopes of constructing a future as well as a past."[3]

Given the wide range of scholarship on May '68 in France, one question that emerges is how to revisit this topic today using a new approach. Our perspective in this book is that although scholarship exists on the late 1950s and 1960s new waves, little research puts cinemas of and on 1968 into dialogue across national boundaries. Most of the published scholarship focuses on the celebrated films of the French New Wave,[4] especially those of François Truffaut and Jean-Luc Godard,[5] and of the Left Bank cinema of Chris Marker.[6] Significant studies consider the legacies of Third Cinema, such as Mike Wayne's *Political Cinema: The Dialectics of Third Cinema*, as well as on individual movements such as Brazilian Cinema Novo.[7] Research on movements such as the British New Wave,[8] and the so-called Angry Young Men,[9] as well as the Czech New Wave has expanded understandings of cinematic new waves during this period.[10] The cinema of the global 1960s has also maintained its various afterlives in part through screenings at film festivals or as special film programming.

Another significant area of research examines the new modes of analysis that began post-1968 due primarily to the influence of Marxism, semiotics, and psychoanalysis on film studies. Sylvia Harvey's *May '68 and Film Culture* focuses largely on the events in France and the broader shifts in film culture and scholarship that developed in and around the politics of the era.[11] In her discussion of these events, Harvey analyzes the critique of modernism and the importance of ideological analysis in the post-1968 landscape. She argues that the specificity of historical cultural struggles must be present in any theory of cultural production, and that the events of May '68 are an instructive instance of this radical new mode of analysis and interpretation.[12] Works such as Peter Wollen's *Signs and Meaning in the Cinema* are exemplary of this shift. Wollen pays particular attention to cinema's relationship to modernism and rethinking the means of representation—an approach that can be found across the cinemas discussed in this volume.[13]

In a different vein, Geoffrey Nowell-Smith suggests that what is signified by "the 1960s" is vastly different and cannot be understood blankly as a narrative of modernization, which he argues has been the dominant characterizations of the period.[14] Rather, he argues the period is rife with discontinuities that, if they had to be reconciled under any narrative, are ones of liberation and independence.[15] Although Nowell-Smith's book examines a wide selection of European cinemas, his admitted limitation of the discussion to Europe does not, in our view, support the notion that "Europe really was the center of most of what went [*sic*] during the period."[16] This notion has guided the study of cinemas of the 1960s, particularly those around 1968. As this volume argues, close investigation of the relationship of cinema to political collectives, anticolonial struggles, workers' groups, feminist movements, and student activism makes it possible to consider "cinemas of and around 1968" in global terms. The politics of the long 1968 make it impossible to understand cinemas of the period through a center-periphery model.

Only in recent years have histories of 1968 begun to consider the relationships among social movements globally.[17] Our emphasis on the *global* dimension of 1968 expands not only the geographies of this important historical period but also the history of current "global" cinema studies. In using the term *global*, we point to the ways in which the film productions of multiple nation-states are present and, more importantly, to the fact that the politics and aesthetics of the "long 1968" were so widespread that they constituted particular instances of the global where they appeared. This statement does not suggest a universal aesthetics or politics across the case studies examined in this book (despite the shared interests in realism, ideology, and modernism). Rather, we hope to point to a coeval aesthetic moment that mirrored the politics of international solidarity. From the vantage point of contemporary film studies, it is our goal to expand what is implied by newly viable terms, such as global, by pointing to a longer and more nuanced understanding linked to radical politics.

Recent studies, such as Rosalind Galt and Karl Schoonover's *Global Art Cinema: New Theories and Histories*, point to the complex significations of the term global, which include not only affiliations across cultures and movements but also the influence of capital and its articulation in organizational structures, for example, in international film festivals.[18] Without suggesting that the term *global* and its appearance in various academic disciplinary discourses can be wrenched away from this connection with capital and the processes of globalization, our goal in this volume is also to point to what was once an entirely different approach to understanding the global, often signified under different terms such as *international*. Thus our approach expands "global cinema" to a longer and more varied history, while also suggesting that the potential then implied by the term ought not lose its potency simply due to the way it is understood in contemporary discourses.

In using the term *1968*, we are taking what that year means or conjures up and including it in a longer periodization of the "global sixties." Geoffrey Nowell-Smith suggests that in terms of film, the 1960s begin in the late 1950s and end "with a gentle fade-out" in the mid-1970s.[19] Focusing on feminist film in the United States, Paula Rabinowitz argues that "the long 1968 for the integration of feminism and film in the United States stretches between 1965 and 1972."[20] The essays in this volume discuss film movements spanning the 1960s and 1970s and produce a longer history of "1968" in addition to a peripheral, horizontal understanding of its global reach. One of the ways that we might organize the cinemas of the long sixties themselves hinges not only on a longer timeline but also on the question of the politics of form. This period differs from the era following World War II (with its exploration of new realisms) insofar as film culture displays an awareness of its role in articulating broader political concerns. As Hermann Kappelhoff notes, "consistent film poetics arose in this time precisely from the diagnosis of the failure of political publics."[21] What Kappelhoff describes as a film poetics refers to an explicit attention to changing the forms of representation. This shift in film language, arguably influenced by Brechtian method, can be seen in political cinemas around the globe. The volume's emphasis on a *global* 1968 seeks to examine the simultaneity of envisioning cinema as a response to the "failure of political publics." Thus, where international solidarity occurred during this period in response to global politics, this volume wagers that this solidarity also manifested in the cinematic circuit.

When conducting research on available publications devoted to the topic, two things immediately became apparent. First, a significant body of scholarship exists on various new waves, such as Italian Neorealism, French New Wave, and Brazilian Cinema Novo. Second, most of this scholarship focuses on the cinema of one nation and rarely moves across national boundaries. Recent publications, such as *Cinéma Militant: Political Filmmaking and May 1968*, have added to understandings of the role of cinema in the French 1968 context by exploring underrepresented elements of the political scene, such as workers, Marxist-Leninist collectives, and militant groups.[22] But the period of the 1960s and 1970s has not been the subject of an analysis of *global* cinema like recent collections that take a particular subfield and examine its global iterations.[23] Although each highlights important and often overlooked dimensions of specific film genres or national cinemas, the contributions to this edited volume move beyond national boundaries to examine international dialogue and collaboration of cinemas around 1968.

One way to consider the shortage in research and publications on a global 1968 is as a reflection of the disciplinary boundaries set by area studies or departments, each devoted to a nationally demarcated linguistic, literary, and cinematic tradition. Yet cinemas around 1968 often engaged—drew inspiration from and in turn inspired—the political content and aesthetic innovations of new wave movements in other countries. Additionally, research in area studies has often been slow to take up the (frequently dissident) work of diasporic filmmakers so pivotal in and to this era. In the disciplines of film and media studies, the question of countercinema, political cinema, and the legacies of the 1960s are often limited to discussions of Europe and Latin America. For example, while the interplay between what Fernando Solanas and Octavio Getino call "Second" and "Third Cinema" is taught in the context of the relationship between Europe and Latin America, countless other "new wave" and political film movements were participants in the broader culture of 1968. These film movements, such as the Polish and Iranian New Waves, often intersect with the political aims of the era of cultural decolonization and anti-imperialism. In this way, film movements outside the context of Europe are intricately connected with political movements in Asia, Africa, and Latin America. Thus, it seems existing discourses of "1968" have not yet been capacious enough to think about this necessary inclusion. Recent research on hitherto overlooked cinemas and film practices in the mid-twentieth century, especially from the non-Western world, demonstrates the need to rethink this crucial moment from the perspective of the global. Works such as Yuriko Furuhata's *Cinema of Actuality: Japanese Avant-Garde Filmmaking in the Season of Image Politics* and James Wicks's *Transnational Representations: The State of Taiwan Film in the 1960s and 1970s*, to name two examples, expand our understanding of the relationship between cinema and radical politics during this period.[24] There has, to date, not been enough analysis of this type of interplay. The goal of this volume is to remedy this gap in the scholarship by examining the relationship among cinemas of the global sixties. It is our wager that this research will generate new insights into film theory, history, and style. This volume seeks to build on the work of transnational cinema studies by undoing the division of cinema studies into fields defined by national boundaries or regions, often designated as "First World" or "Third World." The tendency to organize by national boundaries seems especially unsuited to discerning the specificity of film culture around 1968. Most accounts of non-Western radical cinemas center on the Third Cinema movement of Latin America. Third Cinema, coined by Argentine filmmakers and writers Fernando Solanas and Octavio Getino, mirrored the tripartite "worlding" familiar to the era. Productively, this mirroring provides a counternarrative to the binary landscape created by a Cold War–fixated geographic and political account.

While research in the area of transnational film studies has addressed these concerns, it is our contention that a new conceptualization is needed that considers how the global interplay of the 1960s shifted film language. The contributions to *1968 and Global Cinema* provide a historical and an aesthetic foundation for rethinking global cinemas around 1968. Historically, the volume's contributions engage the era's politics with which many of the films grappled or to which they responded. Select contributions revise notions about cinemas deemed less political, for example, on Satyajit Ray's Apu trilogy, or focus on cinemas less frequently discussed associated with politics as a result of the repressive regimes then in power, for example, the Cinema Novo created during Salazar's rule in Portugal or militant cinema produced during Franco's dictatorship in Spain.

The 1960s, International Solidarity, and (Political) Cinema

It is the wager of this volume that the cinema of the long sixties cannot be understood without taking into account the very real impact of the then ongoing anticolonial and anti-imperial movements taking place and, crucially, efforts to build solidarity alliances worldwide. The post–World War II context or Cold War era certainly hinged on the bifurcated political landscape of the United States (and its allies) versus the Soviet Union (and its allies) or China (and its allies) epitomized by the countries split by the capitalist and communist divide, such as West and East Germany, North and South Korea, or North and South Vietnam. But to read the era solely in terms of this so-called First and Second World landscape leaves the majority of the globe out of the picture, during a time when momentous changes were taking place around the world. Decolonization and independence struggles were being waged throughout the 1950s and 1960s in Southeast Asia and Africa. The Indochina Wars, including the US-Vietnam War, reflected this situation and should be considered part of this wave of anti-imperial movements. Between 1957 and 1977, thirty of Africa's fifty-three nations (including island territories) achieved independence. In 1960 alone ten African nations secured independence from colonial regimes. In countries that had not yet thrown off the shackles of colonization, wars raged and were protracted.

In keeping with our conception of a long 1968, this volume begins with films predating 1968 that articulated these anticolonial struggles taking place in Africa and Latin America respectively: Gillo Pontecorvo's *La battaglia di Algeri/The Battle of Algiers* (1966) and Glauber Rocha's *Terra em Transe/*

Entranced Earth (1967). In his previous *Deus e o Diabo na Terra do Sol/Black God, White Devil* (1964), Rocha had already articulated the legacy of colonization in Brazil and a desire for something new, expressed metaphorically and literally as hunger in his influential essay "The Aesthetics of Hunger" (1965), one of a number of articles that established "Third Cinema." In 1969, Argentine directors Fernando Solanas and Octavio Getino's essay "Towards a Third Cinema"—published in the Cuba-based *Tricontinental*, the journal of the Organization of Solidarity of the People of Asia, Africa, and Latin America (OSPAAAL), together with their codirected film *La Hora de los Hornos/The Hour of the Furnaces* (1968)—put forward key concepts in content and form of Third Cinema. *The Hour of the Furnaces* drew on earlier political cinema and inspired subsequent political cinema. It referenced Sergei Eisenstein's *Stachka/Strike* (1925) and Dziga Vertov's *Shestaya Chast Mira/The Sixth Part of the World* (1926). It also influenced films by the Dziga Vertov Group, which included Jean-Luc Godard and Jean-Pierre Gorin, such as *British Sounds* (1969) and *Pravda* (1969), as well as the L.A. Rebellion's *Repression* (1970).[25] The fact that *The Hour of the Furnaces* was produced under a dictatorship was also a lesson for other countries under authoritarian regimes in Europe, such as Portugal under Salazar or Spain under Franco, or in Latin America, where dictatorships were often brought about by CIA-assisted coups and supported by the US government. *Hour of the Furnaces* pointed out that dissenting films could be made in countries under dictatorships and suggested some strategies for their production and their content. Additionally, Third Cinema not only looked at prior colonial powers but also grappled with ongoing US imperialism. For example, Bolivian director Jorge Sanjinés's *Yawar Mallku/Blood of the Condor* (1969) exposed and critiqued the forced sterilization of indigenous women in the Andes by the US Peace Corps. These writings and films were to a large extent inextricably interwoven with the Third World political movements, such as OSPAAAL and the Non-Aligned Movement.

Julio García Espinosa's "For an Imperfect Cinema" (1969)[26] and Sanjinés's "Problems of Form and Content in Revolutionary Cinema" (1976)[27] also put forward issues of form with regard to political cinema. In his essay, García Espinosa raised pivotal questions about access to the tools and distribution networks related to filmmaking; about the relationship between filmmaking and other forms of labor and of audience; and about whether or not a perfect cinema was even desirable for political cinema. His article suggested, with lasting consequences to the present day, an imperfect or amateur cinema, especially for political cinema.[28] Solanas and Getino's widely read essay addresses similar concerns about models of production, distribution, and exhibition that can stage or enact the changes in representation and film language.

Returning to the interplay among films of the late 1960s, evident in the aforementioned films and texts from South America, *The Battle of Algiers* (1966), which brought the Algerian resistance to French colonization to audiences worldwide, provides an incisive example of international dialogue during this time. The film was screened extensively in Latin America, especially in Argentina, in the United States, where it influenced the Black Panthers, and in western Europe. In the US context, Cynthia A. Young discusses the screening of *The Battle of Algiers* by leftist groups such as the 1199 National Healthcare Workers' Union, which recommended it to members during the 1960s and 1970s as one of many films they should see. Young argues that 1199's film festivals exposed members to films, thereby "shoring up her or his nascent opposition to colonialism or police brutality."[29] Drawing on stylistics associated with Italian Neorealism, the film put forward a gritty black-and-white documentary newsreel aesthetic, combining it with reenactments of guerrilla action, and using many nonprofessional actors. Furthermore, it revised previously hegemonic narratives about the order of influence, historically, politically, and cinematically; that is, its synchronicity with the French New Wave and its focus on decolonization suggests the necessity to shift the conversation on 1968 and cinema from the north to the south.

This argument about *The Battle of Algiers* suggests a new approach to thinking the relationships between European and so-called Third World cinemas, and it underpins the articles in this volume. In collecting these essays under the title *1968 and Global Cinema*, our aim is to put forward the argument that the political forces that led to Third Cinema—namely, colonization and imperialism, influenced the cinema produced in the so-called Third World and that, in content and in form, it impacted the cinemas of the so-called First World. The impact of the Algerian resistance, for example, was not only felt in France. As Claus Leggewie puts it, "What for the older generation was represented by 'Spain' [the Spanish Civil War], was represented for the younger generation by 'Algeria'—[it formed] the early history and layer of the protest movements of the sixties."[30] This reading of the events as they unfolded has, however, shifted since 1968.

Recently, historians and film scholars have revisited these narratives by putting new emphasis on the importance of anticolonial militants and workers, and their solidarity.[31] This shift also underpins the current volume. In *May '68 and Its Afterlives*, Kristin Ross writes that dominant narratives about the 1960s in France reduce events temporally to May 1968 and spatially to Paris's Latin Quarter, which erases workers' strikes[32] and French colonization from history books. Ross argues, however, that "the massive politicization of French middle-class youth in the 1960s took place by way of a set of polemical relations and impossible identifications with two figures so conspicuously absent from this picture: the worker and the colonial militant."[33] Additionally, not only are these two population groups erased, a politics of solidarity is as well.[34] We contend that to insist on returning workers and anticolonial militants by bringing together political cinemas of the 1960s and 1970s is to reject the "grip" of the present, or what Ros Gray and Kodwo Eshun, in a special issue of *Third Text* on the militant image, call "the accreted condescension that the present, in all its accumulated superiority, bears towards the recent yet distant pasts of Tricontinental militancy."[35]

Aesthetically, the volume considers how the new waves of disparate geographic locations influenced one another. In his 2004 article, Dudley Andrew speaks of "An Atlas of World Cinema," which allows film history to be seen as a sequence of "waves . . . rolling through adjacent cultures."[36] Andrew begins with the example of French New Wave, which "buoyed French film in 1959 and rolled around the world, affecting in different ways and under dissimilar circumstances the cinema lives of Britain, Japan, Cuba, Brazil, Argentina, Czechoslovakia, Yugoslavia, Hungary and later Taiwan."[37] While the contributions to the volume attest to this breadth, they also challenge existing genealogies of influence. Despite the range of scholarly works that examine the politics of 1968 in relation to western European cinemas, there is considerably less analysis of this relationship to non-Western cinema. A recent collection of reprinted film manifestos, *Film Manifestos and Global Cinema Cultures*, suggests that the oversight in the scholarship does not reflect a lack of self-identified political film movements that took place during the 1960s. At least sixteen manifestos in the collection relate to radical cinema and come from anticolonial and Third World contexts.[38]

The stylistics of Italian Neorealism after World War II, particularly the use of nonprofessional actors and the focus on class politics and on social reality, would influence subsequent film movements in Europe, such as the French New Wave and Portuguese Cinema Novo, but also farther afield, traceable in Brazilian Cinema Novo, Indian Parallel Cinema, the Iranian New Wave, the Japanese New Wave, and the L.A. Rebellion. The innovations of the French New Wave, stylistically—often deemed to be self-reflexive, calling attention to the very medium itself through its penchant for long takes and tracking shots, as well as its use of jump cuts and break with the 180-degree rule or organization of space—impacted future cinematic movements worldwide, including but not limited to the British and Czech New Waves.

Politically, the cinema of Left Bank directors often encompassed collectively produced films, such as *Loin du Vietnam/Far from Vietnam* (dir. Joris Ivens et al., 1967).[39] Although it is underexamined in the literature on political film, collective cinema played a pivotal role during the era. Chris Marker created the group Société pour le lancement des oeuvres nouvelles (SLON, Society for the Creation of New Works), which encouraged workers to create film collectives and, in turn, to film workers' struggles and the widespread uptick in workers' strikes that took place nationwide in France throughout the 1960s. For example, in 1968, SLON produced *À bientôt, j'espère* (*Rhodiacéta*) about the strike at the eponymous factory. Thus, aside from collective cinema, workers' films also formed an important part of sixties political cinema, focusing on workers' struggles. Moreover, as a number of essays in this volume discuss, cinema that rested at the intersection of collective cinema, produced by workers or by students, and of workers' cinema, played a pivotal role in the long sixties.

While many countries around the world were actively engaged in anticolonial and anti-imperial struggles, numerous nations, including in not only eastern but also western Europe, were living under dictatorships. In countries such as Portugal under Salazar and Spain under Franco, 1968 thus took on a different meaning. In Portugal, Cinema Novo often drew on the hallmarks of earlier Italian Neorealism, focusing on stories of everyday life, using nonprofessional actors and examining the experiences of the working class. In the context of a dictatorship, however, this focus also allowed for a depiction of the quality of life in an authoritarian context, contrasting sharply with a reductive definition of the sixties as revolving solely around sex, drugs, and rock 'n' roll. In reopening discussions of the era's cinema and politics it is our hope that we can shift the conversation about the sixties from one of failure to a more generative analysis of global film cultures and their lasting legacies to the present day: politically and aesthetically.

Overview of the Book

The goal of this book is to revitalize our understanding of film cultures in and around 1968, both by expanding temporally when 1968 signifies, that is, by using the year to refer to the sixties as a period of its own, and by expanding the geography that is implied by "1968." The volume's contributions are organized chronologically, so that as one moves through the analyses, one sees the shifts and developments in aesthetics in different geographic contexts. This organizational approach could also be understood as offering a history of cinematic new waves. In examining the conversations among traditions, the book foregrounds the relations among global political cinemas, particularly those formerly occluded from view by academic, institutional, and disciplinary boundaries.

The first part, "The Long Sixties: Cinematic New Waves," considers the rolling waves of the 1960s, examining the aesthetics of new cinemas and offering new readings of the period's politics in various geopolitical iterations. Robert Stam's essay, "The 'Long 1968' and Radical Film Aesthetics," opens the volume and explores the collaborations between the north and south around 1968. Stam argues that while the impact of Italian Neorealism and the French New Wave on subsequent global new waves is undeniable, the inverse influence of cinemas of the so-called Global South is pivotal for the era's cinema as well. Stam's discussion includes an analysis of the influence of Marxism, semiotics, and psychoanalysis and the changes they brought to the discipline of film studies. In her essay, "'What Am I Doing in the Middle of the Revolution?' Ennio Morricone and *The Battle of Algiers*," Lily Saint also considers a broader relationship, focusing on *The Battle of Algiers* (1966) by Italian director Gillo Pontecorvo, and the anti-Apartheid message being sent by Ennio Morricone's musical composition for the film and other films of his that were often deemed to be less political. In "Before the Revolution: The Radical Anxiety of Paulo Rocha's Cinema," Rocco Giansante examines the development of Cinema Novo in Portugal by a Portuguese filmmaker who had encountered the aesthetic and political revolution of the French New Wave and used it to express opposition to Portugal's authoritarian regime under António de Salazar. Rocha, who had studied filmmaking at the Institut des hautes études cinématographiques (IDHEC, the Institute for Advanced Cinematographic Studies) in Paris, was one of Cinema Novo's initiators. While his first feature, *Os Verdes Anos/The Green Years* (1963), expresses alienation, his subsequent *Mudar de Vida/Change of Life* (1966) inquires into the living conditions of a Portuguese fishing community and expresses opposition to the colonial wars that Portugal was waging in Africa. Peter Hames's article, "The Czechoslovak New Wave Revisited," engages the national and international links of Czech New Wave, looking at the cinematic influences of both the Soviet Union and western Europe. In "Internationalism and the Early Student Films of the German Film and Television Academy Berlin (dffb)," Christina Gerhardt considers the influences on and of early student short films produced at the deutsche film- und fernsehakademie berlin (dffb, German Film and Television Academy in [West] Berlin). While the essay focuses on the relationships among cinemas of various countries manifest in the early dffb, it also touches on the pivotal role early students of the dffb played in sowing the seeds for later workers' films and the second wave feminist movement in West Germany. Rita de Grandis, in "*The Hour of the Furnaces*: A Film 'Happening,'" argues that Fernando Solanas and Octavio Getino's 1968 film must be read in relation to the Argentine Revolution of June 1966 and the proscription of Peronism, which would dominate Argentina in the 1970s, and that the film is a happening, in its suggestion of an active audience that can interrupt at any moment during the film's projection.

In "Toward a New Mode of Study: The New Student Left and the Occupation of Cinema in *Columbia Revolt* (US, 1968) and *The Battlefront for the Liberation of Japan—Summer in Sanrizuka* (Japan, 1968)," Morgan Adamson analyzes two documentaries: The Ogawa Pro's *The Battlefront for the Liberation of Japan—Summer in Sanrizuka* (1968) and the Newsreel Collective's *Columbia Revolt* (US, 1968), and how they electrified the student movements in their respective countries and how the students used cinema as a tool to articulate students' positions in light of the radical transformations taking place in higher education in the late 1960s. Continuing a focus on Japanese cinema but with a decidedly different focus, in "Oshima, Korea, and 1968: *Death by Hanging* and *Three Resurrected Drunkards*," David Desser considers two films by Oshima Nagisa, both released in 1968 and both about Koreans in Japan. Desser discusses the construction of Korean-ness in each film, linking this discussion to the transnational ideals of May 1968.

In "The Hypothetical and the Experimental: Reading Lindsay Anderson's *If . . .* (1968) Alongside Pier Paolo Pasolini's *Teorema* (1968)," Graeme Stout examines how each film breaks with narrative structure—Pasolini's film neglects dialogue and continuity and Anderson's breaks a little over halfway through, opting for a surrealistic collage of images—and uses music to provide a more experimental mode of critique. In "Obscurity, Anthologized: Non-Relation and Enjoyment in *Love and Anger* (1969)," Mauro Resmini focuses on the film *Love and Anger* as an often-overlooked experiment in collective filmmaking. It includes episodes by Carlo Lizzani, Bernardo Bertolucci, Pier Paolo Pasolini, Jean-Luc Godard, and Marco Bellocchio and is emblematic of the global scope of 1968, using an anthology form not only to bring different styles, influences, and political positions into conversation but also to transgress national boundaries. The anthology film, Resmini argues, also prefigures the radical effacement of individual authorship in the work of the Dziga Vertov Group.

The second part of the volume, "Aftershocks," considers the lasting impact of 1968 and related cinematic new waves into the 1970s. The essays in this section range from an examination of Satyajit Ray's Calcutta trilogy and its engagement of the Naxalite movement in Bengal to the greater influence than hitherto acknowledged of French New Waves on the Maysles brothers' films; from China's Cultural Revolution in cinema to militancy and industrial struggle in 1970s workers' films in Spain; and from Hong Kong after 1967 to the dissident cinema of the Iranian New Wave. In these ways, the volume provides fresh takes and allows for new discoveries of the cinemas of the long 1968.

Man-tat Terence Leung's essay, "Re-presenting the 'Just Image': Godard-Gorin's *Vent d'est* and the Radical Thwartedness of Maoist Solidarity after May 1968," focuses on one of the most representative works of the Maoist-leaning Dziga Vertov Group, a collective established in 1968 by Godard, Jean-Pierre

Gorin, and an ensemble of young European Maoists. Reexamining this particular militant film produced shortly after May '68 might actually advance and showcase a new kind of dialectical thinking in political filmmaking that radically departs from, if not violently supplements, the aesthetic paradigm of what Peter Wollen called "counter-cinema." Paula Rabinowitz's "Medium UnCool: Women Shoot Back; Feminism, Film, and 1968—A Curious Documentary" examines feminist filmmaking of the long sixties and its contributions, often overlooked and often experimental, to the era's cinema. Allyson Nadia Field's essay, "Third Cinema in the First World: L.A. Rebellion and the Aesthetics of Confrontation," focuses on the influence of Third Cinema on the filmmakers of the Los Angeles School, arguing that Third Cinema itself was transformed in the process.

Two contributions to the volume take canonical figures of the global 1960s and provide counter-readings of their work, producing new genealogies and configurations of radical cinema. In their examinations of Satyajit Ray and the Maysles brothers, respectively, Sarah Hamblin and J. M. Tyree reject the disavowal of humanist and realist aesthetics in the search for a political cinema. Hamblin's essay, "The Politics of (In)Action: Humanism, Violence, and Revolution in Satyajit Ray's *Pratidwanti/The Adversary*," begins with the notion that although Ray is considered the least radical of the Bengali filmmakers, his work in *The Adversary* demands rethinking this classification. Paying special attention to how dreams and hallucinations organize the style and narrative of the film, Hamblin suggests that the film's humanist aesthetic is integral to its utopian vision. In his essay, "Maysles Films: Some Paradoxes of Direct Cinema in the 1960s and 1970s," Tyree considers cinéma vérité under the rubric of its transnational dimensions. In contrast to arguments that charge Direct Cinema with being apolitical, Tyree provides a historical framework for reexamining the films of the Maysles brothers. Tyree makes the significant argument that the Maysles brothers' emphasis on a realist humanism, rather than on an argumentative cinema, forces us to rethink "the core idea developed in the post-1968 context that radical formalism and political critique inevitably must go hand in hand."

Two essays in the volume's latter half provide compelling new constellations of East Asian film cultures. Victor Fan's essay, "The Rhetoric of Parapraxis: The 1967 Riots and Hong Kong Film Theory," explores the relationship between the leftist riots and film theory in Hong Kong. Fan suggests that a ban on discussing the riots caused film theory to be used as a liminal space wherein the discourse of sociopolitical failure could be reimagined. Fan's essay illuminates how non-Western film theory participated in thinking the relationship of cinema to radical politics. This work constitutes an important dimension of the present volume, for it expands the critical discourse around cinema and the long sixties. In "Cultural Revolution Models on Film: The Third World Politics of Self-Reflexivity in *On the Docks* (1972)," Laurence Coderre reads the Chinese film *On the Docks* as a moment of rejection of the realist imperative in favor of a more radical film aesthetic that mobilizes Third World politics. Coderre regards the transition from the theatrical to the cinematic model as a key moment for Chinese cinema, one in which film's relationship to other media recasts its communicative power.

As stated in the opening of this introduction, one of the aims of the present volume is to draw attention to film movements of the 1960s and 1970s that have been routinely left out of conversations on the era's cinema. To that end, the final two essays in the volume illuminate radical film culture in Spain and Iran. In his essay, "Workers Interrupting the Factory: Helena Lumbreras's Militant Factory Films between Italy and Spain (1968–78)," Pablo La Parra-Pérez examines militant and collective filmmaking, focusing on its relationship to industrial workers who were organizing in nonhierarchical, autonomous assemblies, positing a particular oppositional politics. Through an analysis of the films of Helena Lumbreras, La Parra-Pérez makes a persuasive case for reexamining Spanish cinema under Franco. Like several other essays in the volume, La Parra-Pérez's essay maps a new landscape for cinema in the long sixties by offering a close examination of a previously ignored film movement and by demonstrating its links to better known cinematic movements, in this case in Italy. Closing the volume is Sara Saljoughi's essay, "Political Cinema, Revolution, and Failure: The Iranian New Wave, 1962–79," which examines the diversity of dissident cinema in Iran. Saljoughi argues that Iranian cinema of the 1960s has been ignored due to the association of revolutionary politics with the establishment of the Islamic Republic as well as the politics of the Pahlavi regime. Focusing on films produced prior to the 1979 Iranian Revolution, Saljoughi argues for a re-reading of the Iranian New Wave, one that detaches it from the discourse of failure attached to the 1979 Revolution.

Through an examination of social realist documentary, the political modernism of narrative cinema, and feminist experiments with film form, Saljoughi contends that although it has been overlooked in film history and overshadowed by the postrevolutionary Iranian art cinema, the Iranian New Wave of the 1960s and 1970s was active in the global conversation around cinema and radical politics.

The essays in this volume cover a breadth of cinematic movements that were part of the era's radical politics and independence movements. Focusing alternately on history, aesthetics, and politics, each contribution illuminates conventional understandings of the relationship of cinema to the events of 1968, or the long sixties. The volume aims to achieve balance between new readings of well-known films, filmmakers, and movements as well as new research that engages lesser-known bodies of films and film texts. Through the juxtaposition of these approaches, it is our hope to create new understandings of the period. We seek, in putting these works in dialogue, to encourage new lines of affiliation and new critical genealogies, and to renew interest in a period that has suffered from the discourse of failure attached to radical politics in what is now firmly the era of late capitalism. It is our contention that the interplay of global cinemas so evident in this collection of essays will encourage a new generation of scholars to think anew cinema's relationship to both the "global" and the "radical."

Notes

1. Fredric Jameson, "Periodizing the 60s," *Social Text* 9–10 (Spring–Summer 1984): 178–209. See also Daniel J. Sherman, Ruud van Dijk, Jasmine Alinder, and A. Aneesh, eds., *The Long 1968: Revisions and New Perspectives* (Bloomington: Indiana University Press, 2013).
2. Jameson, "Periodizing the 60s," 178.
3. Sylvia Harvey, *May '68 and Film Culture* (London: BFI, 1980), 1.
4. Peter Graham and Ginette Vincendeau, *The French New Wave: Critical Landmarks* (London: Palgrave/BFI, 2009); Richard Neupert, *A History of French New Wave Cinema* (Madison: University of Wisconsin Press, 2007); Michel Marie, *The French New Wave: An Artistic School*, trans. Richard Neupert (New York: Wiley-Blackwell, 2002).
5. Studies on Godard are too plentiful to tally up. Recent studies include Tom Conley and T. Jefferson Kline, eds., *A Companion to Jean-Luc Godard* (New

York: Wiley-Blackwell, 2014); Douglas Morrey, Christina Stojanova, and Nicole Côté, *The Legacies of Jean-Luc Godard* (Waterloo, ON: Wilfrid Laurier University Press, 2014); Michael Witt, *Jean-Luc Godard, Cinema Historian* (Bloomington: Indiana University Press, 2013).

6. Recent studies include Adrian Martin and Raymond Bellour, *Chris Marker: Owls at Noon Prelude; The Hollow Men* (Brisbane, Australia: Institute of Modern Art, 2008); Nora Alter, *Chris Marker* (Urbana: University of Illinois Press, 2006); and Laurent Roth and Raymond Bellour, *Qu'est-ce qu'une Madeleine? A propos du CD-ROM Immemory de Chris Marker* (Paris: Centre Georges Pompidou, 1997).
7. Mike Wayne, *Political Cinema: The Dialectics of Third Cinema* (London: Pluto Press, 2001). On Brazilian Cinema Novo, see Tatiana Signorelli Heise and Andrew Tudor, "Dangerous, Divine, and Marvelous? The Legacy of the 1960s in the Political Cinema of Europe and Brazil," *The Sixties* 6, no. 1 (2013): 82–100; Lúcia Nagib, *Brazil on Screen: Cinema Novo, New Cinema, Utopia* (New York: Tauris, 2007); Ana del Sarto, "Cinema Novo and the New / Third Cinema Revisited: Aesthetics, Culture and Politics," *Chasqui* 34, no. 1 (2005): 78–89; Robert Stam and Randal Johnson, "Brazil Renaissance, Introduction: Beyond Cinema Novo," *Jump Cut: A Review of Contemporary Media* 21 (November 1979): 13–18.
8. B. F. Taylor, *The British New Wave: A Certain Tendency?* (Manchester: Manchester University Press, 2012); John Hill, *Sex, Class, and Realism: British Cinema, 1956–1963* (London: BFI, 2008); Peter Wollen, "The Last New Wave: Modernism in the British Films of the Thatcher Era," in *Fires Were Started: British Cinema and Thatcherism*, ed. Lester Friedman (Minneapolis: University of Minneapolis Press, 1993).
9. Colin Gardner, *Karel Reisz* (Manchester: Manchester University Press, 2012).
10. Alice Lovejoy, *Army Film and the Avant Garde: Cinema and Experiment in the Czechoslovak Military* (Bloomington: Indiana University Press, 2015); Jonathan L. Owen, *Avant-Garde to New Wave: Czechoslovak Cinema, Surrealism, and the Sixties* (New York: Berghahn, 2013); Peter A. Hames, *The Czechoslovak New Wave* (New York: Wallflower Press, 2005).
11. Harvey, *May '68 and Film Culture.*
12. Harvey, *May '68 and Film Culture*, 117.
13. Peter Wollen, *Signs and Meaning in the Cinema* (London: BFI, 1972).
14. Geoffrey Nowell-Smith, *Making Waves: New Cinemas of the 1960s* (London: Bloomsbury, 2013), 9.

15. Nowell-Smith, *Making Waves*, 11.
16. Nowell-Smith, *Making Waves*, 14.
17. C.f. Kristin Ross, *May '68 and Its Afterlives* (Chicago: University of Chicago Press, 2002); and Quinn Slobodian, *Foreign Front: Third World Politics in Sixties Germany* (Durham, NC: Duke University Press, 2012).
18. Rosalind Galt and Karl Schoonover, *Global Art Cinema: New Theories and Histories* (New York: Oxford University Press, 2010).
19. Nowell-Smith, *Making Waves*, 1–2.
20. Paula Rabinowitz, "Medium Uncool: Women Shoot Back; Feminism, Film, and 1968—A Curious Documentary," *Science and Society* 65, no. 1 (2000): 72–98, at 74.
21. Hermann Kappelhoff, *The Politics and Poetics of Cinematic Realism*, trans. Daniel Hendrickson (New York: Columbia University Press, 2015), 14.
22. Paul Douglas Grant, *Cinéma Militant: Political Filmmaking and May 1968* (London: Wallflower Press, 2016).
23. C.f. Galt and Schoonover, *Global Art Cinema*.
24. Yuriko Furuhata, *Cinema of Actuality: Japanese Avant-Garde Filmmaking in the Season of Image Politics* (Durham, NC: Duke University Press, 2013); and James Wicks, *Transnational Representations: The State of Taiwan Film in the 1960s and 1970s* (Hong Kong: Hong Kong University Press, 2014).
25. For a discussion of *Repression*, see David E. James, "Anticipations of the Rebellion: Black Music and Politics in Some Earlier Cinemas," in *L.A. Rebellion: Creating a New Black Cinema*, ed. Allyson Nadia Field, Jan-Christopher Horak, and Jacqueline Najuma Stewart (Berkeley: University of California Press, 2015), 156–70.
26. Originally published in the 1966/67 issue *Cine cubano*. Reprinted as Julio García Espinosa's "For an Imperfect Cinema," *Jump Cut* 20 (1979): 24–26.
27. Reprinted as Jorge Sanjinés, "Problems of Form and Content in Revolutionary Cinema," in *New Latin American Cinema*, ed. Michael T. Martin (Detroit: Wayne State University Press, 1997), 62–70.
28. C.f. Hito Steyerl, "In Defense of the Poor Image," *e-flux* 10 (November 2009). http://www.e-flux.com/journal/10/61362/in-defense-of-the-poor-image/, accessed August 15, 2017.
29. Cynthia A. Young, *Soul Power: Culture, Radicalism, and the Making of a U.S. Third World Left* (Durham, NC: Duke University Press, 2006), 98.
30. Claus Leggewie, *Kofferträger: Das Algerien Projekt der Linken im Adenauer Deutschland* (Berlin: Rotbuch Verlag, 1984), 9. Translation our own.

31. See Grant, *Cinéma Militant.*

32. Ross, *May '68 and Its Afterlives*, 32. On the Rhodiacéta strike, see also Chris Marker and Mario Marret, directors, *A bientót, j'espère*. Film documentary, 1968, broadcast on French television, station Antenne 2, in February 1968.

33. Ross, *May '68 and Its Afterlives*, 10.

34. Ross, *May '68 and Its Afterlives*, 9.

35. Kodwo Eshun and Ros Gray, "The Militant Image: A Ciné-Geography," *Third Text* 25, no. 1 (2011): 1–12.

36. Dudley Andrew, "An Atlas of World Cinema," *Framework* 45, no. 2 (2004): 9–23, at 21–22.

37. Andrew, "Atlas of World Cinema," 21–22.

38. C.f. Scott MacKenzie, ed., *Film Manifestos and Global Cinema Cultures: A Critical Anthology* (Berkeley: University of California Press, 2014).

39. The collective production of *Loin du Vietnam* can also be considered to account for its "pluralist aesthetic." See Matthew Croombs, "*Loin du Vietnam*: Solidarity, Representation, and the Proximity of the French Colonial Past," *Third Text* 28, no. 6 (2014): 489–505.

I

The Long Sixties: Cinematic New Waves

The "Long 1968" and Radical Film Aesthetics

Robert Stam

What might be called the "long 1968"—for my purposes here roughly from 1966 to 1972—generated scores if not hundreds of radical films in many countries. Here, I will focus on three national cases—France, Brazil, and the United States—in terms of the films themselves and, more importantly, in terms of the debates that swirled around larger issues of politics and aesthetics. At the same time, I will sketch out some of the crucial contextualizations—both political and aesthetic—germane to a deeper comprehension of the films and of the debates.

We can begin with the country often thought to be the epicenter of 1968 radicalism—France. In May 1968, a student-led insurrection almost toppled the Gaullist regime. In the background of the "events" was the crisis of Western Marxism triggered by two 1956 events: the Soviet Communist Party's acknowledgment of Stalin's crimes and the crushing of the Hungarian uprising. In general, 1968 was the product not of the "Old Left"—that is, the Stalinist bureaucratic left of the orthodox communist parties—but rather of the "New Left," which found communist parties strangely passive and complicitous with the bourgeoisie. The revolt failed partly because of the middle-class students' failure to connect with workers, but also because of the refusal of the French Communist Party (PCF) to support a student revolt that the CP ridiculed as "adventurist." Antiauthoritarian, socialistic, egalitarian, and antibureaucratic, the New Left began to move away from a single-minded preoccupation with class and economy toward the integration of the insights of anticolonialism and feminism as part of a broad critique of social hierarchy and alienation.

The phrase "May '68" often serves as shorthand for a much larger phenomenon extending over decades of insurgent thought and practice in many countries. The events in France, while the most spectacular, in some cases actually *followed* events elsewhere. Students and intellectuals in Berkeley and West Berlin, Rio de Janeiro and Tokyo, Bangkok and Mexico City, had all participated in student-led revolts against injustice and oppression as well as against authoritarian forms of communism. In many countries, the mass media and especially network news served to amplify the impact and reach of the social movements.

There was no single, unified 1968. In very broad terms, we can say the movement was Marxist-Leninist in France and in much of western Europe, anti-Stalinist in eastern Europe (with "Socialism with a Human Face" the theme during the "Prague Springtime"). It was Maoist in China, countercultural and antimilitarist in North America, and anticolonialist in the Third World. In some cases, 1968 movements combined the enthusiastic embrace of certain aspects of the American lifestyle with an angry repudiation of US foreign policy, whence Godard's formula (in *Masculin féminin*)—the "children of Marx and Coca-Cola."

Some of the slogans of the time, taken from all three sites, give a sense of the surrealist and anarchist-tinged flavor of the period: "power to the imagination"; "be realistic: demand the impossible"; "chase the cop from your head"; "We are all German Jews"; "Open the doors of the prisons, the asylums, and the high schools"; "don't trust anyone over thirty"; "tune in, turn on, and drop out"; "make love not war"; "two, three, many Vietnams"; "women hold up half the sky"; and "it's forbidden to forbid."

The Seismic Shift and the Decolonization of Culture

Rather than attempt an impossible coverage of the hundreds if not thousands of radical films produced in the three countries in this period, I will address some of the contexts for the radical films and the debates about their politics and aesthetics. First, the film debates take place against the discursive and political backdrop of what Ella Shohat and I have called "the postwar seismic shift" in the thinking about colonialism and empire in the wake of decolonization in what was then called the "Third World" (now the "Global South") and in the wake of the antiracist, anti-imperialist, and antiwar movements in the

"First World" (now the "Global North"). While anticolonial movements were transforming relations *between* nations (colony and metropole), minority liberation movements were transforming social and racial relations *within* nations. Just as newly independent Third World nations were freeing themselves from colonial oppression, so racialized minorities were challenging the white-supremacist protocols of their own societies.

Hundreds if not thousands of writers and activists in the early postwar period participated in this epistemic shift. An early warning of the shift came in 1948 with Sartre's "Orphée Noir" incendiary preface to Senghor's *Anthologie de la nouvelle poesie nègre et malgache de langue française*: "What would you expect, when the muzzle that silenced the voices of black men is removed? That they would thunder your praise? . . . Do you expect to read adoration in their eyes?"[1] Here, the collective self-image of Europeans was being rudely challenged by the dramatically altered subjectivities of the colonized, leaving a severe narcissistic wound and, at times, new openness to the non-European "other." While building on the progressive wing of the Enlightenment, and on the anticolonial thinkers and activists who preceded them, figures such as Hồ Chí Minh, Che Guevara, Julius Nyerere, Kwame Nkrumah, Abdias do Nascimento, Sékou Touré, Amílcar Cabral, Malcolm X, Patrice Lumumba, and Martin Luther King Jr. began to dismantle taken-for-granted racial hierarchies and the intellectual scaffolding of the colonial architecture of the world.

France was a key site in this postwar shift in thinking about race and colonialism. At first, the French government maintained an intransigent colonial posture in the immediate postwar period, initially in Southeast Asia, where the French suppressed Vietnamese independence until the 1954 French army defeat at Dien Bien Phu—when it was replaced by US "advisers"—and then in Algeria, where colonialism ended in 1962 after bitter related political battles in France, too. Much of the French contribution to the intellectual shift formed part of these battles, as anticolonial writers such as the Martinicans Aimé Césaire and Frantz Fanon, Algerians such as Gisèle Halimi, and the Tunisian Albert Memmi, alongside African American expatriates such as Richard Wright, found white French allies in figures such as Henri Alleg, Jean-Paul Sartre, Simone de Beauvoir, Edgar Morin, Francis Jeanson, and François Maspero.

The diverse 1968s had much in common. France, Brazil, and the United States all had their anti-imperialist, anticapitalist, antiracist, antisexist, and antiauthoritarian movements that culminated in the "long 1968" in ways that had serious repercussions within the arts. Such projects were transnational not only in the sense of being allied metaphorically but also in being concretely linked in transnational networks of activism. The movements varied in their emphases, however, depending on whether they took place in the formerly imperial and now authoritarian France of de Gaulle, or in a neocolonized Brazil oppressed by a US-supported dictatorship, or in the United States, which José Martí called the "Belly of the Beast." In France, the vociferously Third Worldist May '68 movement offered its support to revolutions (in China, Vietnam, Cuba, Algeria) and minority US "internal colony" movements (the Black Panthers, the American Indian Movement, the Young Lords), seeing them as partial models for First World revolutionaries. A "tricontinental" united front combined a left-tinged revolutionism with an ardent anticolonialism.

Yet each national situation had its own historically shaped specificities. Fueling the US debates were the first Civil Rights marches and massive antiwar demonstrations. After having helped defeat Nazism in Europe, African American veterans confronted apartheid-style racism in the United States itself. In 1954, the Supreme Court struck down the law dictating "separate but equal" schools on the grounds that "separate" could never be "equal." Rosa Parks refused to sit in the back of the bus, "freedom riders" turned Greyhound buses into vehicles for protest, and many blacks (and a few white supporters) were murdered by white racists. In Birmingham, Alabama, in 1963, thousands of protesters faced police clubs, dogs, and high-powered water hoses. Martin Luther King Jr., in his struggle against segregation, drew on the taproot of two foundational American rhetorics—first, the biblical language of justice, exodus, and the "promised land," and second, the Enlightenment language of the Bill of Rights and the Declaration of Independence—in order to move the larger public toward the preamble's "more perfect union."

The postwar shift in Brazil, meanwhile, took forms both similar to and different from those in France and the United States. In political terms, the post–World War II period was a time of relative democratization after the demise of Getúlio Vargas's authoritarian New State. Right-wing "Integralism" was on the defensive, and democratic movements were on the upswing. Many left Brazilian intellectuals sympathized with anticolonial movements, including in the Portuguese colonies (Angola, Mozambique, Guinea-Bissau, and São Tomé). It was also in this postwar period that Brazilian intellectuals such as Fernando Henrique Cardoso and other shapers of "dependency theory," began to speak of Brazil's status as a "dependent," "peripheral," and "neocolonized" nation. Since Brazil, unlike the United States and France, was not an imperial power, there was no need for a movement against "Brazilian imperialism," only one against US imperialism. And since Brazil was not a legally segregated country, there was no perceived need for massive Civil Rights marches against de jure segregation, which is not to suggest that Brazil should be idealized as a "racial democracy." In Brazil, unlike France (but like the United States), issues of racial difference had always been part of the debate about national identity, whether in the form of romantic "Indianist" discourses or of racist theories of "degeneracy" or of "racial democracy" discourses, or of the black consciousness movements that gathered strength in the late 1960s and 1970s.

From Fanon to the Battle of Algiers

One figure whose work shaped political and aesthetic debates globally was activist and intellectual Frantz Fanon. As a virtual personification of the "seismic shift," Fanon's work deeply affected intellectual life, activism, and the cinema in all three zones. Fanon, whose work built on Césaire's call in *Discourse on Colonialism* for a "Copernican revolution" in thought, became best known as an eloquent critic of colonial oppression and as an astute diagnostician of the twinned pathologies of whiteness and blackness. His work forged a strong link between anticolonial struggles in the Third World with antiracist struggles in the First World (and in the Americas). Forging a link between colonialism and racism, Fanon called attention to metropolitan racial tensions, in *Black Skin, White Masks* (1952), and to Third World revolutions, in *The Wretched of the Earth* (1961). Fanon inspired black liberation thinking around the diaspora, even while he himself was inspired by the Algerian revolution.[2]

Fanon's work was subsequently disseminated not only in France and the Francophone world but also throughout much of the Americas, Africa, and Asia. In Brazil, Fanon became a key reference for African and Afro-diasporic intellectuals-activists, such as Abdias do Nascimento, Clóvis Moura,

Lelia Gonzales, and Yedo Ferreira. Fanon's work helped inspire the "pedagogy of the oppressed" developed by Paulo Freire and the "theater of the oppressed" staged and theorized by Augusto Boal, and anticolonialist artistic manifestos such as filmmaker Glauber Rocha's "An Esthetic of Hunger."[3]

In the United States, Fanon's work became exceedingly well known among black activists and among the left-wing academics who regularly assigned his work in a wide array of fields. Speaking more generally, Fanon provided a formative text for Latin American intellectuals articulating the neocolonial dimension of their histories. Fanon's key anticolonial concepts radiated outward through other movements, impacting feminism (which "gendered" Fanon's three-stage theory of disalienation), situationism (which denounced the metaphorical "colonization" of everyday life), and sociological radicalism (which saw French peasants as "the wretched of the earth").

Although Gillo Pontecorvo's *The Battle of Algiers* (1966) was not a French film, it had everything to do with France and with Fanon, and by implication with colonial-inflected racism in all three of our countries. An Italian Algerian production, the film resonated around the world because it was seen as the first major European fiction feature to treat Third World independence struggles in a sympathetic manner. More specifically, the film reenacts the Algerian war for independence from France, a war that raged from 1954 to 1962, costing France twenty thousand lives and Algeria infinitely more—with estimates ranging as low as half a million deaths and as high as a million and a half deaths. Banned in France and threatened by plastic bombs of the partisans of Algérie Française, *Battle of Algiers* offers a marked contrast with the timidity of 1960s French cinema in treating the war in Algeria.

To a remarkable extent, the film adhered to the actual historical events. In many cases, the names of the characters and their prototypes are the same: Ben M'hidi and Ali-la-Pointe actually existed. Elsewhere, the prototypes existed but their names were changed. Yacef Saadi, the Algerian leader of the "Battle of Algiers" and author of a memoir on which the film was partially based, plays himself in the film but under the name "Djafar." The prototype of Colonel Mathieu was actually General Jacques Massu. As in the film, the French police did actually place their bombs in the Rue de Thebes, the only street in the casbah wide enough for their getaway car. The terrorist bombs were actually placed in the sites depicted: a milk bar, a cafeteria, and an Air France office.

(The Criterion Box 3-F+DVD Box Set includes interviews with the principal actors from various sides of the conflict: the guerrilla leaders who planned the insurrection; the women who carried the bombs; the French generals who conducted the war; and even the secret agents, like Paul Aussaresses, who tortured and killed Algerian fighters.)

But relative historical accuracy was not the only innovation of the film: its innovations were also aesthetic and narrational. First, the film hijacked the apparatus of "objectivity" and the formulaic techniques of mass-media reportage—hand-held cameras, zooms, long lenses, voice-over narrations, TV-News-like titles, technical inadequacies as signs of "authenticity"—to express political views usually anathema to the dominant media. The "reality effect" was so convincing that many spectators took the film to be a documentary, obliging the filmmakers to append a caveat stating that the film contained no archival or documentary footage.

Second, *The Battle of Algiers* went beyond being simply a realistic representation of an anticolonial struggle to become a Fanon-informed analysis of the very revolution about which Fanon wrote in *The Wretched of the Earth*. The film "sees" the events through a Fanonian anticolonialist prism, a result not only of close collaboration with the Algerians during the filming but also of Pontecorvo and Solinas's passionate reading of Fanon. Rather than simply depict the struggle accurately, Pontecorvo "reads" it through Fanonian concepts such as the colonial "two cities" and the violence of the colonized as the reciprocal response to the violence of the colonizer. At times, it seems as if Fanon had written the script. Sequence after sequence provides audiovisual glosses on key passages from *The Wretched of the Earth*, beginning with the film's dualistic conceptualization of a socially riven urban space. The iterative pans linking the native medina and the French city contrast the settler's brightly lit and well-fed town with the native town as a place of ill repute. The dividing line between these two worlds, for the film as for Fanon, is formed by barbed wire and barracks and police stations, where the policeman and the soldier are the official go-betweens and agents of the settler rule of oppression. While the French are in uniform, the Algerians wear everyday civilian dress. For the Algerians, the casbah is home; for the French, it is a frontier outpost. The iconography of barbed wire and checkpoints remind us of other occupations, eliciting our sympathy for a struggle against a foreign occupier. While never caricaturing the French, the film exposes the crushing logic of colonialism and fosters our complicity with the Algerians.

The immense worldwide impact of *The Battle of Algiers* had less to do with factual accuracy than with its deployment of the identificatory mechanisms of the cinema on behalf of the colonized, presenting the Algerian struggle as an inspirational exemplum for other colonized peoples. Interestingly, the issue of identification is at the heart of the work of Fanon and of the cinema itself. For Fanon, the struggle between competing identifications and projections exists at the very core of the colonial encounter. The revolution, for Fanon, mobilizes popular identification; it exorcises the colonizing power that has "occupied" and "settled" even the intimate spaces of the colonized mind. Nation and psyche exist in a relation of homology. National revolution promotes a massive transfer of allegiance away from the metropole as introjected ideal ego. "Identification" formed part of the very process of production of *The Battle of Algiers*. The film became known as the "film where the extras cried." The Algerian extras "identified" so much with the struggle, staged for the cameras just a few years after the events themselves, that they actually wept as they "performed" their grief over the destruction of the casbah.[4]

Subsequent to its release, *The Battle of Algiers* intersected with historical change in very dramatic and multifarious ways. While inspiring tricontinental revolutionaries everywhere and winning awards around the world, the film was banned and bombed in France by the nostalgic partisans of Algérie Française. During the "long 1968," the film resonated with First World resistance movements and Third World and minoritarian struggles and revolts. In the United States, it resonated with the activism against the war in and with the African American liberation struggle, particularly for the Black Panthers who took it as a possible model for urban insurrection.

1968 and Film Culture

In terms of film, the 1960s and early 1970s proliferated in radical movements of political, artistic, and cinematic renovation. In the wake of Neorealism and the new wave, the period saw the emergence of many national film movements, whose names usually included variations of the word "new": Cinema Novo in Brazil, Nueva Ola in Mexico, Neues Deutsches Kino in Germany, New

American Cinema in the United States, Tercer Cine in Argentina, New Indian Cinema in India, and Giovane Cinema in Italy.

The events of 1968 had momentous repercussions in the world of the arts generally and in film specifically. Many of the films, and the theories on which they were based, conducted a struggle on two fronts, the political and the aesthetic. In France, the student-led May insurrection was preceded and foreshadowed by "L'affaire Langlois," the attempt by the French left (including filmmakers Truffaut, Godard, and Rivette, along with Roland Barthes) to reinstate Henri Langlois as director of the French Cinémathèque after he had been fired by the Minister of Culture André Malraux. In May, in the name of solidarity with striking students and workers, prestigious French filmmakers called for the closing of the Cannes Film Festival, a movement that culminated with Godard and Truffaut literally "closing the curtain" on the festival. Calling up the memory of the French revolution and the "three estates" (nobility, clergy, and the people), leftist filmmakers also tried to create an updated cinematic equivalent of the French revolution through the short-lived États Generaux du Cinéma. Among its audacious proposals were the complete abolition of censorship and the Centre National du Cinéma (CNC, National Center of Cinematography), free movie screenings, the development of new screening venues such as factories, farms, the publicly financed film screenings, state support for noncommercial films, universal education in filmmaking, and, more generally, a cinema unencumbered by the profit motive. (Long thought utopian, some of these measures have been realized, at least within the French school system.)

May 1968 was preceded by Guy Debord's manifesto-book *Society of the Spectacle* (1967) in which the leader of the Situationist International, in an aphoristic style, argued that life in modern society displays itself as an immense accumulation of spectacles. For Debord, the state capitalism of the socialist bloc and the market capitalism of the West alienated workers through the ghastly unity of a passively consumed "spectacle." (In 1973, Debord turned the book into a compilation film that superimposed Marxist commentary on found film materials.) The Situationists also challenged the art system itself, calling not for a "critique of revolutionary art" but rather for "a revolutionary critique of all art."

The first "1968 film," ironically, was released in 1967. The film was Godard's *La Chinoise*, an ironic portrayal of a Maoist cell in Paris. At first dismissed as wildly improbable, the film came to be seen as prescient and even prophetic as the public became aware of the massive role of Maoist activists in the "events of May." In 1967 the collective anti–Vietnam War film *Loin de Vietnam* was released, produced by Chris Marker and featuring sequences and materials by Jean-Luc Godard, Agnès Varda, Alain Resnais, Claude Lelouche, Joris Ivens, and American expatriate William Klein. The year 1968, meanwhile, brought *Weekend* (1968), Godard's anarchistic satire of French bourgeois society, and Chris Marker's *Le Joli Moi de Mai* (1968) about the mass rallies and the police repression during May.

During May '68, one form of filmic intervention consisted of anonymous *ciné-tracts*, which orchestrated still photos of demonstrations, the recorded sounds of militancy, voice-over commentary, and intertitles relaying the slogans of the day. One of the most famous *ciné-tracts* featured a photo of a Parisian graffiti equating the CRS (de Gaulle's militia) with the Nazi SS. Chris Marker was a key figure in the largely student-fueled *ciné-tract* movement and a guiding force in the attempts to "put cameras in the hands of the workers," through his efforts with Société pour le lancement des oeuvres nouvelles (SLON, Society for the Creation of New Works) in collaboration with French factory workers.

Acknowledging the internationalism of 1968, the radical French filmmakers did not limit their endeavors to their own country of origin. Godard made films about the student movements in the United States and Italy. Chris Marker made radical films about politics in the other two countries under discussion here. In Brazil, he made a film about torture under the dictatorship (*Speaking of Torture in Brazil*, 1969) and about a famous Marxist writer, politician, and guerilla, in *Speaking about Brazil—Carlos Marighela* (1970). And in the United States, Marker's *The Sixth Face of the Pentagon* (1968) addressed the mass rallies of the antiwar movement and specifically the March on the Pentagon. Agnès Varda, meanwhile, made films about African American radicalism (*Black Panthers*, 1968) and the American counterculture (*Lion's Love* [. . . *and Lies*] in 1969).

In the United States, meanwhile, 1968 brought such iconic radical films as the Godard-influenced film *Medium Cool* (1969) by Haskell Wexler. The film, whose final shot of a camera aimed at the spectator forms an homage to the opening shot of Godard's *Contempt* (1963), mingles actors with actual events, specifically the violent police repression of the antiwar protests during the 1968 Democratic Convention in Chicago. The period also brought counterculture films like the San Francisco–set *Revolution* (1968) by Jack O'Connell, along with more whimsically antiwar films like *Alice's Restaurant* (1969). In terms of documentaries, the radical collective Newsreel, founded in 1967, produced revolutionary films about a wide array of topics: black activism (*Black Panther*, 1967); the March on the Pentagon (*No Game*, 1968); student activism (*Columbia Revolt*, 1968); labor struggles (*Richmond Oil Strike*, 1969); and police brutality (*Pig Power*, 1969).

Another collective produced a searing account of a war crimes trial conducted by Veterans against the Vietnam War in Detroit in 1971. The film, titled *Winter Soldier* (1972), featured young veterans bearing witness to the brutality they saw (and sometimes themselves committed), expressing their utter rage and visceral contempt for the militaristic and classist system that sent them to Vietnam to kill and be killed. Pointing to a photo of himself grinning next to a heap of Vietnamese corpses, one veteran exhorts the audience to "never let any government do that to you . . . never let them turn you into the fool you see in that image!"

If in the United States the major issues were racism and war, and if in France the major issues were primarily Gaullist authoritarianism, the class system and a colonial Vietnam War, which France itself had perpetrated even before the Americans, in Brazil the major issues had to do with hunger and injustice in the northeast, social oppression in the favelas, and the US-supported dictatorship imposed in 1964. By 1968, the situation had evolved from what Brazilians punningly called the *Ditamole* (Soft Dictatorship), to *Ditadura* (Hard Dictatorship), which brought increasing censorship, political repression, and the murder of dissidents as "internal enemies" of the state. This political moment generated socially powerful and artistically innovative Cinema Novo films treating the favelas (the anthology film *Cinco Vezes Favela*, 1962), poverty in the arid northeast (e.g., *Vidas Secas* in 1963, *Black God, White Devil* in 1964) along with allegorical films about dictatorship and imperialism such as Glauber Rocha's *Terra em Transe* (1967), a trance-modernist parable about the "tragic carnival of Brazilian politics"; Joaquim Pedro de Andrade's

Macunaima (1968), a revisionist and updated antimilitarist version of Mario de Andrade's 1928 modernist novel; and Nelson Pereira dos Santos's *How Tasty Was My Frenchman* (1971), a lesson in cultural relativism and a cannibalistic allegory that deployed a sixteenth-century story about the French colony in Brazil to indirectly address twentieth-century genocide and authoritarianism.

From the Avant-Gardes to Transmodernism

The long 1968 period was also marked by the proliferation of Marxist and left-leaning film journals such as *Positif*, *Cinétique*, *CinémAction*, and (the newly leftish) *Cahiers du Cinéma* in France; *Screen* and *Framework* in England; *Cine-Tracts* and later *Cine-Action* in Canada; *Jump Cut* and *Cineaste* in the United States; *Ombre Rossi* and *Filmcritica* in Italy; *Hablemos de Cine* in Peru; and *Cine Cubano* in Cuba and *Filme Cultura* and *Cine-Olho* in Brazil. The leftist film theory of the period asked such questions as the following: What is ideology and how are ordinary people deluded by it to misrecognize their own social conditions? What is the ideological role of what Frankfurt School theorists called the "culture industry"? What are the social determinants of the film industry? Is the cinematic apparatus itself bourgeois in orientation or is it a neutral instrument that can be used by any political tendency? How do class and gender and sexuality operate within the process of filmmaking? Should films be the creations of auteurs, or of political collectives? Should revolutionary films first of all be revolutionary *as art*, as Walter Benjamin suggested? Should films imitate mainstream entertainments in order to win over an audience accustomed to such entertainments? Is there a Marxist aesthetic? An anarchist aesthetic? A Maoist aesthetic? What is the role of social class in the production and reception of films? What style and narrative structures should filmmakers adopt, and what strategies should critics deploy to analyze film politically? How can films advance social struggles for justice and equality?

But to understand why these were the questions being asked, we have to open a parenthesis about another key historical context—artistic modernism. The term refers to the various movements in the arts (both in and outside of Europe) that emerged in the late nineteenth century, flourished in the early decades of the twentieth century, and became ambiguously institutionalized as "high modernism" after World War II. The agenda of a series of movements forming the historical avant-gardes—"expressionism," "cubism," "surrealism,"

"Dada," "anthropophagy"—often became synonymous with the aspirations of radical artists. Radical forms of modernism were rooted in the utopia of a transformative liaison between the aesthetic and the political avant-gardes. The filmic possibilities of such a liaison were best glimpsed, perhaps, in Eisenstein's unrealized project of an adaptation of Karl Marx's *Das Kapital*, which would show spectators how to "think dialectically" in a film whose style would be inspired by Joyce's *Ulysses*. The phrase "political modernism" embedded the prospect of a euphoric tryst between the two avant-gardes by mobilizing the energies of these movements in favor of the transformation of social and political life. Peter Bürger, in *Theory of the Avant-Garde*, refined the argument by distinguishing between a radical avant-garde—for example, surrealism and Dada—which attacked the bourgeois canons and institutions of art in the name of transforming social life, as opposed to an apolitical high modernism that merely institutionalized the formal innovations of movements like cubism and abstractionism.[5]

The radical cinemas of the late 1960s built on the heritage of the *two avant-gardes* that achieved a tentative symbiosis during certain privileged historical moments, for example, in the experimental 1920s films and theories of Eisenstein and Vertov in the postrevolutionary Soviet Union, movements that later inspired some of the 1968 movements. Working against the backdrop of the remarkable flowering of experimentation in theater, painting, literature, cinema, and theory, these filmmaker-theorists combined radical ideas with the practical challenge of constructing a socialist film industry. Mingling creative audacity with political efficacy, these artists—despite the diversity of their theories and styles—privileged montage as the basis for a socialist cine-poetics. In incendiary essays and manifestos, Dziga Vertov pronounced a death sentence on "profiteering" cinema. The filmmaker's obligation, for Vertov, was to expose mystifications as part of the "communist deciphering of the world" while also celebrating socialist collectivity. Rather than see art as transcendently above the fray of the everyday life of social production, Vertov saw art as existing on a continuum with that production.[6]

Four decades later, the *two avant-gardes* converged again in the 1960s film movements, notably in the various new waves around the world: Jean-Luc Godard and Chris Marker in France; Glauber Rocha and Leon Hirzman in Brazil; Haskell Wexler and Joseph Losey in the United States, Tomás Gutiérrez

Alea and Santiago Álvarez in Cuba; Fernando Solanas and Octavio Getino in Argentina; Alexander Kluge and Rainer Werner Fassbinder in Germany; Mrinal Sen in India. In Brazil, Glauber Rocha proposed the reinvention of Latin American film language through a synthesis of the neorealism of Zavattini and the transrealism of Eisenstein. Many Latin American filmmakers cited Eisenstein in their writing and alluded to his work in their films: Rocha evoked the "Odessa Steps" and the rotting-meat sequence from *Potemkin* in his satirical portrayal of right-wing dictatorship in *Terra em Transe*, while Silvio Tendler in *Jango* juxtaposed Eisenstein's staging of the Potemkin mutiny with footage showing popular support for a real-life mutiny in the Brazil of the early 1960s. Filmmaker and theorist Gutiérrez Alea, for his part, in his essay book *Dialectics of the Spectator*, proposed a "viewer's dialectic"—a synthesis of Eisensteinian "pathos" and Brechtian "distance," with both seen from the vantage point of Latin American cultural politics. Citing Brecht, Gutiérrez Alea rejected the emotion/reason dichotomy, seeing emotion as stimulating reason, and reason as purifying emotion.[7]

Gutiérrez Alea was not alone in referencing German dramatist Bertolt Brecht, for leftist film theory and practice of the 1960s and 1970s in Europe and the Third World generally drew from the taproot of Brecht's Marxist-inflected critique of the dramatic realist model operative in traditional theater and in the Hollywood film. The performances of *Mother Courage* by the Berliner Ensemble at the Theater of Nations in Paris in 1956, the year of Brecht's death, attended by many French critics and artists, and the subsequent laudatory essays penned by Roland Barthes and Bernard Dort, fueled the Brecht mania in France. In 1960, the film journal *Cahiers du Cinéma* dedicated a special issue to the German playwright, marking the first stages of a politicizing tendency within art cinema that reached its apogee in the late 1960s and the 1970s. The Brechtian critique influenced not only countless film theorists, such as Jean-Louis Comolli, Peter Wollen, Colin MacCabe, but also countless filmmakers, among them Orson Welles, Joseph Losey, Jean-Luc Godard, Alain Resnais, Marguerite Duras, Glauber Rocha, Ruy Guerra, Jean-Marie Straub and Danièlle Huillet, Dušan Makavejev, R. W. Fassbinder, Alexander Kluge, Tomás Gutiérrez Alea, Alain Tanner, Nagisa Oshima, Mrinal Sen, Herbert Ross, Haskell Wexler, and myriad other filmmakers.

Already hostile to the "First Cinema" of Hollywood, politically radical filmmakers drew on Brecht to shape their alternative aesthetics. In the various essays collected in *Brecht on Theatre*, Brecht theorized his general goals for the theater and detailed specific techniques for their realization, many of them subsequently extrapolated to the sister-art of film.[8] Repelled by the reactionary exploitation of pathos in the sentimental form of bourgeois drama and in the racist form of Nazi spectacle, Brecht rejected the totalizing aesthetic of the Wagnerian *Gesamtkunstwerk*, that is, the total work of art that enlisted all the theatrical "tracks" (lighting, staging, acting, music) in the service of a single, overwhelming emotion. The redundant Hollywoodean style, whereby all of the various tracks coax the spectator toward exactly the same visceral/emotive effect—attractive stars plus profilmic kiss plus backlighting plus romantic Chopinesque music equals a romance effect—could be called Wagnerian in the totalizing sense of the word. The ultimate goal, for Brecht, was to use alienation effects (*Verfremdungseffekt*) to decondition spectators and "estrange" their lived social world, freeing socially conditioned phenomena from the "stamp of familiarity," and revealing them as other than "natural."[9]

Sur-realismo and an Aesthetics for the Global South

In still another discursive-cultural context, 1968 was the highpoint of "Third World Cinema" also known as "Tricontinental Cinema" in a reference to filmic representatives of the colonized or formerly colonized regions of the world. In relation to cinema, the term "Third World" was empowering in that it called attention to the collectively vast cinematic productions of Asia, Africa, and Latin America and of minoritarian cinema in the First World. Just as peoples of color form the global majority, so the cinemas of people of color form the majority cinema, and it is only the notion of Hollywood as the only "real" cinema that obscures this fact. The notion of "Third Cinema" emerged from the Cuban Revolution, from Peronism and Peron's "third way" in Argentina, and from such film movements as Cinema Novo in Brazil. Aesthetically, the movement drew on currents as diverse as Soviet montage, Brechtian epic theater, Italian Neorealism, and even the Griersonian "social documentary." The term was launched as a rallying cry in the late 1960s by Fernando Solanas and Octavio Getino, who define Third Cinema as "the cinema that recognizes in [the anti-imperialist struggle in the Third World and its equivalents within the imperialist countries] . . . the most gigantic cultural, scientific, and artistic manifestation of our time . . . in a word, the decolonization of cultures."[10]

In the wake of the Vietnamese victory over the French in 1954, the Cuban Revolution in 1959, and Algerian independence in 1962, Third-Worldist film ideology was crystallized in a wave of militant film manifesto-essays not only by Solanas and Getino but also by figures such as Glauber Rocha and Julio García Espinosa, in formulations that strove both to incorporate and to go beyond Brecht. That a country was economically underdeveloped, Glauber Rocha suggested, did not mean that it had to be artistically underdeveloped. For Rocha, Italian Neorealism and Soviet-style socialist realism and even Brecht were flawed models for Third World cinema. Playing on the Spanish word for "south" (*sur*), Rocha called for "sur-realismo" or a sur-realism for the Global South.

In a 1965 manifesto-essay, Rocha called for an "aesthetics of hunger," expressed in a "hungry" cinema of "sad, ugly films," which treated hunger not only as a theme but also as a low-cost production strategy, turning scarcity into a carrier of affect and meaning.[11] In a displaced form of mimesis, the material poverty of a low-budget style would form the two-dimensional filmic correlative of poverty and the bodily pangs of hunger in the three-dimensional world depicted in the film. Breaking with humanist paternalism and the folklorization of misery, Rocha argued that Latin America's originality was inseparable from its hunger, the noblest cultural manifestation of which was violence, including the symbolic violence to cinematic decorum. In a displaced form of Fanonian insurrectionism, social violence would be performed and allegorized not only in socially typical realist depictions but also through the aesthetic violence to the norms and production values of dominant cinema.

Even before Rocha coined the talismanic phrase "the aesthetics of hunger," that aesthetic was embodied in Nelson Pereira dos Santos's *Vidas Secas*, a film about hungry migrant peasants from Brazil's arid northeast. In a perfect isomorphism that simultaneously embraced austere production method, backlands theme, pitiless backlands light, and a "famished" aesthetic, the film offered a sterling example of Rocha's aesthetic model. In an aesthetic proposal realized brilliantly in his 1967 film *Terra em Transe*, meanwhile, Rocha argued for a politicized auteurism generative of films that would be technically imperfect, dramatically dissonant, poetically rebellious, and sociologically imprecise. Questioning the bedrock foundations of dramatic-realist entertainments, Rocha excoriated cinematic populism as the expression of a pseudo-radical and authoritarian regime of political representation relayed by a populist style of filmic representation. Paternalistically assuming that art should speak to the people in simple and transparent language in the name of facile communication, cinematic populism, for Rocha, practices a sugar-coated pill theory of art. It packages popular Brazilian culture in a Hollywood format—coconut milk in a Coca-Cola bottle. To get its message across, film populism gives the public its habitual dose of saccharine gratifications—a Manichaean conflict, a charming love story, a luxuriant spectacle, a happy resolution—in order to make the ideological medicine, as it were, "go down." Populism treats the audience as intellectually handicapped, in need of a prettified and simplistic version of social complexities. Like populist politics, cinematic populism turns the people into mere extras; they lose their collective identity as a class and become an amorphous mass of obedient individuals and spectators.

The debates, as we have seen, were both similar and distinct in the various countries. In Brazil, radical filmmakers were fighting a military dictatorship. Whereas the Vietnam War was a major concern in the United States especially, and secondarily in France, it was not in the foreground in Brazil. Filmmakers and theorist/critics at the time of the long 1968 were asking themselves such questions as: How could cinema struggle against the dictatorship in an era of censorship? What strategies might be effective? What production strategies were most appropriate to Brazil's situation as a neocolonized country where Hollywood dominated distribution and exhibition? What was the role of the state? Was it the disinterested protector of national cinema vis-à-vis foreign interests or was it allied with them and with conservative forces in Brazil? How could Brazilian cinema capture the market in the face of Hollywood domination? What cinematic language was the most appropriate? Should it wrap radical content in Hollywood forms, in order to attract an audience, or make a radical break through an aggressive "aesthetics of hunger" or an "aesthetics of garbage?" To what extent should Brazilian cinema incorporate popular cultural forms such as *samba*, *candomble*, and *literatura de cordel*? Should the films adopt classical narrative and dramatic storytelling strategies, or be anti-illusionist, reflexive, antinarrative, antispectacular, in short avant-garde? What was the relation between the largely middle-class directors and the "people" whom they purported to serve and represent? Should they be a cultural vanguard speaking ahead of and for the people, or merely be the passive mouthpieces of the people, the advocates of popular and mass culture, or the critics of its alienation? Many of these questions have to be modified in the light of changes in the medium and historical shifts in power—for example, the digital revolution, the decline of movie theaters, postcelluloid film, globalization, financialization, and so on—but with some reformatting they remain highly relevant to twenty-first-century concerns.

Notes

1. See Jean-Paul Sartre, "Orphée Noir," in *Anthologie de la Nouvelle Poesie Nègre et Malgache de Langue Française*, ed. Léopold Sédar Senghor (Paris: Presses Universitaires de France, 2015), 7. Translation the author's.
2. See Aime Césaire, *Discourse on Colonialism* (New York: Monthly Review Press, 1972). See Frantz Fanon, *Black Skin, White Masks* (New York: Grove Press, 1967) and *The Wretched of the Earth* (New York: Grove Press, 1964).
3. See Paulo Freire, *Pedagogy of the Oppressed* (New York: Continuum, 2007); Augusto Boal, *Theater of the Oppressed* (New York: Theatre Communications Group, 1993); Glauber Rocha, "An Esthetic of Hunger," in *Brazilian Cinema*, ed. Randal Johnson and Robert Stam (New York: Columbia University Press, 1995), 68–71; and Tomás Gutiérrez Alea, *Dialéctica del Espectador* (Havana: Union de Escritores y Artistas de Cuba, 1982).
4. For an analysis of *Battle of Algiers*, see Robert Stam and Ella Shohat, eds., *Unthinking Eurocentrism: Multiculturalism and the Media* (London: Routledge, 1994). For a detailed account of the production of *Battle of Algiers*, see Irene Bignardi, "The Making of *The Battle of Algiers*," *Cineaste* 25, no. 2 (2000): 14–22; and Alan O'Leary, "The Battle of Algiers at Fifty: End of Empire Cinema and the First Banlieu Film," *Film Quarterly* 70, no. 2 (2016): 17–29.
5. Peter Bürger, *Theory of the Avant-Garde* (Minneapolis: University of Minnesota Press, 1984).
6. Annette Michelson, ed., *Kino-Eye: The Writings of Dziga Vertov*, trans. Kevin O'Brien (Berkeley: University of California Press, 1995).
7. See Tomás Gutiérrez Alea, *Dialéctica del Espectador* (Havana: Union de Escritores y Artistas de Cuba, 1982).
8. See Bertolt Brecht, *Brecht on Theatre* (New York: Hill and Wang, 1964).

9. For an extensive discussion of the serious limitations as well as the artistic/political potentialities of a Brechtian approach, see Robert Stam, with Leo Goldsmith and Richard Porton, *Keywords in Subversive Film/Media Aesthetics* (Malden, MA: Wiley-Blackwell, 2015).
10. Octavio Getino and Fernando Solanas, "Hacia un Tercer Cine (Towards a Third Cinema)," *Tricontinental* (1969): 107–32. https://ufsinfronteradotcom.files.wordpress.com/2011/05/tercer-cine-getino-solonas-19691.pdf, accessed April 9, 2016.
11. See Rocha, "An Esthetic of Hunger," 68–71.

Bibliography

Bignardi, Irene. "The Making of *The Battle of Algiers*." *Cineaste* 25, no. 2 (2000): 14–22.

Boal, Augusto. *Theater of the Oppressed*. New York: Theatre Communications Group, 1993.

Brecht, Bertolt. *Brecht on Theatre*. New York: Hill and Wang, 1964.

Bürger, Peter. *Theory of the Avant-Garde*. Minneapolis: University of Minnesota Press, 1984.

Césaire, Aime. *Discourse on Colonialism*. New York: Monthly Review Press, 1972.

Fanon, Frantz. *Black Skin, White Masks*. New York: Grove Press, 1967.

———. *The Wretched of the Earth*. New York: Grove Press, 1964.

Freire, Paulo. *Pedagogy of the Oppressed*. New York: Continuum, 2007.

Getino, Octavio, and Fernando Solanas. "Hacia un Tercer Cine (Towards a Third Cinema)." *Tricontinental* (1969): 107–32.

Gutiérrez Alea, Tomás. *Dialéctica del Espectador*. Havana: Union de Escritores y Artistas de Cuba, 1982.

Michelson, Annette, ed. *Kino-Eye: The Writings of Dziga Vertov*. Trans. Kevin O'Brien. Berkeley: University of California Press, 1995.

O'Leary, Alan. "The Battle of Algiers at Fifty: End of Empire Cinema and the First Banlieu Film." *Film Quarterly* 70, no. 2 (2016): 17–29.

Rocha, Glauber. "An Esthetic of Hunger." In *Brazilian Cinema*, edited by Randal Johnson and Robert Stam, 68–71. New York: Columbia University Press, 1995.

Sartre, Jean-Paul. "Orphée Noir." Preface. In *Anthologie de la Nouvelle Poesie Nègre et Malgache de Langue Française*, edited by Léopold Sédar Senghor, ix–xliv. Paris: Presses Universitaires de France, 2015.

Stam, Robert, and Ella Shohat, eds. *Unthinking Eurocentrism: Multiculturalism and the Media*. London: Routledge, 1994.

Stam, Robert, Leo Goldsmith, and Richard Porton. *Keywords in Subversive Film/Media Aesthetics*. Malden, MA: Wiley-Blackwell, 2015.

2

"What Am I Doing in the Middle of the Revolution?"

Ennio Morricone and *The Battle of Algiers*

Lily Saint

In 1966, two years before the events that would come to be known as '68, Ennio Morricone scored thirteen different films including Gillo Pontecorvo's landmark work of anticolonial political cinema, *La battaglia di Algeri/The Battle of Algiers* (Italy, 1966). Five of his other soundtracks that year were composed for that less discernably political genre, the western, including scores for Sergio Leone's celebrated *Il Buono, Il Brutto, Il Cattivo/The Good, the Bad, and the Ugly*, Sergio Corbucci's largely forgotten *Navajo Joe*, and Sergio Sollima's *La resa dei conti/The Big Gundown*. That year Morricone also composed soundtracks for Pier Paolo Pasolini's *Uccellacci e uccelloini/The Hawks and the Sparrows*, and for Franco Zeffirelli's only documentary, about the 1966 flooding of the Arno in Florence, *Per Firenze/Florence: Days of Destruction*. This cross section of a year epitomizes Morricone's renowned productivity and the eclectic and catholic reach of his aesthetic and commercial commitments.[1] Yet this wide generic variety also stymies attempts to discern political or ideological affinities in Morricone's film music, even though the 1960s were particularly turbulent years in postwar Europe that produced many outspoken responses by artists, musicians, and filmmakers.

This essay argues that within Morricone's approaches to form, style, and instrumentation during this period, we can discover an oeuvre considerably invested in making film music do revolutionary work akin to that being done by the more overt expressions in visual and textual media. Morricone's film music communicates its own radicalism, often transcending the image to which it is tethered, and serving in place of any politicized verbal enunciations that might have jeopardized his career. Such a political orientation is clearly palpable in Morricone's scores for overtly political films like *The Battle of Algiers* and *Sacco and Vanzetti* (1971)[2] but carries over, also, into the music he wrote for more popular films, such as the globally successful spaghetti westerns. By turning our attention to the music in *The Battle of Algiers*, this chapter insists on film music's political import, urging scholars of this highly charged political moment, in the Global South as much as in the Global North, to attend to those other cultural signs of political urgency that were often as influential, if less tangibly so, as the more overt political and cultural manifestos produced during that volatile period now known by the shorthand "1968."[3] Indeed music, particularly, operates powerfully within a nexus of the "psychoaffective," thus eliciting a bodily, experiential, phenomenological politics of the everyday (in contrast to the more programmatic politics of the elite, or educated, vanguard classes).[4]

In Morricone's film music during this highly prolific period, we can discern a *tone* of prophecy, particularly, that gestures toward a more just, less fascistic future. While this sonic tone or mood of utopian longing bears no causal relation to governmental policy or law, it conveys and elicits affective forms of political aspiration that are operative outside the officially designated spheres for political transformation. Such politico-affective experiences, I argue, were as likely to occur through engagements with popular culture in the form of the spaghetti western as they were through more obviously political films such as *The Battle of Algiers*. Because film music operates through more diffuse circuits than the official channels of state power, it can inspire or evoke political vision and feeling in opposition to state dictates, even when the terrain of politics proper is largely inaccessible.

The Battle of Algiers depicts Algeria's anticolonial struggle for national independence in a black-and-white aesthetic that mirrors the Manichaeism of the political climate. Film scholars, critics, and postcolonial thinkers have extensively studied the film,[5] and in its more recent history it gained notoriety because it was screened in the George W. Bush Pentagon as a primer on "terrorism." When it originally appeared in 1966, its overt anticolonial message prevented the film from being shown both in France and apartheid South Africa.[6] This essay turns away from scholars' focus on the film's visual import to insist that the politics discernable in Morricone's soundtrack for *The Battle of Algiers* appeared also in those scores he wrote for other movies that same year, even in those ostensibly disinterested in and detached from politics. Moviegoing populations in South Africa and France were exposed to the same affect and tone of revolution present in *The Battle of Algiers*' score, via circuitous but nonetheless influential routes through Morricone's music for westerns. Despite the fact that French and South African audiences were not able to watch, or listen, to *The Battle of Algiers*, a substitution of meaning and interpretation across transatlantic space occurred through the consumption of popular cowboy films and spaghetti westerns, so that viewers were able to access the film's anticolonial affects through more hidden codes, like music.

My title comes from *Che c'entriamo noi con la rivoluzione?/What Am I Doing in the Middle of the Revolution*? (Italy, 1972), a spaghetti western comedy by Sergio Corbucci that completes his "Zapata trilogy" about the Mexican Revolution. While a recent scholarly monograph finally accords the spaghetti westerns radical undertones, both at the time of their making and subsequently, spaghetti westerns have been thought devoid of politics, or to have any nascent political subtext thwarted by the movies' conflicting commercial aims.[7] As with most dismissive responses to popular culture, spaghetti westerns are generally designated as escapist and are rarely considered to be politically influential, but as Austin Fisher argues, several preeminent directors working in the genre "sought to replenish the form with radicalized doctrine, addressing contemporary issues in direct and uncompromising terms."[8] Audiences everywhere, voraciously consuming spaghetti westerns, experienced these radical undertones in both emotional and intellectual forms.

It is, after all, a curious truth that the same people working on explicitly political films like *The Battle of Algiers*, and Pontecorvo's next film, *Queimada/Burn!* (1969), were also integral to the production of many of the spaghetti westerns being made in Italy at the same time, an overlap Pauline Kael called "incestuous."[9] A quick look at the credits shows, for instance, that Franco Giraldi, Leone's assistant on *Per un pugno di dollari/A Fistful of Dollars* (1964), went on to direct the popular *Sette pistole per i MacGregor/7 Guns for the Mac-*

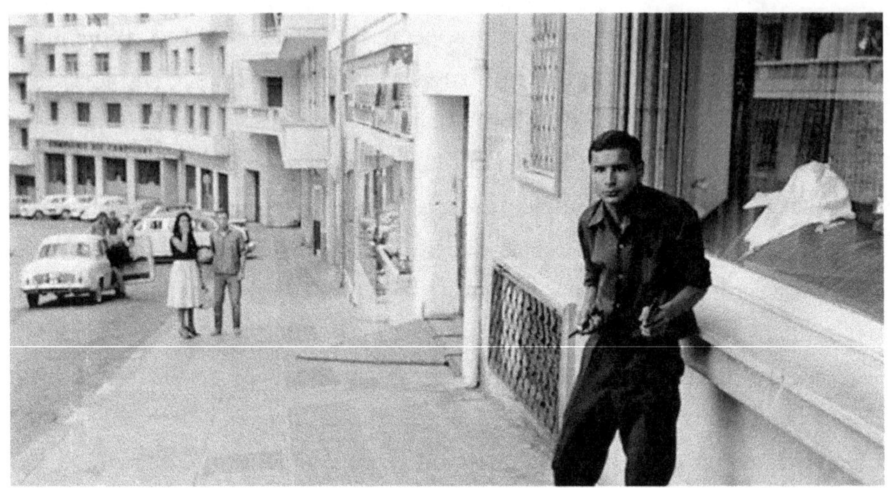

Still from *The Battle of Algiers* (1966).

Gregors in 1966, the same year that *The Battle of Algiers* was made, and it, too, featured a score by Morricone. Or we might note that Franco Solinas, the scriptwriter for *The Battle of Algiers* who traveled to Algeria with Pontecorvo for the first meeting with the Front de Libération Nationale (FLN) leader Saadi Yacef, also wrote the script for Sergio Sollima's *The Big Gundown* in 1966, and "fathered the 'political western'" in his screenplay for *Quién Sabe?/A Bullet for the General* that same year.[10] Of course, this entanglement of writers, directors, and composers effected the films' generic manifestations as well, so that it is not entirely unsurprising that a reviewer in *Cahiers du Cinéma* suggested that Pontecorvo, in *The Battle of Algiers*, "had succumbed to the mysticism of action and produced a 'Western.'"[11]

The Italian western was thus all mixed up in the political film world that produced it, and in its musical tropes, too, we can see a kind of multidirectional exchange of ideas and influences, rendering it political in ways that have frequently been elided in studies of the genre. While distinctions are frequently drawn between so-called political genres and apolitical or nonpolitical genres of "entertainment," this imbrication of moviemakers, topic, and form renders such categorizing moves suspect, since they sequester all modes of political engagement within a few unpopular films, thereby dismissing the political content within all filmic forms.

This essay thus emphasizes the formative, if indirect, role of cultural reception in the production of individual and collective political consciousness. In an interview, *The Battle of Algiers* scriptwriter, Franco Solinas, admits that

> movies have an accessory and not a decisive usefulness in the various events and elements that contribute to the transformation of society. It is naïve to believe that you can start a revolution with a movie and even more naïve to theorize about doing so. Political films are useful, on the one hand, if they contain the correct analysis of reality, and on the other [hand], if they are made in such a way to have that analysis reach the largest possible audience.[12]

Westerns were of course precisely that genre of film with mass popularity, and so their affective communiqués could influence a larger number of spectators than was possible for overtly political movies. The music in these popular films from 1966 influenced both Africans and Europeans in its ability to communicate proleptic tones of revolutionary fervor, enhancing anti-apartheid sentiment in South Africa, and anticipating the soundtrack of 1968's collective action. For Kristin Ross, the Algerian War and the protests of May '68 were inextricably linked. She writes that "the prehistory of the [May '68] uprising . . . goes back at least to the ending of the Algerian War in the early 1960s."[13] Indeed, "the first appearance of a durable radical current within the student milieu" occurred when a small group of students joined the Algerians in Paris who were protesting a curfew they had been placed under. This protest resulted in the undermemorialized massacre of Algerians on October 17, 1961, by the police.[14]

Contestations over sound and the soundtrack of life are, after all, political.[15] Ross notes that in France during the pro-Gaullist demonstrations in 1958, certain rhythmic patterns of a honking car horn—"three short, then two long horn blasts"—was a way to claim sonic ownership over a disputed political landscape.[16] Returning during the turbulence of '68,

> this brief but powerful mnemonic device, a kind of soundtrack to the whole of the Gaullist regime, was sounded out loud one more time; the rhythmic honking signal that had once meant "De-Gaulle-au-

pouvoir" in 1958, and then "Al-gé-rie fran-çaise" during the following years, and "O-A-S vaincra" most recently, was now sounded to signify "de-Gaulle-n'est-pas-seul."[17]

This repurposing of an aural cue was meant "to drown out what was for the forces of order the most terrifying sound of May '68: the catcalls and hisses from Billancourt [workers on strike]."[18] Solinas, Pontecorvo, and Morricone knew that sound in film could also be put to political ends. Combining image work (montage, close-up), textual devices (plot, narrative, dialogue), and film music, these men created a triadic foundation for the dissemination of political ideology, solidifying and intensifying its psychoaffective impact.

The Battle of Algiers experienced "relative invisibility . . . in French film culture," due, in part, to its belated 1970 commercial release eight years after Algerian independence.[19] At the very same time, one commentator noted in 1968, "the prestige of [the western] is now at an all-time high. Each week dozens of Westerns are shown on Paris movie screens. They not only attract the mass audience but also are popular with highbrow critics and Sorbonne intellectuals."[20] The genre's popularity, as in many other parts of the globe, was also expressed through fashion: "on the Left Bank . . . youths dressed in cowboy clothes are no uncommon sight. The young people may be observed buying their boots, bandanas, and ten-gallon hats at the Western House clothing store, near the Arc de Triomphe. They also congregate at Jacky's Far West Saloon, an American-run discotheque in the Montparnasse district."[21] The popularity of all things cowboy related was not confined to the Global North.[22]

Much farther south, at the other end of the African continent from Algeria, black South Africans similarly repurposed cowboy films for their own ideological and sartorial uses. In an account of a party in his memoir, *Down Second Avenue* (1959), Es'kia Mphahlele recounts the arrival of his friend and novelist, Bloke Modisane: "Bloke had come in cowboy outfit [*sic*]. We got a secret little audience together for him to do a dramatic scene from the film, *The Fastest Gun Alive*."[23] And in his book about growing up during apartheid, Jacob Dlamini recalls his mother's penchant for country western songs. She was "a woman of modest schooling and little interest in Western popular music—except . . . the crooning of Jim Reeves, the Texan folk singer."[24] "We had a whole stack of Reeves's vinyls when I was growing up. My mother was not alone in her liking of Reeves and his music. Apparently, Reeves had armies of supporters among the black working class in South Africa."[25] Reeves's and other country music stars' popularity was partially due to the usually restrictive apartheid censorship board's lax policy vis-à-vis westerns, which were thought to be innocuous, distracting, and possibly stultifying. In contrast, overtly political, antiracist or anticolonial films were banned for release, in black theaters particularly.[26] Yet as I argue, it was still possible for black South Africans to engage with politics via the medium of the cinema, even though it was not communicated through any explicitly revolutionary prism. The music in spaghetti westerns contributed to audiences' ability to imagine forms of life alternative to colonial conquest and domination, even when the spaghetti westerns provided the soundtrack for seemingly retrogressive historical and narrative plotlines. By looking at the overlap between the film music in *The Battle of Algiers* and in spaghetti westerns also composed by Morricone, we get closer to understanding the role music played in contravening colonialism, and in suggesting alternative futures and ways of living and thinking. Since filmic properties can elicit affective and intellectual responses that one might associate with the political, it was possible all the same, under a regime such as apartheid that censored explicitly left-wing political films, for audiences to experience politics in cinematic space.

I am largely concerned here with film music's contributions to political meaning that works outside of any mere diegetic function. While discussions of music necessarily deploy a medium of signification—words—generally disavowed by music, music operates at the symbolic level, too, as Sergio Miceli notes with regard to Morricone. Miceli states that

> a constant in Morricone's work . . . consists precisely in making formal values semantic and semantic values formal. What is purely building-block material is organized in such a way that it assumes a character analogous to that which pertains to the narrative context. The musical elements "act" like "actors" on the stage, responding to the script, which is then a precise, incorporated study of symbols.[27]

Critics, composers, and filmmakers generally agree that music can serve an autonomously symbolic role in film, though the degree and purpose of this autonomy differs from film to film and from composer to composer.[28] According to Anderson, Morricone, for instance, "is not interested in melody per se. . . . He tries to compose music that is not just descriptive of what is already communicated by the image and that maintains its own internal logic. While doing what the director wants, he tries to add something that only the music can."[29] Pontecorvo also felt that this is what film music should do, as Morricone himself explains: "Pontecorvo maintains that the music in a film has to be that which they cannot express in the film's colors, movements, or dialogue. It has to be something else entirely."[30] How do we get at this "something that only the music can [do]," this "something else entirely"?

For Pontecorvo, soundtracks are neither secondary nor supplementary to his films' images. In an interview with Edward Said, Pontecorvo refers to the "music-image," to describe those moments in a film during which the sensory experience of the viewer-auditor is dominated by the musical or aural information in the film, moments, indeed, when the visual supplements the sound, rather than operating in reverse. Such a moment occurs when the familiar twang of Morricone's cowboy music initiates the film's depiction of the 1956 Algerian insurrection as a violent western (see figure 2.1).[31] In this scene a policeman walking down a street stops to look into a shop window. Here, an ostinato alternates menacingly between two notes, first plucked out on a bass guitar, gradually accompanied by strings to augment the moment's tension. An Algerian man appears around the corner, nonchalantly walking behind the policeman. After a quick check behind, he suddenly stabs the policeman in the neck, a synchronization point marked in the music by the introduction of an insistent four-note piano pattern, Morricone's signature use of a militaristic snare drum, and a two-note refrain on a brass instrument that wails like an ambulance or police car siren. Finally, with increased agitation, the Algerian man retrieves the policeman's gun from his holster and runs off backward down the street facing the camera and the onlookers with his weapons bared as the brass takes up the piano's theme, the drum increases the unrest, and the tempo accelerates. Kael wrote that "in *The Battle of Algiers*, music becomes a form of agitation: at times, the strange percussive sound is like an engine that can't quite start, pounding music gives the audience a sense of impending horror at each critical point."[32] Forty years after the film's initial release, critics still insist that "Morricone's soundtrack, which contrasts French martial music with a percussive representation of the emotions of the Algerian people (a musical idiom close to an Algerian *baba saleem*), more than any other aspect of the film, delivers the affective register of the political struggle."[33] This independently politicized musical soundtrack of *The Battle of Algiers* was surprisingly easy to transfer into the westerns Morricone scored during the same period.

The political urgency conveyed by the ululations of women in various scenes in *The Battle of Algiers* reappear, for instance, in the screaming in Morricone's orchestration for *Navajo Joe*. The film's title song begins with a chorus of voices yelling a syllabic pattern—"aaaah-a-á-a-á-a-á-aaaah"—in call and response, with the voices becoming increasingly untethered from their allegiance to melody, sounding more and more like voices screaming in pain. These opening bars of the song enhance the emotional register of the film's horrific first scene in which a group of white, marauding bandits inexplicably massacre a community of Navajos. The central bandit, Duncan, is shown taking great pleasure as he first shoots and then scalps a Navajo woman, which is precisely the moment that the screaming soundtrack kicks in.

Although his music is often praised for its catchy melodies, Morricone decries this thematic obsession of audiences and movie directors. For him, "[voice] is the principal instrument. . . . But what interests me very much goes beyond the melodic business."[34] He lists the "possibilities with which [voice] can intervene in the cinema."[35] This can happen through the production of whispers, recitations, exhales and inhales, sighs, gasps, catcalls; "ugly sounds in general"; "sounds of war, sounds of love, sounds of protest"; sounds "produced by the larynx and digestive sounds; animal sounds; choruses (classic, liturgical, and 'ethnic'); collective buzzing"; or with "crowds that emit phonemes and unorganized words."[36] It is of note that the first word spoken by an Algerian in *The Battle of Algiers* is also simultaneously a cry of torture. The long "nooooooo" yelled by the man who does not want to betray his countrymen and reveal the whereabouts of FLN fighter Ali La Pointe, is a refusal that also inaugurates the resistance that is the film's topic, placing human sound at the forefront of the film's methods for communicating that feeling that is also a political stance.

For Pontecorvo, film music is essential to directing. Discussing his filmmaking process, he explains: "the most beautiful moment for me in movies . . .

is when you begin to work on the sound. It is then that I am really happy."[37] "Although [he] acknowledges that for many people music is not intrinsic to film, he believes that in his work themes are conveyed *principally* through music, providing the focus of his mode of communication."[38] One central idea he sought to foreground in *The Battle of Algiers*, for instance, was that a hero could be a collective hero, much as in Sergei Eisenstein's 1925 *Battleship Potemkin*. Michael Shapiro points out that Pontecorvo used the language of music to ascribe heroic status to an entire populace by "describ[ing] the Algerian people as a whole in his film as a 'chorus,'" thus "figur[ing] his main protagonist musically."[39] Pontecorvo thus inverts the expected pairings of conventional storytelling that subordinate film music to images and the chorus to the hero or protagonist, turning things upside down, revolving the status quo of filmic organization, thereby exposing the politics inherent in form and sound.

Morricone's experimentation with sound—or noise—featured these formal revolutions. Such musical experimentation and improvisation appear in his playful score for Pasolini's *Uccellacci e uccelloini/The Hawks and the Sparrows*, written the same year, in which he shows a willingness to disturb film music conventions.[40] He recounts being deeply moved at a performance at the association of the Vita Musicale Contemporanea in the 1960s, recalling:

> The concert was supposed to start at 9 pm. The public waited with much courtesy, but 9:15 passed, and the concert did not begin. At a certain point, a man in a normal suit arrived and climbed onto the tiny stage . . . took off his coat, hung it on a coat rack, took a ladder, put it against a little balcony, and climbed onto it. It was 9:30, and the people naturally talked, in expectation that the concert would begin, without paying attention to that man on the ladder, who in the meantime had begun to act in a very strange way, producing creaking noises . . . 9:40, 9:45. . . . Then the public began to ask itself whether that man up there represented something that perhaps it should pay attention to, and little by little silence fell. The man continued, undaunted, in absolute silence. 10:15 arrived. The man descended the ladder, took his coat, and left. End of the first half. The happening left the public very perplexed.[41]

Morricone learns from this Cageian performance that "[a] sound, any sound from our life, taken out of the context that produces it, assumes with time, in silence, another value, another meaning. The buzz of a fly in front of a microphone, isolated from all the rest, listened to in silence, is no longer what we thought but something completely different."[42] Morricone's innovation extended to his use of everyday sounds, and he regularly deployed the dodecaphonic, or twelve-tone, scale pioneered by Schoenberg, in conjunction with more classical forms of composition. His approach is a hybrid one, and he is not averse to using music written by others in his soundtrack, when it makes sense for him to do so. *The Battle of Algiers* repurposes J. S. Bach's *St. Matthew's Passion*, for instance, as well as popular music from the period. In the famous scene in which an Algerian woman plants a bomb in a milk bar in the French Quarter, a song, "Rebecca," plays on the jukebox with the central refrain—"*hasta mañana*" ("til tomorrow" or "I'll see you tomorrow)."[43] As the dancers move back and forth oblivious of the presence of a bomb in their midst, the song ironizes the idea of the future, since the future that is to come is suffused with violence and tragedy. Indeed, both music and film are often described as media that are inherently future oriented or prophetic. Morricone notes himself that "cinema and music are joined by one element characteristic of their nature: temporality."[44]

Philosophers seem taken by the idea that film and music are advents of what is to come. In a 2001 interview in *Cahiers du Cinéma*, Algerian philosopher Jacques Derrida reminds us: "On apprend ce qu'est un baiser au cinema, avant de l'apprendre dans la vie."[45] For Derrida, sensual and erotic culture comes to us from the cinema, through its representations, before we know it experientially. Our desire to know desire is first fulfilled on screen and then, subsequently (one hopes) in reality. Cinema's oracular function—its ability to depict in advance the fulfillment of our desires that we may hardly even know to recognize *as* our desires until we see them on screen, is enhanced by the central symbolic role of cinema in childhoods across the globe. Cinema works not only to depict the fulfillment of desire (revolutionary as well as erotic) but also to *program* that desire, to give it shape and make it known. Desire is characteristically associated with the future tense, with the hope of the fulfillment of a utopia to come, and as such cinema appears the medium best able to represent these desires for the future still yet to come.

Similarly, philosophers like Lydia Goehr and Jacques Attali claim that *music* is a prophetic medium.[46] Goehr writes of the sense music provides of "getting beyond a specific condition, the sense that one can reach for something that presently is not so or does not exist."[47] "This reaching," she proposes, "suggests that individuals or societies strive to surpass the identity or the particular condition that currently defines them. They can see past who they are to what they could (or should) be. 'While listening to great music,' Schopenhauer once wrote, 'everyone feels distinctly what his ultimate worth is, or, much more, what his worth could be.'"[48] For Goehr building on Schopenhauer, music is "prophetic and can articulate a 'politics for the future.'"[49]

Goehr argues that music is the medium that gets closest to allowing people to be in touch, however momentarily, with the affective experiences of hope, optimism, and utopia. This relation is not apart from reality but rather like the car horns in French symbolic culture, "rooted in the real nature of things and of man." What Schopenhauer refers to as music's "autonomy[,] does *not* deprive it of a metaphysical and moral involvement with the world."[50] But what it does offer us, however temporarily, is "a release from our perpetual suffering."[51] Writing of the impossibility of a harmoniously perfect music, Goehr explains that "temporary alleviation from the world does nothing to change its essential condition; it only hints at what the world would be like if our experience were different, if we had no illusions and no unfulfilled desires."[52] It is in the combinatory effect of these two genres, then, in the possibility represented by music (as articulated by Goehr via Schopenhauer) and that represented by cinema (Derrida, Pontecorvo), that sound films become thus *doubly* prophetic, solidifying their power to render the experience of utopia, however short-lived, palpable.

While it is well known that both Solinas and Pontecorvo wanted to make a film about the protracted Algerian struggle for independence, it is perhaps less clear what Pontecorvo's motivations were. By focusing on an insurrection that took place between 1956 and 1957, a revolt suppressed by the French that did not put an immediate end to the French occupation, the film archives history, with Pontecorvo himself acting as the historian who can expose the "dictatorship of the truth."[53] Pontecorvo's choice of a neorealist black-and-white granular reportage aesthetic helps us to think of the film as a historical document, a powerful aide-mémoire resuscitating the role of the Algerian people in the teleological production of history.

Yet Pontecorvo's active participation in politics (he was the leader of the clandestine communist youth movement during the early 1940s in Italy) makes clear, if it is not already obvious, that his filmmaking was meant to do more than merely document the past.[54] Despite Solinas's injunction against naively thinking that culture could incite revolution, Pontecorvo had future-oriented goals. While the films he made before and right after *The Battle of Algiers*—*Kapò* (1960) and *Queimada/Burn!* (1969)—were both set in antecedent moments of historical upheaval, their thematic, affective, and formal commitments propose a forward-looking political agenda that aims, however intangibly, to influence audiences' and auditors' political commitments. As late as 1992, Pontecorvo stated: "I'm still a man of the left . . . searching . . . for a way to change the terrible things in our world."[55] That *The Battle of Algiers* was shown at the Pentagon many years after it was made only testifies to the success of Pontecorvo's quasi-Marxist agenda: the film works to influence the global politics of the future, and it aimed to do so at the time of its production as well. While it remains difficult to assess the degree to which cultural practices influence political consciousness and action, what I have argued here is that affect, particularly, is mobilized through film music to do precisely this. Reception practices vary widely, and are certainly not inherently resistant. Often, they can reproduce hegemonic discourses of the most dangerous kind. But popular film genres, particularly, have been largely overlooked as a source for the formation of political consciousness during this highly politicized period in world politics. Revolutionary or oppositional ideologies might inhere in spectatorship practices despite the fact that the films being watched gesture toward antirevolutionary, static, or conservative agendas. And conversely, revolutionary aims can belie other oppressions. Films certainly influence spectators, then, but not as direct transmitters of pure ideological meaning embedded in the films themselves, but through a negotiation between the material, social, and historical positions of the spectators; the images, stories, and characters; and as I have argued here, through the affective, emotional, and psychological effects of music.

Notes

1. Pontecorvo told Morricone: "I should never ask your opinion of the film that you are making because you like all of them so much," in Ennio Morricone and Sergio Miceli, *Composing for the Cinema: The Theory and Praxis of Music in Film*, trans. Gillian B. Anderson (Lanham, MD: Scarecrow Press, 2013), 230.
2. The title song, "The Ballad of Sacco and Vanzetti," was sung by Joan Baez with lyrics taken from Vanzetti's letters.
3. Yasiin Bey, known as the politically engaged rapper Mos Def, samples a section of *The Battle of Algiers* soundtrack in his 2009 track, "The Auditorium," appearing on the album *The Ecstatic*. Thanks to Sean Jacobs for bringing this to my attention.
4. Frantz Fanon, *The Wretched of the Earth*, trans. Richard Philcox (New York: Grove Press, 2004).
5. Since its release, academics and critics have consistently found the film worthy of attention and debate. The film's recent 2016 fiftieth anniversary initiated several new scholarly engagements in journals such as *Film Quarterly*, *Screen*, and *Radical History Review*, among other venues, as well as a monograph, *Fifty Years of The Battle of Algiers: Past as Prologue*, by Sohail Daulatzai (Minneapolis: University of Minnesota Press, 2016). Coinciding with its fortieth anniversary in 2007, *Interventions: International Journal of Postcolonial Studies* devoted a special issue to *The Battle of Algiers*.
6. In other countries, it passed censorship boards though it received different assessments, receiving an "X" rating in the United Kingdom, deeming it suitable for "those aged 16 and over" but a "PG" rating in Canada, which merely stipulated a need for parental caution around child viewers.
7. Austin Fisher writes that "[by] 1966, a radicalized sub-*filone* variously offering critiques of latent fascism, engaging with contemporaneous protest movements and expounding bravura anti-imperialist doctrine had arisen from within the Italian Western." See Austin Fisher, *Radical Frontiers in the Spaghetti Western: Politics, Violence, and Popular Italian Cinema* (London: I. B. Tauris, 2011), 40.
8. Fisher, *Radical Frontiers in the Spaghetti Western*, 73.
9. Pauline Kael, "Politics and Thrills," *New Yorker*, November 19, 1973, 243.
10. Franco Solinas, ed., PierNico Solinas, *The Battle of Algiers* (1973), Criterion Collection DVD booklet, 29.
11. Quoted in Patricia Caillé, "The Illegitimate Legitimacy of *The Battle of Algiers* in French Film Culture," *Interventions* 9, no. 3 (2007): 382. Jean-Pierre Gorin

recalls that there was a time when "every Marxist on the block wanted to make a Western." Quoted in Fisher, *Radical Frontiers in the Western*, 71.

12. Solinas, *Battle of Algiers*, 37–38.
13. Kristin Ross, *May '68 and Its Afterlives* (Chicago: University of Chicago Press, 2002), 8.
14. Ross, *May '68 and Its Afterlives*, 56.
15. C.f. Alexander G. Weheliye, *Phonographies: Grooves in Sonic Afro-Modernity* (Durham, NC: Duke University Press, 2005).
16. Ross, *May '68 and Its Afterlives*, 60.
17. Ross, 60.
18. Ross, 60.
19. Caillé, "Illegitimate Legitimacy of *The Battle of Algiers*," 372.
20. Kent L. Steckmesser, "Paris and the Wild West," *Southwest Review* 54, no. 2 (1969): 168–69. Steckmesser notes that "even the Communists applaud Westerns on occasion, although *l'Humanité* is apt to praise only those that are based on such contemporary problems as racism or the struggle between 'possessors and disposed.'"
21. Steckmesser, "Paris and the Wild West," 173.
22. MaryEllen Higgins, Rita Keresztesi, and Dayna Oscherwitz, *The Western in the Global South* (New York: Routledge, 2015); Lily Saint, "'You Kiss in Westerns': Cultural Translation in Moustapha Alassane's *Le retour d'un aventurier*," *Journal of African Cinemas* 5, no. 2 (2013): 203–17.
23. Ezekiel Mphalele, *Down Second Avenue* (London: Faber and Faber, 1959), 199.
24. Jacob Dlamini, *Native Nostalgia* (Auckland Park, South Africa: Jacana Media, 2009), 26.
25. Dlamini, *Native Nostalgia*, 82.
26. See Mphahlele, *Down Second Avenue*; Bloke Modisane, *Blame Me on History* (Johannesburg: Ad Donker, 1963); Hortense Powdermaker, *Copper Town: Changing Africa* (Westport, CT: Greenwood, 1973).
27. Morricone and Miceli, *Composing for the Cinema*, 177.
28. Claudia Gorbman, *Unheard Melodies: Narrative Film Music* (Bloomington: Indiana University Press, 1987).
29. Gillian B. Anderson, "Translator's Note," in Morricone and Miceli, *Composing for the Cinema*, vii.
30. Morricone and Miceli, *Composing for the Cinema*, 191.
31. Morricone explains: "The western helped me, because the genre, at least

as Leone intended it, is picaresque, exaggerated, excessive, playful, dramatic, entertaining, and caustic . . . it was necessary for me to use unusual sounds that would be equal to these excesses. . . . Everything, including the soundtrack, had to appear to be much more than it really was. Thus, therefore, I called for bells, whip, whistling, anvil, clay whistle, voices, and . . . so many other things. The necessity of making [*A Fistful of Dollars*] seem epic caused me to augment the tone of the instrumentation and to resort to a chorus, to crescendos, to strings with their galloping rhythm," in Morricone and Miceli, *Composing for the Cinema*, 167.

32. Kael, "Politics and Thrills," 238.
33. Michael J. Shapiro, "Slow Looking: The Ethics and Politics of Aesthetics," *Millennium—Journal of International Studies* 37, no. 1 (2008): 181–97, at 193.
34. Morricone and Miceli, *Composing for the Cinema*, 223.
35. Morricone and Miceli, 224.
36. Morricone and Miceli, 224.
37. Joan Mellen, *Filmguide to the Battle of Algiers* (Bloomington: Indiana University Press, 1973), 13.
38. Mellen, *Filmguide to the Battle of Algiers*, 14.
39. Shapiro, "Slow Looking," 193.
40. Domenico Mudugno sings the opening titles, exquisitely delivering a laugh when the song arrives at the credit: "Ennio Morricone, compositore."
41. Morricone and Miceli, *Composing for the Cinema*, 191–92.
42. Morricone and Miceli, 192.
43. "Rebecca" is by Les Chakachas and was released in 1959.
44. Morricone and Miceli, *Composing for the Cinema*, 249.
45. Jacques Derrida, "Le cinema et ses fantômes: Interview with Antoine de Baecque et Theirry Jousse," *Cahiers du Cinéma* (2001): 74–85, at 76. "We learn what a kiss is at the cinema—before we learn it in life." Translation the author's.
46. "Music is prophecy . . . [I]t makes audible the new world that will gradually become visible, that will impose itself and regulate the order of things; it is not only the image of things, but the transcending of the everyday, the herald of the future." Jacques Attali, *Noise: The Political Economy of Music*, trans. Brian Massumi (Minneapolis: University of Minnesota Press, 1985), 11.
47. Lydia Goehr, *The Quest for Voice: On Music, Politics, and the Limits of Philos-*

ophy; *The 1997 Ernst Bloch Lectures* (Berkeley: University of California Press, 1998), 27.

48. Goehr, *The Quest for Voice*, 27–28.
49. Goehr, *The Quest for Voice*, 1.
50. Goehr, 24.
51. Goehr, 24.
52. Goehr, 26.
53. This phrase is ascribed to Pontecorvo in numerous articles and interviews as a description of his documentary style of cinematography, but I have been unable to locate its original source.
54. Alexander Billet, "A Marxist Poet: The Legacy of Gillo Pontecorvo," *Monthly Review*, October 19, 2006. https://mronline.org/2006/10/19/a-marxist-poet-the-legacy-of-gillo-pontecorvo/. Pontecorvo was in the Parti communiste italien (PCI) from 1944 to 1956. Solinas was a member his whole adult life.
55. Quoted in Billet, "Marxist Poet."

Bibliography

Anderson, Gillian B. "Translator's Note." In *Composing for the Cinema: The Theory and Praxis of Music in Film*, vii–viii. Lanham, MD: Scarecrow Press, 2013.

Attali, Jacques. *Noise: The Political Economy of Music*. Translated by Brian Massumi. Minneapolis: University of Minnesota Press, 1985.

Billet, Alexander. "A Marxist Poet: The Legacy of Gillo Pontecorvo." *Monthly Review*, October 19, 2006.

Caillé, Patricia. "The Illegitimate Legitimacy of *The Battle of Algiers* in French Film Culture." *Interventions* 9, no. 3 (2007): 371–88.

Daulatzai, Sohail. *Fifty Years of The Battle of Algiers: Past as Prologue*. Minneapolis: University of Minnesota Press, 2016.

Derrida, Jacques. "Le cinéma et ses fantômes: Interview with Antoine de Baeque et Thierry Jousse." *Cahiers du Cinéma* (2001): 75–85.

Dlamini, Jacob. *Native Nostalgia*. Auckland Park, South Africa: Jacana Media, 2009.

Fanon, Frantz. *The Wretched of the Earth*. Translated by Richard Philcox. New York: Grove Press, 2004.

Fisher, Austin. *Radical Frontiers in the Spaghetti Western: Politics, Violence, and Popular Italian Cinema*. London: I. B. Tauris, 2011.

Goehr, Lydia. *The Quest for Voice: On Music, Politics, and the Limits of Philosophy*.

Ernest Bloch Lectures. Berkeley: University of California Press, 1998.

Gorbman, Claudia. *Unheard Melodies: Narrative Film Music*. Bloomington: Indiana University Press, 1987.

Higgins, MaryEllen, Rita Keresztesi, and Dayna Oscherwitz. *The Western in the Global South*. New York: Routledge, 2015.

Kael, Pauline. "Politics and Thrills." *New Yorker*, November 19, 1973, 236–44.

Mellen, Joan. *Filmguide to the Battle of Algiers*. Bloomington: Indiana University Press, 1973.

Modisane, William Bloke. *Blame Me on History*. Johannesburg: Ad Donker, 1963.

Morricone, Ennio, and Sergio Miceli. *Composing for the Cinema: The Theory and Praxis of Music in Film*. Translated by Gillian B. Anderson. Lanham, MD: Scarecrow Press, 2013.

Mphahlele, Ezekiel. *Down Second Avenue*. London: Faber and Faber, 1959.

Powdermaker, Hortense. *Copper Town: Changing Africa*. Westport, CT: Greenwood, 1973.

Ross, Kristin. *May '68 and Its Afterlives*. Chicago: University of Chicago Press, 2002.

Saint, Lily. "'You Kiss in Westerns': Cultural Translation in Moustapha Alassane's *Le retour d'un aventurier*." *Journal of African Cinemas* 5, no. 2 (2013): 203–17.

Shapiro, Michael J. "Slow Looking: The Ethics and Politics of Aesthetics." *Millennium—Journal of International Studies* 37, no. 1 (2008): 181–97.

Solinas, Franco. The Battle of Algiers booklet accompanying the Criterion Collection DVD release, edited by PierNico Solinas. 1972.

Steckmesser, Kent L. "Paris and the Wild West." *Southwest Review* 54, no. 2 (1969): 168–74.

Weheliye, Alexander G. *Phonographies: Grooves in Sonic Afro-Modernity*. Durham, NC: Duke University Press, 2005.

3

Before the Revolution

The Radical Anxiety of Paulo Rocha's Cinema

Rocco Giansante

The Cinema Novo (New Cinema) was created by a young generation of Portuguese filmmakers influenced by the aesthetic and political revolution of the French Nouvelle Vague (New Wave). In their films, they brought to the screen not only the 1960s angst, which would fully manifest itself with the events of 1968, but also the suffocating life they lived under the corporatist authoritarian regime of António de Salazar—the Estado Novo (New State).

One of the initiators of the Cinema Novo was Paulo Rocha, who studied filmmaking at the Institut des hautes études cinématographiques (IDHEC, Institute for Advanced Cinematographic Studies) in Paris. In his first two films, Rocha created an original cinema that inserted the radicality of the Nouvelle Vague inside the visual tropes and narrative structures of traditional Portuguese cinema. His first feature, *Os Verdes Anos/The Green Years* (Portugal, 1963), is a dramatic story of alienation taking place in the typical locations of the conservative comedies produced by the regime in the 1930s: Lisbon's neighborhoods. The love story of a fisherman in *Mudar de Vida/Change of Life* (Portugal, 1966) can be read as a text critical of the wars that Portugal was waging against the liberation movements in its African colonies. The film also provides a realistic inquiry into the living conditions of the fishing communities of the Furadouro region. Rocha's characters do not act politically; on the contrary, they dig themselves deeper into their alienation, waiting for the situation to explode. In his 1960s productions, Rocha unveiled the cracks of a system that was imploding under its surface; the encounter between the authoritarian image of Portugal and the Nouvelle Vague creates a short circuit that signals an imminent liberation.

Paulo Rocha is unanimously considered to be among the initiators of the Cinema Novo, the Portuguese New Wave.[1] His first film, *The Green Years*, represented a stylistic and narrative departure from prior Portuguese cinema and received critical attention abroad. That year, it won the Best First Film prize at the Locarno Film Festival. While many commentators have detected Neorealist elements in the story of Júlio, the poor provincial shoemaker arriving in Lisbon to start a new life, the influence of the French Nouvelle Vague on the film is far more significant.

After abandoning his law studies at the University of Lisbon and thanks to a generous scholarship of the Gulkenkian Foundation,[2] Rocha traveled to Paris to study filmmaking at the prestigious IDHEC. Here, he attended the premiere of Godard's *À bout de souffle/Breathless* (France, 1960); developed an interest for Japanese cinema, in particular for Kenji Mizoguchi; and worked as Jean Renoir's assistant in *Le caporal épinglé/The Elusive Corporal* (France, 1962). Once back in Portugal, with the support of producer António da Cunha Telles, Rocha began work on his first film. *The Green Years* tells the story of Júlio, a nineteen-year-old shoemaker, who leaves the province he grew up in to go work in Lisbon. Unable to fit in to the new environment, he starts a relationship with the housemaid Ilda. The more he feels alienated and unsatisfied with his surroundings, the more Júlio gets attached to Ilda, seeing her as the only person who can save him from his predicaments. When Ilda refuses his marriage proposal, Júlio kills her, thus performing a desperately tragic act of revolt.

The novelty of Rocha's film appears not only through the adoption of solutions and elements of the French Nouvelle Vague—for example, the low-budget nature of the film projects carried out by first-time actors and crews, or the telling of stories about individuals trying to make their way in a hostile environment—but also through the insertion, inside the visual forms and storytelling structures of the French movement, of themes and tropes belonging to classic Portuguese cinema. In this sense, the Nouvelle Vague not only becomes a critical tool to reflect on Portuguese cinema and society but also reveals hidden aspects of the country that had not been represented on the screen before, potentially activating new forms of social and political engagement.

According to French philosopher Jacques Rancière, "aesthetic acts [are] configurations of experience that create new modes of sense perception and induce novel forms of political subjectivity."[3] In the years immediately after World War II, the Neorealist filmmakers chose to film stories and characters that had been excluded from the Fascists screens, on the one hand, thus successfully creating a novel image of post-Fascist Italy that incorporated its newly established democracy; on the other hand, the young artists of the Nouvelle Vague built a representation of France that stood firmly in opposition to Vichy's reactionary heritage and the nationalist hubris of the war in Algeria. Without being overtly critical of the Estado Novo, Rocha established a basis for the creation of the image of democratic Portugal: inserting new elements inside the Salazarian frame, Rocha filmed and made visible the profound crisis that the Portuguese nation was living out, stuck between the colonial wars it was waging in Africa and the desire for European modernity and freedom. A radical anxiety marks his films, which are inhabited by characters whose emotional lives are out of sync with the reality in which they are immersed. Divided between a desire for independence and the rigid norms of the authoritarian state, Rocha's protagonists live in a state of constant unease, seeing the object of their desire escaping from their reach.

The convergence between the Nouvelle Vague paradigm and the traditional Portuguese cinema that structures Rocha's *The Green Years* finds its most visible manifestation in three moments: the urban-rural binary, the young love story, and the rebellious, antiauthoritarian stance.

The relationship between the city and the country forms one of the major topoi of the Nouvelle Vague. In particular, Paris is both the destination of choice for characters in search of freedom and the location where their disillusion takes place. The roads of the French capital provide the location for Truffaut's alter ego Antoine Doinel to find refuge from the oppressive atmosphere of his own home and school but the final shot of *Les Quatre Cents Coups/The 400 Blows* (France, 1959), carrying the promise of endless adventures, takes place on the ocean's edge. In *Breathless*, the small gangster Michel avoids imprisonment (and death) only temporarily when hiding in the Ville Lumière. Rivette's *Paris nous appartient/Paris Belongs to Us* (France, 1961) describes the life of twenty-something actors whose lives are marred by the suicide of one of their peers. The Nouvelle Vague city is, thus, a stage for life and death, freedom and imprisonment, love and disappointments.

The film industry under the Estado Novo gives ample space to the treatment of the relation between the city and the country. The identification of the regime with the rural population affected the representation of the city on screen: "Lisbon neighborhoods, where urban comedies take place, resemble small isolated villages in an expanding metropolis."[4] Lisbon as a village is the set for stories that convey the conservative values Salazar cherished. At the same time, Lisbon as a city is condemned for favoring licentious and amoral lifestyles, for harboring crime, and for corrupting the healthy body of the nation: films like Leitão de Barros's *Maria Papoila* (Portugal, 1937) contrast the purity of country life with the shallow conduct of the decadent urban bourgeoisie.

The love story that happily concludes the *comedias lisboetas*—confirming through marriage the place of the couple inside the Portuguese society—in the Nouvelle Vague films serves to explore the relations between the sexes in postwar France. The French authors exhibit, according to Naomi Greene, "a disregard for the social conventions—particularly those governing sexuality—that marked their parent's generation."[5] While the Portuguese love stories are the manifestation of a social order perpetuating itself, the love relations of the French cinema challenge the country's moral and social mores.

The antiauthoritarian stance of the Nouvelle Vague reverberates in Rocha's films with its opposition to established authority. If in Rocha the visible targets of this opposition are Júlio's uncle and boss, the young French filmmakers rise up against the "collaborationist" mentality of the French Right and the imperial vision of the Gaullist regime (namely, the colonial war in Algeria).[6]

The convergence between the Nouvelle Vague and Portuguese cinema creates a short circuit that will lead to a crude and devastating political act. In fact, Rocha's aesthetic operation carries along a radical political declaration: although failed, the tragic rebellion of the young shoemaker creates the condition for an alternative to the present reality, dominated by the suffocating authoritarian power of Salazar's corporatist regime.

The Urban/Rural Binary

Despite being a small industrial reality (in the year 1955 no films were produced[7]), Portuguese cinema had been developed under Salazar to become a propaganda tool. Films had to convey the image of the country that the regime was building,[8] an image that was based on nationalism, social conservatism, obedience, and order. The most successful products of the Portuguese film industry were the so-called *comedias lisboetas* (Lisbon comedies), musical comedies set in one of Lisbon's historical neighborhoods depicting innocent love stories that did not challenge the status quo. In these films, the city of Lisbon is treated like a country village; the plot, in fact, generally develops around a courtyard or a patio where the main characters live. The films tell stories of communities in which everyone knows one another, where there is no social mobility, and the individual is aware of his or her role and place in society.

The cinematic Lisbon turned village became the ideal setting for the promotion of the values of the regime, whose supporters lived mainly in the countryside, a location more in tune with the conservatism the Salazarian regime promoted: "archaic, isolated and puritanical, rejecting industrialization as a harbinger of class and labor problems, glorifying a sanitized peasant and folkloric tradition, Salazar's Portugal was firmly set against the twentieth century."[9] Turning the city into a village had a specific propaganda function: the rural policy of the regime was based on the idea that the authentic Portuguese spirit was to be found in the countryside, where Salazar's regime had its power base and where the masses could be easily manipulated through the help of the Catholic Church.[10]

To better understand the relation between the urban and rural settings in the Portuguese cinema under the eye of Salazar, it is useful to consider António Lopes Ribeiro's propaganda film *A Revolução de Maio/The May Revolution* (Portugal, 1937). César, a dangerous agitator, returns to his home country in order to prepare a revolution that he intends to start on May 28, on the same date as the regime's "National Revolution." Instead of arresting him, the police follow him to find his accomplices. In this way, the viewer is taken on a tour of the country. In the north, César goes to visit his family (he will not find his father at home because he is participating in the regime's Labor Day celebrations; a documentary sequence of those celebrations is inserted in the film so that the spectator can learn about the country's situation). We then follow César to Braga, where he witnesses the commemoration of the National Revolution, the military coup that put an end to Portugal's First Republic and paved the way for the dictatorship of the Estado Novo. As the film progresses, a symbolic process takes place: César's real father is replaced by the nation's father, António de Salazar. Arriving in Lisbon, the dangerous subversive, who has witnessed the achievements of the country, abandons his revolutionary proposals and fully embraces the regime.

Lopes Ribeiro's cinematic journey through Portugal highlights the opposition between the values of the countryside and the corrupted morals of the foreign-backed traitors operating in the dark streets of the capital. Despite this contrast, there is no contradiction in the regime's favoring of Lisbon as the location for its films: the Lisbon of the comedies may well serve as an example of urban cinema but takes the shape of villages so as to reconcile the traditional values of the countryside with the city.[11] Rocha set his first film in Lisbon, thus apparently continuing a certain Portuguese filmic tradition, but the Lisbon of Rocha—an expanding metropolis menacing the countryside at its borders—is a city in which the protagonist sets out to create a new network of relations. Writing about cinema and cities, Barbara Mennel describes the city of the Nouvelle Vague as "the setting for affective relationships substituting for conventional family structures: coffee-houses, bars, and the street become home for the young protagonists."[12] The Lisbon of Rocha follows this description up to a certain point because, contrary to what happens in the city of the Nouvelle Vague, the urban space turns, during the course of the film, into an alienating environment from which the protagonist, Júlio, increasingly withdraws. What is missing in Rocha's film is the Nouvelle Vague sense of freedom in the city, enabled by its alternative forms of community. In Rocha's film, in fact, the loneliness of the main character—disconnected from his surroundings—evokes the rigid separation within society; drawing on Georg Simmel's suggestion that the city is "not a spatial entity which entails sociological characteristics but a sociological entity that is formed spatially,"[13] it can be affirmed that the Lisbon filmed by Rocha provides an image of the relationship between its inhabitants, a relationship affected by the authoritarian powers stifling society. The urban space is the setting of Júlio's estrangement from society, not of his liberation. Cut off from the natural settings of his home, those same settings that he looks for in his long Sunday walks on the border of the city, the young shoemaker crosses the city like a foreign body. And indeed, he is an outsider: living with his uncle in an old farmhouse located outside the urban perimeter, Júlio symbolically needs to cross a bridge each time he wants to reach the city.

Young Love

The Nouvelle Vague was an artistic movement made by young people about young people. "The *Nouvelle Vague* was youth, it did not recreate it," film critic and historian Antoine de Baecque once declared.[14] It brought to the screen the image of a generation that had grown up in a world that—because of the freedoms and possibilities it offered—was completely different from the one their parents had lived in. In the same way, the twenty-eight-year-old Rocha made a film about two youngsters who spend their free time wandering through the streets and bordering areas of Lisbon, timidly sharing their thoughts, and tentatively trying to imagine a future together. The film is structured around the making of this relationship as the "New Wave stories tended to be loosely organized around rather complex, spontaneous young characters."[15] While the theme of romantic love is central to the *comedias lisboetas*, Rocha adds to this material a sense of doom that can be found also in contemporary French productions like Louis Malle's *Ascenseur pour l'échaffaud/Elevator to the Gallows* (France, 1958) or Claude Chabrol's *Les cousins/The Cousins* (France, 1959). Especially in Malle's or Chabrol's films, one sees the representation of a new "lost" generation "feeling doomed amid the prosperity of the highly capitalized postwar economy."[16] If the doom felt by the French youngsters is the product of society's postwar changes and of the developments of contemporary events like the war in Algeria, the doom enveloping Júlio is the unmediated reaction to a condition of poverty and a lack of possibilities. Once Ilda refuses his marriage proposal, Júlio—stuck in a low-paying job and surrounded by patronizing adults—surrenders to the inevitability of his condition.

The lack of democracy in Portugal and the crisis of parliamentary democracy in France would bring about revolts initiated by young people: the "1968 Movement" in France with its students and the "Carnation Revolution" of 1974 in Portugal with its junior officers and soldiers. In the years preceding those events, cinema became a space in which society's tensions could be safely evoked and the representation of an alternative reality was offered to the audience's eyes.

Against Established Authority

In the Nouvelle Vague we can find a desire for freedom in a statement against authority: this political dimension can be traced back to the historic experience of the French Resistance. At the end of World War II, the Liberation freed the country not only from its occupiers and their collaborators but also from a certain mentality, introducing a real need for communication, expression, reflection, and knowledge. The aesthetic choices of the Nouvelle Vague were founded on essentially moral grounds. The young directors felt that "beauty" could be achieved only through goodness and truth, lucidity and struggle—in brief, through the spirit of the Resistance. This commitment toward truth, struggle, and deliverance redeployed in the Portuguese context, carried a renewed urgency in the absence of a democratic system.

Júlio's alienation derives from his impatience toward authority, in the film, physically embodied by his uncle Afonso—with whom he lives and who acts as his tutor—and Raúl, his boss at the workshop. Like his counterparts across the Western world, Júlio does not subscribe to the previous generation's way of life. He cannot see himself living like his uncle, who takes special care to remind his young nephew to take things *devagarinho* (slowly). While his girlfriend, Ilda, has a more conservative outlook on life—for example, she encourages him, to no avail, to study or to look for another position, with the confidence that, slowly and surely, the reward of a successful life will come—Júlio feels the suffocating restrictions of the models imposed on him by society and he rejects them. Júlio has no political conscience and no desire to change the political landscape; his dissatisfaction is an intimate affair that starts and ends with him. The absence of a political solution may be the reason for his descent toward self-destruction. Unable to see alternatives, even when his girlfriend seems to desert him, he can only dig himself deeper into his alienation waiting for the situation to finally explode.

A year after the release of *The Green Years*, filmmaker Fernando Lopes made *Belarmino* (Portugal, 1964), considered together with Rocha's work as one of the founding films of the Cinema Novo. In this docufiction, Lopes presents the life of Belarmino Fragoso, a once mildly successful boxer who, exploited by managers and promoters, ended his career with little money. Similar to *The Green Years*, *Belarmino* is built around sequences that document the main character's wandering through the streets of Lisbon. Isolated against the urban background, Fragoso makes a living by polishing shoes and retouching photographs. Like Júlio, the former boxer is excluded from the city's life and its rewards; the world around him is indifferent to his bright past and gray present. The city doesn't offer the boxer any opportunities, turning instead into a prison in which he stands alone. While Júlio escapes the city-prison by walking to the outskirts of Lisbon (where he can momentarily reconnect with the countryside of his childhood), Fragoso finds refuge in smoky nightclubs—where for the night, as a member of the audience, he can feel part of a collective—and at the gym containing the traces of his former glory. But even the gym turns out to be a prison with Fragoso working out behind a metal fence, his still agile movements framed by the narrow spaces of the architecture.

The lack of freedom of Rocha's characters is visually suggested by their obedience to the lines of the space: they constantly move inside an invisible grid that prevents improvisations and transgressive moves. The train that brings Júlio to Lisbon enters the station crossing the frame diagonally like the bridge that connects Afonso's house to the road and that leads to the city. The sequence shot in front of the university is built around the modernist lines of the building's architecture.

The architecture imposes its lines and elements on the characters: each time Júlio enters the workshop where he works, he needs to bend his head because of the low ceiling. Finding himself in the entrance hall of Ilda's condominium, the young shoemaker is trapped because he does not know how to operate the electric door. And in the final scene of the film, the murderer cannot escape his fate because he is literally blocked by a line of cars stopping in front of him.

In the films of Kenji Mizoguchi—the Japanese auteur whose work Paulo Rocha knew and admired—the characters are framed and oppressed by windows and sliding doors' frames and tatami lines. Like Júlio, the Japanese characters are denied their freedom by the *giri*, the social conventions and obligations. When Júlio proposes to Ilda, the two are visually separated by a tree dividing the frame in two parts: spatially separated from Júlio, Ilda refuses his marriage offer. Conversely, at the beginning of their love story, the distance between the two is completely canceled: filming from afar, in wide shot, the couple walking on the outskirts of the city becomes one body—the product of the superimposition of the two figures. The space also does not impose itself in the same way on the rich as it does with the poor: the apartment of Ilda's employers is vast and allows the enjoyment of life. The poor are crammed one onto the other, without space or privacy.

The Nouvelle Vague's antiauthoritarian stance—against the official film industry, that is, the *cinéma de papa*, the universities, the parents, the institutions—in Rocha acquires a new dimension: although not overtly challenging the regime, the film still registers a signal of mounting dissatisfaction toward authority that will inevitably be directed toward the political powers. The murder of Ilda symbolically sanctions the end of the Portuguese comedies and the vision behind it: the violent death of the maid—replicating the state-sanctioned violence against political opponents and the military brutality of the colonial wars—is the (distorted) manifestation of a desire for freedom that will soon take over Portuguese society in full.

Paulo Rocha's second film, *Mudar de Vida/Change of Life* (Portugal, 1966), carries the promise of a better future, a promise that was denied to young Júlio in the first film. *Change of Life* tells the story of Adélino, a veteran from the war in Angola who returns home to find his former girlfriend married to his own brother.

In the film's first shot, we see a woman working the fields; behind her, at a cross road, a coach is approaching. Traveling on the coach is Adélino, who finally returns home after many years of absence. A character returns to a place and he is transformed by it, exactly like Júlio in the Lisbon of the *Green Years*. Adélino, the soldier in Africa, who has fought the colonial wars Portugal waged to keep alive the imperial dream, returns to the miserable life of his birthplace in an attempt to revive his past life.

For the first time, although marginally, Portuguese cinema engages the theme of the colonial wars.[17] Rocha doesn't show battlefields or movements of troops, nor do we hear gunshots or bombings; instead, the war is interiorized, manifesting itself in the traces it leaves behind on the spirit of Adélino, in the defeating realization of having fought on the wrong side of history. In the same way, the Algerian war appears in the Nouvelle Vague: "not the scene of national historical drama—as Vietnam for American cinema—but that of a fragile and bewildered individual's doubts in the face of history."[18] In films like *Le Petit Soldat/The Little Soldier* (France, 1963), *Les Parapluies de Cherbourg/The Umbrellas of Cherbourg* (France, 1964), *Muriel* (France, 1963), or

Cléo de 5 à 7/Cleo from 5 to 7 (France, 1962), the Algerian War and its atrocities silently contaminate the life of the characters who, as a consequence, lose their innocence. Cinema reveals the corrupting effect that wars of domination have on societies; the African war fought with the intention of ruling over another population highlights the failings of the Western model (both democratic and nondemocratic). Rocha's Adélino returns to his hometown a stranger: changed by the war, his movements seem out of place in the landscape of his youth, which is fading away. The war has also affected the community of fishermen at home; bereft of its young members who carry the promise of future, the community is sinking in the sands of oblivion.

Reality enters the cinema of Paulo Rocha, and his characters are left dealing with it: the war, the poverty of the fishing community of the Furadouro, the proletarianization of the former fishermen now working in the factory nearby, emigration, the condition of women. All of these aspects of Portuguese society are present in *Change of Life*, hidden in the dialogues and scarring the characters' bodies. The documentary-like sequences of the fishermen going out to sea in their wooden boats can be read as a critique of the difficult living conditions of the poverty-stricken communities of the Furadouro, as they are trapped between the choice of the mortal dangers of life at sea and the alienation of work in the factory. But Rocha's film transcends the difficulties of daily life to show that there is a possibility for redemption. If the films' characters at the end take control of their lives, why can the spectators not do the same?

The return home is not a happy one for Adélino. The dream of rekindling the relation with his former girlfriend reveals its impossibility while a health issue prevents him from going back to the sea with the other fishermen. He applies for a job at the local factory, unsuccessfully. But when everything seems lost, the chance encounter with the free-spirited Albertina provides the opportunity to change his life for the better.

Albertina differs intensely from the quiet Ilda of Rocha's first film; while the servant was knifed to death, Albertina possesses a knife to defend herself. This young woman expresses a new era; free-spirited and independent, she is not afraid to speak her mind and to look people directly in the eye. And it is Albertina who dares first to imagine a new life, an alternative to the present state. She runs away, abandons her family and house; her brothers look for her to bring her back home but she manages to escape and, beyond the river, meet

Adélino. It is Albertina again who asks him if he wants to go away with her; she gives him an exit strategy and the possibility to free himself from the ghosts of the past that still torment him.

While Júlio of *The Green Years* "changes his life" by killing the woman he loves, Adélino, through Albertina, grabs the possibility of restarting anew, maybe in another country. Having experienced the colonial wars, the discharged soldier Adélino can be seen as an anticipation of the junior officers of the Movimento das Forças Armadas (MFA, Armed Forces Movement), who carried out the revolution in 1974. In witnessing the disappearance of his fishing community, visually suggested by the sand eating away the houses on the beach, Adélino moves beyond his anxiety by taking control of his life; in this way, he anticipates the political liberation awaiting the country. As the film becomes "blurred and light, it leaves behind misfortune and moves on toward a place still to be found, freedom."[19]

Conclusion

Paulo Rocha captured on film the tensions of the Portuguese society to reveal a country ready for change, eagerly waiting to usher in a new era. The personal stories of his characters highlight the crisis of Salazar's authoritarian regime that, out of history, cultivated the anachronistic dream of a colonial empire and the outdated policy of denying democratic freedom to its citizens. The "Carnation Revolution" of 1974 will bring parliamentary democracy but also a diffuse disillusion caused by many unfulfilled promises. Rocha will leave democratic Portugal and its imperfections to find refuge in the Far East where, collecting the remnants of legendary Portuguese men like Wenceslau de Moraes and Luís de Camões, he will continue to reflect on the events of his country and produce images carrying the possibility of a new beginning.

In the meantime, more outsiders keep arriving in Lisbon: inhabiting the frames of Pedro Costa's *Ossos/Bones* (Portugal, 1997), African immigrants from the former colonies land—amid general indifference—with their load of pain and desperation in the city. Trapped in the slums of Fontainhas, they share their poverty with a young couple and their unwanted baby. Júlio and Ilda are still in Lisbon waiting for their redemption.

Notes

1. "Paulo Rocha foi, com Fernando Lopes, António de Macedo e alguns outros, un nome fundamental no arranque e estabelecimento do Novo Cinema Português dos anos 60 do Século XX." Carlos Melo Ferreira, "Paulo Rocha no Cinema Português," *Cinema Journal of Philosophy and the Moving Image* 5 (2014): 157–74, at 157.
2. Established in 1956, the Calouste Gulbenkian Foundation functioned, especially up to the 1990s, as a "super ministry of culture" that has decisively transformed the Portuguese artistic life.
3. Jacques Rancière, *Politics of Aesthetics: The Distribution of the Sensible* (New York: Continuum, 2004), 9.
4. Patricia Vieira, *Portuguese Film, 1930–1960: The Staging of the New State Regime* (London: Bloomsbury, 2013), 97.
5. Barbara Mennel, *Cities and Cinema* (London: Routledge, 2008), 66.
6. "On trouve les noms de cinq jeunes cinéastes (Doniol-Valcroze, Kast, Resnais, Sautet, Truffaut) parmi les signataires du 'Manifeste des 121,' cette prise de position radicale d'une poignée d'intellectuels courageux contre la guerre coloniale, en septembre 1960." Jean-Michel Frodon, *Le Cinéma Français: De la Nouvelle Vague à nos jours* (Paris: Cahiers du Cinéma, 2010), 163.
7. In the time period that ends in 1974, excluding the films that were autonomously produced in the colonies or the ones funded mainly by foreigners, only the following years saw more than five films produced in Portugal: 1963 (six films), 1964 (nine films), 1965 (seven films), 1972 (seven films) and 1974 (seven films). Augusto M. Seabra, ed., *Portogallo: "Cinema novo" e oltre* (Venice: Marsilio, 1988).
8. The Secretariado de Propaganda Nacional was created in 1935 to help publicize the regime's achievements.
9. Kenneth Maxwell, *The Making of Portuguese Democracy* (Cambridge: Cambridge University Press, 1995), 17.
10. "The Portuguese Catholic Church not only contributed to the shaping of the regime's ideology, it also functioned as one of its principal tools to be used in the political arena." Silas Cerqueira, "L'Église catholique et la dictature corporatiste portugais," *Revue française de sciences politique* 23 (June 3, 1973): 473–513.
11. Augusto M. Seabra, *Portogallo: "Cinema novo" e oltre* (Venice: Marsilio, 1988), 12.

12. Mennel, *Cities and Cinema*, 67.
13. Georg Simmel, *Simmel on Culture: Selected Writings*, ed. David Frisby and Mike Featherstone (London: Sage, 1997), 11.
14. Antoine de Baecque, "Nouvelle Vague: 50 Years On," the French Institute Cine Lumière, London, March 2009.
15. Richard John Neupert, *A History of the French New Wave Cinema* (Madison: University of Wisconsin Press, 2002), xviii.
16. Neupert, *History of the French New Wave Cinema*, 108.
17. Only on very few occasions has Portuguese cinema taken an interest in the colonies or in the colonial wars that were fought between 1961 and 1974. Surprisingly, also among the propaganda films, very few films recognized the colonial reality: among them, *O Feitiço do Império/Spell of the Empire* (Portugal, 1940) by António Lopes Ribeiro and *Chaimite/Chaimite* (Portugal, 1953) by Jorge Brum do Canto. In 1966, Faria de Almeida's *Catembe/Catembe* (Portugal, 1965)—shot in Mozambique—was censored. Interestingly, *29 Irmãos/29 Brothers* (Portugal, 1965) by Augusto Fraga is considered a sister film of *Mudar de Vida* because its main character is a returning soldier. After the Revolution of 1974, Portuguese cinema dealt with the colonies and the wars with more frequency in *Um Adeus Português/A Portuguese Farewell* (Portugal, 1985) by João Botelho; *Não o a vã gloria de mandar/No or the vain glory of command* (Portugal, 1990) by de Oliveira; and in *Tabu* (Portugal, 2012) by Miguel Gomes.
18. Antoine de Baecque, *Camera Historica* (New York: Columbia University Press, 2012), 148.
19. Bruno Fornara, "Qui e Altrove: Il cinema di Paulo Rocha," *Cineforum* 10 (1995): 24–28.

Bibliography

Baptista, Tiago. "Nationally Correct: The Invention of Portuguese Cinema." *Portuguese Cultural Studies* 3 (Spring 2010): 3–18.

Cerqueira, Silas. "L'Église catholique et la dictature corporatiste portugais." *Revue française de science politique* 23 (June 3, 1973): 473–513.

De Baecque, Antoine. *Camera Historica*. New York: Columbia University Press, 2012.

Gallagher, Tag. "Mizoguchi and Freedom." *Screening the Past* 13 (2001): 44–53.

Maxwell, Kenneth. *The Making of Portuguese Democracy*. Cambridge: Cambridge University Press, 1995.

Melo e Castro, Paul. *Shades of Grey: 1960s Lisbon in Novel, Film, and Photobook.* London: MHRA, 2011.

Melo Ferreira, Carlos. "Paulo Rocha no Cinema Português." *Cinema Journal of Philosophy and the Moving Image* 5 (2014): 157–74.

Mennel, Barbara. *Cities and Cinema.* London: Routledge, 2008.

Neupert, Richard John. *A History of the French New Wave Cinema.* Madison: University of Wisconsin Press, 2002.

Rancière, Jacques. *Politics of Aesthetics: The Distribution of the Sensible.* New York: Continuum, 2004.

Seabra, Augusto M. *Portogallo: "Cinema novo" e oltre.* Venice: Marsilio, 1988.

Simmel, Georg. *Simmel on Culture: Selected Writings.* Edited by David Frisby and Mike Featherstone. London: Sage, 1997.

Vieira, Patricia. *Portuguese Film, 1930–1960: The Staging of the New State Regime.* London: Bloomsbury, 2013.

4

The Czechoslovak New Wave Revisited

Peter Hames

Writing about Věra Chytilová's 1966 film *Sedmikrásky/Daisies*, Jonathan Rosenbaum argued that whereas critics had been preoccupied with the innovations of the French New Wave in the 1960s, their attention should really have been directed toward Eastern Europe, where the changes were formally and politically much more radical. He was referring, in particular, to the work of Chytilová and of the Hungarian director Miklós Jancsó.[1] Rosenbaum's comments were in celebration of the first ten years of the British DVD company, Second Run, which had then released over fifty Eastern European titles, most of them from the 1960s. In 2015, a massive forty-five-film tribute to the Czechoslovak New Wave was launched in Warsaw and, in 2015–16, there were retrospectives in London devoted to two of its leading female directors, Chytilová and Drahomíra Vihanová.

If *Daisies* has acquired a certain cult following, the same can be said of *Valerie a týden divů/Valerie and Her Week of Wonders* (dir. Jaromil Jireš, 1970) and *Marketa Lazarová/Marketa Lazarova* (dir. František Vláčil, 1967). Vláčil's work went virtually unnoticed in international circles in the 1960s but has excited a powerful "late" interest leading to retrospectives in New York, London, and Moscow, among others. One suspects that it is the formal originality of these films that appeals, since they are at total variance with the structures of most contemporary mainstream cinema. They are certainly being received out of their original context.

The Czechoslovak New Wave of the 1960s attracted international attention when two films, *Obchod na korze/The Shop on Main Street* (dirs. Ján Kadár and Elmar Klos, 1965) and *Ostře sledované vlaky/Closely Watched Trains* (dir. Jiří Menzel, 1966), won Hollywood Oscars (1966 and 1967) in quick succession. Miloš Forman's films *Lásky jedné plavovlásky/Loves of a Blonde* (1965) and *Hoří, má panenko/The Firemen's Ball* (1967) were also nominated in 1966 and 1968 respectively. At Cannes, Vojtěch Jasný won the Special Jury Prize in 1963 for *Až přijde kocour/Cassandra Cat* (1963) and Best Direction in 1969 for *Všichni dobří rodáci/All My Good Countrymen* (1969). In 1968, the year of the May events in Paris and the Soviet invasion of Czechoslovakia, no less than three Czechoslovak films were in competition—*O slavnosti a hostech/Report on the Party and the Guests* (dir. Jan Němec, 1966), *Rozmarné léto/Capricious Summer* (dir. Jiří Menzel, 1967), and *The Firemen's Ball*. Czechoslovak films also regularly won awards at other European festivals such as Locarno and Mannheim. This essay assesses the significance of the Czechoslovak New Wave for the politics and culture of the 1960s within both a national and international context.

In 1964 the Czech critic Antonín J. Liehm described how his peers had only just realized that the Czech "film miracle" had occurred.[2] While the impact of the New Wave can be traced to the arrival between 1961 and 1963 of a new generation of directors, such as Chytilová, Forman, and Jireš, the roots go deeper, to what the novelist and screenwriter Josef Škvorecký described as the Ur-wave,[3] which made significant breakthroughs in the late 1950s. Here, he is referring to the work of Jasný, Vláčil, and Karel Kachyňa. While his book only describes Czech cinema, this generation also included Slovak directors such as Peter Solan and Štefan Uher.

Alice Lovejoy suggests that the tendency to see the history of Eastern European cinema in terms of Cold War parameters leads to a simplification of history—that there is diversity, struggle, and continuity underlying even the worst years of Stalinism.[4] There are also, I would argue, links with the prewar era, which are notably absent, for instance, in the case of British cinema. The films of the prewar director Martin Frič were much in evidence during my first visit to Czechoslovakia in the early 1970s, and other filmmakers who began their careers before the war lectured at Filmová a televizní fakulta, Akademie múzických umění (FAMU, Film and TV School of the Academy of Performing Arts in Prague). Among them were Otakar Vávra, Václav Krška, Elmar Klos, and Jiří Weiss. Many of these directors also continued to win international attention with their films during the 1950s. One should also mention the fact that Czech animation, particularly the work of Jiří Trnka and Karel Zeman, flowered in the 1950s in the unlikeliest of climates. I would also argue, along with Škvorecký,[5] that "artistic common sense" gnawed at the system from the beginning.

Nonetheless, little doubt exists that the innovations of the 1960s would not have taken the same form without the work of the film school. The first film school in Czechoslovakia was set up in 1937 in Slovakia by the ethnographer and photographer, Karel Plicka, director of the classic documentary *Zem spieva/The Earth Sings* (1933) and was attended by the then young Ján Kadár. Plicka became the first dean of FAMU when it was established after the war in 1946. The school consisted of seven departments, with the early staff including Jiří Weiss (who had worked during the war with the British Crown Film Unit) as head of directing.

In the 1960s, however, the figure of Vávra was the most important, introducing a curriculum based on Institut des hautes études cinématographiques (IDHEC, the Institute for Advanced Cinematographic Studies) in Paris and Vsesoyuznyi gosudarstvennyi institut kinematografii (VGIK, All-Union State Cinema Institute) in Moscow. It stressed the importance of studies in literature and art history in addition to the more technical aspects of training. Vávra himself conducted one cohort of students (Chytilová, Menzel, Evald Schorm, Jan Schmidt) through all four years of the course. As is evident from his films, he adopted a rigorous and often classically "academic" approach to filmmaking. But, as Chytilová once said, she wanted to learn everything from the conventional perspective so that she knew how to break the rules.

This leads to a second factor in the school's approach: the development of personal expression and individual creative ability. The dean at that time, A. M. Brousil, despite, as Jan Němec put it, "being a Bolshevik," presided over a regime where students could see most of the latest international films when they were brought to Prague for potential distribution. Thus, students had the opportunity to see work by Fellini, Antonioni, Resnais, Godard, Bresson, and Buñuel, among others. During this period, the novelist Milan Kundera also lectured at FAMU and exerted an influence. Three of his works were filmed, most notably Jireš's adaptation of his novel *Žert/The Joke* (1968). FAMU rapidly acquired an international reputation with directors such as Jerzy Passendorfer (Poland) and Frank Beyer (German Democratic Republic) studying there in the 1950s and Agnieszka Holland (Poland) studying there in the 1960s. In the 1970s virtually the whole of the "Yugoslav School" (Rajko Grlić, Emir Kusturica, Goran Paskaljević, Goran Marković, Srdjan Karanović, Lordan Zafranović) studied at FAMU.

The first generation of Czech and Slovak students to graduate from FAMU included Jasný, Kachyňa, Solan, and Uher. Given the show trials and the execution of leading Communists and the Stalinist repression of the early 1950s, and the adherence to the most rigid criteria of socialist realism, they did not have the same opportunities as their colleagues of the 1960s. Nonetheless, Alice Lovejoy's recent study points out the importance of the Czechoslovak Army Film Unit during this period.[6]

The Army Film Unit was set up in the 1930s and was principally associated with the name of Jiří Jeníček, a career soldier but also a professional photographer with close links to the avant-garde. He was much influenced by the model of sponsored filmmaking adopted by the Empire Marketing Board and the General Post Office (GPO) Film Unit in the United Kingdom under John Grierson. Much like the British documentary movement, it was also seen as a training ground for feature filmmakers. Most filmmakers worked for the unit during their two years of national service. Others worked for longer periods—Jasný and Kachyňa for five years. Vláčil, one of the few major directors not to go to film school, owed virtually all of his training to the film unit. Many leading cinematographers, as well as composers and editors, collaborated on army films.

Thus, many of the directors to attract attention in the 1960s—Jasný, Kachyňa, Vláčil, Solan, Uher, to which one can add Ján Kadár, who made his debut in 1945, and Zbyněk Brynych, who entered the industry around the same time—had served their apprenticeship in the 1950s. Even Miloš Forman, who graduated in 1956, had already worked as an assistant to Martin Frič and Alfréd Radok (in both film and theater) before making his debut in 1963.

If one looks at the films of the 1960s overall, with the exception of veterans like Frič and Vávra, one is looking at two groups. The older directors, who made their debuts in the 1940s and 1950s, were filmmakers who had experienced the war and, in many cases, supported the attempt to create a "socialist" society. Despite their conflicts with authority, this was certainly the case with Kadár and Klos, and both Jasný and Kachyňa made ideologically committed films. The second group consisted of directors who had grown up under what passed for socialism and for whom it was their overall life experience. Lovejoy suggests that many of these younger filmmakers were then in their twenties and were making their films for an audience 80 percent of which was in the same age group. Since official policies favored youth, considerable latitude was given to those "born under socialism."

The Czechoslovak New Wave films were clearly not anticapitalist but neither were they obviously antisocialist even if, in films such as *The Joke*, *All My Good Countrymen*, or *Report on the Party and the Guests*, they supplied obvious criticisms of the 1950s or of current bureaucratic excesses. Here, it is important to recognize that the Czechoslovak New Wave developed alongside and contributed to the Czechoslovak reform movement leading to the Prague Spring of 1968.

It can be argued that the reform movement of the 1960s was not directed against socialism as such but was in opposition to the Soviet model, aiming for a progression toward a more democratic and open society. In 1968, Alexander Dubček, who had been appointed General Secretary of the Party that year, spoke of the widest democratization of the whole social and political system, censorship was abolished, and workers' councils were established. This was a potential realization of the objectives of the reform movement. There is no reason therefore to suppose that most filmmakers, whether Party members or not, did not share in these overall objectives.

Debates within the Party, the Writers' Union, and the Film Makers' Union were clearly of significance in their reflection of changing attitudes and in the movement toward reform. While the Communist influence was strong in the period of the democratic interregnum between 1945 and 1948, it was not until the "February events" of 1948, the establishment of total power, and the rigorous persecution of the democratic opposition, that ideological conformity was genuinely established. Given the fact that both Stalin and the Czech Communist leader Klement Gottwald died in 1953 and that Khrushchev's denunciation of Stalin took place in 1956, one is looking at a short if traumatic period of historical time.

The attempt to reform the Communist system from the inside is too large a subject to address here, but it is clear that there was a movement within the system on political, economic, philosophical, and cultural levels.

Marxist philosophers such as Karel Kosík and Ivan Sviták supported the changes, speaking out in favor of the new developments and, in particular, the role of film. Articles appeared as early as 1956 and 1957, and Kosík's important study, *Dialektika konkrétního* (*Dialectics of the Concrete*) was published in 1963. He argued that bureaucratic rule had led to a "false totalization" and that the (Marxist) dialectic expressed "the movement of human praxis," expressing contradictions.

In 1963, the legendary Kafka conference was held in Prague. It was in response to a speech Jean-Paul Sartre gave in Moscow the previous year where he had argued for the universality of Kafka and the need for a Marxist study. Kosík described "the Kafkaesque world" as "the world of absurdity of human thoughts and action, of human dreams, a world of a monstrous and unintelligible labyrinth, a world of human powerlessness in the network of bureaucratic machines, mechanisms, reified relations."[7] Examples from "socialist" society were not hard to identify. In his recent film *Vlk z Královských Vinohrad/The Wolf of Royal Vineyard Street* (2016), Jan Němec dramatizes an interview with a member of state security in which Kafka is assumed to be a present-day (that is, 1970s) leader of the counterrevolution.

Vera Blackwell argued in 1966 that since Czechoslovakia was a "closed society," ideas could circulate very rapidly among the intelligentsia and that "serious and basic questions about human existence," based on common experience, could rapidly become a moving force for society as a whole.[8] While a number of the 1960s films can be linked fairly directly to Kafka, it is this shared experience that led Sviták to link a whole range of films to "the alienated hero,"[9] which can be seen as one of the defining characteristics of the New Wave. In Kosík's words, "in contrast to the regime's official or implicit assumptions, Czech culture emphasizes Man as a complex creature, continually active, elastic, striving to overcome conflicts, a being irreducible to a single dimension."[10]

As suggested earlier, the roots of criticism can be traced to the late 1950s when a number of films began to challenge the system. The work of Ladislav Helge was of particular significance. His first two features, *Škola otců/School for Fathers* (1957) and *Velká samota/Great Seclusion*, 1959), dealt respectively with the problems of a teacher confronting a school life corrupted by ideology, and a committed communist confronting the less-than-perfect reality of his village cooperative. Other directors committed to Communism who challenged the system included Ján Kadár and Elmar Klos, whose work included *Hudba z Marsu/Music from Mars* (1955) and *Tři přání/Three Wishes* (1958), both adapted from scripts by the satirical writer Vratislav Blažek. At a conference in Banská Bystrica in 1959, a number of these films were criticized and banned, including *School for Fathers*, *Three Wishes*, Jasný's *Zářijové noci/September Nights* (1956), and Václav Krška's *Zde jsou lvi/Hic sunt leones/Here There Are Lions* (1958). Criticism was launched at other filmmakers, including Brynych. As already noted, many of these directors went on to make major contributions to the films of the 1960s. Furthermore, major names, who later collaborated with the younger directors, such as cinematographers Jaroslav Kučera and Jan Čuřík, began their careers in the mid-1950s. Others, such as composer Zdeněk Liška and film editor Miroslav Hájek, had begun their careers even earlier. It is possible to argue that had the "New Wave" not happened, critical and aesthetic changes would still have occurred. The reality, of course, is different. The generations interacted in a wider, international sociocultural sphere of influence and not solely in the context of Czech and Slovak culture.

The particular visual flavor of the Wave can be linked to national traditions in cinematography. The visual qualities of Czech cinema had already manifested themselves in the 1930s in films such as Gustav Machatý's *Extase/Ecstasy* (1933), Josef Rovenský's *Řeka/The River* (1933), and František Čáp's and Václav Krška's *Ohnivé léto/Fiery Summer* (1939). Cinematographers such as Jan Stallich, Karel Degl, and Ferdiinand Pečenka all taught at FAMU. Thus, it can be argued that there is a continuing tradition through to Kučera and Čuřík. Similarly, both Jasný and Kachyňa also studied cinematography, as did "New Wave" director Jireš. These qualities were often linked to the lyrical presentation of landscape—the sense of the countryside as a homeland or lost paradise.

Yet the question of style and influence needs to be treated with extreme care. Most filmmakers do not set out to imitate one another, and influence is at best a springboard for future work. Influence is also more widely disseminated than audiences and critics might expect on the basis of films distributed to cinemas. Nonetheless, each generation has its own models and terms of reference. If one looks at Antonín Liehm's collection of interviews with key directors recorded in the late 1960s, those of the older generation are more likely to reference Soviet cinema (Eisenstein, Dovzhenko, Pudovkin) alongside Italian Neorealism and Ingmar Bergman. The younger directors reference Antonioni, Fellini, Resnais, and Godard. Incidentally, with reference to the Slovak director Juraj Jakubisko, Liehm himself draws parallels with Glauber Rocha and Alejandro Jodorowsky.

While the system may not have exerted such a monolithic grip from the late 1950s as is normally suggested, there was nonetheless a conformity to be challenged both in subject and content. It is frequently (and accurately) argued that, for the young directors of the early 1960s, the objective was to put "real life" on the screen and to attack the "stupidity" of the standard product. Miloš Forman has often commented on how he "salivated" at the image of real people on the screen.

Probably the first to achieve this new realism was Věra Chytilová, although she habitually combined the influence of cinéma vérité with formal innovation. This is most notable in her graduation film *Strop/Ceiling* (1961), where she combines a "documentary" account of the life of a fashion model with a fictional account of the model's internal and emotional life. She makes striking use of this formula in her film *Pytel blech/A Bagful of Fleas* (1962), where she examines the lives of young factory girls through the eye of a subjective camera. Her feature debut, *O něčem jiném/Something Different* (1963) saw her combine an account of the life and training of the champion gymnast Eva Bosáková with a fictional account of the life of a housewife. Miloš Forman's two films *Konkurs/Talent Competition* and *Černý Petr/Black Peter* were released the same year, to be followed by *Loves of a Blonde* (1965) and Ivan Passer's *Intimní osvětlení/Intimate Lighting* (1966).

With his cowriters, Ivan Passer and Jaroslav Papoušek, Forman worked with nonprofessional actors and semi-improvised dialogue to provide a view of working-class life free from official stereotypes, combining this with a profound social analysis and a relaxed approach to narrative. Drahomíra Vihanová's graduation film *Fuga na černých klávesách/Fugue on the Black Keys* (1964) demonstrated—as did Chytilová—a desire to combine the reality of street scenes with a subjective story. To some extent, the desire to reflect real life together with formal experiment is also apparent in Štefan Uher's Slovak production *Slnko v sieti/The Sun in a Net* (1962), the one feature film considered a genuine forerunner of the "Wave."

The realist tendency, which arguably had the most immediate international influence, was relatively short-lived. By the time of *The Firemen's Ball*, Forman's approach and humor was already more self-conscious and deliberate and, in *Daisies*, Chytilová more or less abandoned cinéma vérité for her highly sophisticated investigation into the possibilities of film language.

It is worth considering the example of Chytilová in more detail, as her work in many respects mirrors the developments of the 1960s. While all of the directors shared in the objectives of opposing the stereotypes of socialist realism, this aesthetic dogma had also been inevitably linked to conventional film forms. In addition to attempts to portray everyday reality, there was, therefore, also a revolt against formal convention. While this rebellion shared elements with similar movements such as British Free Cinema and the French New Wave, it also reflected a greater political content and significance.

Although Chytilová objected to films being produced that resembled one another "like so many eggs," she also aspired to put real life experience, especially that of women, on screen. Despite being a student film, *Ceiling* attracted a good deal of international attention. When first shown, its merits as a documentary impressed. It is in fact, however, artfully constructed with a use of creative montage and subjective commentary. The final sequence, in which Marta walks through the city streets at night, shows her as a decorative object among neon lights and shop window displays. City streets at night also recall traditions in avant-garde film.

In her little seen short film, *A Bagful of Fleas*, Chytilová comes most close to cinéma vérité influences, but it is certainly not a documentary, despite its surface appearance. It was filmed in the town of Náchod, a center of the textile industry, where the factories created dormitories for their female workers. While she used nonactors throughout and allowed some improvisation of dialogue, the scenes are nonetheless constructed. The central character, Eva, joins a work team, and the action is principally seen through her eyes. Her voice is heard off camera both interacting with and commenting on the action. Besides immersing us in a female reality far from approved stereotypes, set principally in the dormitory, the film also provides scope for formal invention. One scene is conducted in virtual darkness, the camera circling an almost abstract space as disembodied voices talk at night.

Chytilová's first feature film, *Something Different*, was one of the films that—together with Forman's *Black Peter* and Jireš's *Křik/The Cry* (1963)—was considered a breakthrough film of the New Wave. Here, she experimented with telling the parallel stories of two women experiencing different life situations—one filmed as documentary and the other as fiction. The first is a cinéma vérité style account of the training and competitions of the gymnast Eva Bosáková. The second is the story of Věra, a housewife living in a world of domestic boredom and marginalization. In focusing on the hopes and aspirations of women in a male-dominated society, the film was clearly ahead of its time. It won awards in West Germany (Mannheim), Italy, and Poland and was featured in the First International Festival of Women's Film held in 1972 in New York City. While Věra's story is fairly conventional in narrative terms, the film is also an exercise in the pure pleasure of filmmaking. The gymnastic exercises, in particular, are presented with a great deal of formal sophistication. In form, it anticipates many later ideas developed around feminist cinema.

In *Something Different*, Chytilová worked with the cinematographer Jan Čuřík, who had previously worked with Vláčil. With *Daisies*, she turned to Jaroslav Kučera, who had contributed much to the success of Jasný's films. Kučera, who was married to Chytilová, was intensely interested in visual experiment and certainly wanted to make a film in which the image could go beyond mere illustration. The script was cowritten by Ester Krumbachová, who was also responsible for design. While the film had precise dialogues, to "safeguard its meaning," Chytilová and Krumbachová otherwise left themselves open to improvisation and free thinking. The result was controversial and the film remains unique even in today's context.

Here, it is clear that Chytilová has finally abandoned any pretense at "realism" (even if her two protagonists are played by nonprofessionals). She once described the film as a "philosophical documentary in the form of a farce." Two girls live in a kind of vacuum with no past or future, and their cheating and provocation leads to the destruction of both themselves and everything around them. In place of conventional narrative, the film takes the form of a sequence of "happenings" based on the game "It matters—it doesn't matter." The girls are variously framed in a garden, a nightclub, with a lover, with old and middle-aged men (whom they exploit), climaxing with the destruction of a large banquet (presumably destined for Communist bureaucrats).

Although impossible to summarize, Herbert Eagle makes a persuasive case for the film's links with Dadaism, in its use of montage and its "radical collisions of signs from disparate cultural and artistic orders." Since women have been excluded from productive behavior, they have turned to art and play. "There is a semantic linkage," Eagle writes, "between the spoiled but creative characters and the spoiled (in terms of violating norms) and creative female artists (Chytilová and Krumbachová)."[11]

Daisies caused an immediate scandal, and twenty-one deputies signed a protest demanding its withdrawal from distribution alongside Němec's *Report on the Party and the Guests* (also coscripted by Krumbachová). The films were alleged to "have nothing in common with our Republic, socialism, and the ideals of Communism." Both films were given restricted distribution but were eventually released. In Chytilová's final film from this era, *Ovoce stromů rajských jíme/The Fruit of Paradise* (1969), a coproduction with Belgium, she also sought to make the maximum use of film language. While avoiding the fragmentation and montage of *Daisies*, its storyline is deliberately obscure. It is more, as Jan Žalman suggests, a kinesthetic experience in which a logical storyline becomes irrelevant.[12] Ignored until relatively recently, it is finally receiving the attention it deserves. The most experimental of the New Wave films, it is a film in which different lines of expression—narrative, acting, design (Krumbachová), cinematography (Kučera), and music (Zdeněk Liška)—exhibit independence and interaction. Iveta Jusová and Dan Reyes suggest that the film's "dynamic and intersubjective encounters" reflect feminine subjectivity.[13]

The real significance of the 1960s lies in the promotion of individual expression both in terms of form and content. If one looks at the directors contributing to the development, the numbers are striking and generalization other than the superficial becomes inadequate. As Jaroslav Brož put it in 1967: "when there suddenly emerged not five or ten but fifteen or twenty promising individuals we are fully justified to face the future with optimism."[14]

Nonetheless, if one is forced to simplify, then the late 1950s can be seen to be characterized by the poetic cinema of Vláčil, Uher, Jasný, and Kachyňa—an approach that they continued through the 1960s albeit with a progressively more radical social and political content. While some of the new generation exhibited elements of this tradition—arguably Jireš and Menzel—the more general stylistic legacies of the New Wave comprised the already described "realist" developments of the early 1960s, the personal cinema of directors such as Němec and Juraj Jakubisko, and the unique exploration of film form developed by Chytilová.

Toward the end of the 1960s, increased collaboration with Western European countries also took place. This was particularly true of Slovakia, where there was collaboration with France (Jakubisko's *Vtáčkovia, siroty a blázni/ Birds, Orphans, and Fools*, 1969) and Italy (Jakubisko's *Zbehovia a pútnici/The Deserter and the Nomads*, 1968 and *Dovidenia v pekle, priatelia!/See You in Hell Fellows*, 1970–90).[15]

In considering the international influence and reception of the Czechoslovak New Wave, it is necessary to look at both critical responses and the wider influence on filmmakers. While much of the evidence is inevitably inconsistent and inconclusive, positive responses and influences are clear. Given Czechoslovakia's links with nonaligned countries, many films were able to exhibit an influence beyond purely European boundaries. The influence is, however, most apparent in the United States, France, United Kingdom, and Central Europe.

The wide range of festival and other awards gained during the 1960s does not automatically convert to a wider influence or a significant (as opposed to temporary) journalistic or academic response. The main American impact was, of course, achieved through the Academy Award for Best Foreign Film won by *The Shop on Main Street* in 1965, followed by that awarded to *Closely Watched Trains* in 1967 together with the shortlisting of Forman's *Loves of a Blonde* and *The Firemen's Ball*. This perhaps explains why Kadár and Forman were the first Czechoslovak directors to establish American careers. Both Kadár's *The Angel Levine* (1970) and Forman's *Taking Off* (1971) were the results of initiatives that predated the Soviet invasion. Kadár's film featured Ida Kamińska, the Polish star of *The Shop on Main Street*, along with a score and soundtrack by his regular composer Zdeněk Liška (subsequently reedited), and Forman's regular cinematographer, Miroslav Ondříček, photographed *Taking Off*.

If one looks at critical responses in film magazines, *Film Comment* and *Film Quarterly* made the most significant interventions. Kadár and Klos were interviewed in *Film Comment* in the fall 1967 issue, while articles by Kirk Bond and Antonín J. Liehm appeared in the fall 1968 issue. *Film Quarterly* featured Harriet Polt's study of Czech animation (1964) and Jan Žalman's "Some

Question Marks on the New Czech Cinema" (1967). Both Liehm and Žalman were, of course, providing Czech accounts of the developments. *Film Quarterly* also published French critic Claire Clouzot's reviews of *Intimate Lighting* and *Daisies*, while the review of Vláčil's *Marketa Lazarova* by Ernest Callenbach and Emory Menefee provided the only significant recognition for a film that Czech critics later, in 1998, voted the best Czech film ever made. Needless to say, most of the articles came out in 1968, the year when the Prague Spring itself was headline news. They served almost as a valediction, as the Soviet invasion came in August and the shutters progressively came down during the following year.

The same was largely true of French responses. Here, interest was largely directed at the work of Forman, with articles in *Cahiers du Cinéma* and the publication of the screenplay of *Loves of a Blonde* in *L'Avant Scène du Cinéma* in 1966. Forman's French connections were reinforced when Claude Berri and François Truffaut arranged foreign sales for *The Firemen's Ball*, which was smuggled to Paris with the help of Jan Němec and Pavel Juráček. Berri coproduced Forman's US-based *Taking Off* as well as *Valmont* (1989). Jean-Claude Carrière collaborated on the scripts of both films as well as on *Goya's Ghosts* (2006) and the ill-fated (unproduced) *Embers* and *The Ghost of Munich*.

In 1968, as already mentioned, three Czech films were scheduled to compete for the Palme d'Or at the Cannes Film Festival: *The Firemen's Ball*, *Report on the Party and the Guests*, and *Capricious Summer*. It was the year, of course, that the festival was closed down by Godard and others in support of the May events in Paris. In his final film, *The Wolf of Royal Vineyard Street*, Němec refers to them as "left wing fools" and stages a mock assassination of Godard. He also criticizes Godard for his *Pravda* (1969), shot in Prague, for its negative portrayal of the Prague Spring.

The most substantive critical interest, however, was via the extensive interview with Chytilová by Michel Delahaye and Jacques Rivette in the February 1968 issue of *Cahiers du Cinéma*.[16] It remains one of the most significant critical interventions not least because of the parallels that developed between Rivette and Chytilová. It highlights the doubling of the female "heroines" in both *Something Different* and *Daisies*. Rivette speaks of how he found the double narrative of *Something Different* progressively more mysterious. In an accompanying article, Paul-Louis Martin points out that in

Something Different the two heroines never meet "in reality," whereas in *Daisies* they are always together but never truly distinct.[17] He also suggests that her refusal of realism is even more systematic than that of Godard. The influence of these ideas is readily apparent in Rivette's *Out 1* (1970–71), *Céline et Julie vont en bateau/Celine and Julie Go Boating* (1974), and *Duelle/Twilight* (1975–76). This merely demonstrates the fact that ideas traveled from east to west as well as from west to east.

In the United Kingdom, there was little significant critical coverage, although *Sight and Sound* addressed Forman's films and Claire Clouzot wrote "Sons of Kafka" for the winter 1966 issue. Yet the monthly magazine *Films and Filming* sponsored a major festival of Czech film in 1965 at which Jan Němec's *Demanty noci/Diamonds of the Night* (1964) won a major award. Lindsay Anderson, a systematic champion of both Czechoslovak and Polish cinema, lent his support by supervising the subtitles for the British release of *The Shop on Main Street*.

Anderson had visited Czechoslovakia the same year, where he was received by Forman, Passer, and Jireš, among others. Forman has commented on his admiration for Anderson's film *This Sporting Life* (1963), and Anderson visited the sets of both *Loves of a Blonde* and Němec's *Mučedníci lásky/Martyrs of Love* (1966), where he played a walk-on role. Anderson noted in his diaries that *Loves of a Blonde* was "full of superb and delicate poetic things."[18] He also described its similarity to the British "Free Cinema" films with which he had been associated along with Karel Reisz and Tony Richardson in the 1950s. The director of photography on both Czech films was Miroslav Ondříček, which led directly to Anderson's offer for him to work with him on his adaptation of Shelagh Delaney's *The White Bus* (1967). This subsequently led to his work with Anderson on *If. . .* (1968) and *O Lucky Man!* (1973).

Ken Loach, whose work is quite close to that of early Forman, has often cited *Loves of a Blonde* and *Closely Watched Trains* as two of his favorite films. He has also acknowledged the indirect influence of Ondříček since his director of photography, Chris Menges, worked as an assistant to Ondříček on *If. . .* before working on Loach's *Kes* (1969). Despite the occasional similarities between British and Czech humor, it is difficult not to see a more direct influence in films such as Bill Forsyth's *Gregory's Girl* (1981) and

Mark Herman's *Brassed Off* (1996) in terms of their working-class themes and low-key approach.

In the case of the United States, the country most favored by Czechoslovak cinematic exiles, the influence tended to work in reverse. Although early films such as *Taking Off* and Passer's *Born to Win* (1971) seemed to mark a continuation of Czech sensibilities, this did not last long. As Forman has noted, American audiences (and producers) expected clear narratives, and his improvisatory style proved difficult to replicate in a foreign language. Consequently, he decided to make "American" films based on known literary or dramatic subjects—Ken Kesey, Ragni's and Rado's *Hair*, E. L. Doctorow—and continued the practice with his Czech-made *Amadeus* (1984, from Peter Shaffer) and the French *Valmont* (1989, from Laclos). The original scripts of Scott Alexander and Larry Karazewski for his films on Larry Flynt and Andy Kaufman were quintessentially American. Ondříček photographed most of his films while at the same time working on other American films and maintaining a Czech career. With the exception of the classic *Cutter's Way* (1981), Passer seemed content to inject an unusual sensitivity into a variety of commercial projects that ranged from his Emmy-award-winning biopic of *Stalin* (1992) to Stevenson's *Kidnapped* (1995). Kadár's brief American career (he died in 1979), despite the international success of the Canadian-made *Lies My Father Told Me* (1975), was also star-crossed. Generally, one could argue that Czech culture was absorbed by American culture rather than the reverse.

Since the Prague Spring and the culture it produced was suppressed in Central and Eastern Europe, one could not expect direct allegiances, but there are overt references in a number of films, including Krszysztof Kieslowksi's *Amator/Camera Buff* (1976). There is little doubt that the films of the New Wave not only made a significant impact in Poland but also more generally. Grzegorz Zariczny's recent film *Fale/Waves* (2016) also draws strongly on the tradition of early Forman, showing just how fruitful the observation of everyday life and work with nonactors can still be. A continuing influence in the Czech and Slovak Republics seems to have been intermittent. In the early days following the fall of Communism, a number of directors drew sustenance from the observational tradition (Saša Gedeon, Alice Nellis, Jan Hřebejk), but this mode has continued mainly through a strong documentary movement. More recently, a number of Slovak films seem to have followed the same path.

Under market conditions, it proved difficult for the older directors to resume their careers. Chytilová and Menzel achieved limited success, while Němec opted for a low-budget personal cinema. In retrospect, it seems likely that Němec's films—*Noční hovory s matkou/Late Night Talks with Mother* (2001), which won an award at Locarno, and *Toyen* (2005)—may have the more lasting resonance.

Little doubt exists that the New Wave is being rediscovered via DVD releases and internet resources—notably the release of *Marketa Lazarova* and *Valerie and Her Week of Wonders* by Criterion in the United States and multiple releases by companies such as the UK Second Run and the French Malavida. This rediscovery, in turn, has led to a wide range of interest from filmmakers and critics along with a good deal of internet writing and discussion. Vláčil's work has been discovered, and Chytilová's films have attracted the attention of feminist critics, a comprehensive three-month season was organized in Warsaw, and a month-long discussion was mounted online in the United States. The influence lives on and is in some ways wider and more informed than it was in the 1960s.

Notes

1. Jonathan Rosenbaum, in *10 Years of Second Run* (2015): 22.
2. Antonín J. Liehm. "Argument," *Literární noviny* 17 (April 25, 1964): 3, quoted in Alice Lovejoy, *Army Film and the Avant Garde: Cinema and Experiment in the Czechoslovak Military* (Bloomington: Indiana University Press, 2015), 161.
3. Josef Škvorecký, *All the Bright Young Men and Women: A Personal History of the Czech Cinema*, trans. Michael Schonberg (Toronto: Peter Martin Associates, 1971), 45.
4. Lovejoy, *Army Film and the Avant Garde*, 10.
5. Škvorecký, *All the Bright Young Men and Women*, 54.
6. Lovejoy, *Army Film and the Avant Garde.*
7. Karel Kosík, "Hašek and Kafka," trans. Karel Kovanda, *Telos* 23 (Spring 1975): 84–88.
8. Vera Blackwell, "Literature and the Drama," *Survey* 59 (April 1966): 41–47.
9. See Ivan Sviták, "Les héros de l'aliénation," *Image et Son* 221 (November 1968): 51–69.
10. Karel Kosík, interviewed in Antonín J. Liehm, *The Politics of Culture*, trans.

Peter Kussi (New York: Grove Press, 1973), 398–99. In addition to the "rediscovery" of Kafka, one should also mention the theater productions of Beckett, Ionesco, and Václav Havel in the period 1963 and 1965. The Czech production of Edward Albee's "Who's Afraid of Virginia Woolf?" was retitled "Who's Afraid of Kafka?"

11. Herbert Eagle, "Dada and Structuralism in Chytilová's 'Daisies,'" in *Cross-currents 10: A Yearbook of Central European Culture*, ed. Ladislav Matejka (New Haven, CT: Yale University Press, 1991), 223–34, at 229. *Daisies* has sometimes been described as surrealist. Despite Kučera's interest in the work of the surrealist animator, Jan Švankmajer, the leader of the Prague surrealist group, Vratislav Effenberger, dismissed it as "decorative cynicism," preferring the presentation of "objective humor" in the work of Forman and the presentation of "a reality that has turned sour."
12. Jan Žalman, "Le Fruit du Paradis/Ovoce stromů rajských jíme," in *International Film Guide 1971*, ed. Peter Cowie (London: Tantivy Press, 1970), 106–7.
13. Iveta Jusová and Dan Reyes, "Věra Chytilová's 'Fruit of Paradise,' a Tale of a Feminine Aesthetic, Dancing Color, and a Doll Who Kills the Devil," *Camera Obscura* 29, no. 3 (2014): 65–91, at 81.
14. Jaroslav Brož, *The Path of Fame of the Czechoslovak Film* (Prague: Československý Filmexport, 1967), 83.
15. Jakubisko's film style exhibits a stylistic freedom reminiscent of Godard combined with inspirations from folk culture. He was also influenced by the Soviet cinematographer, Sergei Urusevski, who photographed Mikhail Kalatozov's *Letyat zhuravli/The Cranes Are Flying* (1957) and *Soy Cuba/I Am Cuba* (1964). The French and Italian links were purely commercial and all three of the films were banned. Other coproductions with western Europe included *Třicet jedna ve stínu/Ninety Degrees in the Shade* (dir. Jiří Weiss, 1965), with United Kingdom and, with France, *Muž, ktorý luže/L'Homme qui ment/The Man Who Lies* (dir. Alain Robbe-Grillet, 1968), *Tělo Diany/Le Corps de Diane/The Body of Diana* (dir. Jean-Louis Richard, 1969), and *Eden a potom/L'Eden et après/Eden and After* (dir. Alain Robbe-Grillet, 1970).
16. Michel Delahaye and Jacques Rivette, "Le champ libre: Entretien avec Věra Chytilová," *Cahiers du Cinéma* 198 (February 1968): 46–73.
17. Paul-Louis Martin, "Le métamorphoses de l'impertinence," *Cahiers du Cinéma* 198 (February 1968): 58–61.
18. Lindsay Anderson, *The Diaries*, ed. Paul Sutton (London: Methuen, 2004), 107.

Bibliography

Anderson, Lindsay. *The Diaries*. Edited by Paul Sutton. London: Methuen, 2004.

Blackwell, Vera. "Literature and the Drama." *Survey* 59 (April 1966): 41–47.

Brož, Jaroslav. *The Path of Fame of the Czechoslovak Film*. Prague: Československý Filmexport, 1967.

Delahaye, Michel, and Jacques Rivette. "Le champ libre: Entretien avec Věra Chytilová." *Cahiers du Cinéma* 198 (February 1968): 46–73.

Eagle, Herbert. "Dada and Structuralism in Chytilová's 'Daisies.'" In *Crosscurrents 10: A Yearbook of Central European Culture*, edited by Ladislav Matejka, 223–34. New Haven, CT: Yale University Press, 1991.

Jusová, Iveta, and Dan Reyes. "Věra Chytilová's *Fruit of Paradise*: A Tale of a Feminine Aesthetic, Dancing Color, and a Doll Who Kills the Devil." *Camera Obscura* 29, no. 3 (2014): 65–91.

Kosík, Karel. "Hašek and Kafka." Translated by Karel Kovanda. *Telos* 23 (Spring 1975): 84–88.

———. "Interview." Translated by Peter Kussi. In *The Politics of Culture*, by Antonín J. Liehm, 398–99. New York: Grove Press, 1973.

Liehm Antonín J. "Argument." *Literární noviny* 17 (April 25, 1964): 3.

Lovejoy, Alice. *Army Film and the Avant Garde: Cinema and Experiment in the Czechoslovak Military*. Bloomington: Indiana University Press, 2015.

Martin, Paul-Louis. "Le métamorphoses de l'impertinence." *Cahiers du Cinéma* 198 (February 1968): 58–61.

Rosenbaum, Jonathan. *10 Years of Second Run* (2015): 22.

Škvorecký, Josef. *All the Bright Young Men and Women: A Personal History of the Czech Cinema*. Translated by Michael Schonberg. Toronto: Peter Martin Associates, 1971.

Sviták, Ivan. "Les héros de l'aliénation." *Image et Son* 221 (November 1968): 51–69.

Žalman, Jan. "Le Fruit du Paradis/Ovoce stromů rajských jíme." In *International Film Guide 1971*, edited by Peter Cowie, 106–7. London: Tantivy Press, 1970.

5

Internationalism and the Early Student Films of the German Film and Television Academy Berlin (dffb)

Christina Gerhardt

The demonstrations that took place in West Berlin during the late 1960s exemplify the international nature of West Germany's 1968. Many of these protests were documented by cinema of the then newly founded German Film and Television Academy Berlin (dffb, deutsche film- und fernsehakademie berlin), which was established in 1966. The dffb was created, in part, in response to the Oberhausen Manifesto, an appeal put forward at the International Short Film Festival Oberhausen by twenty-six directors on February 28, 1962, which radically revamped the television and film industry in West Germany, demanding, not explicitly but de facto, among other things, a revision of its funding mechanisms as well as the establishment of more film schools.[1] Scholarship, by focusing on the Young German Cinema and New German Cinema that emerged after Oberhausen, has eclipsed the early cinema of the dffb and other film schools founded in response to the Oberhausen Manifesto and of the era's cinematic countermovements in West Germany.[2] This essay considers the student films of the early dffb, focusing on their relationship to the era's unfolding global political events and their local iterations, on the one hand, and, on the other hand, on their relationship to the era's cinematic new waves.

Parts of this essay were published previously as "1968 and the Early Cinema of the dffb," in "1968 and West German Cinema," ed. Christina Gerhardt, special issue, *The Sixties* 10 (2017): 26–44.

On the thirtieth anniversary of the dffb's founding, film and media theorist Tilman Baumgärtel argued: "The short documentary and agitation films, which the collective of politically active students produced during this time at the DFFB, have now been almost completely forgotten witnesses of the student movements."[3] Baumgärtel's claim continues to hold true to the present day; with the exception of Farocki, the early work of dffb filmmakers has been neglected in English-language scholarship.[4]

The reasons for this oversight of early dffb cinema are numerous. Some early dffb films have been destroyed or lost. A lack of availability is responsible: the majority of early dffb cinema was, until recently, only available in 16 mm and in archives.[5] Additionally, the early dffb student films consist mostly of amateur shorts and thus are rarely publicly screened. Yet again, Farocki's films form the major exception, both in being publicly screened and in their availability.[6]

Revisiting the films of the early dffb proves worthwhile for rethinking what constituted 1968 in West German politics and cinema for at least the following three reasons. First, since the notion of what constitutes West German cinema around 1968 has focused mostly on Young German Cinema and more so on New German Cinema, arguably West Germany's best-known post–World War II era cinema, the contributions of the dffb to political cinema, in form and content, have been, by and large, left out of (West German) film histories of the 1960s. Second, the early dffb directors both drew on and contributed to the political cinemas of other countries, helping to form an international vocabulary of the practice of radical filmmaking. Third, the early dffb directors sought to rework the relationship *between* political content and aesthetic form. That is, when lesser-known cinemas of the era are discussed, the avant-garde cinema is cast as devoid of political content,[7] and inversely, political cinema is reduced to its thematics, while the politics of its form is disregarded or underexamined.[8] Revisiting the latter point with regard to the dffb reveals how they stood in conversation with then contemporary traditions, across national boundaries.

This essay focuses on early short films produced by dffb directors Helke Sander, Ulrich Knaudt, and Harun Farocki. Concentrating on their early dffb films, this essay reveals how the early student films illuminate the era's key political preoccupations and engage the era's cinematic stylistics in ways that revise notions of what constituted West German cinema around 1968. These films demonstrate that the dffb, both the institution and its cinema, is important to the histories of 1960s politics and 1960s cinema, in West Germany and beyond. Thematically, the films examined engage with the era's main issues: corporate media coverage of the social movements and international self-liberation and self-determination struggles. Inseparable from these political concerns are the films' use and reworking of techniques ranging from Soviet montage to Italian Neorealism and French New Wave.

International Film Schools, Global New Waves, and dffb Films of the Late 1960s

When scholarship does engage the early cinema of the dffb, it tends to read it as political, which makes sense. Shortly after the school opened, in 1966, demonstrations and student uprisings in West Berlin escalated. Given the school's location in relative proximity to the political actions, its early cinema often engaged the unfolding demonstrations. On September 17, 1966, West Berlin mayor Willy Brandt cut the ribbon, officially opening the dffb. Founding codirectors were Erwin Leiser and Heinz Rathsack.[9] Of over 850 applicants, thirty-four were selected for the dffb's inaugural class.[10]

To be sure, the early dffb made efforts to recruit an international roster of students. The incoming classes of the late 1960s included the Mexican director and cameraman Carlos Bustamante; the Yugoslav filmmaker Irena Vrkljan (from current-day Croatia); the African American filmmaker and former actor Skip Norman; and Farocki, whose father had immigrated to Germany from India in the 1920s. Farocki was born in the Sudetengau region of the Nazi regime. Farocki's father "was a supporter of the militant Indian anti-colonial movement led by Subhas Chandra Bose and acted as Bose's doctor during his wartime years in Germany."[11] The family moved to India and then Indonesia, returning to West Germany in 1958 when Farocki was fourteen years old.

Film scholar Julia Knight underscores that the school offered an important opportunity to female aspiring directors within a still male-dominated profession. The inaugural class of fifteen included three women: Gerda Katharina Kramer, Helke Sander, and Irena Vrkljan.[12] Additionally, Cristina Perincioli, Gisela Tuchtenhagen, Gardi Depe, Barbara Kasper, and Marianne Lüdcke were early attendees of the dffb and directed feminist films.[13] In 1970 as many women as men were accepted. And in 1979, for the first time, more women than men were accepted into the incoming class.

The early dffb was globally focused in its intent. In 1963, dffb founding director Heinz Rathsack planned to establish a film school in West Germany and compared four European film schools, in Rome (established 1935), Paris (established 1943), Łódź (established 1947), and Madrid.[14] Previously, Rathsack had also studied and referenced the Vsesoyuznyi gosudarstvennyi institut kinematografii (VGIK, All-Union State Cinema Institute, established 1919). Rathsack noted that the Institut des hautes études cinématographiques (IDHEC) in Paris could count 301 international students among its 681 alumni since its founding in 1944. "This number alone," Rathsack argued, "gives an impression of the extent to which this institute reached beyond France. The list of former students shows that aside from students from the US and Brazil, students from Africa and Asia make up most of the international studies of the IDHEC."[15] While the VGIK and the Hochschule für Film- und Fernsehen (hff) in Potsdam constituted the main film schools for the Soviet Union and East Germany respectively, training an international roster of students from countries in Africa, Asia, eastern Europe, and Latin America, West Berlin lacked any such institution, an untenable situation during the Cold War era that fomented rivalry between the two German states. Thus, an attempt was made to establish a film school on the western side of the Berlin Wall, one that was equally as international in its draw and influence. A suggestion was made, for example, to provide three positions to people working with the Grupo Cine Liberación, cofounded by Fernando Solanas, Octavio Getino, and Gerardo Vallejo.[16]

While this never came to pass, during the first decade, dffb students, in addition to the aforementioned international students, also included people from Greece (which had suffered the CIA-assisted military junta and dictatorship starting in 1967 and lasting until 1974), Iran, Namibia (then South West Africa, ruled by South Africa), Israel, Sierra Leone, the United States, Mexico, and Yugoslavia, as outlined by Madeleine Bernstorff.[17] According to statistics compiled by Hans Helmut Prinzler, director of studies (*Studienleiter*) from 1969 to 1979, in the first decade of the dffb, of 258 students, fifty-four were international.[18]

The internationalism of the early dffb manifested not only in its demographics but also in the cinematic traditions taught and screened. One of the school's key early figures was Ulrich Gregor, who taught film history and film theory at the dffb from its founding in 1966 until 1972. Aside from teaching at the dffb, Gregor initiated key other forums that impact German cinema to this day. In 1963, Erika Gregor and Ulrich Gregor along with others cofounded the Freunde der Deutschen Kinemathek (Friends of the German Cinematheque, FDK). Films screened included a range of eras, directors, and styles. Students who were active in the social movements, such as Rudi Dutschke, and students who later attended the dffb, such as Harun Farocki, regularly attended its screenings. The screenings, which took place at the Akademie der Künste (the Berlin Academy of Arts) and other venues, sought "to connect old and new films, in order to ensure that film history was lively."[19] In 1970, through the FDK, the screenings found a permanent home and the Kino Arsenal was established. Also in 1970, the Forum des jungen Films (Forum of New Cinema), which had been established in 1968 as a counterweight to the Berlin International Film Festival, became part of the film festival, preserving, however, its own directorship.[20] Both Kino Arsenal and the International Forum of New Cinema exist to the present day.[21]

The list of films screened by the Kinemathek in the late 1960s provides a snapshot not only of the film history but also of the international range of then contemporary cinemas to which attendees were exposed.[22] While the Kinemathek screened classics of French surrealism, German expressionism, and early Russian cinema—Sergei Eisenstein's *Strike* (1925) and *Alexander Nevsky* (1938), and Dziga Vertov's *Man with a Movie Camera* (1929)—it also featured then new works associated with direct cinema and cinéma vérité, as early as 1964 and again in 1966, such as the early films of D. A. Pennebaker, Richard Leacock, Robert Drew, and the Maysles brothers, including *Daybreak Express* (1954) and *Primary* (1960). Also in 1964, the Kinemathek screened contemporary cinema from East Germany, including Frank Beyer's *Karbid und Sauerampfer/Carbide and Sorrel* (1963) and Konrad Wolf's *Der geteilte Himmel/The Divided Heaven* (1964), as well as Jonas Mekas's film of the theater production *The Brig* (1964). In 1965, series were devoted to Chris Marker's *Letter from Siberia* (1957), *Description d'un Combat* (1960), *La Jetée* (1962), and *Le joli Mai* (1963); to new cinema from then Czechoslovakia; from

Poland; and from the Soviet Union. In 1966, three series focused on Soviet cinema of the 1930s, on Griffith, and on cinéma vérité, respectively. In 1967, a series featured New American Cinema, and in 1969 a series focused on Polish New Wave cinema. And in 1970, one series featured contemporary cinema from Hungary and another series contemporary cinema from Algeria. As this list shows, through the Kinemathek, dffb students had access to the latest cinematic new waves of other countries.

Gregor's courses, too, introduced students to a range of films, including silent Soviet films, especially of Dziga Vertov, Vsevolod Pudovkin, Alexander Dovzhenko, and Sergei Eisenstein; French avant-garde and surrealist films of the 1920s, especially of René Clair and of Luis Buñuel; Italian Neorealism films of the 1940s, such as Luchino Visconti's *La Terra Trema* (1948); and both the short and long work of D. W. Griffith. Gregor also worked to establish the dffb archive, which at the time consisted mostly of 35 mm prints.[23] As will be discussed in the closing section, this international array of influences informed the aesthetics of early dffb films.

dffb Films of the Late 1960s and Global Protest Movements

In the late 1960s, as the social movements were approaching their peak, the West Berlin dffb rested at the front lines of the uprisings. West Germany's and West Berlin's 1968, too, as elsewhere, began earlier. In 1961, in response to the assassination on January 17 of Patrice Lumumba, the first democratically elected prime minister of the then Republic of Congo, and two other ministers, Maurice Mpolo and Joseph Okito, which was not made public until three weeks later, protests took place worldwide.[24] Although often overlooked by historians, Slobodian argues "the global protest wave following the death of Lumumba in 1961 would be a more appropriate starting point for historical narratives of the global 1960s."[25]

The year 1961 was also a key starting point for the international demonstrations in West Germany. Early in 1961, the "Tehran University [was closed] after a demonstration against parliamentary fraud," Slobodian writes, continuing: "On February 19, a female Iranian medical student led a march in Cologne of three hundred Iranian, Egyptian and West German students to protest the Iranian university's closure with further protests in Munich, Erlangen, Göttingen and Düsseldorf."[26] The day after, "on February 20, in Bonn, . . . African students protested Lumumba's murder" with "further demonstrations . . . held in Hamburg, Erlangen, Kiel and Frankfurt."[27] This revision of historical narratives about West Germany's 1960s expands both the temporal span, stretching it back to 1961, and the geographic scope, widening to include the international solidarity expressed by demonstrations often initiated and coorganized, at great risk, by foreign dissidents.

The focus on the Congo continued in 1964 in West Berlin as students protested the arrival of Congolese leader Moïse Tshombe, given his role in the murder of Lumumba.[28] The solidarity demonstrations that included both West German and Congolese students marked a broader political shift toward analyses of imperialism. As Slobodian puts it: "Before the Vietnam War, West German New Leftists saw the Congo conflict as the key case in understanding how the dynamics of imperialism could persist after decolonization."[29] Bernd Rabehl, one of the coorganizers of the Sozialistischer Deutscher Studentenbund (SDS, Socialist German Students' Union),[30] laid out the implications of the demonstrations against Tshombe for broader analyses of imperialist politics: "The Tschombé demonstration outlined the relationship between the third world and the metropolises . . . and the intervention of the strongest imperial world power as a figurehead of capitalism against all self-liberation movements became self-evident."[31] These earlier solidarity demonstrations also include the 1966 demonstration, organized by African students and the SDS in West Berlin, protesting the screening of the film *Africa Addio* (1966).[32]

By most historical accounts, West Germany's 1968 began in 1967. Amid the Vietnam War protests, on June 2, 1967, two demonstrations protested the visit of Iranian Mohammad Reza Shah Pahlavi and his wife. They instantiated yet again how international 1960s social movements in West Germany were.[33] The June 2 demonstrations were organized by Iranian dissidents affiliated with the Confederation of Iranian Students National Union (CISNU), a student organization of the Iranian Tudeh and the National Front political movements, which existed in various countries, such as England, France, West Germany, the United States, and India.[34] The SDS eventually joined to coorganize the demonstration.

Information about political repression in Iran had been disseminated in West Germany in the 1960s through domestic newspapers, such as *Die Zeit*, and Iranian newspapers, such as *Iran Azad*, the paper of the National Front, which had been available in West Germany since 1962 and in German since 1964.[35] Additionally, Bahman Nirumand's *Persia: A Model Developing Country* was published in March 1967.[36]

The demonstration took place in front of West Berlin's Opera House where the Shah and his wife were going to see a performance of Mozart's *Magic Flute*. About 4,500 demonstrators and dissidents participated. Nonviolent demonstrator Benno Ohnesorg was attempting to flee the increasingly chaotic scene, which included police mounted on horseback charging into the crowds, when police officer Karl-Heinz Kurras fatally shot him. Kurras was acquitted of all charges. Activists often cite this shooting as a key event in radicalizing the student movement.

Students of the early dffb often engaged the movements' main preoccupations.[37] Not only did the students concentrate on the uprisings thematically in their films, they also acted in solidarity with them.[38] For example, after the emergency laws—which allowed the suspension of civil liberties, permitting the government to intercept personal mail or telephone communications when in a state of emergency—were ratified on May 30, 1968, students occupied the dffb from May 30 to June 10, 1968, renaming it the Dziga Vertov School. Social movements had consistently protested the ratification of the emergency laws; given how the Nazis used the declaration of a state of emergency and the suspension of civil liberties to consolidate and take over power, many West Germans, especially of the 1968 generation, were eager to avoid having the emergency laws enshrined in the constitution. The eighteen dffb students who protested the emergency laws by occupying the dffb for ten days were expelled on November 18, 1968, on the grounds of, or charges of, trespassing.[39] According to one account, a higher court later dismissed the decision and reinstituted the students' right to attend the dffb.[40]

dffb Films of the Late 1960s: Protest Movements, Media, and Solidarity

Dffb students Thomas Giefer and Hans Rüdiger Minow filmed the June 2, 1967, demonstrations and produced the film *Berlin, 2. Juni 1967* (1967) based on this footage.[41] The film included eyewitness accounts and spontaneous interviews, photographs provided by demonstrators, and footage provided by journalists from the United States and the United Kingdom.[42] As Priscilla Layne argues, the "manipulation of sound, focus, editing and inter-titles" drew on Vertovian techniques and contrasted starkly with Oberhausen documentary filmmaking.[43] Subsequent dffb films often included footage from it, for example, Knaudt's graduation film, *Unsere Steine/Our Stones* (1968).

In response to the June 2 shooting, a group of politically engaged and active students participating in a seminar taught by Otto Felix Gmelin formed the "Gruppe 3" (Group 3). It included, among others, Bitomsky, Farocki, Thomas Hartwig, Knaudt, Jean-François Le Moign, Meins, Norman, Sander, Günter Peter Straschek, and Christian Ziewer. Students affiliated with this group directed each of the following films that I will discuss.

Sander's documentary, *Brecht die Macht der Manipulateure/Break or Stop the Power of the Manipulators* (January 1968),[44] funded by Suomen Televisio (Finnish television), is one of the first to show the preoccupation with media coverage of the Springer press.[45] The black-and-white, 16 mm film was shot between December 1967 and February 1968, thus right after the shooting of Ohnesorg. Sander's film sought, as she put it, "to communicate to people for whom the argumentation of the APO [Ausserparlamentarische Opposition or Extraparliamentary Opposition] was foreign. The realization that what was in the papers is not only 'information' but that it also edits, comments on, distorts, and can serve particular interests really hit me hard back then."[46] Sander's film shows two men riding in the back of a car, being chauffeured along the autobahn to West Berlin to negotiate the political preconditions for saving the West Berlin economy. Their dialogue consists of quotes or headlines from Springer-owned newspapers. Mouthed by representatives of West German companies, the dialogue shows or expresses the nexus of corporate media, economic interests, and politics.[47]

Another sequence shows Sander at the annual Presseball, an extravagant annual dinner and dance ball attended by leading figures in the press industry on January 15, 1968.[48] She had secured credentials as journalists for herself and fellow dffb students Farocki (sound) and Skip Norman (cameraman). (Knaudt was responsible for the film's sound but could not attend the ball because the group was only allocated three tickets, so Farocki filled in for him.) Behind the table at which Axel Springer was seated, Sander and Farocki unfurled and held a banner that read "Mit Geld Politik Machen, Mit Politik Geld Machen" (Use

Money to Make Politics, Use Politics to Make Money), while Norman filmed the action. The group was quickly escorted out by security guards and spent the night in jail for using their credentials to disrupt the dinner and ball with their political action.[49]

A subsequent dffb production, Knaudt's thirty-five-minute thesis or graduation film *Unsere Steine/Our Stones* (February 1968), shot in black and white and 16 mm, is even more provocative in its suggestions about the direction actions against the Springer press might take.[50] The film opens with a black screen and Sander's voice-over narration, stating "the tradition of all dead beings weighs like a nightmare on mind of the living." The opening visuals consist of found footage of US soldiers deplaning (presumably in Vietnam); then the film cuts to a panning shot of the bodies of dead Vietnamese, mostly children, lined up on the ground. Then the film cuts to a headline: "This is how America defends our freedom." Later, the film focuses on the consumption of the media. A long tracking shot shows a woman reading the Springer-owned daily the *Berliner Morgenpost*. The film cuts to a slow vertical pan down the photojournalist Eddie Adams's well-known and oft-reprinted photo "Saigon Execution," from February 1, 1968, showing South Vietnamese police chief Nguyễn Ngọc Loan holding a gun to the head of Vietcong soldier Nguyễn Văn Lém.

Then, the film shifts from media consumption to action. The film cuts back to the woman, who wraps the paper around a cobblestone and throws it. An intertitle reads "Steine" (Stones). Found footage shows masses of bombs being dropped from military planes. The film cuts to a hand-held camera in a high-angle close-up shot, showing a cobblestone sidewalk. The person holding the camera begins to run. The ground floor of the West Berlin office of the Springer press is shown with the name of one of its papers, *Berliner Morgenpost*, illuminated in neon letters. Displayed against the window are copies of the press's newspapers. The camera zooms in to the front page of one issue of *Berliner Morgenpost* taped to the window; the headline reads: "Vietnam: Worum es wirklicht geht" (Vietnam: What it is really about). The film cuts to a window (no newspapers); behind the window, the black-and-white photo, included in Sander's previously discussed film, showing US Vice President Humphrey and of Axel Springer. A projectile hits and cracks the window; the sound of shattering glass can be heard.

The film cuts back to the wobbly hand-held camera, and the legs and feet of a person running across the cobblestones. It cuts back to the window cracking and the photo in the background. The film cuts back and forth four more times between the broken window with the photo in the background and the person running across the cobblestones. To explain the action, after the first two crosscuts between cobblestones and broken window, the montage includes newspaper images of Vietnamese people who have been beaten, or found footage of them being physically abused, faces bloodied and bruised. Then the film cuts to a long shot of the West Berlin headquarters of the Springer offices where smoke, as if from a fire burning but off screen, blows across the screen's bottom third. Knaudt's film connects political events (Vietnam War), press coverage (Springer), and the action taken. Together, these films mount a critique of the role of the Springer press in legitimating the violence of wars being waged in Southeast Asia.

Farocki's seventeen-minute short agitprop film *Ihre Zeitungen/Their Newspapers* (February 1968), shot on black-and-white film and in 16 mm, also focuses on the campaign against the Springer press.[51] The film opens with three fast cuts, showing three Springer papers respectively—*Berliner Morgenpost*, *B.Z.*, and *Bildzeitung*. It continues with three fast jump cuts, showing a man reading two different editions of *B.Z.* and one of the *Bildzeitung*, as in an auditory approximation of the jump cut, a male voice-over says "as news," a female voice-over says "as mutilated news," and a male voice continues, "Vietnam arrives in Berlin." Toward the film's end, members of a collective wrap cobblestones in newspapers. "The stones," a voice-over states, "weigh down the paper. The paper dictates [to the stone] the direction to take." In other words, the stones are directed toward the newspapers. Then, one hears the sounds of windows shattering off screen. The film ends. Like Knaudt's film, Farocki's short suggests which newspapers to target. Thomas Elsaesser refers to this film as "among the most notorious of these instructional shorts" of Farocki's early oeuvre.[52]

Lastly, Farocki's *Drei Schüsse auf Rudi/Three Shots Targeting Rudi* (1968), a four-minute black-and-white 16 mm short, picks up on the discourse surrounding the Springer press, outlining its role in leading to the assassination attempt on SDS leader Rudi Dutschke by focusing on its tabloid BILD. A balloon caption reads, "Students protesting against mass murder in

Vietnam."[53] Then, an arrow points; a new caption appears, stating "BILD speaks of rowdies and ring-leaders." The short film progresses like a flowchart until at the end only two circles remain. Farocki slips off his shoes, leaves them in the circles, and exits the frame. The two shoes left in the frame reference the widely circulated photograph after the 1968 assassination attempt on Dutschke, where—after Dutschke had been shot and taken to the hospital—his bicycle and two shoes, laying on the sidewalk, encircled by chalk as part of the police investigation of the crime scene, were all that remained for press photographers. By moving from the headlines to an image of Dutschke's shoes, Farocki's short film suggestively links inflammatory rhetoric of the Springer press with the assassination attempt on Dutschke. When he was on trial for the attempted assassination, Josef Bachmann revealed he had "taken [his] daily information from the *Bild-Zeitung*."[54] Additionally, Bachmann was carrying a copy of the right-wing paper *National-Zeitung* with images of Dutschke and the headline: "Stoppt Dutschke jetzt! Sonst gibt es Bürgerkrieg" ("Stop Dutschke Now! Otherwise there will be a civil war!").

The responses to the assassination attempt on Dutschke were immediate. Roughly 2,500 people blockaded the streets in front of the Springer's West Berlin headquarters and demonstrated against the publisher across West Germany over the long Easter holiday weekend in riots that resulted in four hundred injured and two dead. Over the course of the weekend, 20,000 demonstrated and 60,000 police officers were deployed in West Berlin. Across West Germany, an estimated 300,000 participated in the demonstrations in front of Springer offices and publishing plants including in Cologne, Frankfurt, Hamburg, and Munich.[55] Solidarity demonstrations took place at West German embassies around the world. While these actions bespeak the solidarity of era, the early dffb films do as well. Each of the aforementioned films engages the Vietnam War, arguably then the key focus of international social movements. At the same time, as will be discussed in the next section, the early dffb films stand in conversation with the era's political cinemas of other countries.

dffb Films of the Late 1960s: The Aesthetic Interplay with Global New Waves

The early films of the dffb, as discussed, clearly exhibit a concern with the era's international political events, in particular the self-liberation and self-determination wars being waged with a specific focus on the Vietnam War, with domestic solidarity demonstrations, and with the ongoing debates about the press's coverage of them. Yet to read the early dffb films as political only due to their thematic content to the neglect of their aesthetics would give short shrift to the early dffb students' keen engagement with form. For the early dffb filmmakers, politics and aesthetics were inseparable. In this stance, they were not unique, taking a page from earlier film movements. But precisely this focus on the interplay of aesthetics and politics has gone underexamined; lacking is an analysis of which influences and an elaboration on what techniques were used, by whom, and to what end—and how they exhibit the conversations among international new waves. This section grapples with these questions.

As mentioned, one of the key influences on the aesthetics of the dffb's political cinema was undoubtedly Gregor. The influence of the earlier Soviet montage cinema, of French New Wave, and of D. W. Griffith is palpable in the aforementioned early dffb films. Revisiting the films and their aesthetics allows for a reconsideration of what makes these films political or of what constitutes the political in film. It also shifts the way the early dffb films have typically been read or pigeonholed. I will just call attention to a few traces of this influence.

In Knaudt's *Our Stones*, started shortly after and finished concurrent with Sander's film, the sequence featuring the quick crosscut back and forth between the window cracking with the photo of Humphrey and Springer in the background, and the image of someone running across cobblestones is further complicated formally by nondiegetic inserts: high-angle shots show various ingredients that could be used to make a cake or a pudding. Taken together with the image of Humphrey and of Springer, they reference the "Pudding Attentat" (pudding attack). In conjunction with US Vice President Humphrey's April 6, 1967, visit to West Berlin, the collective and activist household Kommune I planned to stage an action or "Happening."[56] While Humphrey visited Schloß Charlottenburg, the police raided the nearby Kommune 1 building and arrested eleven, stating they feared an assassination attempt. While the Springer papers asserted, "Assassination Attempt on Humphrey Foiled by Criminal Police,"[57] and that "An Attack Consisting of Bombs and Highly Explosive Chemicals"[58] had been prepared, it quickly emerged that, in fact, the communards had nothing more than pudding cakes, consisting of flour and blancmange, to throw at Humphrey. The event became known as the "Pudding Bombing Assassination Attempt" (*Pudding Bomben Attentat*).

The use of nondiegetic inserts to disrupt narrative continuity editing had featured prominently in Godard's *La Chinoise* (1967). In one sequence, one of the main characters talks about the ancient Egyptians and their language. Godard then cuts to two close-up nondiegetic inserts: one of a lion at the bed of King Tutankhamen and one of the king's mask. In both Godard's and Knaudt's films, the disruption invites the viewer to search for the relationship among and the meaning of the sequence's constituent parts.

In Farocki's near contemporaneous short film *Their Newspapers*, he uses three fast jump cuts early on, to show the same man reading two editions of *B.Z.* and one of the *Bildzeitung*. It draws on a technique often associated with Vertov's *Man with a Movie Camera*. Godard used jump cuts extensively in *À bout de souffle/Breathless* (1960) in order to disrupt graphic, spatial, and temporal continuity, creating a jarring effect. Often associated with Brechtian techniques that aim to alienate, that is, to keep an emotional distance, jump cuts call the viewer's attention to the constructed nature of the film. Farocki uses the technique commonly associated with early Soviet avant-garde and revolutionary cinema of Vertov and Eisenstein or the French New Wave cinema of Godard and Truffaut, but he does so in order to call attention to the constructed nature of the corporate media's message and to engage the ongoing debates about the Springer press.

Lastly, in the final sequence of *Brecht die Macht der Manipulateure*, Sander, Knaudt, and Farocki sit around a table and read texts related to the relationship among media, politics, and economics. Norman, as cameraman, is off screen, filming, and behind the camera. Nonetheless, he, too, reads texts, often in English.[59] The sequence, as is common for early dffb films, scrupulously avoids shot/reverse shots, taking a page from Godard, as one of many strategies to shun Hollywood continuity editing. Norman's off-screen voice reading from behind the camera adds another element. As Noël Burch has argued, focusing on Jean Renoir's *Nana* (1926), there are six zones off screen: the one behind each side of the frame; the fifth behind the set; and the sixth behind the camera.[60]

The sixth off-screen zone space also features prominently early on in the films of D. W. Griffith, such as his fourteen-minute short silent film *A Corner in Wheat* (1909). Gregor included Griffith, both the long and short films, in his dffb seminars. And to Gregor's surprise, Farocki was fascinated by and presented on Griffith.[61] By having Norman participate in this scene not only by filming silently but also by reading audibly from off screen, Sander calls attention to the off-screen space(s) and also to the space behind the camera. Additionally, Farocki looks off screen intently, not into the camera lens but rather in the direction of the camera, again calling attention to what Burch calls the sixth off-screen space. By drawing on these techniques, Sander's film underscores the very construct of the film and its message.[62]

The audience must imagine what is happening in the off-screen space. Must assemble. Must put together. Must remember off-screen space. Must remember the constructed nature of cinema. In so doing, these strategies of the early dffb films by Sander, Knaudt, and Farocki remind the viewer to consider the medium in content and in *form* as constructed.

Conclusion

In his 1998 study of Farocki's work, Baumgärtel concludes the section on Farocki's early dffb and early 1970s films as follows:

> In the interviews, which I conducted with Farocki for this book, he repeatedly pointed out the relationship between his activities around 68 and the subsequent interest in his work and also the deep falling out of favor of the West German film scene. Indeed, the films by him and a number of his fellow dffb students have until today remained exceptional cases in the German film history. Through the aesthetic-political radicality of their early short films and statements they embody in some ways the announcement of a "different" cinema, which was never cashed in. That makes them interesting to the present day: quasi as a promise whose fulfillment still remains awaited."[63]

Farocki collaborated with the best-known director affiliated with the contemporary Berlin School of filmmaking, Christian Petzold, on all of Petzold's films up to Farocki's passing in 2014. The Berlin School cinema's engagements, thematically, with the impacts of contemporary neoliberal economics on communities, families, relationships, notions of home, and individuals through a radical aesthetic reconfiguration of the sensible[64] could be read as fulfilling the promise of a cinema to come announced by the dffb, mentioned by Baumgärtel above, in the present day.[65] But if that is the case, and if the Berlin School's cinema is read so intently for its aesthetic articulation of politics, it might behoove to connect the dots. That is, it might behoove to study the early dffb cinema further, focusing on its aesthetics and considering how they articulate politics. The dffb films were both integrally interwoven with the era's pivotal political preoccupations and staged critiques by dint of their very aesthetic form. Reengaging the political and aesthetic preoccupations of the early dffb films revises notions of what constituted West German (political) cinema around 1968.

Notes

1. "Oberhausen Manifesto," in *West German Filmmakers on Film*, ed. Eric Rentschler (New York: Holmes and Meier, 1988), 2. On the history of film schools in Germany, see Peter C. Slansky, *Filmhochschulen in Deutschland. Geschichte—Typologie—Architektur* (Munich: Edition Text + Kritik, 2011); and Christina Gerhardt, "Introduction: Cinema in West Germany around 1968," in "1968 and West German Cinema," ed. Christina Gerhardt, special issue, *The Sixties* 10 (2017): 1–9.
2. On other cinematic countermovements of the long sixties in West Germany, see also Randall Halle, "Xscreen 1968: Material Film Aesthetics and Radical Cinema Politics," in "1968 and West German Cinema," ed. Christina Gerhardt, special issue, *The Sixties* 10 (2017): 10–25; Lisa Haegele, "Beyond the Left: Violence and the Politics of Affect in Roland Klick's *Bübchen* (*Little Vampire*)," in "1968 and West German Cinema," ed. Christina Gerhardt, special issue, *The Sixties* 10 (2017): 45–62; and as well as Christina Gerhardt and Marco Abel, eds., *Celluloid Revolt: German Screen Cultures of the Long Sixties* (Rochester: Camden House, 2019).
3. Tilman Baumgärtel, "DFFB-Studenten bei der Revolte von 1967/68," *Jungle World*, September 27, 1996. Translation the author's. See also Tilman Baumgärtel, "1. February, 1968," in *A New History of German Cinema*, ed. Jennifer Kapczynski and Michael David Richardson (Rochester: Camden House, 2013), 400–404.
4. For book-length studies devoted exclusively to Farocki, see Thomas Elsaesser, ed., *Harun Farocki: Working on the Sight-Lines* (Amsterdam: Amsterdam University Press, 2004); Tilman Baumgärtel, *Harun Farocki:*

Vom Guerrillakino zum Essayfilm (Berlin: b-books, 1998); and Rolf Aurich and Ulrich Kriest, eds., *Der Ärger mit den Bildern; Die Filme von Harun Farocki* (Konstanz: UVK Verlag, 1998). For essays in German, see Volker Pantenburg, "Die Rote Fahne: Deutsche Film- und Fernsehakademie Berlin, 1966–1968," in *Handbuch zur Kultur- und Mediengeschichte der Studentenbewegung*, ed. Martin Klimke and Joachim Scharloth (Stuttgart: Metzler, 2007), 199–206; and Klaus Kreimeier, "Papier—Schere—Stein: Farockis frühe Filme," in *Der Ärger mit den Bildern: Die Filme von Harun Farocki*, ed. Rolf Aurich and Ulrich Kriest (Konstanz: UVK Verlag, 1998), 27–45.

5. As of 2016, the dffb has made some of these early films available online at the official dffb site, https://dffb-archiv.de/, accessed January 26, 2017.
6. His work from 1967 to 2005, including his early dffb films, was released as a box set of DVDs in 2009. Harun Farocki, *Filme, 1967–2005* (Berlin: Absolut Medien, 2009).
7. See Halle, "Xscreen 1968," 10–25, and Haegele, "Beyond the Left," 45–62, for arguments to this effect.
8. On this point, see also Baumgärtel, *Harun Farocki*, 47–53.
9. Leiser resigned on March 28, 1969, after an escalation in tensions between him and students.
10. Günther Peter Straschek states thirty-four students were accepted. Günther Peter Straschek, *Wider das Kino* (Frankfurt am Main: Suhrkamp, 1974), 357. The official dffb historiography lists thirty-four original students, dffb official site, http://www.dffb.de/html/de/akademie/die_dffb, accessed January 26, 2017. Website updated; original number accepted in 1966 no longer posted, accessed January 24, 2018.
11. Quinn Slobodian, *Foreign Front: Third World Politics in Sixties West Germany* (Durham, NC: Duke University Press), 177.
12. Pantenberg, "Die Rote Fahne," 199. Madeleine Bernstorff, "Film Feminisms in West German Cinema," in Gerhardt and Abel, *Celluloid Revolt*. See also Julia Knight, "The Absent Directors," in *Women and the New German Cinema* (New York: Verso, 1992), 1–21, at 9. And see Fabian Tietke, "Filming the Tenants' Movement: Independent Film Production between Feminism and Workism," in Gerhardt and Abel, *Celluloid Revolt*, 128–51, and Christina Gerhardt, "Helke Sander's dffb Cinema and West Germany's Feminist Movement," in Gerhardt and Abel, *Celluloid Revolt*, 78–103.
13. Knight, "The Absent Directors," 9; Tietke, "Filming the Tenants' Movement," 128–51.

14. Rathsack originally examined three and then expanded the analysis to include Madrid. Published as Heinz Rathsack, "Drei Filmhochschulen," *Filmkritik* 4, no. 64 (1964): 174–84, quoted by Ralph Eue, "Vorgeschichte der dffb 1962–66," dffb official site, https://dffb-archiv.de/editorial/vorgeschichte-dffb-1962–66, accessed January 26, 2017. Website page taken down, attempted access January 24, 2018.
15. Heinz Rathsack, *Vier Filmhoschschulen. Strukturen—Aufgaben—Ergebnisse* (Bonn: FIAG 1964), 33, quoted in Madeleine Bernstorff, "Transnationales Lernen," dffb official site, https://dffb-archiv.de/editorial/transnationales-lernen, accessed January 26, 2017.
16. Lukas Foerster, Nikolaus Pernetzky, Fabian Tietke, and Cecilia Valenti, eds., *Spuren eines Dritten Kinos: Ästhetik, Politik und Ökonomie des World Cinema* (Bielefeld: Transcript, 2013), 11, quoted in Bernstorff, "Transnationales Lernen."
17. Bernstorff, "Transnationales Lernen."
18. Bernstorff, "Transnationales Lernen." Bernstorff underscores that thirteen students were from Switzerland, which did not have a film school until the 1990s.
19. "Vereinsgeschichte," Arsenal Berlin, official site, http://www.arsenal-berlin.de/ueber-uns/geschichte/verein.html, accessed August 31, 2017. Translation the author.
20. Erika and Ulrich Gregor codirected the Forum until 2000.
21. In 2000, Kino Arsenal moved to the Filmhaus am Potsdamer Platz, the same building that now houses the dffb.
22. Ulrich Gregor, email to author, September 14, 2016.
23. Ulrich Gregor, email to author, September 14, 2016.
24. Thomas Kanza, "Lumumba's Murder," in *Conflict in the Congo: The Rise and Fall of Lumumba* (London: Penguin, 1972), 322–24. See also Kwame Nkrumah, "The Murder of Lumumba," in *The Challenge of the Congo* (London: International Publishers, 1967), 119–33; Ludo De Witte, *The Assassination of Lumumba* (London: Verso, 2001); and Raoul Peck, dir. *Lumumba*, 2000, Zeitgeist Films. For a list of the worldwide demonstrations that took place worldwide to express solidarity, see also Slobodian, *Foreign Front*, 62.
25. Slobodian, *Foreign Front*, 14.
26. Slobodian, 15.
27. Slobodian, 15.
28. George Katsiaficas, *The Imagination of the New Left: A Global Analysis of*

1968 (Boston: South End Press, 1987), 49; Niels Seibert, *Vergessene Proteste: Internationalismus und Antirassismus, 1964–1983* (Münster: Unrast Verlag, 2008), 27–34.

29. Slobodian, *Foreign Front*, 13.
30. The West German SDS has no relation to the US SDS.
31. Bernd Rabehl, "Von der antiautoritären Bewegung zur sozialistischen Opposition," in *Rebellion der Studenten oder die neue Opposition*, ed. Uwe Bergmann, Rudi Dutschke, Wolfgang Lefevre, and Bernd Rabehl (Hamburg: Rowohlt, 1968), 160–62.
32. See Slobodian, "Corpse Polemics," in *Foreign Front*, 137–46; and Seibert, "Alte Themen, neue Protestformen: Der Film *Africa Addio* (1966)," in *Vergessene Proteste*, 35–42.
33. They also include the 1967–68 demonstrations in Hamburg against the Wissman statue. See Seibert, "Geschichtspolitische Denkmalstürze: Die Wissmann-Statue," in *Vergessene Proteste*, 51–58.
34. CISNU was established in 1962. Ervand Abrahamian, *A History of Modern Iran* (Cambridge: Cambridge University Press, 2008), 144. See also Slobodian, "The Missing Bodies of June 2," in *Foreign Front*, 101–34; and Arif Dirlik, "The Third World in 1968," in *1968: A World Transformed*, ed. Carole Fink, Philipp Gassert, and Detlef Junker (Cambridge: Cambridge University Press, 1998), 295–320.
35. Slobodian, *Foreign Front*, 104. The National Front was the democratic political opposition group that had brought Mohammad Mossadegh to power in 1949.
36. Nirumand had studied in Germany and then returned in 1960 to Iran, where he taught first at the Tehran University and then, due to repression from the Iranian government, at the Goethe Institut. As a result of the increasingly repressive political situation in Iran, Nirumand returned to West Germany in 1965, where he published the book with an epilogue by Enzensberger. It quickly went through numerous print runs.
37. Pantenburg, "Die Rote Fahne," 199–206; Karl-Heinz Stenz, *Kampfplatz Kamera: Die filmkulturelle Bedeutung der filmstudierenden '68er Generation; Am Beispiel der Protestaktivitäten an der neu gegründeten Deutschen Film- und Fernsehakademie Berlin (dffb)* (Munich: GRIN Verlag, 2008).
38. See also Tilman Baumgärtel, "Die Rolle der DFFB-Studenten bei der Revolte von 1967/68," *Junge Welt*, September 27, 1996, and October 2, 1996.
39. The number of students expelled varies from seventeen to nineteen.

Baumgärtel puts the number at seventeen; newspaper accounts of 1968 put the number at eighteen; and Pantenburg puts the number at nineteen, relying on the official dffb publication "10 Years dffb," according to which fourteen students, who started in 1966, and five students, who started in 1967, were expelled. See Baumgärtel, *Harun Farocki*, 56–78; Werner Kließ, "Eindruck willkürlicher Maßnahmen," *Film* (1969): 1; and Hans Helmut Prinzler, ed., *10 Jahre DFFB* (Berlin: DFFB, 1976), 57–120.

40. Film Portal, "Holger Meins," http://www.filmportal.de/node/240917/gallery, accessed January 26, 2017.
41. *Der 2. Juni 1967.* Directors: Thomas Giefer and Hans-Rüdiger Minow. 47 mins. 1967. Laika Verlag. Hamburg.
42. Priscilla Layne, "Ideological Rupture in the dffb: An Analysis of Hans-Rüdiger Minow's 2. Juni, 1967," in Gerhardt and Abel, *Celluloid Revolt*, 57–77.
43. Layne, "Ideological Rupture in the dffb," 60.
44. *Brecht die Macht der Manipulateure* (Stop the Power of the Manipulators), dir. Helke Sander. Made for Finnish television, Suomen televisio, although not aired; 48 minutes.
45. According to Sander's website, the film never aired in Finland due to pressure from the Springer Verlag. Sander would become known especially for her feminist filmmaking. Her first dffb four-minute short *Subjektitüde* (1966) already focused on sexism. In 1968 Sander cofounded the Aktionsrat zu Befreiung der Frauen (Action Committee for the Liberation of Women) and participated in an action at an SDS conference, in which she denounced the sexism of male SDS. As she did so, she was yelled at in an attempt to shut her up and or down. To support feminist filmmaking, she co-organized with Claudia von Alemann the first international women's film seminar in 1973 in West Berlin, and in 1974 she founded *Frauen and Film* (Women and Film), one of the first feminist film journals in Europe, which continues to the present day. See also Christina Gerhardt, "Helke Sander's dffb Cinema and West Germany's Feminist Movement," in Gerhardt and Abel, *Celluloid Revolt*.
46. For the quote: "Brecht die Macht der Manipulateure," *Helke Sander*. http://www.helke-sander.de/filme/brecht-die-macht-der-manipulateure/, accessed January 26, 2017. Translation the author's. See also Marc Silberman, "An Interview with Helke Sander," *Jump Cut* 29 (February 1984): 59.
47. See also Elsaesser, "'It Started with These Images'—Some Notes on Political Film-Making after Brecht in Germany: Helke Sander and Harun Farocki," *Discourse:*

Journal for Theoretical Studies in Media and Culture 7 (Fall 1985): 95–120.

48. "Brecht die Macht der Manipulateure," deutsche film und fernsehschule berlin, https://dffb-archiv.de/dffb/brecht-die-macht-der-manipulateure, accessed January 26, 2017.
49. "Brecht die Macht der Manipulateure."
50. *Unsere Steine/Our Stones*, dir. Ernst-Ulrich Knaudt. See also Baumgärtel, *Harun Farocki*, 27.
51. *Ihre Zeitungen/Their Newspapers*, dir. Harun Farocki.
52. Elsaesser, *Harun Farocki*, 38n10.
53. *Drei Schüsse auf Rudi/Three Shots Targeti*ng Rudi, dir. Harun Farocki. Description based on Harun Farocki's official website, http://www.farocki-film.de/, accessed January 27, 2017.
54. "Siebzig Prozent reiben sich die Hände," *Spiegel*, March 10, 1969. Translation the author's.
55. Wolfgang Kraushaar, *1968: Das Jahr, das alles verändert hat* (Munich: Piper, 1998), 108.
56. Dieter Kunzelmann, *Leisten Sie keinen Widerstand! Bilder aus meinem Leben* (Berlin: Transit, 1998), 63–65.
57. "Attentat auf Humphrey von Kripo vereitelt," *Berliner Morgenpost*, April 6, 1967.
58. "Mit Bomben und hochexplosiven Chemikalien, mit sprengstoffgefüllten Plastikbeuteln—von den Terroristen 'Mao-Cocktail' genannt—und Steinen haben Berliner Extremisten einen Anschlag auf den Gast unserer Stadt vorbereitet," *Bild*, April 6, 1967.
59. Norman spoke fluent English and German and is shown speaking both languages in the film. He was African American, grew up in Baltimore, then moved to West Germany. After a successful acting career, he began studies at the dffb, finishing his degree in 1969. He completed a PhD at Ohio State University and then taught at Eastern Mediterranean University in Cyprus. He died in 2015.
60. Noël Burch, "*Nana*, or the Two Kinds of Space," in his *Theory of Film Practice* (Princeton, NJ: Princeton University Press, 1981), 17–31. See also Robert L. Adams Jr., "D. W. Griffith and the Use of Offscreen Space," *Cinema Journal* 15, no. 2 (1976): 53–57. I thank Quinn Slobodian for an edifying discussion of this sequence in Sander's film.
61. Ulrich Gregor, interview by Frederik Lang und Fabian Tietke, "Im Interview: Ulrich Gregor," Kino Arsenal; Berlin, Germany, June 22, 2015,

https://dffb-archiv.de/editorial/ulrich-gregor, accessed January 26, 2017.

62. *I Am Curious (Yellow)* (1967), directed by Vilgot Sjöman, is mostly remembered for the controversy surrounding its sex scenes, but in one scene the main characters, Lena and Börje, are arguing in a car and the director suddenly points out that Börje has forgotten part of a line. I thank Sarah Hamblin for the helpful exchange about off-screen space in 1960s cinema.
63. Baumgärtel, *Harun Farocki*, 101. Translation the author's.
64. See also Marco Abel, *The Counter-Cinema of the Berlin School* (Rochester: Camden House, 2013).
65. As numerous scholars have pointed out, the moniker "Berlin School" is a bit of a misnomer, since not all directors associated with the school studied at the dffb.

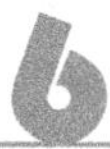

The Hour of the Furnaces

A Film "Happening"

Rita de Grandis

Unlike Patricio Guzmán's *La batalla de Chile/The Battle of Chile* (1975)—an epic project about what could have been, but was not—or Chris Marker's *Fond de l' air est rouge/A Grin without a Cat* (1977)—a magnum opus of an era of revolutionary movements—*La hora de los hornos/The Hour of the Furnaces* (1965–68) is an epic that anticipates *what would come to be* with apparently unquestionable certainty. Much has been written about this full-length film-manifesto of Third Cinema—"Tercer Cine," "Cine Liberación" or Liberation Film, "Cine Militante" or Militant Cinema—especially in terms of its cinematographic influences, European and Soviet as well as Latin American.[1] Yet there has been insufficient exploration of how *The Hour of the Furnaces* relates to, and dialogues and connects with, other avant-garde innovations in the Argentine artistic field of the 1960s, particularly the "happening" in its extreme political expression and *Tucumán arde* (Tucumán Burns), another expression of conceptual political art.

In this essay, I analyze *The Hour of the Furnaces* as an avant-garde event within the wide range of artistic expressions and political-ideological positions that were driven by the pressing need to renew artistic language and by Jean-Paul Sartre's call for the action and engagement of intellectuals. The film fuses the political and the artistic realms with the conviction that the rift between art and life, and between art and politics—the concern of the historic avant-gardes of the 1920s and 1930s in Europe and the Soviet Union—would finally be bridged on Latin American and Argentine soil. I plot an itinerary that runs from April to November 1968 through three avant-garde expressions,

"El Happening inoportuno" (The Untimely Happening), *The Hour of the Furnaces*, and the exhibition *Tucumán arde*, as aesthetic, cinematic, and plastic art practices that were also political-conceptual "happenings." More specifically, I frame *The Hour of the Furnaces*, released in Italy in 1968, between a "before"—"El happening inoportuno" of April 3, 1968[2]—and an "after"—the exhibition *Tucumán arde*, which opened on November 3, 1968, in the city of Rosario and later in Buenos Aires. In formal terms, these three expressions share the idea of staging and questioning the institution of art. The happening was a precursor of and antecedent to a foreign-centered tendency from avant-garde internationalism, which was highly institutionalized in Argentina under the auspices of the Instituto Di Tella.[3] *Tucumán arde* was also an expression of an artistic-political vanguard that stood in tension with the system of artistic enshrinement of the Instituto Di Tella but not entirely outside of it. A comparison of *The Hour of the Furnaces*—as a work of political, national, and Third World cinematic art—with the happening and with *Tucumán arde*, reveals some of the formal, conceptual, and ideological transactions among Peronism, 1960s modern art, and the cultures of the Left. The avant-gardes presented paradoxes as part of the imperative to bring together the aesthetic and political vanguards, paradoxes that led to a constellation of ruptures, repositionings, and mutual appropriations that responded to the national and international political situation and to conditions inherent in the intellectual field.[4]

"El happening inoportuno," as Ana Longoni and Mariano Mestman note, took place in the Museum of Modern Art (then located in the Centro Cultural San Martín) on the occasion of the inauguration of the Ver y Estimar prize. Eduardo Ruano, a young artist invited to participate in the event, entered the room, followed by a few friends,[5] interrupting the proceedings, shouting "¡Fuera yanquis de Vietnam!" ("Yankees, out of Vietnam!") and other political slogans. The group then headed to the installation that Ruano had prepared several days previously and that, until that point, everyone had considered his artwork. It consisted of an illuminated display case containing a large poster of President John Fitzgerald Kennedy, along with literature about his 1963 assassination. A few meters away was a lead brick with which Ruano then destroyed both the display case and the image of Kennedy. With this act, evoking Duchamp (*The Large Glass*, 1915–23, and *To Be Looked At (from the Other Side of the Glass) with One Eye, Close to, for Almost an Hour*, 1918), the happening constituted an "attack," "a lightning act," as the press referred to it and other interventions in the streets carried out by leftist political groups. The violent action of stoning the display case was a political and artistic gesture against Kennedy's official image, "under the auspices of the artistic institution."[6]

The Hour of the Furnaces is also an "attack." Produced amid the local echoes of France's May '68 and of anticolonial movements—screened across four continents, translated into scores of languages, and considered a sacred text for hundreds of collective projects[7]—the film forms an important object of study because of its artistic richness and because of the subsequent depletion of the revolutionary imaginary. Reality would come to render it obsolete as a revolutionary political project, but as a singular artistic expression of its moment, *The Hour of the Furnaces* allows us to analyze, beyond its specific framework, how the Argentine intellectual field received and placed its specific stamp on the era's philosophy, culture, and revolution. The peak of existentialism, the development of structuralism, the Cuban Revolution (1959), the impact of Fanon's thinking about neocolonialism, the rupture of the modernist canon, and national liberation movements all made an indelible impression on the general configuration of the field at the time. *The Hour of the Furnaces*, running approximately 260 minutes or 4 hours and 33 minutes, is a "trilogy originally filmed in 16 mm, by a team made up of no more than four or five people over 30 months of work . . . in one of the most reactionary periods of Argentine history: 1966–1968."[8] The collective that made the film was the Grupo Cine Liberación (Liberation Cinema Group),[9] which formed shortly before the dictatorship of Juan Carlos Onganía (1966–70) and continued under the dictatorship of his successor Alejandro Agustín Lanusse (1970–73)[10] until 1976 when a military junta comprising Jorge Rafael Videla, Orlando R. Agosti, and Eduardo E. Massera took power in a coup d'état.

The collective's members were young people from various leftist tendencies that in the years of the prohibition of Peronism, the 1960s and 1970s, gradually became associated with Peronism's most radicalized elements: Juventud Peronista (the Peronist Youth) and its armed wing, the Montoneros. Making use of the avant-garde in the political sense, the Grupo Cine Liberación adopted clandestinity as a political objective, making anonymous films that would favor the process of collective creation, thus constituting a collective discourse independent of the individualistic bourgeois system.

The collective began to film the first interviews in mid-1965, and in 1966–67 they made several trips to the interior of the country in order to dive directly into the reality of the provinces, especially Tucumán, which was undergoing a profound social transformation as a result of economic restructuring and accelerated industrialization. Fernando Solanas had been active in the Communist Party, and Octavio Getino, having grown up in working-class neighborhoods, had connections with workers' representatives and Peronist resistance movements.[11] The idea of erasing the mark of authorship, conceived primarily so as to develop a collective voice that would coincide with the "voice of the people" (the ideologeme of the time), meant that the progressive intellectuals and artists would join the political demands of the working class and students. Furthermore, the proposal of a clandestine cinema allowed its members to protect themselves from the state's political repression.

This approach was abandoned in the brief democratic interregnum between the 1973 elections and the death of Perón in 1974. In this short-lived break, the Grupo Cine Liberación decided to incorporate itself into the new institutional process, abandoning clandestine action in favor of screenings in traditional movie theaters. They prepared cinematographic policy proposals as some of the group's members took up public office (Getino was in charge of the Cinematographic Rating Body in 1973). *The Hour of the Furnaces* was no longer thought of as a clandestine document meant only for militants but as a film for the general population. Before the return of Perón, the first part of *The Hour of the Furnaces* had been screened in conventional cinemas, but only after the filmmakers made modifications, such as cutting the final image of the dead Ernesto "Che" Guevara, a frozen image projected for five minutes that, as Robert Stam says, renders it transcendental.[12] The halo of sacrificial myth is removed from this eternalized face that even in death is omnipresent across these five long minutes, showing the imperfections of its decomposing materiality. For Julianne Burton, this cut, along with the declaration of support by Solanas, Getino, and Gerardo Vallejo for Isabel Perón, demonstrates the Group's inconsistencies, representing a 180-degree turn from their cinematographic position of using the camera as a weapon and clandestine screenings as political activism. The irony of this endorsement arises from the fact that, with the elimination of Guevara's image, the revolutionary myth was rendered questionable for its own supporters because of its defense of violence and call for political martyrdom at a time of generalized violence from paramilitary and parapolice groups. With this regrettable declaration of support for Isabel Perón, the repression unleashed after the military junta deposed her placed those who remained true to their principles and those who did not on the same level.[13]

In *The Hour of the Furnaces*, the two avant-gardes—the formal and the theoretical-political—converge. From Third World radicalism and artistic innovations (for example, conceptual art, pop art, concrete art) arises a fertile appropriation of the procedures of both fields. Solanas and Getino provide a new interpretative slant on the metaphor of the *fusil cinématographique* of the photographer and forerunner of cinema, Étienne-Jules Marey.[14] The camera is conceived of as a weapon loaded with revolutionary provocation, taking on cinema as commodity with its rules of "the 35 mm camera, 24 frames a second, arc lights, and a commercial place of exhibition."[15] The camera is a "beautiful weapon," write Solanas and Getino, that shoots "carefully selected" targets.[16] In their well-known essay "Towards a Third Cinema," as in other texts, the notion of "film action," one of the conceptual bastions of their film practice, reappropriates "the well-known quote from Marx . . . [that] it is not sufficient to interpret the world; it is now a question of transforming it."[17] Under this theoretical-political mandate, aesthetic quality is subordinated to political and communicative effectiveness:

> Pamphlet films, didactic films, report films, essay films, witness-bearing films—any militant form of expression is valid, and it would be absurd to lay down a set of aesthetic work norms. . . . The *effectiveness* of the best films of militant cinema show that social layers are able to capture the exact meaning of an association of images, an effect of staging, and any linguistic experimentation placed within the context of a given idea.[18]

In this idea of film action as communicative *effectiveness* resides echoes of Sartre's influential call in *Les temps modernes* for a literature of social commitment. Sartre proposes the notion of commitment not as service to a political party but as a way to reestablish literature's social function through a focus on communication in terms of its effects: "The 'engaged' writer knows that words are *action*. He knows that to reveal is to change and that one can reveal only by planning to change."[19] Commitment, communication, effectiveness, action, and act are all fundamental ideas that traverse the activities of the field. *Action* (the political act) is key to avant-garde experimentation, both artistic and political. The struggle for the signifier *action* becomes highly productive in transactions between art and politics.

The happening, which comes from the strictly artistic field, also calls on action. Conceived of as an event (as "theater of chance," "action theater," "total theater," or "kinetic theater"), it is irruptive and provocative, performed anywhere (in the street, basements), and requires the active participation of the spectator because it reduces the distance between spectator and spectacle, eliminates interventions, and promotes direct communication between people and objects. The happening may achieve the old aspiration of participatory art that Duchamp and the Dadaists so desired. In Argentina, this art was strongly associated with Oscar Masotta, a central and controversial figure in the modernization of the Argentine intellectual and artistic field from the 1950s to the 1970s, who was closely connected to the Instituto Di Tella.[20]

The acts that happenings create are not spontaneous, but then neither are strictly political "lightning acts." The characteristic that they share is connoted action, a performance in the sense of dramatization, of acted representation. What differentiates them is that the one attacks the institution of art, while the other forms a strategy of revolutionary action. In the case of happenings, their "spatial" aspect, according to Masotta,[21] is fundamental for creating a milieu, a setting for the materials and objects spread or organized in a composition that engulfs the spectator. Moreover, a link to Brechtian theater is evident in the way that the happening presents a "story" and a "plot" by virtue of logical connections and ideological functions. This spatial or dramatized aspect of the happening and of the revolutionary political act is present in the conception of "Third Cinema" that aims to displace both commercial cinema (First Cinema) and auteur cinema (Second Cinema). In *The Hour of the Furnaces*, the setting emerges in the screenings, as it was common in film festivals to adorn the screen with banners and flags, creating the ambience of a happening that fused spectator and object in a dramatization of the cinematographic act. Solanas and Getino recall that at the premiere of *The Hour of the Furnaces* at the Pesaro Film Festival in June 1968, before the screening of the second part,

"Acts for Liberation": "we played revolutionary songs and marches from the Third World . . . we put up Argentine flags on both sides of the screen and put a banner right across it, 10 metres long, that said *Every spectator is either a coward or a traitor—Fanon.*"[22]

The Hour of the Furnaces, like the happening, proposed an active spectator. Among its strategies for involving the spectator, a narrator directly addresses the audience, creating an "I-to-You" relationship. The film also ends without a conclusion, inviting the audience to continue it: "Now it is time for you to conclude." The cinema combats the spectator's passivity in that the story's protagonist is not on screen but is the audience itself. All three parts of the film begin with overtures, grand slogans, shouts, and demonstrations, suggesting that spectators should not sit comfortably and allow themselves to relax or be entertained but should participate in the cinematographic act. This strategy forms an attack on the audience's voyeurism. Encouraging the spectator to intervene, the film employs a series of strategies: each screening aims to create a space of liberation, a decolonized space. Through this approach a film of this sort can appeal to a transcontinental audience and be premiered, not clandestinely as in Argentina, but in a large festival in Italy, despite addressing a local (Argentine) experience. In 1968, the group took sixty rolls of film out of Argentina,[23] which Solanas edited in Rome through the production company of Juliani de Negri and Valentino Orsini, and in the laboratories of the Taviani brothers before its debut at the IV Mostra Internazionale del Cinema Nuovo, in Pesaro, Italy, from the June 1 to 8, 1968.[24] The movie was awarded the Critics' Grand Prize, the first of its many awards.

The idea of the act is connected to another of the film's experimental strategies: its open character. It is not that the movie's *political meaning* is open (it is absolutely not), but that it transmits its concept of the creative process as an act in which the spectator can interrupt the screening and participate in the political interpretation or political discussion. In "Towards a Third Cinema," Solanas and Getino theorize this as follows:

> Moreover, each projection of a film act presupposes a different setting, since the space where it takes place, the materials that go to make it up (actors-participants), and the historic time in which it takes place are never the same. This means that the result of each projection act

will depend on those who organize it, on those who participate in it, and on the time and place; the possibility of introducing variations, additions, and changes is unlimited.[25]

Yet despite coinciding with the idea of the act, the traditional Left did not look well on happenings, condemning the experiments of the 1960s avant-gardes promoted by the Instituto Di Tella as frivolous, shallow, foreign, and depoliticized. Controversies about the role of the artist in society therefore arose around Masotta, placing the happening in a dilemma: "Either happenings or politics of the Left."[26] But the impact of the happening on the Argentine artistic scene at the beginning of the 1960s and the subsequent radicalization of the political scene led to an aesthetic transaction—in which pop, happenings, media art, the Grupo Espartaco (Spartacus Group), Antonio Berni's social collage,[27] and the Otra Figuración (Other Figuration)[28] group all had a part—such that the organizations of the Left could be expected to incorporate it into their political practice. The decline of the dictatorships of Onganía and Lanusse, along with the radicalization of the armed groups, opened the way to an art that was much more committed to local political circumstances.

The Revolution as Imminent Present with the Return of Peronism

The title of *The Hour of the Furnaces* comes from a famous phrase of José Martí's ("It's the hour of the furnaces and only the light shall be seen," uttered in the context of Cuba's war of independence against Spain), taken up by Che Guevara in a speech to support his transcontinental socialist enterprise.[29] The title thus indicates the anticolonial drive of this decolonizing cinema and the close relationship between Grupo Cine Liberación and both the Cuban Institute of Cinematic Art and Industry (ICAIC) and the Cuban cause, a model for all revolutionary movements in Latin America. The film's dedication, "To Jorge Abelardo Ramos," is also significant. Ramos (1921–1994) was a left-wing Argentine essayist and a revisionist historian of Argentina and Latin America whose work formed the basis of the film, defined by the directors as a "film-essay." Ramos had moved from Trotskyism to the conviction that national liberation was a basic imperative of the Argentine Left. He argued that the Latin American nation was no more than a reaction against Spanish domination in 1810 and was still a mere intellectual creation by 1910, the centennial of the May Revolution. The Revolution only began to solidify with the Cuban Revolution, and Ramos proposed a Marxist-Bolivarian synthesis that would take into account the specificity of the revolutionary process in Latin America. The national bourgeoisie, he added, was incapable of coming to power in the context of nation-states balkanized by colonialism, and therefore Bolívar's task was inherited by the disciples of Marx. These disciples of Marx were called to take on this mission, without forgetting the national movements and always respecting the Bolivarian tradition. In *The Hour of the Furnaces*, Ramos's thinking takes another twist in the wider context of tricontinental revolution under the symbolic leadership of Frantz Fanon, Hồ Chí Minh, and Che Guevara.

The Hour of the Furnaces presents an essay in celluloid about the development of neocolonial oppression in Latin America in general and in Argentina in particular, represented as a contradictory history. It has a three-part structure. The first part, "Neocolonialism and Violence," and the third, "Violence and Liberation," are both concerned with the continental situation, while the second part, "Act for Liberation," analyzes the social-political conflict in Argentina. "Neocolonialism and Violence" examines the international context, revealing a palimpsest of European influences. It consists of thirteen notes on neocolonialism, to show its impact on Argentina in terms of history, geography, politics, and culture. It also covers how Argentina is seen in the world, and particularly in Europe, following the great European immigration of the end of the nineteenth and beginning of the twentieth centuries. The film's second part, "Act for Liberation," is subdivided into two sections: "Chronicles of Peronism" (100 minutes), from the movement's emergence in 1945 to its defeat in 1955, and "Chronicles of Resistance" (100 minutes), on the struggles during Peronism's prohibition. The third part, "Violence and Liberation" (the shortest, approximately 45 minutes long), contains documents, testimonials, and interviews of which the most notable are with Julio Troxler, one of the survivors of the massacre in José León Suárez,[30] and with an octogenarian symbol of Peronist resistance and living memory of the struggles against Peronism's prohibition, who predicts the coming socialist revolution.[31]

The film's discourse is characterized by a systematic use of binaries and a Manichaean opposition between popular national forces and an "enemy" (the oligarchy, the *cipayos* or sellouts, neocolonialism, Europe, the United States, and so on) whose goal is to destroy national memory and identity. Peronism is presented as the embodiment of the revolution and the last hope for the bourgeoisie and revolutionaries alike. This dialectical binary involves a danger: basing the affirmation of one's own identity (revolutionary Peronism) exclusively on a rejection of the enemy's colonizing oligarchical identity implies that the eventual extermination of the latter (the colonizing oligarchical identity) would mean the simultaneous self-annihilation of the former (one's own identity as defined by revolutionary Peronism), as Stam has shown.[32] Subsequent events would confirm the consequences of this binary logic. The very day of Perón's return to the country after eighteen years of exile in Spain (June 20, 1973), confrontations played out between Peronist factions. These shootings and deaths took place in the fields around Buenos Aires's Ezeiza Airport, where crowds waited for the longed-for leader. They would be a harbinger of a veritable civil war within the movement that would continue beyond the death of Perón (on July 1, 1974) and the military coup of 1976.

In sum, *The Hour of the Furnaces* constructs an anticolonial film-essay by way of 1960s revolutionary Peronism, amalgamating the proposal of Perón's "Third Position" (between capitalism and socialism) to anticolonial Third World Fanonism and the artistic conception of a "Third Cinema" characterized by experimentation in film language, independent production, and political militancy. Furthermore, this Latin America–centered position, built on the foundation of a binary history, is rooted historically in the period of the independence movements and the formation of nation-states, finding support in quotations from Simón Bolívar, José de San Martín, José Martí, and other patriots from what left-wing Peronism termed the "first war of liberation." This was the war against the Spanish empire from the beginning of the nineteenth century. The "second war of liberation" would then be the one to be fought in the 1960s, against national governments that had betrayed the tradition of San Martín and Bolívar, by acting as agents of neocolonialism and of the oligarchical groups that had become its servants. These concepts are translated into slogan-phrases such as "Latin America = The Greater Homeland, The Unfinished Continent."

In the film, the quotations emphasize the supposed original unity of the Spanish American people, recall the genocide of pre-Columbian peoples, and hold that "Imperialism aspires to exterminate the peoples of Latin America."

These sentences are presented as titles against a black screen, requiring the spectator to concentrate on reading and interpreting them; some, like "liberation," flash forward and back, dynamically in a close-up or zoom, in order to further attract the spectator's attention. Others, like "heroes" and "fathers of the homeland," point to the meaning of official colonized culture. The camera is a combination of *caméra-stylo*, as Bazin had conceptualized it, and camera-rifle. Another type of quotation recalls the ideas of Argentine Marxist-revisionist historians, notably Jorge Abelardo Ramos, but also Juan José Hernández Arregui, Raúl Scalabrini Ortiz, and Arturo Jauretche. Jauretche and Hernández Arregui, thinkers of the so-called national Left, had studied national consciousness, criticizing the identity crystallized under neocolonial domination. Scalabrini Ortiz, historian, economist, and man of letters, had been repudiated by both the right and the communist Left but had sought to clarify the economic aspects of dependence.

Part of the strategy of this film-essay is to use spoken commentaries from an off-camera narrator. *The Hour of the Furnaces* is rich in spoken as well as written discourse superimposed on the image. As the structuring center of the film, the essay is simultaneously abstract and concrete. Between images, the screen irrupts intermittently but insistently into a black screen, transformed into an audiovisual blackboard invaded by provocative titles, or simply left empty in the hope that the audience will inhabit it with their participation. Thus, *The Hour of the Furnaces* generates its own self-reflection on cinematic writing in which the spoken text, the written text, and the images interact as they de-familiarize each other within the film composition.

Solanas and Getino proposed their theory of revolutionary cinema in the essay "Towards a Third Cinema" of October 1969,[33] as well as in the later essays "Militant Cinema: An Internal Category of Third Cinema" (March 1971) and "Cinema as Political Fact," and in other documents that were published in the group's journals and collected in the book *Cine, cultura y descolonización* in 1973 in the middle of the euphoria of the election of Héctor José Cámpora. In "La cultural nacional, el cine y *La hora de los hornos*" ("National Culture, Cinema, and *The Hour of the Furnaces*"),[34] Solanas and Getino contend that Third Cinema should break from the aesthetic contemplation of art and from a bourgeois conception of man. Instead, they propose "forms of dialogue and communication that, while at the margin of all regular conception of cinema as spectacle, work to develop—more than *film screenings*—acts, in which the reaction, the internal or open debate, and the unrest of the participant-actors are more important than the films themselves."[35] Besides the sections defining first cinema (Hollywood), second cinema (auteur film), and the proposed third cinema ("our" cinema),[36] is the introduction of the category of "film action" that emerged not only for political reasons (the need for clandestine discussion during Peronism's prohibition and the subsequent military dictatorship)[37] but also as part of a search for a new language of representation. In the film-act, the film as an object is rejected in favor of a collective activity to be completed by the film's viewers: "What is important is not the cinematic image, rather the live act that each screening makes possible; the film is an instrument for calling forth the act."[38] Solanas and Getino conceptualize this as follows:

> The act is guided by one or more mediators in the room that can interrupt the screening when the participants believe it to be necessary so that the relationship between the film and the protagonist *can definitively eliminate the spectator* . . . Provoking, more than screening, film *acts*. To establish a strong link between the artistic and the political avant-gardes; to make our cinema a beautiful weapon that fires at targets. . . . Comrades, we said at the beginning of "Act for Liberation," this is not only the projection of a film or a spectacle; above all it is an *act*, an act of anti-imperialist unity.[39]

The entire film is a call to action. From the first image of Che Guevara to the end, everything is partisan, factional—nothing is objective. This strategy evokes Brecht, who believed one had to divide the audience, forcing it to take sides. In the Argentine context, the message of *The Hour of the Furnaces* is clear: the intellectuals must take sides, for or against Peronism. The quotation from Fanon, "Every spectator is either a traitor or a coward," was provocative and uncomfortable, as was the call for martyrdom, to choose a life that meant choosing death, as Stam suggests.[40] But this was the call of the time and such revolutionary mystique permeates the experimentalism of *The Hour of the Furnaces*, making it an instance of a masochistic vanguard, as Renato Poggioli and Massimo Bontempelli remark.[41]

Another of the film's strategies is the choice of the testimonial genre, rooted in Italian postwar Neorealism. The film was inspired by the theorist and filmmaker Fernando Birri, considered by many to be the father of New Latin American Cinema.[42] In fact, the second part of *The Hour of the Furnaces* includes sequences from *Tire dié*, Birri's well-known 1958 documentary. On Birri's return from Rome, where he had studied cinema in the Centro Sperimentale di Roma, he founded Santa Fe's Cinema School in 1956, where one of his most outstanding students was the Tucumán native Gerardo Vallejo. Vallejo later joined Solanas and Getino as they filmed in his province, and he also participated in the creation of the Grupo Cine Liberación.[43] Getino and Velleggia, in a later critical essay, note that the inclusion in the film of the sequence from *Tire dié*—a sequence of children running along a bridge, looking up to a passing train, and asking for ten-cent coins ("*dié*" in popular language) that never come—"incorporates his or her own reading of the quotation, transforming it into allegory"[44] of the marginalization of poverty. It cites a precedent but also renews the interpretation of the cited sequence by inviting the spectator to take action against this poverty. For Birri, the citation points to an Argentine and Latin American precedent that the Grupo Cine Liberación recognizes as a peer, but it goes beyond this model by adding new meaning to it. The same thing happens with other sequences that the film cites, as well as in its use of fragmentary materials, either the filmmakers' own documentary images or collage-like incorporations of advertisements and archival materials.

The idea of montage is central to *The Hour of the Furnaces* and would become a trademark of Solanas's aesthetics, making his later films a form of auteur cinema. The montage feeds off of the aesthetics of the collage in the sense of dissonant visual fragments that find narrative coherence in the promise of Peronism. Paradoxically, this formal experimentation would be compatible with the idea of film as instrument of politics and with noninstrumental political cinema; that is, a cinema whose advanced aesthetics affirms its autonomy with respect to politics, even as the filmmakers do not deny their political ideas.[45] Yet Birri is not the only one cited in *The Hour of the Furnaces*: images are also taken from other documentaries to represent the resistance to imperialist aggression of all the peoples of the Third World. Examples include the documentary *Maioria absoluta/Absolute Majority* (Brazil, 1964) directed by

León Hirszman, and an allegorical dance of Vietnamese children taken from Dutch documentarist Joris Iven's *Le ciel—La terre/The Threatening Sky* (Netherlands, 1967).

The organizing logic of *The Hour of the Furnaces* governs these aesthetic strategies: the dialectical montage, which predominates in the film, distinguishes it from other political documentaries such as *The Battle of Chile*.[46] *The Hour of the Furnaces* puts forward a montage of different revolutionary aesthetics and recalls the silent films of Sergei Eisenstein, earning it the nickname of "the Latin American *Potemkin*." A great deal of the film's persuasiveness comes from the montage of idea-images or visual ideas, concepts such as "the oligarchy" that become concrete through the mention of the fifty families that dominate the country and through the presentation of images of the establishment. These include the writers of the Argentine Society of Writers represented by Manuel Mujica Láinez, the oligarchy's cemetery—*La Recoleta*—the Rural Society in which the best Argentine cattle are selected and awarded prizes. *La Recoleta* is presented superimposed with lights and sound effects, using techniques reminiscent of Alain Resnais's documentary art. The images of the cemetery statues create an artificial space and time. An excursion through Buenos Aires is parodied with monumental buildings and travelogues accompanied by caustic commentary. The titles and subtitles demystify the images of the wealth of Buenos Aires, a wealth immediately undermined by images of poverty in marginal neighborhoods. Shots of abstract geometrical buildings coincide with the sound of sirens, creating an atmosphere of urban anxiety evocative of the cinematic style of Godard.

In a sequence inspired by the avant-garde, Sergei Eisenstein (in an echo of his 1924 film *The Strike)* and Andy Warhol (in a gesture to the icons of superficial propaganda, pop art) are fused with images of a slaughter yard, a metaphor consecrated in nineteenth-century Argentine literature by Esteban Echeverría's short story "The Slaughter Yard." This slaughter yard, originally an allegory of the fratricidal nineteenth-century struggles between Unitarians and Federalists, is resignified in terms of the conflict between an agro-exporting oligarchy (representing neocolonial interests) and the revolutionaries that affirm national self-determination. A Brechtian ethos of sociopolitical commitment through politicized aesthetic representation permeates the film, along with poetic realism taken from French cinema of the 1930s.

This aesthetic of the montage extends to the soundtrack, which is a true musical compendium and a complex exercise in the theory of asynchronous and dialectical sound, as proposed in "A Statement" by Eisenstein, Pudovkin, and Alexandrov in 1928, combined in parodic fashion with the Swingle Singers metamorphosing into Bach by way of Ray Conniff.[47]

The film's strategies of aesthetic representation, organized by dialectical montage, synthesize a varied avant-garde arsenal at the service of awakening a continental and intercontinental historical-political consciousness that calls for the brotherhood and sisterhood of people in the struggle for liberation. Artists, as Adorno put it in his "The Essay as Form," do not create but assemble "preformed" cultural materials, leaving the mark of their own style. The collage or patchwork that constitutes the formal fabric of *The Hour of the Furnaces* is a means to construct anticipation for the revolutionary return of Peronism at a moment in which historic and mythical time coincide, as Ana Amado notes.[48] This space and temporality of "the national" is inscribed, furthermore, in a larger temporality of Third World movements in which other times and spaces coincide.

The Hour of the Furnaces and Tucumán arde

Any truly avant-garde intention is revolutionary.

—Declaration of the exposition *Tucumán arde*. Rosario, November 1968

Besides the transactions between Peronism and modern art in the aesthetic frame of the happening, as well as other avant-garde forms of the time, another case of transactions exists among Peronism, modern art, and the cultures of the Left: the collective Grupo de Artistas de Vanguardia (Group of Avant-Garde Artists). This collective brought together a sector of the artistic vanguard of the city of Rosario that also broke away from "the so-called avant-garde attitude of the artists that worked in the Instituto Di Tella."[49] The collective carried out an exhibition-act called *Tucumán arde* that represents another eminently political happening, also in the tumultuous year of 1968. A well-studied milestone in Argentine conceptual art,[50] *Tucumán arde* shares numerous conceptual and formal aspects with *The Hour of the Furnaces* that indicate a wider dialogue between media culture and the Left. Both projects were presented to the public in 1968, although, like the happening, they were the outcome of political and artistic processes that had begun in previous years. Both share the use of the testimonial genre and the media, though in *Tucumán arde*, the written press, photography, and investigative materials predominate. Both share the ideas of montage drawn from collage, of political action through art, and of aesthetic creation as a collective and violent act that does away with the bourgeois myth of artistic individuality and with the traditionally passive character attributed to art. Each operates outside the circuits of artistic consecration, albeit in the different spaces and institutions of its own artistic medium.[51]

In Argentina, 1968 was a turning point for the dematerialization of art as it increasingly became exclusively an art of *actions*. Artists such as Juan Pablo Renzi,[52] one of the prominent plastic artists of *Tucumán arde*, considered how to make avant-garde art that would have a public impact: "We were becoming aware of the relationship between the aesthetic avant-garde and the political avant-garde and of the possibilities for uniting them."[53] The extent of the rupture in 1968 was due not only to politicization but also to extreme experimentation. If there was an urgency to make collective art that would act directly on reality and denounce the social, political, and economic conditions that afflicted the country, the crisis in the province of Tucumán seemed to offer an opportunity for such an experiment. The collective appropriated and reformulated the slogan of the military dictatorship—"Operation Tucumán"—that, promoted by the media, drove a program of modernization intending to replace the national bourgeoisie with North American capital through the liquidation of small and medium-size sugar companies. The participants' central goal was to denounce the distance between publicity and reality. They therefore planned their action as an instrument of *counterinformation*. Theories of communication, especially Marshall McLuhan's *Understanding Media*, affected the plastic art avant-garde, making the power of the media a central question of debate. The importance of the media in manufacturing events had been the theme of a happening carried out by Eduardo Costa, Raúl Escari, and Roberto Jacoby, who spread word through the newspapers of a happening that had not taken place and that, thus, only existed in the media. This act led to the manifesto "An Art of the Mass Media," signed by these artists in 1966.[54]

In this context, *Tucumán arde* forms a clear attempt to address communication. The deliberate distortion and defamation of the communications media exist in the planning of events, which sought to generate a circuit of counterinformation that would expose official propaganda. The group's growing politicization through media art made them a target for political repression that would begin soon after.[55] The group began a *Ciclo de Arte Experimental* (Experimental Art Series) at the end of May 1968 in Rosario, with a 300,000 peso subsidy for the project from the Instituto Di Tella.[56] Those involved included, in addition to Juan Pablo Renzi, artists such as Eduardo Favario, León Ferrari, Graciela Carnevale, Rubén Naranjo, Jaime Rippa, and others, as well as academics who had resigned or been expelled from the university in 1966 under Onganía's dictatorship. These former professors included Adolfo Prieto, Nicolás Rosa, and María Teresa Gramuglio, whose base for discussion and alternative studies was a large house in downtown Rosario where they operated the Centro de Estudios de Filosofía y Ciencias del Hombre (Center for the Study of Philosophy and the Human Sciences).

The exhibitions culminated with a departure from the traditional space of the artistic institutions and a shift to a new venue. The artists organized and presented in the Primer Encuentro Nacional de Arte de Vanguardia (First National Gathering for Avant-Garde Art), held in Rosario on the weekend of August 10 and 11, 1968. From this gathering, new modes of political organization were adopted, with Marxism imbued with the Third World perspectives of the time as a theoretical-political guide. León Ferrari notes the capacity of art institutions to absorb all critical manifestations within their borders. This observation is crucial for explaining the movement from modernizing institutions (the Instituto Di Tella) to institutions outside the artistic field. An example is the Central General de Trabajadores Argentinos (General Confederation of Argentine Workers), which rallied around the figure of Raimundo Ongaro, director of the union of graphic workers, and opposed the Central General de Trabajadores (General Confederation of Workers) in clear dispute with Peronist unions led by Augusto Vandor.[57]

The experiment of *Tucumán arde*, traversed by all the discourses of aesthetic dematerialization, unfolded more as a process than as a viewable object. The main goal was *effectiveness* in unmasking the official press's campaign of concealment. The action took place in several stages. First, research was conducted and material collected in the province of Tucumán. Two trips to Tucumán were carried out—the first in mid-September; the second starting on October 22—accompanied by a dissemination campaign on the second trip to the province and in the days preceding the exhibitions in the cities of Rosario, Santa Fe, and Buenos Aires. A team from the Centre for Social Research produced a report on the economy of Tucumán that was publicized by covering the walls of these cities with the word "Tucumán." Shortly before they left for Tucumán, the word "Arde" was added. During the trip, participants gathered testimonial material. A few days after the second trip to Tucumán, on November 3, 1968, the exhibition opened on Central General de Trabajadores Argentinos (CGTA, General Confederation of Argentine Workers) premises in Rosario, attracting approximately a thousand people according to Longoni and Mestman.[58] On the street, ironic signs proclaimed the "First Biennial of Avant-Garde Art." The material that had been collected (films, recordings, photographs) was displayed on the different floors of the dissident workers' headquarters. The public was not traditional art spectators but militants and workers. The intention was to provoke the audience to *take a position.* One wall featured a montage of newspaper cuttings, assembled by the conceptual collagist León Ferrari.

The relationship of *Tucumán arde* to the repertory of conceptual art like *The Hour of the Furnaces* has largely been ignored in the local artistic milieu. This absence may be due to the negative ideological baggage associated with Peronism in large sectors of Argentine criticism.[59] The link to conceptualism does not lie in the tautological and self-referential form of conceptualism that may reconfirm the modernist paradigm[60] in which language does not refer to language (that is, to the specificity of the artistic act) but in the contextual relationships in which reality is no longer considered a field of reflection and becomes the way to transform society. Although the audiences that attended the clandestine screenings of *The Hour of the Furnaces* or the exhibition *Tucumán arde* were not as large as the public that the Instituto Di Tella could attract, they were a different kind of audience: a politicized audience inspired to participate in the construction of a revolutionary struggle.

Conclusion

I have examined *The Hour of the Furnaces* within the Argentine intellectual field of the 1960s, and 1968 specifically, as a series of conceptual and ideological transactions among Peronism, the cultures of the Left and the artistic tendencies of the avant-gardes in relation to the centers of legitimization and institutionalization, and to the era's philosophical, ideological, and cultural paradigms. My goal was to chart an itinerary between artistic and political expressions. Beyond their semiotic, ideological, and institutional specificities, these expressions interacted in a productive synergy. I believe the happening to be a transactional intersection between an avant-garde aesthetic that questions the institution of art and a political radicalization. *The Hour of the Furnaces*, a militant Peronist film happening, and *Tucumán arde*, a "conceptual political 'happening'" according to Beatriz Sarlo,[61] allow us to navigate a constellation of transactions within Latin American political-artistic conceptualism.[62]

Starting in the mid-1960s, politicized art took a leading role in the political panorama, initially in opposition to the United States' intervention in Vietnam and Santo Domingo, and later as part of the international repercussions of the events of May 1968 in France. Within this international and Argentine context of the 1960s and 1970s, particularly between 1966 and 1976 with the emergence of a Marxist variant of Peronism, the revolution was thought to be both real and imminent. This led to the configuration of a complex network of overdeterminations, heterogeneities, sharp shifts, and changes, all imbued with multiple self-destructive binaries and a sacrificial revolutionary logic.

—*Translated by Ross Swanson*

Notes

1. In the words of Robert Stam, it "inherits" and "prolongs" the legacy of Sergei Eisenstein, Dziga Vertov, Joris Ivens, Glauber Rocha, Fernando Birri, Alain Resnais, Luis Buñuel, and Jean-Luc Godard ("*The Hour of the Furnaces* and the Two Avant-Gardes," in *The Social Documentary in Latin America*, ed. Julianne Burton [Pittsburgh: University of Pittsburgh Press, 1990], 251–66, at 256–57). See also Julianne Burton, "The Camera as Gun: Two Decades of Culture and Resistance in Latin America," *Latin American Perspectives* 5, no. 1 (1978): 49–76; Julianne Burton, ed., *Cinema and Social Change in Latin America* (Austin: University of Texas Press, 1986); Stam, "*The Hour of the Furnaces* and the Two Avant-Gardes,", 251–66; Zuzana Pick, *The New Latin American Cinema: A Continental Project* (Austin: University of Texas Press, 1993).
2. Ana Longoni and Mariano Mestman note that this happening was not the first of its kind, but it took on an inaugural character since it "began a series of

artistic-political actions carried out collectively by a significant core group of the vanguard . . . posing an exceptional form of crossover between politics and art" ("Del Di Tella a 'Tucumán Arde,'" in *Vanguardia artística y política en el '68 argentino* [Buenos Aires: El Cielo por Asalto, 2000], 79).

3. The Instituto Di Tella was the most important art institution of this decade that proposed the modernization of art in Argentina, promoting artistic internationalism. John King, in *El Di Tella y desarrollo cultural argentino en la década del sesenta* (Buenos Aires: Asunto Impreso Ediciones, 1985), analyzes the institution's international network. But Andrea Giunta argues that King does not consider the underlying motives of this project or its correlations with "a web of institutions organized in the United States as part of the proposed inter-American dialogue generated in relation to the Alliance for Progress program." Andrea Giunta, *Avant-Garde, Internationalism, and Politics: Argentine Art in the Sixties*, trans. Peter Kahn (Durham, NC: Duke University Press, 2007), 8, 102.
4. Giunta, *Avant-Garde, Internationalism, and Politics*, 245.
5. Roberto Jacoby and Pablo Suárez, both from Buenos Aires, and Juan Pablo Renzi, from Rosario, were among those who participated in the "happening" (Longoni and Mestman, "Del Di Tella a 'Tucumán Arde,'" 77).
6. Longoni and Mestman, "Del Di Tella a 'Tucumán Arde,'" 78.
7. Guy Hennebelle, "Préambule: La nostalgie est toujours ce qu'elle était," in *Fernando Solanas ou la rage de transformer le monde, 1978, CinémaAction* (Paris: Éditions Corlet, 2001), 9–17, at 10.
8. Fernando Solanas and Octavio Getino, *Cine, Cultura y Descolonización* (Buenos Aires: Siglo XXI Editores, 1973), 13.
9. There were other collectives that also practiced political militancy through cinematic innovation. The best known and most coherent was the Grupo Cine de la Base (Cinema from the Base Group). Formed in the early 1970s, it included the film director Raimundo Gleyzer, who produced *Los traidores/The Traitors* (1972–73) and was later "disappeared" on May 27, 1977. The group's members were associated with the Worker's Party and its military arm the Ejército Revolucionario del Pueblo (People's Revolutionary Army). Like the Grupo Cine Liberación, the Grupo de Cine de la Base was motivated by concerns over Latin American integration and neocolonialism. Both groups proposed violence as an alternative method to combat hegemonic power. The fundamental difference between the two was in their positions on Peronism: the Grupo de Cine de la Base was critical, mainly because of

official unionism. Nevertheless, the Grupo de Cine de la Base fed off the conceptual principles of "Third Cinema" as theorized by Solanas and Getino, and its cinematic practice was much more coherent than that of the Grupo Cine Liberación in maintaining the goal of making a clandestine political cinema. See Burton, "Camera as Gun," 60–61.

10. Lanusse was Argentina's president between 1971 and 1973. He negotiated with the Montoneros for the return of Eva Perón's body to the country and ended the prohibition of Peronism. During his presidency, repression increased alongside the radicalization of armed groups. In 1972, sixteen leftist prisoners from the Ejército Revolucionario del Pueblo were executed in Trelew Prison, as is reconstructed in Tomás Eloy Martínez's *Passion according to Trelew* (1973). Lanusse finally led an opening to democracy, calling elections that would result in the triumph of Peronism in 1973.
11. René Prédal, "1936–1976: 40 ans de cinéma politique; Premier entretien avec Fernando Solanas," in *Fernando Solanas ou la rage de transformer le monde, 1978, CinémaAction* (Paris: Éditions Corlet, 2001), 18–33, at 25–26.
12. Stam, "*The Hour of the Furnaces* and the Two Avant-Gardes," 259.
13. Burton, "Camera as Gun," 60.
14. Marey's design of a light, portable camera in the shape of a rifle allowed him to photograph a figure in movement in twelve poses. Although he only used it for a few months, it became famous in the history of photography and cinema. Stam also mentions that Walter Benjamin in "The Work of Art in the Age of Mechanical Reproduction" uses a ballistic image to describe the Dadaist project. See Stam, "The *Hour of the Furnaces* and the Two Avant-Gardes," 254.
15. Fernando Solanas and Octavio Getino, "Towards a Third Cinema," *Tricontinental* 14 (October 1969): 120. Javier de Taboada points out the contrast between this proposal and that of the *caméra-stylo* of the auteur film promoted by André Bazin. See Javier de Taboada, "Tercer Cine: Tres Manifiestos," *Revista de crítica literaria latinoamericana* 73, no. 1 (2011): 37–60, at 44.
16. Solanas and Getino, "Towards a Third Cinema," 52.
17. Solanas and Getino, "Towards a Third Cinema," 124.
18. Solanas and Getino, "Towards a Third Cinema," 124. My emphasis.
19. Giunta, *Avant-Garde, Internationalism, and Politics*, 246. My emphasis.
20. As an intellectual who promoted the international avant-gardes, Masotta gave talks on pop art and other experimental movements of the time. He edited *Happenings*, a collection of articles with the publishing house Jorge

Álvarez in 1967, which includes essays by him and by those from his context (Eliseo Verón, Roberto Jacoby, Eduardo Costa, Raúl Escari, Alicia Páez, Madela Ezcurra).

21. Oscar Masotta et al., *Happenings* (Buenos Aires: Jorge Álvarez Editor, 1967), 29.
22. Solanas and Getino, *Cine, Cultura y Descolonización*, 42.
23. Prédal, "1936–1976: 40 ans de cinéma politique," 27.
24. Pesaro was then the capital of alternative Third World cinema (Prédal, "1936–1976: 40 ans de cinéma politique," 9). The link to the Taviani brothers is not coincidental; in their films, the brothers express a deep interest in the oppressed classes in marginal regions of Italy, and their work has been taken as an example of political-cultural practice understood in Gramscian terms. In 1960s Argentina, Gramsci's texts were much read, partially because certain tendencies on the Left questioned Argentina's stagnant Communist Party.
25. Solanas and Getino, "Towards a Third Cinema," 132.
26. Ana Longoni, "Óscar Masotta: Vanguardia y revolución en los años sesenta," Segundo Simposio Prácticas de comunicación emergentes en la cultura digital, Córdoba, Argentina, 2005, 31. In 1966, in the midst of the Onganía dictatorship, Masotta planned to implement a cycle of happenings in the Instituto Di Tella, though it had to be postponed because of the tumult of the coup d'état. Finally, he carried it out in October of that year. Masotta hired twenty auctioneers of the kind that sell off cheap jewelry, paying them for their work and displaying them to the audience while he emptied twelve fire extinguishers. This happening placed Masotta in a difficult position when his friends from the Left asked him about its meaning. He replied that it was "an act of social sadism made explicit." Cited in Giunta, *Avant-Garde, Internationalis, and Politics*, 187.
27. See especially Antonio Berni's series "Juanito y Ramona."
28. This group included Rómulo Macció, Luis Felipe Noé, Ernesto Deira, and Jorge de la Vega.
29. James Roy MacBean, "*La hora de los hornos*," *Film Quarterly* 24, no. 1 (1970): 31–37, at 31.
30. José León Suárez is a district of greater Buenos Aires where a group of prisoners (some Peronist, some not) were taken and executed by the Revolución Libertadora (Liberating Revolution) on June 9, 1956, as martial law was imposed in the context of a Peronist revolt. This massacre did not appear

in official newspapers but was researched by the writer, journalist, and later member of the Montoneros, Rodolfo Walsh, and published in what would become a celebrated text of Argentine literature: *Operación masacre*. Later, in 1976, both Troxler and Walsh were victims of another military repression, when they were disappeared under the military dictatorship of Videla, Agosti, and Massera (1976–83).

31. See MacBean, "*Hora de los hornos*," 32, and Stam, "*The Hour of the Furnaces* and the Two Avant-Gardes," 255.
32. Stam, "*The Hour of the Furnaces* and the Two Avant-Gardes," 263.
33. This essay was the era's best-known essay, written at the request of the Organization of Solidarity of the People of Asia, Africa, and Latin America (OSPAAAL), an organization that brought together the Third World countries and processes working for self-liberation. The essay was published in OSPAAAL's Havana-based journal *Tricontinental* 13 (October 1969). (The English translation of it was published in *Tricontinental* 14 [October 1969]. In the subheading of the Spanish text, a quote by Frantz Fanon appears that gives meaning to the goals of Grupo Cine Liberación: "need to discover, need to invent" (cited in Octavio Getino and Susana Velleggia, *El cine de las historias de la revolución: Aproximación a las teorías y prácticas del cine político en América Latina, 1967–1977* [Buenos Aires: Grupo Editor Altamira, 2002], 48). Javier de Taboada ("Tercer Cine") comments that "in a more prophetic than calculated manner," publication in this Cuban journal gave the article an international dissemination that anticipated the global reach of the New Latin American Cinema.
34. Response to a questionnaire presented by *Cine Cubano* 56/57 (March 1969), Havana, Cuba.
35. Solanas and Getino, *Cine, Cultura y Descolonización*, 41.
36. "Third Cinema" is a term that also has specific Peronist connotations in that it evokes the third position that Perón proposes in his political theory, between socialism and capitalism. Most critics overlook this fact, with the exception of Robert Stam, as De Taboada points out ("Tercer Cine," 40).
37. Hennebelle, "Préambule," 25.
38. Solanas and Getino, *Cine, Cultura y Descolonización*, 42.
39. Solanas and Getino, *Cine, Cultura y Descolonización*, 43–48.
40. Stam, "*The Hour of the Furnaces* and the Two Avant-Gardes," 262–63.
41. Cited in Stam, "*The Hour of the Furnaces* and the Two Avant-Gardes," 262.
42. Julianne Burton's pioneering study of Birri's cinema as an indispensable prec-

edent for *The Hour of the Furnaces* has not been sufficiently recognized. She notes Birri's seminal role in shaping an entire generation of Latin American filmmakers, as well as his participation in the creation of the Cuban Institute of Cinematic Art and Industry (ICAIC).

43. Gerardo Vallejo (1942–2007) was a cofounder along with Solanas and Getino of the collective Grupo Cine Liberación. In 1975, he fled to Panama and later to Spain due to the Argentine dictatorship. In 1979, he founded a film school in Madrid that had 150 students in the three years that it was open.
44. Getino and Velleggia, *Cine de las historias de la revolución*, 47.
45. Cited in Getino and Velleggia, *Cine de las historias de la revolución*, 48.
46. Ana López points out a large difference: *The Battle of Chile* abounds with extensive sequences, like the majority of political documentaries, to organize and construct a later reading of the social and political events, while *The Hour of the Furnaces* gives privilege to the idea of montage. See Ana López, "*The Battle of Chile*: Documentary, Political Process, and Representation," in *The Social Documentary in Latin America*, ed. Julianne Burton (Pittsburgh: University of Pittsburgh Press, 1990), 267–87, at 277.
47. Stam, "*The Hour of the Furnaces* and the Two Avant-Gardes," 254–59.
48. Ana Amado, *La imagen justa: Cine argentino y política, 1980–2007* (Buenos Aires: Colihue, 2009).
49. María Teresa Gramuglio and Nicolás Rosa, "Artistas de vanguardia responden con Tucumán Arde," *Transatlántico* 5 (2008): 1. http://ccpe.org.ar/artistas-de-vanguardia-responden-con-tucuman-arde-por-maria-teresa-gramuglio-y-nicolas-rosa/, accessed November 25, 2017.
50. See Longoni and Mestman, "Del Di Tella a 'Tucumán Arde'"; Giunta, *Avant-Garde, Internationalism, and Politics*; Luis Camnitzer, *Conceptualism in Latin American Art: Didactics of Liberation* (Austin: University of Texas Press, 2007).
51. *The Hour of the Furnaces* would contribute, together with Cuban film and other militant films in the region, to the establishment of alternative distributors in the First World. Some of these include the following: The Other Cinema (London); Third World Cinema Group and Tricontinental Film Center (USA); MK2 (France); Cinéma d'Information Politique Champ Libre (Montreal); Collettivo Cinema Militante, San Diego Cinematográfica, and Centro Documentazione Cinema e Lotta de Classe (Italy). Other projects for the dissemination of political film existed. Getino and Velleggia, *El cine de*

las historias de la revolución, 49.

52. A name that Ricardo Piglia reclaims as a fictitious representation of the avant-garde writer in his famous novel *Artificial Respiration*.
53. Cited in Giunta, *Avant-Garde, Internationalism, and Politics*, 267.
54. Giunta, *Avant-Garde, Internationalism, and Politics*, 187.
55. This is the case of the painter Eduardo Favario, one of the founders of the Grupo de Artistas de Vanguardia de Rosario (Group of Avant-Garde Artists of Rosario), which led to a deep break in the vision of art as a political tool. He participated in Tucumán Arde until deciding to abandon artistic activity and to join the PRT-ERP (Hugo Montero, "Eduardo Favario: De Tucumán Arde al PRT-ERP," Revista Sudestada, http://www.revistasudestada.com.ar/articulo/591/eduardo-favario-de-tucuman-arde-al-prt-erp-/, accessed November 21, 2017, n.p.).
56. Longoni and Mestman, "Del Di Tella a 'Tucumán Arde,'" 115.
57. Longoni and Mestman, 129.
58. Longoni and Mestman, 163.
59. A certain critical resistance exists with respect to *The Hour of the Furnaces* and its aspects of formal experimentation that establish a dialogue with artistic conceptualism in Latin America. It may be due to an ideological prejudice that considers productions associated with Peronism to lack conceptual or aesthetic depth. The collective that created *Tucumán arde* came from different formations of the Left, more associated with socialism and the Grupo Cine de la Base; some of its members participated in the Revolutionary Workers' Party and its armed wing, the Ejército Revolucionario del Pueblo. There is no doubt that *Tucumán arde* has received much more attention and is seen as a milestone in the local artistic field. In Tucumán, there is the Casa de Cultura Tucumán Arde and the word '*Arde!*" has been taken up by the collective "Arde! Arte de acción colectiva," that formed amid the political-economic crisis of December 19 and 20, 2001, and continues its activities even now. Likewise, La Casa por la Memoria de Rosario (House for the Memory of Rosario) held an exhibition of photographs and documents from *Tucumán arde*. The Instituto Di Tella's book on *Tucumán arde* was reprinted, proof of continued interest in this exhibition's meaning for Argentina's artistic and political fields. The connections between the two collectives (the Grupo Cine Liberación and *Tucumán arde*) seem to come from outside local criticism: Luis Camnitzer in *Conceptualism in Latin American Art*, dedicates a chapter to *Tucumán arde* (chapter 8) and one to politics and identity

(chapter 19), discussing the impact of the manifesto of Third Cinema and its artistic correlate, *The Hour of the Furnaces.*

60. Giunta argues that the nexus with the ideological variant of conceptualism should be made even more explicit.
61. Cited in Longoni and Mestman, "Del Di Tella a 'Tucumán Arde,'" 172.
62. As is to be expected, in *La máquina cultural*, Beatriz Sarlo refers to *The Hour of the Furnaces* and *Tucumán arde* as cinematographic and plastic practices that "needed to foretell what the Revolution would bring about concretely: the unification of the spheres that modernity had separated" (*La máquina cultural* [Buenos Aires: Ariel, 1998], 254; cited by Longoni and Mestman, "Del Di Tella a 'Tucumán Arde,'" in note 208).

Bibliography

Amado, Ana. *La imagen justa: Cine argentino y política, 1980–2007.* Buenos Aires: Colihue, 2009.

Arte nuevo. "Inventario 1965–1975. A 40 años de Tucumán Arde." http://arte-nuevo.blogspot.com/2008/10/inventario-1965-1975-40-aos-de-tucumn.html, accessed November 21, 2017.

Burton, Julianne, ed. *Cinema and Social Change in Latin America.* Austin: University of Texas Press, 1986.

______. "The Camera as Gun: Two Decades of Culture and Resistance in Latin America." *Latin American Perspectives* 5, no. 1 (1978): 49–76.

Camnitzer, Luis. *Conceptualism in Latin American Art: Didactics of Liberation.* Austin: University of Texas Press, 2007.

De Taboada, Javier. "Tercer Cine: Tres Manifestos." *Revista de crítica literaria latinoamericana* 73, no. 1 (2011): 37–60.

Getino, Octavio, and Susana Velleggia. *El cine de las historias de la revolución: Aproximación a las teorías y prácticas del cine político en América Latina (1967–1977).* Buenos Aires: Grupo Editor Altamira, 2002.

Giunta, Andrea. *Avant-Garde, Internationalism, and Politics: Argentine Art in the Sixties.* Translated by Peter Kahn. Durham, NC: Duke University Press, 2007.

Gorini, Florian. "Arde! Arte de acción colectiva: Centro Cultural de Cooperación." December 21, 2011. www.marcha.org.ar.

Gramuglio, María Teresa, and Nicolás Rosa. "Artistas de vanguardia responden con *Tucumán Arde.*" *Transatlántico* 5, 2008. http://ccpe.org.ar/artistas-de-vanguardia-responden-con-tucuman-arde-por-maria-teresa-gramuglio-y-nicolas-rosa/, accessed November 21, 2017.

Hennebelle, Guy. "Préambule: La nostalgie est toujours ce qu'elle était." In *Fernando Solanas ou la rage de transformer le monde, 1978, CinémaAction*, 8–17. Paris: Éditions Corlet, 2001.

Longoni, Ana. "Óscar Masotta: Vanguardia y revolución en los años sesenta." Segundo Simposio Prácticas de comunicación emergentes en la cultura digital. Córdoba, Argentina, 2005.

Longoni, Ana, and Mariano Mestman. "Del Di Tella a 'Tucumán Arde.'" In *Vanguardia artística y política en el '68 argentino*. Buenos Aires: El Cielo por Asalto, 2000.

López, Ana M. "The Battle of Chile: Documentary, Political Process, and Representation." In *The Social Documentary in Latin America*, edited by Julianne Burton, 267–88. Pittsburgh: University of Pittsburgh Press, 1990.

MacBean, James Roy. "La hora de los hornos." *Film Quarterly* 24, no. 1 (1970): 31–37.

Masotta, Óscar, et al. *Happenings*. Buenos Aires: Jorge Álvarez Editor, 1967.

Montero, Hugo. "Eduardo Favario: De Tucumán Arde al PRT-ERP." Revista Sudestada. http://www.revistasudestada.com.ar/articulo/591/eduardo-favario-de-tucuman-arde-al-prt-erp-/, accessed November 21, 2017.

Pick, Zuzana. *The New Latin American Cinema: A Continental Project*. Austin: University of Texas Press, 1993.

Prédal, René. "1936–1976: 40 ans de cinéma politique: Premier entretien avec Fernando Solanas." In *Fernando Solanas ou la rage de transformer le monde, 1978, CinémaAction*, 18–33. Paris: Éditions Corlet, 2001.

Solanas, Fernando E., and Octavio Getino. *Cine, Cultura y Descolonización*. Buenos Aires: Siglo XXI Editores, 1973.

———. "Towards a Third Cinema." *Tricontinental* 14 (October 1969): 107–32.

Stam, Robert. "*The Hour of the Furnaces* and the Two Avant-Gardes." In *The Social Documentary in Latin America*, edited by Julianne Burton, 251–66. Pittsburgh: University of Pittsburgh Press, 1990.

7

Toward a New Mode of Study

The New Student Left and the Occupation of Cinema in *Columbia Revolt* and *The Battlefront for the Liberation of Japan—Summer in Sanrizuka*

Morgan Adamson

> The student graduates. But not all of them. Some still stay, committed to black study in the university's undercommon rooms. They study without an end, plan without a pause, rebel without a policy, conserve without patrimony. They study in the university and the university forces them under, relegates them to a state without interests, without credit, without debt that bears interest, that earns credits. They never graduate. They just ain't ready. They're building something down there. Mutual debt, debt unpayable, debt unbounded, debt unconsolidated, debt to each other in a study group, to others in a nurses' room, to others in a barber shop, to others in a squat, a dump, a woods, a bed, an embrace.
>
> Stephano Harney and Fred Moten
> *The Undercommons: Fugitive Planning and Black Study*

The figure of the student is indelibly seared into the audiovisual archive of the New Left. Images of her protests and occupations, posters and screams become shorthand for a whole set of myths about the 1960s: the idealism of youth, the fragility of the movement, the tenuous and short-lived alliances of an embattled Left. Despite attempts to trivialize them, student movements in India, Thailand, Mexico, Turkey, Egypt, and Nigeria (to list only a few) that erupted in 1968 in tandem with disruptions in industrial centers like the United States, western Europe, and Japan became what George Katsiaficas described as "a force of international relations."[1] The rapid expansion of higher education in the postwar era had enfolded a vastly augmented section of the population into the university system, resulting in the unintended consequence of a new social force with the capacity to analyze and to resist the increasing role of the university industrial complex in imperialist ventures, the production of specialized labor for capital, and the university's role in the reproduction of manifold forms of inequality. Coinciding with the Keynesian era of demands for full employment, Nick Mitchell suggests the swelling of the student population in the postwar period was the implicit strategy to contain and manage a significant portion of the population that would otherwise be seeking jobs. Mitchell proposes the best analogy for the university in the postwar era might not be a "factory" but rather a "warehouse" for the industrial reserve army.[2] Such an understanding of the student in the postwar era provides a fresh lens through which to analyze the student in the event of global 1968 not only as a "force of international relations," as Katsiaficas suggests, but also as a force of capital relations.[3]

As a global force, student movements played a principle role in redefining what constitutes valid academic knowledge. As Roderick Ferguson charts in *The Reorder of Things*, these movements produced interdisciplinary knowledges that emphasized difference and "historical particularities rather than transhistorical universalities."[4] Furthermore, these interdisciplinary forms of knowledge being formed within student movements drew from traditions of thought connected with anti-imperial struggles, such as the model of internal colonialism outlined by Latin American theories of underdevelopment. The cinema is a significant site of investigation for the production of new forms of knowledge arising from New Left struggles as student movements across the United States, Latin America, Europe, Africa, and Asia inspired and participated in the production of films that worked to articulate new epistemologies, not only in their form and content but also in their alternative methods of production, distribution, and exhibition. The themes of internal colonialism and of forging new encounters and collectivities come to the fore in the two cases of militant, student collective filmmaking addressed in this essay: the New York Newsreel's *Columbia Revolt* (US, 1968), and the Ogawa Pro's *Nihon kaiho sensen—Sanrizuka no natsu/The Battlefront for the Liberation of Japan—Summer in Sanrizuka* (Japan, 1968). Each film is situated within social movements that used an analysis of internal colonization in the defense of university and of extrauniversity spaces. Furthermore, these spaces were produced through the language of the commons, each film dramatizing struggles against enclosure by either the university or the state. Like the student movements from which they were born, *Columbia Revolt* and *Summer in Sanrizuka* demonstrate the ways that new knowledges are forged through radical and collective modes of study, thus realizing in cinematic terms Mario Tronti's assertion that "knowledge comes from struggle."[5]

In generating alternative epistemological paradigms, the students engaged in a new mode of study, extending far beyond the walls of the university and participating in encounters that sought to foster new modes of being and thinking in common. I use the term *study* in its broadest sense, constituting what Fred Moten refers to as a "speculative practice" or a "common intellectual practice" that is not necessarily geared toward an end and is often not recognized as valid by authoritative academic standards.[6] Like so many films of the New Left made in the 1960s and 1970s, these cinematic movements actively rejected auteur cinema and developed collective models of filmmaking as a political gesture in a broader attempt to overcome the implicit forms of authority and hierarchy that auteur cinema was thought to engender. Among the student movement—as elsewhere within the New Left—this was an international phenomenon, as indicated by the collective nature of other canonical student films such as *El Grito* (Mexico, 1968) and the *Cinegiornale del movimento studentesco* (Italy, 1968).

I argue that the New Left's essay-film is not simply a formal technique but a cinematic modality that attempts—in the original sense of Michel de Montaigne's use of the term *essai* (as a trial or attempt)—to produce collective enunciations and participatory modes of communication. In different ways, these films are emblematic of how cinema is employed as a tool for study, one capable of generating affects and amplifying antagonisms. Through its unique capacity to use cinema as a tool for study, each film elaborates an essayistic politics of the commons by attempting to express the power of what Kristin Ross, referring to the Paris Commune, has called "communal luxury," which she describes as, "at its most speculative . . . a set of criteria or system of valuation other than the one supplied by the market for deciding what a society values, what it counts as precious."[7] The films do so by cinematically rendering affective dimensions of living behind the barricades and the new forms of knowledge and discourses that materialize in these spaces of collaboration and contradiction, using formal strategies that situate the camera as a tool of struggle rather than as a neutral observer.

Columbia Revolt opens with a homily on the status of the university in modern society:

> The modern university is the cradle of the nation's future. Today it not only preserves and transmits knowledge and values, it serves more and more as a center of research and innovation. It has been called the chief energizing and creative force in our entire social system. The modern university is the cradle of the nation's future: *this be so*. Let us not underestimate the task we face. Meanwhile the explosive growthage [*sic*] still increases the demands upon us. The underdeveloped peoples look to us for training and guidance.

Delivered in a grave tone characteristic of the "voice of god" narration used in midcentury documentary, the voice-over is accompanied by ceremonious organ music and booms over footage of marble columns and statues that line the halls of the university. This lecture, however, is interrupted by the sound of a machine gun and the rapid fire of the famous Newsreel logo on the screen, disrupting the imperious proclamation "*this be so*" with a militant affront to the university and its claims to truth and futurity. In the following sequence, the neoclassical architecture and authoritarian tone of the intro is juxtaposed with footage of rigid, modern university buildings and unattributed voice-overs of students and activists speaking about the increasing militarization and corporatization of the university. These anonymous voice-overs, which Jonathan Kahana has described as "voice-offs," are characteristic of the early Newsreel style, indicating an antiauthoritarian, situated knowledge taken from interviews with participants.[8] In its rejection of the idea that any one voice could represent the totality, the voice-off functions as the primary formal mechanism for foregrounding difference in the film by displacing universalizing claims to truth with disparate voices.

In its formal rejection of the purported neutrality of the university and the knowledge it produces, *Columbia Revolt* expresses an antagonism between universality and difference through a cacophony of voices that both narrate and analyze the events that unfolded in the United States in April and May 1968. In her popular account of the Columbia protests and occupations published in 1969, Joanne Grant identifies what she calls the "Columbia pattern of protest," a mode of student revolt that marks a break from earlier student protests, typified by the 1964 Berkeley Free Speech Movement. Grant locates "black separatism, student occupations of buildings, student and community participation, police battles, reluctance to negotiate, [and] rebel demands for amnesty" as the hallmarks of new campus activism.[9] Although often characterized as an escalation of campus protests against the Vietnam War, the clash at Columbia is inseparable from the increasing black militancy and its effects on the new student Left in the United States. In particular, the Columbia conflict between students and administration was catalyzed by the intensification of hostilities between Columbia and the surrounding Morningside Heights and Harlem neighborhoods. As Stefan Bradley documents in *Harlem vs. Columbia University: Black Student Power in the Late 1960s*, tensions between Columbia and the surrounding black community that had been growing for years came to a head in the aftermath of Martin Luther King Jr.'s assassination and the riots that ensued. In the name of "urban renewal" and crime reduction, Columbia had been in the process of evicting primarily black tenants from its vast real estate holdings in Morningside Heights.[10] The focal point of the Harlem community's protests against Columbia became a gym that the university planned to build in Morningside Park, a small green space that separated Columbia and Harlem. In the years leading up to the Columbia protests, the plan for the private gym built on public land, which would have a separate entrance and facilities for community members in the basement, galvanized the increasingly militant Harlem community, whose leaders such as H. Rap Brown articulated the grievances of the community through the language of Black Power.[11] Building on a sentiment in the movement that Harlem represented an internal colony of the United States, local activists figured the gym as an "invasion" of their community—linking white supremacy and imperialist strategies at home with those abroad.[12] A pamphlet titled "Gym Crow," most likely produced by Columbia students aligned with the Student Afro-American Society (SAS), presented a carefully researched case against the gym and gave ammunition to the struggle to thwart its construction by providing a pithy slogan that captured the project's inherent racism.[13]

In an often chaotic and contradictory manner, *Columbia Revolt* works to underline the disparity between the university's ideals and its reality by foregrounding the struggle around the gym. The film's account of the events that ensued on April 23 and 24, 1968, starts with footage of the gym's fenced-off construction site with voice-offs from participants we assume are members of the Harlem community. "This country went up on violence and this country's going down on violence; as a house go up, a house must come down," states a distinctly African American female voice (one of the few such voices we hear in the film). Footage of a black man, lying in the blade of a large bulldozer defiantly smoking a cigarette, and a black woman, sitting in front of the tank tread of the same machine, visualize the militant posture of the community against the encroachment of Columbia.

Although the Students for a Democratic Society (SDS), led by then-president Mark Rudd, are often given credit for the escalation of protest, it was the Harlem community and black Columbia students that led the charge by rejecting the tactic of an integrated, nonviolent sit-in characteristic of the Berkeley Free Speech Movement. Instead, they barricaded Hamilton Hall and demanded that the white students leave (due to their disorganization, internal divisions, and unwillingness to barricade the building) and let the black students and members of the community take charge in the struggle against the gym. The "black-white split," as it is named in the film, is presented in *Columbia Revolt* through an account of a member of SDS in a moment of self-critique as he narrates the series of events that led to the split over footage of SAS leaders such as Cicero Wilson, Ray Brown, Bill Sales, and Ralph Metcalfe Jr., all of whom go unnamed in the film, unlike Mark Rudd, whose leadership is mentioned at several points. While this voice-off functions as an affirmation of the tactics of the SAS and the participants from the Harlem community in escalating the confrontation, it simultaneously robs the black leadership of a voice at the moment of the clearest assertion of its power. By featuring the images, but not the voices, of the black leadership, this scene reproduces a set of representational hierarchies. Despite its desire to disrupt the discourse of the university by creating a partial account of events, designing the production of the film around the principles of participatory democracy and collective critique, *Columbia Revolt* ultimately falls short by consistently presenting an account of the events from the perspective of the white (primarily male) participants, whose voices crowd out those of the black students and community participants whose militant leadership and tactics precipitated the radical turn of events. The voices heard on screen reflect the complexion of the early New York Newsreel at the time, whose primarily white, male leadership replicated the hierarchies and centralized organization of cinematic meaning that the group purportedly worked to undermine. These contradictions in the group have been well documented and eventually led to the formation of the Third World Newsreel in the early 1970s.[14] As Bill Nichols has argued, the Newsreel collective operated as a kind of barometer for the Left in the United States, and the contestation over the production of radical cinematic meaning that played out in the Newsreel are indices of larger struggles within the New Left itself.[15]

Despite its failure to give voice to the black leadership, *Columbia Revolt* does foreground their tactical innovation, studying the construction and consequences of the barricades in occupying and reclaiming of university territory. It does so by focusing on the importance of building and maintaining the barricades and emphasizing how new possibilities of being-with-in-struggle were magnified behind the barricade walls. A sequence documents the process of building the barricades at Hamilton Hall, using water cannons, chairs, and other furniture in order to prevent a surprise takeover by the police, while another voice-off recounts groups of Harlem high school students, mothers, and other sections of the black community marching on Columbia. In a shot taken from the interior of the building while H. Rap Brown (with Stokely Carmichael by this side) reads the students' demands to onlookers and the press in front of Hamilton Hall, the silhouettes of three black Columbia students looking down on the crowd assembled outside (see fig. 7.1). This shot conveys the power of the barricade as a tactic, creating a dynamic that temporarily displaces the spatial, and racial, order of everyday life at Columbia University. Scenes that anticipate the militant struggles for ethnic studies that would emerge in places like San Francisco State (captured in San Francisco Newsreel's *San Francisco State on Strike*), Cornell University, and numerous campuses across the country, the display of black militancy in reclaiming university spaces and connections with the larger black community engendered a broader claim to knowledge production and dissemination. In defending the commons, Morningside Park, and the surrounding community, a space for an

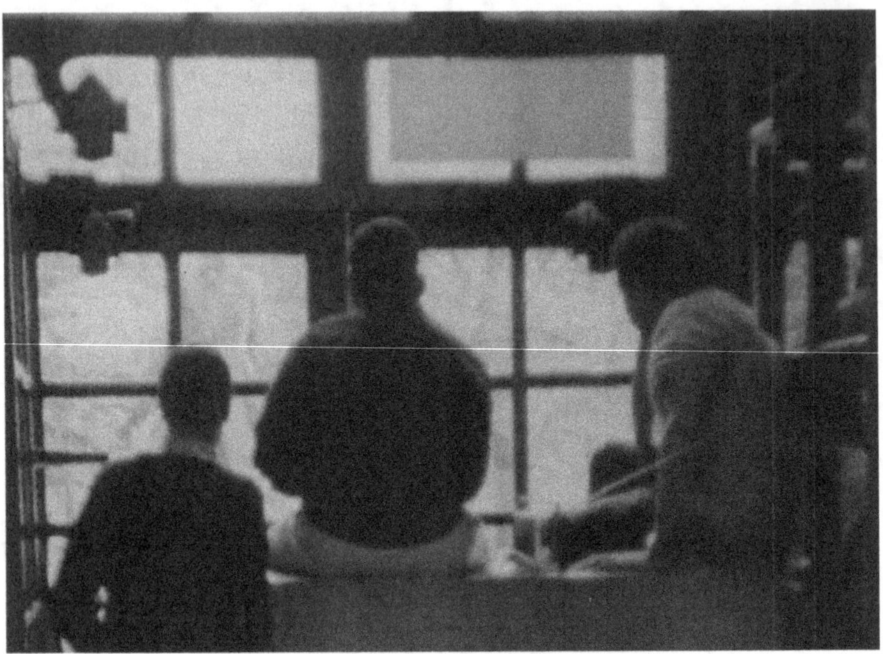

Columbia Revolt.

alternate commons is forced opened within the institution, or better, within its undercommons. This alternate commons is the knowledge, experience, and history of the black community.

In these scenes from Hamilton Hall, *Columbia Revolt* underscores the ways that the epistemological grew from the tactical, generating a situated knowledge made possible by the act of occupation. In a voice-off, we hear a student reflecting on tactical transition from sit-in to barricade: "we realized that our strength was in our militancy, in holding those buildings. It took the example of the blacks to move us." In the following scene, a voice-off explains one of the most controversial moments of the Columbia protests, in which occupying students took over President Grayson Kirk's office and went through his files, discovering ample evidence of Columbia's links to the Institute for Defense Analyses (IDA) and its plans to take over the surrounding neighborhood, further displacing the black and Puerto Rican communities, findings which it disseminated in mimeographed dispatches during the occupation. Enabled by the barricades, this radical form of study that takes the university itself as the object of research was the model for the production of *Columbia Revolt*, which, according to Roz Payne, involved the Newsreel collective actively participating in the occupation, using cameras "as weapons as well as recording events. Melvin has a W.W.II case iron steel bell and Howell camera that could take the shock of breaking plate glass windows."[16] The production of *Columbia Revolt* was modeled on the collective study already at work within the occupation, implicating the filmmakers as participants. Militant study through cinema in the case of *Columbia Revolt* necessitated transforming the camera into a tool of the barricade, one that could uniquely convey the antagonisms by producing a distinctly situated knowledge.

Perhaps the most memorable sections of *Columbia Revolt* are those that convey the affective dimensions of life behind the barricades as the discovery of the intensities formed in communal existence: "the life of the commune was a group of people who were incredibly close to each other on no other level but the level of struggle." The film itself becomes a mode of study that reflects on the possibility of redefining self, home, and family within the occupation. Over a sequence of a milk carton being passed around, a voice-off recounts: "There was a total collective feeling. No one particularly cared about his individual feelings, because you never experienced them. Everything was experienced in the most collective sense that I've ever known. This was one of the new experiences for most the people in the strike, a kind of electric awakening." In an emphatic tone, a participant asserts: "People are living here, it's a home. *It's a home*. I've never been so comfortable on this campus." Scenes of people drumming, dancing, forming a limbo line, and, famously, getting married in the organized chaos of the occupied buildings convey a joyful sentiment of collaboration in the occupied spaces. "We chose to be married at home and with our family," states a voice-off of the bride, and the anonymous officiant declares: "I now pronounce that Andrea and Richard are children of the New Age." *Columbia Revolt* does not linger on the commune but reasserts antagonism by interrupting cheers from the wedding crowd with the sounds of police sirens and the inevitable breaking of the barricades. What is notable in the sequence on communal life is the integrated nature of participants—an unspoken blurring of the "black-white" split that is discussed earlier. The moments in which the film asserts a new definition of home and family convey a utopian camaraderie among different factions of the strike.

Despite its limitations, in conducting a new mode of study by way of a cinema that activates and participates in struggles to redefine the university, *Columbia Revolt* served as a catalyst for student uprisings in the United States and globally by redefining and affirming the epistemological and affective values discovered, however briefly, in life behind the barricade.

Like many of the cinematic moments of the New Left, *Columbia Revolt* is significant for the independent networks of distribution and exhibition through which it circulated.[17] Along with San Francisco Newsreel's *Black Panther: Off the Pig!* (USA, 1968), *Columbia Revolt* became a mainstay of the underground cinema scene in the United States, its screening prompting not only conversation and debate but also actual campus uprisings, such as the burning of an ROTC center at SUNY Buffalo by the film's audience immediately following a screening.[18] As Robert Kramer of the New York Newsreel put it, the purpose of these films was to create "a form of propaganda that polarizes, angers, and excites for the purpose of discussion—a way of getting at people, not by making concession to where they are, but by showing them where you are and forcing them to deal with that, bringing out all their assumptions, their prejudices, their imperfect perceptions."[19]

While the emphasis on alternate forms of production, distribution, and exhibition were simultaneously developing in Latin America, Europe, and the United States in the years leading up to the upheavals of 1968 and the publication of Fernando Solanas and Octavio Getino's "Towards a Third Cinema," some of the most innovative theorization and infrastructure of independent New Left cinema was being cultivated in Japan under the auspices of the Jeiso Collective. Emerging out of a rich culture of independent and avant-garde filmmaking, the group's center was Ogawa Shinsuke, a charismatic figure who, along with prominent filmmakers such as Tsuchimoto Noriaki, abandoned mainstream filmmaking in the midst of a radical transformation in Japanese documentary cinema taking place in the mid-1960s that rejected both commercial cinema and the centralized hierarchies that characterized the documentary cinema associated with the Japanese Communist Party (JCP).[20] Ogawa quickly connected with the student movement in Hanai and formed the Jishu Joei Shoshiki no Kai (Independent Screening Organization), or Jeiso, in 1966. Largely unknown in the United States to this day, Jeiso's early films such as *Seinen no umi/Sea of Youth* (1966), *Assatsu no mori/Forest of*

Pressure (1967), and *Gennin hokusho-Haneda toso no kiroku/Report from Haneda* (1967) galvanized the Japanese student movement in the late 1960s.

As Abé Mark Nornes chronicles in his definitive account of Ogawa's career, Jeiso (renamed "Ogawa Pro" in 1968) redefined movement filmmaking in several ways. First, the collective developed an elaborate, independent distribution and exhibition network that emphasized audience participation and engagement: "Ask an Ogawa Pro member about its 'film movement' and he or she would assume you are talking about the screenings, not the film. The real activism of the collective centered on the reception context."[21] As spaces for networking among different segments of the New Left, especially the student movement, screenings were held across Japan in nontraditional spaces, "from urban art houses to rural gymnasiums to homemade theaters."[22] Second, a method of collective research and production was systemized for each film, in which various working groups—such as screening, production, investigation, and theory—were engaged in carrying out every aspect of production, distribution, and exhibition collectively.[23] The organization of Jeiso was remarkably similar to the cells in the "*film-guerilla* group," described by Solanas and Getino in the "Implementation" section of "Towards a Third Cinema."[24] In fact, both the Newsreel collective and what we assume to be the Jeiso collective are mentioned in Solanas and Getino's groundbreaking essay, indicating the important aspect of the internationalism of the New Left.[25] In addition to networking among the New Left in Japan, the collective developed connections with international New Left organizations, including the Black Panthers, whose minister of propaganda, Elbert Howard, visited the collective in 1969, and New Left film collectives in the United States and France, including Newsreel, and the collective produced dubbed Japanese versions of both *Columbia Revolt* and *Black Panther*.[26] The group was influenced by the theory of avant-garde documentary developed by the New Left filmmaker and theorist Matsumoto Toshio that rejected naturalism and called for a "new realism" that would "unify the documentary and the avant-garde" by way of a dialectical engagement between what he identified as the "inside," the subjectivity of the filmmaker, and "outside," the world conceived of as active rather than inert.[27] This manifested in the active research and engagement with the student movement in the production of *Forest of Pressure*, which included conducting research by making trips to numerous Japanese universities and political organizations.[28] Following Matsumoto's imperative, as Abé puts it, the Jeiso collective's "experimentation with documentary style asserts the subjectivity of the filmmakers in the tissue of the image and sound."[29] While seemingly observational in nature, Jeiso's theorization of collective, subjective engagement through cinema shows the attention to the epistemological and affective consequences of using cinema as a form of social engagement.

The subjects of Jeiso's cinematic explorations followed closely that of the Japanese student movement, beginning in the universities before expanding beyond them. Just as the struggle around "Gym Crow" highlighted links between the local displacement of black communities and imperialism, the Japanese student movement's antagonistic view of the Vietnam War drew connections between US imperialism in Vietnam and imperial and capitalist legacies domestically. These issues converged in the struggle against the construction of the Narita Airport outside of Tokyo, which would become one of the most protracted battles of the long sixties, continuing for over a decade and involving an estimated 750,000 to a million people.[30] The conflict began with farmers being displaced by the construction of the airport, opposing the initial purchase of their land by the government and forming a coalition of villages united under the name of Hantai Dōmei. Resistance to the airport soon became the focal point of the Japanese New Left, particularly the student movement. As David Apter and Nagayo Sawa demonstrate, the intensity of the struggle against the Narita Airport grew out of a legacy of New Left activity in Japan centered on resisting US imperialism, particularly the construction of US airbases, which culminated in 1960 with the AMPO (Anti-US-Japan-Security-Treaty) movement. With the help of New Left student organizations like Zengakuren (a group that had officially split from the JCP in 1958), militants framed the airport struggle in terms of US imperialism:

> The proposed Narita airport became a "military" airport, a symbol of U.S. imperialism and Japanese subservience to American military needs. In turn the farmers saw their own resistance as part of a common "front" with "progressive forces" in Vietnam and elsewhere, and as part of a peasant struggle of classic proportions, especially after some of them had visited China during the Cultural Revolution.[31]

The militant's defense of the farmland was not informed by a nostalgic pastoralism, but rather understood the process of displacing farmers as "part of the process of world capitalism, a form of primitive accumulation" that was intended to "create both an authentic proletariat and an industrial reserve army."[32] Thus, the movement against US imperialism was understood as deeply connected to world processes of capitalism, and the Sanrizuka struggle articulated peasant struggles in Asia and elsewhere with the accelerated industrialization of Japan in the postwar period.[33] With the participation of antinuclear movements and the burgeoning movement around the tragedies of industrial pollution emerging from Minamata, explored in depth in the documentaries by Tsuchimoto Noriaki in the same era, the struggle over the construction of the airport combined a Marxist critique of what David Harvey has called "accumulation by dispossession" with a nascent environmentalism.[34]

The Ogawa Pro collective's sustained involvement in the struggle against the Narita airport, which lasted nine years and yielded seven films, paralleled the trajectory of the Japanese New Left from the late 1960s through the 1970s. When the collective shifted their focus to the Narita struggle in the summer of 1968, they documented the escalation of the conflict around the preliminary survey of the land. In the process, the first major wooden barricades were constructed and basic weapons such as bamboo spears and even buckets of human feces and urine were employed to halt the surveyor's activities.[35] Against any purported neutrality of the documentary image, *Summer in Sanrizuka* makes clear the ways that the collective actively participated in life behind the barricades and shot the conflict from the perspective of the farmers and protesters, with ample footage of the filmmakers engaged in struggles with the police—at one point a cameraman is even arrested. In documenting the battle against the enclosure of the farmland, the collective became deeply entwined in life behind the barricades, living simply and devoting all of their efforts to the task of producing cinematic studies of the unfolding events. According to Adam Bingham, "Ogawa and his collaborators entirely redefined and re-conceptualized discursive filmmaking by becoming one with their subjects, by conceiving of the documentary form not as a record and thus closed reality, but as a continuous, unfolding, and mediated process."[36] Much like the Newsreel, however, the collective exhibited its own internal struggles with difference, particularly around gender, and reproduced some of the most

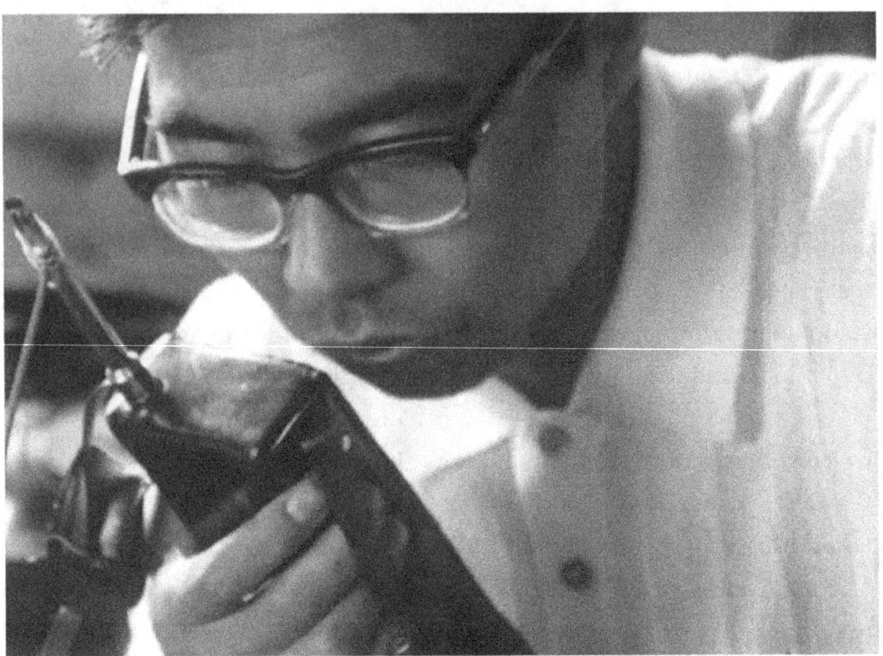

Sanrizuka no natsu.

lamentable internal divisions of labor.[37] While female farmers are given a strong voice within *Summer in Sanrizuka* and other films in the series, the internal structure of the collective most often relegated women to domestic labor, like so many New Left social movements, reproducing the conditions in which the radical politics, and in this case filmmaking, could take place.

Episodic in nature, *Summer in Sanrizuka* explores a series of events in the battle over the land survey that conveys a similar intensity and chaos to *Columbia Revolt*. Rather than using voice-offs, the film privileges a cinéma vérité style, emphasizing the narration of events by the farmers themselves. In the opening sequence, an exterior shot shows a field being battered by a rainstorm. The bucolic beauty of this shot is interrupted by the sound of the rhythmic beating of a drum, which we later discover is villagers striking on steel drums as a call to action to the surrounding residents in the event of an invasion by the police and the land surveyors. The sequence cuts to an interior close-up of a hand-drawn map being discussed and edited by the resistance. In scenes that serve as refrains throughout the film, we observe farmers strategizing battle plans, mapping out barricade locations, and communicating with each other over walkie-talkies. In contradistinction to the knowledge of the

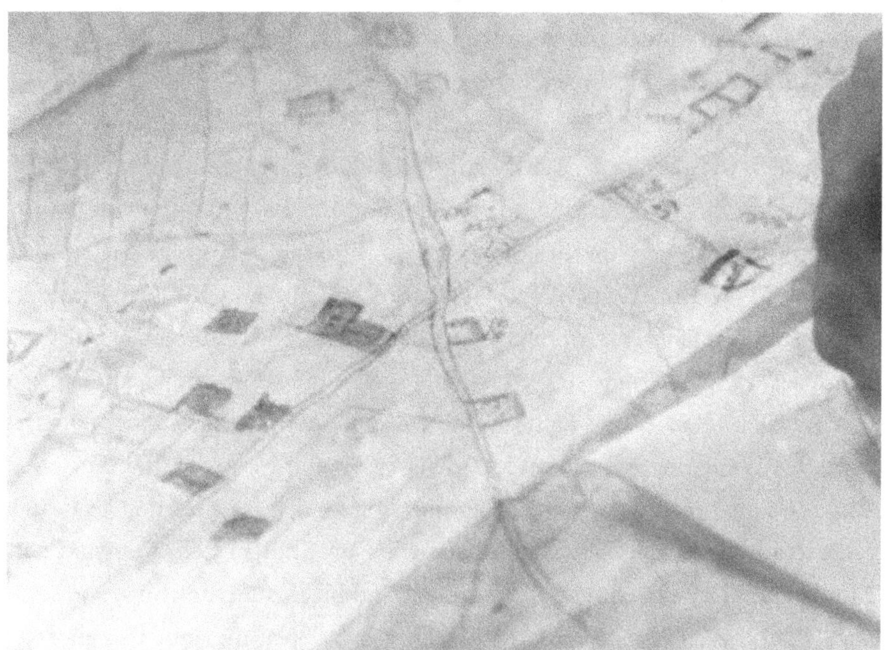

Sanrizuka no natsu.

space being produced by the land surveyors, who we see throughout the film using purportedly neutral tools of measurement to produce knowledge about the land, *Summer in Sanrizuka* charts out a space that is apprehended by way of a fundamental antagonism, and the affective tone of the film registers both the transformation of the knowledge of the space through conflict and the acute sense of intimacy generated by the barricades.

In one of the few formal interviews in the film, a leader of the Hantai Dōmei draws an explicit connection between the struggles of the peasants in Vietnam against the United States and the militant tactics of the farmers against the dispossession of their land. The interview is intercut with footage of a large-scale clash with the police, in which we witness both long, static shots, and jittery hand-held close-ups of protesters being beaten and arrested by the police (see fig. 7.2). Following is a shot of protesters being pummeled by water cannons that formally replicates the field shot in the opening sequence, further painting the landscape through the lens of antagonism. As the camera lens is drenched with water, we understand its position to be not neutral observer but active participant in the struggle against the airport. The film becomes an active participant in drawing out the distinctions between epistemological modes and generates a space of the commons that is actively being produced in and through struggle.

There is much more to say about each of these films and the movements from which they emerged, but I want to conclude by contemplating the ways that these struggles endure in our present and the ways that the cinema was used to formulate new modes of being and thinking in common. It is worth noting that the United States and Japan are the countries with the highest per capita student debt in the world. The financialization of student life in these countries, as I have suggested elsewhere, is a counterrevolutionary technique of control leveled at populations that disciplinary measures had failed to contain.[38] Struggles against student debt today mark our own battle against enclosure and accumulation by dispossession, and it is important to draw a red thread between these struggles and the New Student Left. I opened with Moten and Harney's conversation of debt and black study to think about the ways that new modes of study within New Left social movements generated the inverse of financial debt, a mutual and unpayable debt that is bound up with the communal luxury of life behind the barricades—however fragile or short-lived. Far from giving us the impression of a neutral truth of New Left social movement, these cinematic artifacts produce highly situated and antagonistic knowledges whose collective enunciations work to articulate a prefigurative politics of the commons. In this way, these cinematic collectives participated in what Gigi Roggero calls "militant inquiry" or "co-research": "it is only by taking a partial position that it becomes possible to understand the whole and transform it—that is, to organize the common."[39] In affirming the essayistic, collaborative, and antagonistic knowledge produced in and through the cinema of the New Student Left (recognizing, at the same time its limitations), we also affirm the enduring quality of these struggles in our present. New Left cinematic experiments demonstrate the ways that, in this era, the cinematic image becomes a terrain of struggle more than ever before.

Notes

1. George Katsiaficas, *The Imagination of the New Left: A Global Analysis of 1968* (Boston: South End Press, 1987), 37.
2. Nick Mitchell, "Alternate Trajectories," paper presented at the annual meeting of the American Studies Association, Toronto, Ontario, October 8–11, 2015.

3. For a discussion of the relationship between unemployment and capital, see Fredric Jameson, *Representing Capital: A Reading of Volume One* (London: Verso, 2011), 149.
4. Roderick A. Ferguson, *The Reorder of Things: The University and Its Pedagogies of Minority Difference* (Minneapolis: University of Minnesota Press, 2012), 34.
5. Translation and discussion of Mario Tronti's famous quotation from: Gigi Roggero, "Five Theses on the Common," *Rethinking Marxism* 22, no. 3 (2010): 357–73, at 358.
6. Stefano Harney and Fred Moten, *The Undercommons: Fugitive Planning and Black Study* (New York: Minor Compositions, 2013), 110.
7. Kristin Ross and Manu Goswami, "The Meaning of the Paris Commune," *Jacobin*, May 4, 2015, https://www.jacobinmag.com/2015/05/kristin-ross-communal-luxury-paris-commune.
8. Jonathan Kahana, *Intelligence Work: The Politics of American Documentary* (New York: Columbia University Press, 2008), 177.
9. Joanne Grant, *Confrontation on Campus: The Columbia Pattern of Protest* (New York: Signet Books, 1969), 5.
10. Stefan M. Bradley, *Harlem vs. Columbia University: Black Student Power in the Late 1960s* (Urbana: University of Illinois Press, 2009), 29–30.
11. Bradley, *Harlem vs. Columbia University*, 40–53.
12. Bradley, 61.
13. Bradley, 62.
14. For more on the history of Newsreel, see Bill Nichols, *Newsreel: Documentary Filmmaking on the American Left* (New York: Arno Press: 1980). This book is his 1977 dissertation, which chronicles the Newsreel movement.
15. Nichols, *Newsreel*, 52. See also Michael Renov, "Newsreel: Old and New—Towards an Historical Profile," *Film Quarterly* 41, no. 1 (1987): 20–33.
16. Roz Payne, "Early History of Newsreel," Newsreel Films: Roz Payne's Archives, http://www.newsreel.us/life.htm, accessed November 1, 2015.
17. Bill Nichols sees the Workers Film and Photo League (1928–35) as the only historical precedent to the Newsreel's collective production methods in the United States. Bill Nichols, "Newsreel: Film and Revolution," *Cineaste* 5, no. 4 (1973): 7–13, at 7.
18. Renov, "Newsreel," 24.
19. Robert Kramer et al., "Newsreel," *Film Quarterly* 22, no. 2 (1968–69): 43–48, at 46.

20. Abé Mark Nornes, *Forest of Pressure: Ogawa Shinsuke and Postwar Japanese Documentary* (Minneapolis: University of Minnesota Press, 2007), 38.
21. Nornes, *Forest of Pressure*, 45.
22. Nornes, 45.
23. Nornes, 41.
24. Fernando Solanas and Octavio Getino, "Towards a Third Cinema," in *Film and Theory: An Anthology*, ed. Robert Stam and Toby Miller (Oxford: Blackwell, 2000), 265–89, at 278–79.
25. Solanas and Getino, "Towards a Third Cinema," 266.
26. Nornes, *Forest of Pressure*, 41.
27. Nornes, 154.
28. Nornes, 47.
29. Nornes, 53.
30. David Apter, "A 60s Movement in the 80s: Interview with David Apter," in *The Sixties, without Apology*, ed. Sohnya Sayres (Minneapolis: University of Minnesota Press, 1984), 70–90, at 80.
31. David E. Apter and Nagayo Sawa, *Against the State: Politics and Social Protest in Japan* (Cambridge, MA: Harvard University Press, 1986), 6.
32. Apter and Sawa, *Against the State*, 81.
33. Apter, "A 60s Movement in the 80s: Interview with David Apter," 79.
34. David Harvey, *The New Imperialism* (Oxford: Oxford University Press, 2013), 137.
35. Apter and Sawa, *Against the State*, 89.
36. Adam Bingham, "Filmmaking as a Way of Life: Tsuchimoto, Ogawa, and Revolutions in Documentary Cinema," *Asian Cinema* 20, no. 1 (2009): 166–75, at 168.
37. Nornes, *Forest of Pressure*, 140–41. Also see Barbara Hammer's documentary on Ogawa Pro: *Devotion* (USA, 2000).
38. See Morgan Adamson, "The Financialization of Student Life: Five Propositions on Student Debt," *Polygraph* 21 (2009): 107–20.
39. Roggero, "Five Theses on the Common," 358.

Bibliography

Adamson, Morgan. "The Financialization of Student Life: Five Propositions on Student Debt." *Polygraph* 21 (2009): 107–20.

Apter, David. "A 60s Movement in the 80s: Interview with David Apter." In *The Sixties, without Apology*, edited by Sohnya Sayres, 70–90. Minneapolis: University of Minnesota Press, 1984.

Apter, David E., and Nagayo Sawa. *Against the State: Politics and Social Protest in Japan*. Cambridge, MA: Harvard University Press, 1986.

Bingham, Adam. "Filmmaking as a Way of Life: Tsuchimoto, Ogawa, and Revolutions in Documentary Cinema." *Asian Cinema* 20, no. 1 (2009): 166–75.

Bradley, Stefan M. *Harlem vs. Columbia University: Black Student Power in the Late 1960s*. Urbana: University of Illinois Press, 2009.

Ferguson, Roderick A. *The Reorder of Things: The University and Its Pedagogies of Minority Difference*. Minneapolis: University of Minnesota Press, 2012.

Grant, Joanne. *Confrontation on Campus: The Columbia Pattern of Protest*. New York: Signet Books, 1969.

Harney, Stefano, and Fred Moten. *The Undercommons: Fugitive Planning and Black Study*. New York: Minor Compositions, 2013.

Harvey, David. *The New Imperialism*. Oxford: Oxford University Press, 2013.

Jameson, Fredric. *Representing Capital: A Reading of Volume One*. London: Verso, 2011.

Kahana, Jonathan. *Intelligence Work: The Politics of American Documentary*. New York: Columbia University Press, 2008.

Katsiaficas, George. *The Imagination of the New Left: A Global Analysis of 1968*. Boston: South End Press, 1987.

Kramer, Robert, et al., "Newsreel." *Film Quarterly* 22, no. 2 (1968–69): 43–48.

Mitchell, Nick. "Alternate Trajectories." Paper presented at the annual meeting of the American Studies Association. Toronto, Ontario. October 8–11, 2015.

Nichols, Bill. *Newsreel: Documentary Filmmaking on the American Left*. New York: Arno Press: 1980.

———. "Newsreel: Film and Revolution." *Cineaste* 5, no. 4 (1973): 7–13.

Nornes, Abé Mark. *Forest of Pressure: Ogawa Shinsuke and Postwar Japanese Documentary*. Minneapolis: University of Minnesota Press, 2007.

Payne, Roz. "Early History of Newsreel," Newsreel Films: Roz Payne's Archives. http://www.newsreel.us/life.htm, accessed November 1, 2015.

Renov, Michael. "Newsreel: Old and New—Towards an Historical Profile." *Film Quarterly* 41, no. 1 (1987): 20–33.

Roggero, Gigi. "Five Theses on the Common." *Rethinking Marxism* 22, no. 3 (2010): 357–73.

Ross, Kristin, and Manu Goswami. "The Meaning of the Paris Commune." *Jacobin*, May 4, 2015. https://www.jacobinmag.com/2015/05/kristin-ross

-communal-luxury-paris-commune.
Solanas, Fernando, and Octavio Getino. "Towards a Third Cinema." In *Film and Theory: An Anthology*, edited by Robert Stam and Toby Miller, 265–86. Oxford: Blackwell, 2000.

8

Oshima, Korea, and 1968

Death by Hanging and *Three Resurrected Drunkards*

David Desser

One problem with the critical reception of the films of Oshima Nagisa has been the fundamentally ahistorical nature of their analyses. This is due, in part, to the manner in which Japanese cinema has been deployed in the West—as a tool, sometimes a hammer, with which to beat down Hollywood cinema. Recall that it was in the mid-1970s that academic criticism began to focus on Japan and in the late 1970s and early 1980s when it entered a mature phase; which is to say, some dozen or more years after the films under consideration had been released. In Oshima's case, no film until 1976, with *Ai no korida/In the Realm of the Senses*, was widely distributed and discussed in the West. Following the *succès de scandale* of this antipornographic porno film not only was Oshima's international reputation confirmed but also many of his earlier films were shown in retrospectives and repertory houses. This is not to say that Oshima was a relative unknown at the time, but simply that we can mark this occurrence as his coming-to-consciousness in international cinema.

Koshikei/Death by Hanging (Japan, 1968) was the first Oshima film that toured in Europe and the United States. Oshima and his wife, Koyama Akiko, traveled to Europe to promote the film, which brought them to Warsaw, Prague, Paris, and Cannes.[1] In fact, it was at Cannes that the film had its European premiere, screening at the out-of-competition film market before, as Shota Ogawa reminds us, the festival was closed down by French directors acting in solidarity with the students and workers in Paris.[2] Interestingly, Japan was represented by Shindo Kaneto's *Kuroneko/Black Cat* (1968), which would have screened in competition had the festival continued. Although *Death by Hanging* was well appreciated, the canceling of the festival overshadowed the film, and it would be some years before it returned to cinematic consciousness.

Great Britain's Ian Cameron (1937–2010)—publisher, editor, and film critic for *Movie*—was the earliest commentator on Oshima, publishing a career analysis in 1969/70 and linking Oshima to currents in international cinema with the publication of his edited collection, *Second Wave*, in 1970. Oshima was certainly the only Japanese director in the slim volume, which perforce linked him with the likes of other "radical" filmmakers like Dušan Makavejev, Ruy Guerra, and Glauber Rocha. *Death by Hanging* was central to Cameron's multipronged approach, at once auteur-oriented and formally conscious. Yet Oshima's decreasing production output and the almost total lack of availability of his films led to a kind of hibernation of Oshima criticism and appreciation.

It took the highly theoretical work of Stephen Heath to bring *Death by Hanging* to the newly emergent field of academic film study with "Anata mo," which appeared in the 1976/77 issue of *Screen*. The release of *In the Realm of the Senses* was the immediate contextual appearance of the essay, although it was *Death by Hanging* that most concerned Heath—through the lens of Lacan, as it were. (A second essay by Heath, "The Question Oshima," which dealt with *In the Realm of the Senses*, appeared almost at the same time in the US publication *Wide Angle*.) The influence of *Screen*, the mania for psychoanalytic theory, the concern with "realism" as a critical category for film, the popularization of the theories of Bertolt Brecht, all found *Death by Hanging* suddenly at the center of film studies. Yet the high theory around Oshima and *Death by Hanging*, even the earlier linkage of him to an international "second wave," conspired to suppress the immediacy of Oshima's project for its Japanese contemporary audience. In fact, his other film of 1968, *Kaette kita yoppari/Three Resurrected Drunkards*, is nowhere discussed at all in this period. In order to understand the kind of intervention he made in this period, I will survey Oshima's two films of 1968 by providing a historical analysis of Japanese cinema vis-à-vis 1968 politics, situating where Oshima was located in global cinema and briefly looking at Japanese-Korean relations.

Japan's 1968

> Mobs of screaming students last week swarmed through the vast Shinjuku railway station, Tokyo's largest. Wearing plastic helmets, the lower half of their faces masked with towels as a protection against tear gas, the students scrambled over tracks and platforms, smashing train windows, disemboweling seats, splintering and setting fire to doors, benches and stairways. One rioter shinnied up a pole to smash the signal lights—he touched a high-voltage line and crashed to earth in a shower of sparks, critically injured.[3]

Although this event took place in October 1968, it was against this background that Oshima directed his two films of 1968. In fact, these events of October are documented in his 1969 avant-garde effort, *Shinjuku dorobo nikki/Diary of a Shinjuku Thief.* These protests and riots at the end of the year were just part and parcel of a politics of anger (which one could compare to the frustration in the United States that led to the October 1969 Days of Rage), instigated over a number of years, arguably since the massive Anti-US-Japan-Security-Treaty (AMPO) protests of 1960, which similarly make their way into Oshima's film *Seishun zankoku monogatari/Cruel Story of Youth* (1960).

A relative quietude existed after the 1960 AMPO demonstrations and before 1965, the year 1968 began, so to speak. In 1965, an organization called Beheiren (Citizen's Union for Peace in Vietnam) was established. Perhaps less an organization per se—as it had no formal member system—the movement depended on the independent initiative of its members, and spread nationally, with over three hundred groups joining the organization. Zengakuren (condensation of a Japanese name, All-Japan League of Student Governments), the umbrella organization for left-wing student groups, the Socialist Party, labor unions such as Sōhyō (General Council of Trade Union in Japan), and antiwar youth organizations were central to the movement, and a variety of struggles were developed against the war and against Japanese governmental actions.

These two elements—antiwar sentiment and displeasure at governmental policies—combined in October 1967 when a small group of Zengakuren activists clashed with police near Tokyo's Haneda Airport in an effort to prevent

Prime Minister Satō Eisaku from traveling to South Vietnam. As described by Oguma Eiji:

> Students wearing plastic construction helmets and wielding two-by-fours overpowered lightly armed police. Images of the violent confrontation, in which one student activist was killed, were broadcast on national television news programs in vivid color, at a time when color televisions had only recently become widespread. Younger students and workers who had missed out on the 1960 protests were enthralled by the heroic struggle they witnessed on their televisions and the recently moribund Zengakuren sects saw a surge in membership and participation.[4]

These events are the subject of the early radical documentary *Gennin hokusho—Haneda toso no kiroku* (Report from Haneda, 1967) by Ogawa Shunsuke. The same month saw the proclamation of International Antiwar Day. Demonstrations and meetings were held across the country in which 1.4 million people participated. In January 1968 a small but active struggle took place to prevent the US nuclear submarine *Enterprise* from docking at Sasebo harbor, again part of the overall movement against the Vietnam War and against the Japanese government's collusion with waging it.

As documented in Ogawa Shunsuke's 1968 *Nihon kaiho sensen: Sanrizuka no natsu/The Battle Front for the Liberation of Japan—Summer in Sanrizuka*, February 1968 saw the first mass meeting to prevent the construction of a new airport at Sanrizuka (now known as Narita International Airport).[5] Farmers felt that the decision to build a new international airport on land expropriated from landowners who refused to sell was a violation of postwar democratic reforms. In this month three thousand people battled riot police, more heavily armed and prepared than in October of the previous year. Eventually, these protests would lead to a complex, years-long struggle for many farmers and their allies, especially students who banded together with them for the first time.

Alongside these events and issues was a student movement—as in the United States and France, for instance, developing along specific circumstances but fed by international energies and influences. In the late 1960s in

Japan, then, students of university medical departments and their graduates all around the nation had deployed social movements calling for improvements of treatment of medical interns. The medical department at the University of Tokyo, too, was among those universities, or rather, the most vehement one. In January 1968, the department launched an indefinite strike against the university, and students and administration went into dispute. Unable to reach a compromise, in June, a militant group of students occupied the Yasuda Auditorium. The president of the university brought in riot police to forcibly evict the students.

In June, students at two institutions—the University of Tokyo, Japan's most elite university, and Nihon University, the largest institution of higher learning with approximately one-tenth of Japan's total university student population—established Zenkyōtō (short for *zengaku kyōtō kaigi*, All-Campus Joint Struggle Councils). Armed with hard hats and two-by-fours, they seized and barricaded their campuses against police intrusion. Zenkyōtō was open to any willing participant, regardless of ideological affiliation. The barricaded universities were declared "liberated zones," and the image of students resisting police in the name of greater academic and personal freedom initially elicited sympathetic coverage from the Japanese media. From mid-1968 through early 1969 campus occupations, collectively remembered as the Zenkyōtō movement, spread to hundreds of universities and thousands of high schools nationwide. Oshima's sympathies clearly rested with the militant students fighting for the farmers of Sanrizuka, for greater academic freedom and self-governance and against the escalating war in Vietnam. Students in the United States and in France would have felt right at home as well.

Death by Hanging

Given the status and stature of *Death by Hanging* in the West—where I venture to say it is, along with *In the Realm of the Senses*, the most discussed of Oshima's films and alone among the most critically acclaimed—it might be surprising to learn that it is merely the 143rd best Japanese film of all time as voted by the readers of *Kinema Jumpo*, Japan's most prestigious film magazine.[6] It does not appear at all on *Kinema Jumpo*'s critics list of Top 100 Japanese films of all time, though many other of his films do make the cut, including *A Treatise on Japanese Bawdy Song* at 110 (there are 118 films on the list).[7] When it was released in 1968, however, the journal was quite taken with the film, putting it at number 3 for the year; *Japanese Bawdy* song had placed twelfth the year before.

Released on February 3, 1968, amid the roiling protests and demonstrations rocking Tokyo and other Japanese cities, "viewers in Tokyo experienced the film as an event. In addition to being a daring message against capital punishment, the film was also a pilot scheme for a new initiative undertaken by the independent exhibitor—distributor Art Theatre Guild (ATG), which aimed to provide a platform for experimental films produced on [a] minimum budget."[8] In fact, Imamura Shohei's *Ningen johatsu/A Man Vanishes* (1967) had been partly financed by the ATG the year before. ATG's flagship theater was the Art Theatre Shinjuku Bunka. Shinjuku was the center of youth culture, with its attendant avant-garde media, including theater, art, and alternative cinema, much of it under the umbrella notion of *ungura* (underground). Roland Domenig notes of the Shinjuku Bunka: "The foyer acted as a gallery where well-known painters and illustrators exhibited their work. ATG posters were often designed by famous artists and were utterly different from traditional movie bills."[9]

As is well known by now, Oshima based this bitingly satirical, darkly comic, yet furiously angry film on a real case of a *zainichi* Korean tried and executed for the murder of a Japanese girl. The protagonist of *Death by Hanging* is called "R" to recall the real name of the young Korean, Li Jin-wu (Ri Chin-u). Recall that the "L" sound in Japanese is often confused with "R," especially when Japanese speak English. (The position of the tongue at the roof of the mouth for the Japanese "L" makes the sound ambiguous, somewhere between "L" and "R," and was one of the stereotypical ways that Japanese speakers were rendered in English-language films.)

Oshima had evinced an interest in Korea and the *Chosen mondai* ("Korea Problem") and its possibilities for a Japanese radicalism as early as 1960 with *Seishun zankoku monogatari/Cruel Story of Youth*, in which, as I point out in *Eros plus Massacre*, a television set is broadcasting a newsreel featuring a student clash with police in South Korea.[10] Shota Ogawa notices that "*The Sun's Burial* is the first instance in which Oshima depicts a Korean character, albeit in an indirect manner, as his ethnicity is only alluded to through an exaggerated Korean accent enacted by Oshima's regular Fumio Watanabe, whose performance borders on racist caricature."[11] As Ryan Cook aptly describes it:

> The Korea problem referred broadly to the difficult relations between Japan and the Koreas in the aftermath of the war and decades of colonization (there were no diplomatic relations between the postwar Japanese state and the Republic of South Korea until 1965, and the treaty of that year formally precluded diplomacy with the North in perpetuity), as well as to the conditions of poverty and political instability in the former colony, and especially to the various social troubles associated with the *zainichi* population of resident Koreans in Japan.[12]

With references both to contemporary South Korean protests and the problematic presence of Koreans in postwar Japan, Oshima began a lengthy process of examining the *Chosen mondai*.

Oshima was long aware of the Komatsugawa Incident and the trial and execution that followed. He had originally commissioned a screenplay in 1963, the year after Li Jin-wu was executed, but funding was not forthcoming.[13] Shortly thereafter, Oshima turned to making television documentaries, among them *Wasurerareta kogun/The Emperor's Forgotten Army*, the story of wounded *zainichi* Korean soldiers who fought for the Imperial Army but were denied disability pay. And on April 1, in the momentous year of 1964, Japan lifted overseas travel restrictions, and Oshima's first foray outside of the country of his birth was to South Korea. Unable to make the project he planned, Oshima instead made the film *Seishun no ishibumi/Monument to Youth* (1964), which dealt with the subject of a young Korean woman who had turned to prostitution after sustaining a disabling injury during the student uprising of 1960.[14] The masterpiece of this interest in and trip to South Korea is the famous *Yunbogi no nikki/Diary of Yunbogi-boy* (Japan, 1965). Its use of still photographs that Oshima had taken on his trip was inspired by Chris Marker's 1962 film *La Jetée* with voice-over narration taken directly from *Yunbogi no nikki*, the Japanese translation of a young poverty-stricken Korean boy's work. The narration exceeds the diary, however, in its exhortations to the Japanese audience. In fact, as Cook notes, "the 24-minute film—the first exclusive production for Oshima's company Sozosha—opened in a late-night screening at the ATG Shinjuku Bunka Theater, accompanied by a lecture marking the significance of the date" (the formalization of The Treaty on Basic Relations between Japan and the Republic of South Korea [*Nikkan kihon joyaku*], which had been ratified in June of 1965).[15] It was not only Oshima's most explicitly political film but also marked, in its way, the first collaboration between Sozosha and the ATG, at least in terms of exhibition.

Oshima's next attempt to imagine or depict Koreans and their "use" for the Japanese came with *Nihon shunka-ko/Treatise on Japanese Bawdy Song* (1967), the first of his so-called Korean trilogy and also his most difficult work. In this instance comparisons to Godard's post-1965 films are warranted. Like the Godard of *Pierrot le fou* (1965), *Masculin féminin/Masculine Feminine* (1966), or *La Chinoise* (1967), Oshima made no effort to hide his overtly political intent, combining it with a disruptive, often deliberately inelegant camera style. Long takes combined with a relentlessly panning or tracking camera were used to deliver the film's most challenging sentiments. Cook points out that this film was made partly in response to the "reinstatement of the national holiday *Kigensetsu*, which had been established in the Meiji era to commemorate the founding of Japan, in pre-recorded history, with the accession of the mythical first emperor Jimmu."[16] Renamed Kenkoku kinen no hi (National Foundation Day) in 1966, it was first observed in February 1967. Among other aspects of this difficult film's "treatise" is the presence of a *zainichi* woman singing a folk song associated with Korean "comfort women," then carried off to be raped by a group of Japanese students, and the proposition put forward by an exam proctor (played by Koyama Akiko, Oshima's wife) that the Japanese are descended from Koreans.

Death by Hanging forms the second of the Korean trilogy. Given its status as among the most analyzed of Oshima's films, I will simply make a point or two regarding the film. (For what is among the most interesting of analyses of the film, I suggest Yuriko Furuhata's *Cinema of Actuality*.[17]) The first point is that there are actually two points, two issues, that Oshima wishes to address. The Korean problem is the most obvious, and he deals with it by the surreal efforts of the prison bureaucrats to convince R that he is R, a *zainichi* Korean who committed murder, after his amnesia following what is apparently an unsuccessful execution by hanging ("the body of R refuses to die"). The second

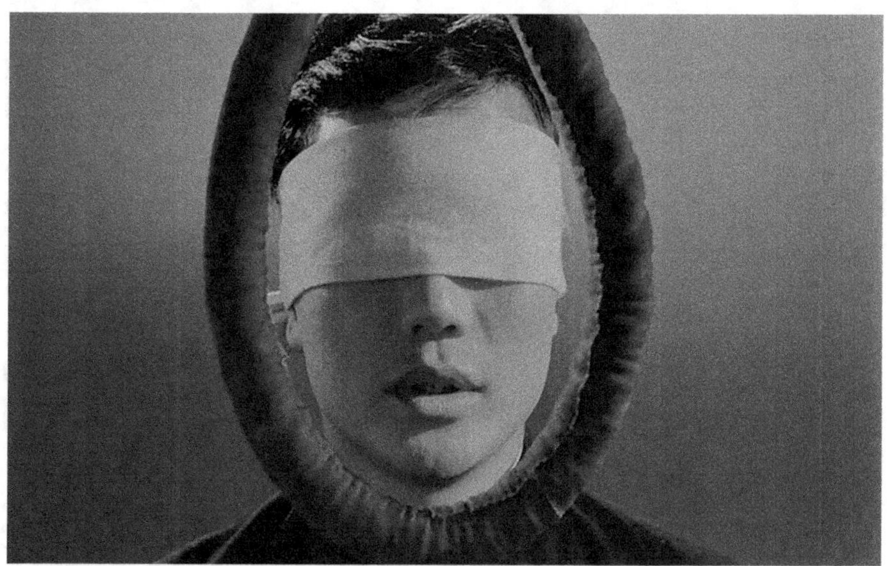

Still from *Death by Hanging* (1968).

concern is a strongly anti-capital-punishment tract. The two concerns come together at film's end.

As the film has progressed, R has become more militant, and thus more Korean. By the final scene he reveals his keen intelligence (Li Jin-wu was an excellent student and a fine writer) and is willing to be executed. Alexander Jacoby gets it just right when he quotes the film, and R, as proclaiming his innocence even as he willingly ascends to the gallows: "As long as the state makes the absolutely evil crime of murder legal through the waging of wars and the exercise of capital punishment, we are all innocent."[18] But Oshima goes further when he has the district attorney insist: "That's right. Now you understand, don't you? We cannot allow you to keep such ideas alive." R then notes, "For the sake of every R, I will consent to being R, and die." He is then hanged, but when the prison officials check to see the body, it has disappeared. Unfazed, the district attorney expresses his satisfaction, first singling out the warden, then the education chief, then the security chief, finally simply saying "and you" (*anata mo*) four times. Then a new, more strident voice (Oshima's) comes on and insists, "And you who have watched this film . . . anata mo." We, too, then are guilty, having done our jobs of supporting capital punishment and insisting that resident Koreans do not deserve full rights while subjecting them to the full power of the Japanese state.

Released almost exactly one year after *Treatise* (the little-discussed *Muri shinjû: Nihon no natsu/Japanese Summer: Double Suicide* [1967] separates the two films), *Death by Hanging* inaugurated an almost unprecedented body of work, most with a resolutely avant-garde film practice and all with an unflinching eye on Japan's unglimpsed social problems and youthful concerns. The first of these works, *Three Resurrected Drunkards,* was released a mere seven weeks after *Death by Hanging* (put into production and completed before Oshima left for Europe to promote the earlier film). Yet while *Death by Hanging* is one of Oshima's best-known and frequently commented on films, *Three Resurrected Drunkards* is one of his least-known and least-written-about films.

Three Resurrected Drunkards

Three Resurrected Drunkards, the third film of Oshima's so-called Korean trilogy, takes its Japanese title, *Kaette kita yoppari,* from a popular song by the trio the Folk Crusaders. The Japanese title is translated as "Drunkard's Return," which has no traction for English-speaking audiences. And the song is not about three Japanese youths who go on the run, mistaken for Korean stowaways. The English title is itself already something of a joke: there may be three protagonists and they are "resurrected," but they aren't drunkards.

There is no question that this is not an easy film to understand or like. One way in which the film is "difficult" comes through on initial viewing. The three nondrunkards (they are actually Japanese schoolboys) are killed halfway through. As Tony Rayns notes, "Oshima simply starts the film again and takes it to a different conclusion. Audiences, [Oshima] noted with delight, thought that the wrong reel had been put on."[19] Puzzlement was often not the only reaction to this seeming mistake. Filmreference.com claims "that at the 1983 Edinburgh Film Festival there was a minor riot from patrons certain that the projectionist was accidentally replaying the opening reel."[20] Had the angry festival attendees waited for seven minutes the repeated footage would have ended and the film would have indeed unspooled to a different conclusion.

That the film remains little known among Euro-American audiences is, despite its difficulties (though not any more so than *Death by Hanging,* and perhaps less so than later films of this period), somewhat puzzling. Oshima cowrote the screenplay with three outstanding collaborators. Sasaki Mamoru had worked with Oshima four times previously, including *Japanese Bawdy*

Song and *Death by Hanging*; Tamura Tsutomu had collaborated with Oshima way back with 1961's *Shiiku/The Catch*, Oshima's first independent production (though long before the formation of Sozosha) as well as *Death by Hanging*, among others. Tamura is the only screenwriter to have worked with Shochiku New Wave stalwarts Oshima, Yoshida Kiju, and Shinoda Masahiro. And then there's Adachi Masao, a politically radical screenwriter (who penned some of Wakamatsu Koji's finest films of the 1960s) and director who, disillusioned with the slow pace of change in 1960s Japan, joined the Japanese Red Army and fought for the Palestinian cause in Lebanon. In one of the many ironies of *Death by Hanging*, Adachi took the role of the chief prison guard. Perhaps its apparent obscurities—situated in a very specific sociopolitical moment; highly puzzling narrative structure; wild shifts in tone from realism to surrealism, from fiction to documentary—made it less attractive to audiences at the time and, as such, the lack of distribution and revival screenings, not to mention its late appearance on the home video market, kept it out of sight and beyond the academic ken.

There is a startling immediacy to the film. Perhaps this immediacy also contributes to the film's difficulty. Its very specific references, its local politics, even its film style—caught in a momentary and specific stream of art cinema—made it problematic outside of Japan at the time of its release and only more beclouded subsequently. Alternately, its virulently anti–Vietnam War message certainly remains clear to most viewers. The two Korean stowaways who land ashore in western Japan, having made their way from Pusan (Busan), come to Japan to avoid service in the Korean Army supporting US troops during the Vietnam War. One of the resurrected trio dreams they are captured by the police who are convinced they are Korean and deport them (by rowboat!) to South Korea where they are immediately sent to the battlefront where they are quickly killed. Interestingly and certainly significantly, both the US flag and the Japanese flag are displayed in the Korean barracks where the boys are briefly held. (Images of the Japanese flag, the *hinomaru*, are everywhere in the film, even in a dank pedestrian tunnel.)

The most prevalent anti–Vietnam War motif is the recurring reference to the infamous photograph taken by Eddie Adams on February 1, 1968, which came to be known as "General Nguyễn Ngọc Loan executing a Việt Cộng prisoner in Saigon." In the photo General Nguyễn stands to the right (screen left)

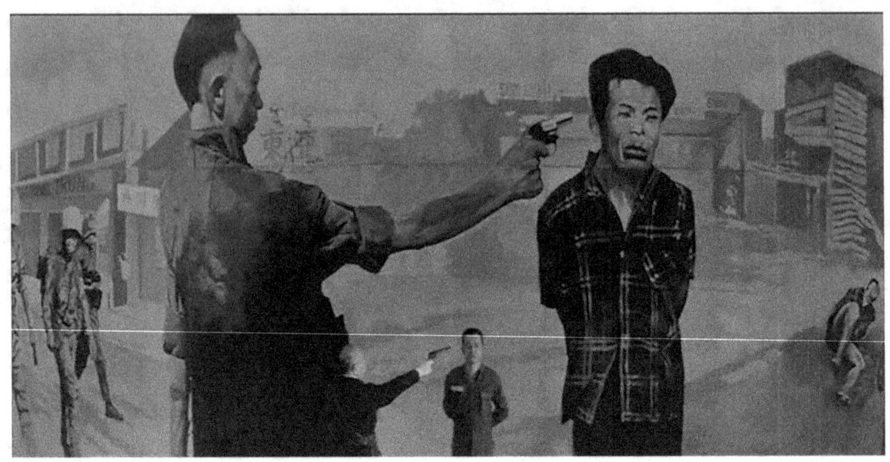

"General Nguyễn Ngoc Loan executing a Việt Cộng prisoner in Saigon."

of a Việt Cộng prisoner, pointing a handgun at his head. This image is restaged many times in the film, from the boys using their fingers for a gun (as early in the film as when they are on the beach in the first sequence) to pointing the gun at the stowaway Korean corporal, to the realistic mural depicting the photo-image at the end with the execution of the Korean corporal staged in the background. Considering that the film was released only two months after the photo was published one can feel the white-hot immediacy of Oshima's film. Outside of the difficulty of the film's many local references or its film style, one difficulty may simply have been the raw wounds still suppurating from the Vietnam War, including its manifest immorality.

Less obvious, but no less immediate, is the film's setting in western Japan, in the Kansai region. This factor is partly a tribute to the Folk Crusaders, who were based in Kansai, but who broke up in 1967. They had a large following, and shortly after their breakup radio play turned two of their songs into mainstream hits. "*Kaette kita yoppari*," as we have seen, gave its title to Oshima's film; "Song of the Imjin River"—an adaptation of a North Korean folk song—has proven to be their most lasting contribution to Japanese music and is sung, at least in part, twice in the film. By 1968, *zainichi* Korean youth living in ghettos began to protest and rebel against the discriminatory Japanese environment and the roving ultranationalist Japanese gangs that confronted them. In 1965, the Japanese government had recognized the South Korean government, but, in keeping with Cold War alliances, did not initiate any negotiations with the

North Korean regime. At that time, Koreans living in Japan were offered South Korean citizenship or remained stateless if they either supported the North Korean regime or preserved their hopes for a unified Korea in the near future by refusing South Korean citizenship.[21] The significance of Kyoto in 1968 can be gauged by the popular *Kinema Jumpo* Best One film of 2004, *Pacchigi!* (Izutsu Kazuyuki)—a film about the love affair between a Korean girl and a Japanese boy and his equal interest in the Imjin River song set in the Kyoto of 1968.[22]

The film's perhaps less immediately timely but most perceptive commentary lies in the way "it looks at the question of Korean immigration in terms of costume and identity. (Three Korean immigrants steal the clothes of three [. . .] Japanese youths. The three Japanese, with nothing to wear and no money, become 'honorary' Koreans and are appropriately persecuted.)."[23] This is an apt and concise description. In a very surreal scene, a hand comes out of a hole in the sand and steals two of the school uniforms and replaces them with the clothing of a Korean soldier and a high school student. Thus, two of the trio dress in the Korean clothing and are continually mistaken for Koreans—even by *zainichi* Koreans themselves. In this instance, clothing doesn't simply make the man, it makes the ethnicity. An old man, coming on the trio, asks to see the feet of one of them, claiming that Japanese sandals leave distinctive marks on feet; thus, Japanese sandals become, literally, one marker of Japaneseness. The inability to distinguish Korean from Japanese is demonstrated not only by the fact that, wearing Korean clothes, the boys are mistaken for Korean, but also by Oshima's casting. Oshima regulars Sato Kei and Watanabe Fumio, who portrayed the prison warden and the education officer, respectively, in *Death by Hanging*, are here portraying the South Korean Army deserter and (at least in the film's second half) a *zainichi* Korean.

Oshima also recognizes the way that discriminatory ideology is embedded within the very linguistic terms used for people and groups. Unfortunately, not apparent in the English subtitles for the film are the different words used for "Korean." "Chosen" is the word most commonly used in the film; it is a continuation of the Imperial term used during the colonial period (1910–45). Although no doubt adapted from the Korean *Joseon* from the long-lived dynastic period just before colonialism, its associations with that period caused the Japanese government to initiate a new term for Korea and Koreans:

Kankoku. Thus, in the old, neo-Imperial manner, Koreans are *Chosen-jin*; in a more enlightened usage they are *Kankoku-jin*. When, in the dream sequence in part one, they near Pusan in their rowboat, they call out "Kankoku-jin" to the waiting South Korean Army. When they are accosted by Japanese citizens they are called *Chosen-jin*.

Just before the trio is killed and then "resurrected," there is a brief cinéma vérité sequence in the film that highlights Oshima's contention that there is no essential difference between Japanese and Korean people. With camera in hand, the boys ask people on a busy Tokyo street: "Are you Japanese (*Nihon-jin*)"? And the answer they invariably get is "No; I'm Korean (*Kankoku-jin*)." The last one to assert his Korean-ness is Oshima himself. There could be no clearer way to deny any essential racial or ethnic profile to Japanese or Koreans nor any clearer sense of identification with Koreans on Oshima's part.

Eventually, the boys themselves, in part two of the film, come to identify completely with the Korean stowaways. In the ultimate Brechtian "epic theater," the boys are aware of what happened in part one, yet they play out their parts with this knowledge. They know, for instance, that the price of Shinsei (an inexpensive brand of Japanese cigarettes) has risen from 40 yen to 50; they know just what the Korean corporal will say to them when he finds them outside the hot springs; one of them wants to wait for the *zainichi* girl to show up to help them, and so on. Of course, this is repetition with difference, the biggest being that the two stowaways are caught by the police and executed—in a quick move on the film's part from farce to ferment. Either in an attempt to stop these executions or in total sympathy with the Koreans, the two boys wearing their clothes claim literal identification with them, the first one proclaiming, "I am Cpl. Yi Cheon-il"; the other one insisting, "I am Kim Hwa." It is perhaps easy for these boys to take on these identities: Oshima has never given the trio any names.

Conclusion

To anyone who lived through May '68, Oshima's films are, at the very least, a nostalgic return to that time. Yet beyond nostalgia for a certain kind of cinema, what do Oshima's two films of that year have to offer? Seeing the films with a contemporary audience, Geoffrey Nowell-Smith poses the question in poignant terms:

> Why was it that films which had so excited audiences in the late 1960s and early 70s no longer seemed to have any drawing power forty or so years later? Was Oshima just a flash in the pan, a 1960s phenomenon whose work could not resonate outside the heady atmosphere that had existed on either side of 1968?[24]

Alternately, Dennis Lim claims quite the opposite: "To call these films products of their times does nothing to diminish their freshness. It is precisely because Mr. Oshima was so furiously engaged with his moment that his movies still have so much to say to ours."[25] The best we can say in the face of these opposite assessments, and what I have tried to accomplish here, is to note Alexander Jacoby's assertion, "Oshima's films demand a fuller understanding of his place in the history of Japan and the history of cinema."[26] Oshima certainly demands to be placed in the canon of filmmakers who responded with intelligence, wit, and wisdom to the events of 1968.

Notes

1. Shota Ogawa, "Reinhabiting the Mock-Up Gallows: The Place of Koreans in Oshima Nagisa's Films in the 1960s," *Screen* 56, no. 3 (2015): 303–18, at 308.
2. Ogawa, "Reinhabiting the Mock-Up Gallows," 309.
3. *Time*, "Japan: Violence in Shinjuku Station." November 1, 1968, http://content.time.com/time/magazine/article/0,9171,839590,00.html, accessed June 8, 2016.
4. Eiji Oguma, "Japan's 1968: A Collective Reaction to Rapid Economic Growth in an Age of Turmoil," *Asia-Pacific Journal* 13 (2015): 1–24
5. For a more sustained analysis of this film, see also Morgan Adamson, "Toward a New Mode of Study: The New Student Left and the Occupation of Cinema in *Columbia Revolt* (US, 1968) and *The Battlefront for the Liberation of Japan—Summer in Sanrizuka* (Japan, 1968)," in this volume.
6. *Kinema Jumpo*, "All Time Best 200 Japanese Movies", https://mubi.com/lists/japanese-movies-all-time-best-200-kinejun-readers.
7. Wildgrounds. "Kinema Jumpo's Top 100 Japanese Movies." http://archive.is/HCBlt, accessed December 1, 2017.
8. Ogawa, "Reinhabiting the Mock-Up Gallows," 305–6.
9. Roland Domenig, "The Anticipation of Freedom: Art Theatre Guild and Japanese Independent Cinema." *Midnight Eye* (2004). http://www.midnighteye.

com/features/the-anticipation-of-freedom-art-theatre-guild-and-japanese-independent-cinema, accessed June 12, 2016.

10. David Desser, *Eros Plus Massacre: An Introduction to the Japanese New Wave Cinema* (Bloomington: Indiana University Press, 1988), 48.
11. Ogawa, "Reinhabiting the Mock-Up Gallows," 307.
12. Ryan Marshall Cook, "Through the Looking Glass: Flirtations with Nonsense in 1960s Japanese Film Culture" (PhD diss., Yale University, 2013), 155.
13. Cook, "Through the Looking Glass," 159.
14. Cook, "Through the Looking Glass," 161.
15. Cook, 165–66.
16. Cook, 166–67.
17. Yuriko Furuhata, *Cinema of Actuality: Japanese Avant-Garde Filmmaking in the Season of Image Politics* (Durham, NC: Duke University Press, 2013).
18. Alexander Jacoby, "In the Realm of Oshima," *Sight and Sound* 19, no. 9 (2009): 48–50.
19. Tony Rayns, "A Samurai among Farmers," *Film Comment* (September–October 2008). http://www.filmcomment.com/article/a-samurai-among-farmers-nagisa-oshima/, accessed June 7, 2016.
20. Film Reference, "Nagisa Oshima—Director." http://www.filmreference.com/Directors-Mi-Pe/Oshima-Nagisa.html, accessed June 12, 2016.
21. Sonia Ryang, *Writing Selves in Diaspora: Ethnography of Autobiographies of Korean Women in Japan and the United States* (New York: Lexington Books, 2008), xxi. https://mouonekorea.wordpress.com/2012/06/07/a-song-to-imjin-river/, accessed June 19, 2016.
22. Oliver Dew, "*Pacchigi!*, the Imjin River Incident and 1968," *Journal of Japanese and Korean Cinema* 6, no. 2 (2014): 134–51.
23. Film Reference, "Nagisa Oshima—Director."
24. Geoffrey Nowell-Smith, "Oshima Revisited," *Film Quarterly* 64, no. 2 (2010): 19–23, at 19.
25. Dennis Lim, "Safeguarding a Japanese Master's Place in Film," *New York Times*, September 25, 2008. http://www.nytimes.com/2008/09/26/movies/26oshi.html?_r=0, accessed June 6, 2016.
26. Jacoby, "In the Realm of Oshima."

Bibliography

Cameron, Ian. "Nagisa Oshima." *Movie* (Winter 1969/70).

______. *Second Wave*. New York: Praeger, 1970.

Cook, Ryan Marshall. "Through the Looking Glass: Flirtations with Nonsense in 1960s Japanese Film Culture." PhD diss., Yale University, 2013.

Desser, David. *Eros Plus Massacre: An Introduction to the Japanese New Wave Cinema*. Bloomington: Indiana University Press, 1988.

Dew, Oliver. "*Pacchigi!*, the Imjin River Incident and 1968." *Journal of Japanese and Korean Cinema* 6, no. 2 (2014): 134–51.

Domenig, Roland. "The Anticipation of Freedom: Art Theatre Guild and Japanese Independent Cinema." *Midnight Eye* (2004). http://www.midnighteye.com/features/the-anticipation-of-freedom-art-theatre-guild-and-japanese-independent-cinema, accessed June 12, 2016.

Furuhata, Yuriko. *Cinema of Actuality: Japanese Avant-Garde Filmmaking in the Season of Image Politics*. Durham, NC: Duke University Press, 2013.

Heath, Stephen. "Anato mo." *Screen* 17, no. 4 (1976/77): 49–66.

______. "The Question—Oshima." *Wide Angle* 2, no. 1 (1977): 49–57.

Jacoby, Alexander. "In the Realm of Oshima." *Sight and Sound* 19, no. 9 (2009): 48–50.

Kinema Jumpo. "All Time Best 200 Japanese Movies." https://mubi.com/lists/japanese-movies-all-time-best-200-kinejun-readers, accessed June 8, 2016.

Lim, Dennis. "Safeguarding a Japanese Master's Place in Film." *New York Times*, September 25, 2008. http://www.nytimes.com/2008/09/26/movies/26oshi.html?_r=0, accessed June 6, 2016.

Macnab G. C., and Guo-Juin Hong. "Nagisa Oshima: Director." *Film Reference*. http://www.filmreference.com/Directors-Mi-Pe/Oshima-Nagisa.html, accessed June 8, 2016.

Nowell-Smith, Geoffrey. "Oshima Revisited." *Film Quarterly* 64, no. 2 (2010): 19–23.

Ogawa, Shota T. "Reinhabiting the Mock-Up Gallows: The Place of Koreans in Oshima Nagisa's Films in the 1960s." *Screen* 56, no. 3 (2015): 303–18.

Oguma, Eiji. "Japan's 1968: A Collective Reaction to Rapid Economic Growth in an Age of Turmoil." *Asia-Pacific Journal* 13 (2015): 1–24.

Oshima, Nagisa. *Oshima Nagisa 1968*. Tokyo: Seido Sha, 2004.

Rayns, Tony. "A Samurai among Farmers." *Film Comment* (September–October 2008). http://www.filmcomment.com/article/a-samurai-among-farmers-nagisa-oshima/, accessed June 7, 2016.

Ryang, Sonia. *Writing Selves in Diaspora: Ethnography of Autobiographies of Korean Women in Japan and the United States*. New York: Lexington Books, 2008, xxi. https://mouonekorea.wordpress.com/2012/06/07/a-song-to-imjin-river/, accessed June 19, 2016.

Time. "Japan: Violence in Shinjuku Station." November 1, 1968. http://content.time.com/time/magazine/article/0,9171,839590,00.html, accessed June 8, 2016.

Wildgrounds. "Kinema Jumpo's Top 100 Japanese Movies." http://archive.is/HCBlt, accessed November 29, 2017.

9

The Hypothetical and the Experimental

Reading Lindsay Anderson's *If . . .* Alongside Pier Paolo Pasolini's *Teorema*

Graeme Stout

If 1968 stands as *the* year of political revolution and rebellion in the postwar era, its status as a revolutionary moment within the history of cinema is less certain. In many ways, 1968 did not produce a politically committed cinematic output, nor need it have done so as the realist project in cinema, and its specific form of political engagement was already making way for something new. With this movement away from the political commitment of realism—a school of thought that had been the approved form of representation throughout the twentieth century[1]—the films of the late 1960s took on a more experimental approach to cinematic form accompanied by an expanded investigation of the notion of the political, one that would also question the modes of deploying pleasure and sexuality.

Both critically successful on their release, Pier Paolo Pasolini's *Teorema* (Italy, 1968) and Lindsay Anderson's *If. . .* (UK, 1968), illustrate this transformation in western European cinema as the two films mark, for both directors, a break with their shared legacy of realist aesthetics and socially committed film from which they emerged in the early 1960s.[2] These two films also mark the point in the oeuvre of both directors, where their particular styles emerged from the larger movements of the early 1960s. This essay does not seek to offer a simple comparison of the two films or to think of them as valuable only due to their place within both directors' creative trajectories. Instead, these films raise larger questions about the political and cultural realities of Western capitalism at a moment when it turned away from heavy industry and moved toward a model of economic organization based on immaterial labor. In both *If . . .* and *Teorema,* this economic shift serves as a backdrop to the unrest that drives both films and the narratives within them. This is not to suggest that they are politically noncommitted, on the contrary; they are both highly critical in that they look ahead to the transformations that will overtake the industrialized countries of western Europe in the decades to come.

These two films break with narrative structure and move to a more experimental mode of critique: Pasolini's neglects dialogue and continuity and Anderson's breaks a little over halfway through, opting for an experimental flow of images. This new mode takes image and sound and imbues them with a transformative status that, in turn, undermines the basic narrative structure with which both films start. The focus here will be based in the visual narrative, but it will also pay close attention to how music operates in these two films, in particular how music is itself an object of consumption and control. In both *Teorema* and *If . . .* music moves between the diegetic and the nondiegetic, blurring the boundaries between the film as a discrete text and the film as a provocation that makes demands of the audience. This experimental nature is one that takes visual and auditory experience seriously as both produce a plurality of pleasures. Here, both films confront the audience in order to break with cinema's "pleasure principle," including that of realism in which the viewing subject is reaffirmed as politically informed and committed. In their titles as well as within their narratives, they offer a hypothesis, an experiment that is enacted in the cinematic experience. The "hypothetical" status of both films allows us to understand them as provocations that confront the audience and ask it to be an active participant in their forms of rebellion. Fifty years later, we can see them as texts that presage the radical economic and political changes that were to take place in the following two decades. As such their "openness" is one that still has force as they interrogate the realities of the last half century.

The White Heat of Technology

If . . . is set in College House, a fictitious amalgam of the English public school experience. The narrative centers on the triumvirate of Mick Travis (Malcolm McDowell), Johnny (David Wood), and Wallace (Richard Warwick)—the

Crusaders—a group of self-appointed outsiders. After a series of encounters and conflicts within the school, the three Crusaders are publicly beaten by the House Whips for being "a general nuisance"; in response, the three, led by Mick, embark on a scheme of revenge where they open fire on students and faculty, resulting in the shooting and bayoneting of the school's vicar. At this point, the film's straightforward and linear narrative breaks down, as the next scene finds the three in front of the headmaster, who forces them to apologize to the vicar, who appears from within a chest of drawers. The Crusaders then prepare for their ultimate assault on the collected body of the College on Founders Day. Having set the school hall on fire, the Crusaders open fire on the fleeing students, family, faculty, and guests with an arsenal of World War II vintage weapons that they discovered when they were tasked to clean up the school's basement. The headmaster appeals to them to stop and claims that he understands them; the enigmatic Girl (Christine Noonan) coldly shoots the headmaster through the forehead, and both sides of the conflict square off. As the camera focuses on Mick Travis firing a Bren gun, the intertitle "if . . ." appears and the film credits roll.

Toward the beginning of *If . . .* , the headmaster addresses the various Whips, explaining to them the value of the institution. This speech, as with the others throughout the film, falls back on the value of College to the empire and vice versa. But what is of particular interest is the discussion of the present moment in the economic and political history of the United Kingdom. Here, it is not the nostalgia for empire that is highlighted, but, rather, the "white heat" of science and industry that Harold Wilson proclaimed in 1963 would guide Britain, once again, to the heights of economic dominance. College House is identified as a laboratory of ideas and innovation, using the school as a training ground for such things as "high standards in the television and entertainment world." The hope for Britain lies in its ability to commercialize talent and export it as a new form of world dominance.

Despite being a film made in the 1960s, *If . . .* refuses many of the obvious popular cultural references of rebellion and youth culture. Produced at the very moment of the events of May '68, Anderson sought to restrict any direct reference to the events in Paris in order to avoid the film turning into an allegory of the student protests.[3] The key site in the film where media plays a central role is in the study of the three main Crusaders: Mick, Wallace, and

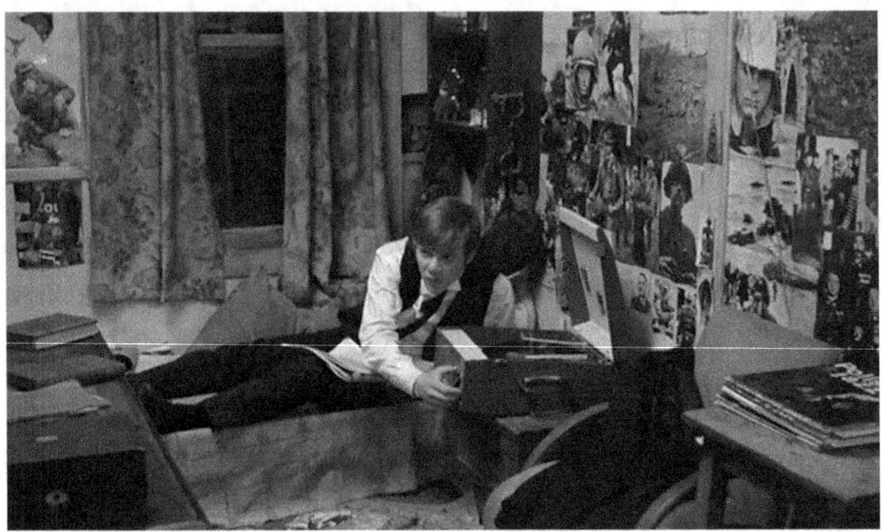

Missa Luba

Johnny. Here, they constantly add to their wall of images taken from the popular press, as a haphazard collage of war, nature, sexuality, and history.

In front of this collage is Mick's phonograph. Early in the film, as we find Mick alone in the study, he introduces us—on the phonograph—to one of the central musical themes of the film: the *Sanctus* of *Missa Luba*. This recording of the Catholic mass by Les Troubadours du Roi Baudouin, arranged by Father Guido Haazen, was a hit throughout the 1960s and, by the end of the decade, had already been featured in a number of films. Mick starts to play the record and, as the tempo picks up, he lifts the needle and returns to the beginning. This act of "reversing" the recording, returning to the moment of anticipation and promise, speaks to the form of aesthetic control that the phonograph offers, something that, in our own digital age, sounds quaint.

Later in the film, we find Mick and Johnny, who, having stolen a motorcycle, come on a roadside café. Entering it, they are met by a singular "Girl" from whom they order coffee. As she turns around to pour it, Mick and Johnny lean over the counter and cast their eyes over her body. She looks back at them, knowing full well their intent. With their coffees in front of them, Mick asks for sugar. Taking two heaping tablespoons, he leans across the counter, seizes her, and kisses her; she pulls back and soundly slaps him across the face. Collecting himself, Mick moves across the room to the jukebox. He selects *Missa Luba* and once again we hear the opening strains of the *Sanctus*. As Mick leans over the jukebox, the Girl approaches from behind, puts her hand on his shoulder, and beckons him to turn around. The shot then turns to a close-up of the Girl's face from over Mick's shoulder. She tells him, "Go on. Look at me . . . and I'll kill you." The shot reverses to Mick who stands with a mixture of guilt and arrogance. She continues, "Look at my eyes." The camera once again focuses on the Girl with an even tighter shot that captures only her eyes. She looks up at Mick and says, "Sometimes I stand in front of the mirror and my eyes get bigger and bigger. And I'm like a tiger. I like tigers." At this point she lunges at Mick with a throaty feline roar. The camera then alternates between Mick and the Girl as they start to sniff each other and, then, hiss and snarl. As they circle around each other, the Girl launches herself at Mick. They wrestle on the café floor, and suddenly they appear completely naked. She grabs his wrist and bites; he silently screams as the *Sanctus* reaches its choral and rhythmic peaks.

What to make of the inclusion of this particular piece of music? On the most obvious level it is an exotic import from the Congo and speaks to the European fascination with, and fetishization of, the other. In the two scenes previously discussed, the song is tied to Mick's desires for control, pleasure, and sexual excess. It is also an inherently colonial text: a version of the Catholic mass set to African melodies by a Belgian missionary and sung by a Congolese choir named in honor of the king of Belgium at the twilight of that country's particularly exploitative empire in Africa. The use of *Missa Luba* is problematic at best as it stands out as a non-European text that will allow Mick to experience some authentic form of religious experience. This implied relationship is given further weight when, after the café scene, we find Mick and Johnny back on the motorcycle riding through a green and pleasant field with the girl standing up between them on the seat. As they circle back toward the camera she runs her hands through her hair, allowing the wind to catch it. As she lowers her arms, they adopt a crucifix-like posture as they drive out of shot. All the while, the opening of the *Sanctus* is heard.

The de-colonial present of *If . . .* is a theme that runs throughout Anderson's film. Even the title consciously references Rudyard Kipling's *If*, a high-colonial text meant to instruct Kipling's son, and all the sons of Britain, on how to be good colonizers. In many ways *If . . .* does not offer a direct and pointed critique of British colonialism, if anything it sees its adherents as fossils who are out of touch with the global realities of the late twentieth century.

The Crusaders do not rebel against College House in order to tear it down; their point is that it is an illusion that masks the changed realities of capitalism and imperialism.

If the use of *Missa Luba* evokes a number of postcolonial critiques, one could also read it as a problematic text within the narrative of the film itself. As a recording heard on a phonograph and a jukebox, it is always introduced into the diegetic world as a commodity and one that speaks to its very status as such. The phonograph record offers Mick the opportunity to control the flow of music and to create a perpetual cycle of sonoric bliss. On the jukebox, it is a direct relationship between money, mechanization, and the experience of listening. If the Crusaders surround themselves with the products of mass media, they do so as willing consumers of that very media; their fantasies are tied more to the forms of rebellion and desire promoted within mass culture than they are to any political cause.

When the Crusaders are called into the headmaster's office after they apparently killed the vicar, the headmaster tells them, "Now you mustn't think that I don't understand. It's a natural characteristic of adolescence to want to claim individuality. There nothing unhealthy about that, it's a quite blameless form of existentialism. This, for instance, is what lies at the heart of the great hair problem. . . . So often I have noticed that it is the hair-rebels who step into the breach when there's a crisis." Here, the headmaster returns to his earlier discussion of the character of College House and its role in contemporary popular culture as a driving force of the British economy. He also identifies a less disciplinary form of control, one that seeks out innovation and individuality as forms of productivity. He sees the Crusaders as those who will go into business as new colonial adventurers of the British Empire.[4]

Writing at the end of the 1980s, Gilles Deleuze described the rise of the societies of control as a general diffusion of the disciplinary forces that Michel Foucault identified as the structures behind the modern forms of power. For Deleuze, the new mode of capitalist production is based on constant restructuring and remodulation, its products, immaterial and relational. As a reflection on the political struggles of the latter half of the twentieth century, Deleuze also questioned the forms of economic activity and political resistance that the new societies of control might produce or allow. He wrote:

> Many young people strangely boast of being "motivated"; they re-request apprenticeships and permanent training. It's up to them to discover what they're being made to serve, just as their elders discovered, not without difficulty, the telos of the disciplines. The coils of a serpent are even more complex than the burrows of a molehill.[5]

Following Deleuze, we could wonder about the forms of resistance that are enacted with *If*. . . . In many ways, what the Crusaders engage in is a series of fantasies centering on violence, revenge, and sexuality. They play with the stuff of mass culture and they have no desire to abandon it. Even if they tarry with the negative, they only see it as part of the collective imaginary of cinema, television, and literature. The headmaster is quite right to see the Crusaders as potential leaders as they are more representative of a critical and creative tendency than any of their fellow students.

"When Do We Live?"

The question of what type of life Mick and his fellow Crusaders might lead is a constant theme throughout the film. Life itself becomes a constant object of discussion and analysis as it is synonymous with the anxieties and energies of young men whose bodies are out of control.

We see this investigation of life unfold in the whipping scene when it moves between a direct, head-on shot of Mick, bent over a pommel horse, being beaten, and a tracking shot of the other students in the sweat room, listening to the punishment. From the various faces, the camera then falls on Peanuts—College House's stereotypical "nerd"—who, after a quick look of disapproval, removes his glasses and stares down through his microscope. We then switch to an "extreme close-up" of bacteria multiplying at an accelerated rate. Within the narrative of the film, this scene marks the point of no return, when the Crusaders will embark on their scheme of revenge that will culminate in an attack on the school's Founders Day celebration.

This view through the scientific apparatus is later echoed when Mick, already concocting his plan of revenge, approaches Peanuts, who is stargazing with his telescope. Mick, instead of looking up to the stars, turns the telescope to earth where he spies the Girl, who, spying him in turn, meets his gaze, stops brushing her hair, and waves to him in a playful fashion. Mick's choice of target points to his earthly desires as opposed to those of Peanuts. When the Crusaders explore the bowels of the College, they discover a series of relics of the school's imperial past:[6] animal specimens from around the world, banners, statues, and architectural details. Here, they come across a cabinet of biological curiosities, from which Mick pulls out a preserved human fetus that he passes to the Girl. She holds the glass container, looks at Mick, shrugs, and passes the fetus back to him. He places it back in the cabinet and reseals it. This exchange of "life" forecloses any possibility of a productive relationship between Mick and the Girl or between any of the other Crusaders. Here, against the biopolitical order of the family and empire, the Crusaders opt for an outburst of destruction made from the images they have collected from mass culture.

The viral growth under the detached eye of Peanuts brings forth images of infection and life out of control. At three moments in the film, Mick asks, rhetorically, "But when do we live?" Here, one can read the question of life as an existential and a biological query. The rebellion that foments under the lashes of the House Whips is a reaction against the institution of class power and privilege in Britain as well as a rebellion against the school as the central player in the concert of power. As Althusser would have it: "Nevertheless, in this concert, one ideological State apparatus certainly has the dominant role, although hardly anyone lends an ear to its music: it is so silent! This is the School."[7] It is important to remember that Althusser did not see the school as a repressive state apparatus but as the sustaining and transformative force in advanced capitalist economies. The final scene of *If . . .* offers a clear, and somewhat comical, allegory of this coming confrontation, when the Crusaders attack, the students, parents, teachers, and alumni break open the school armory and launch a counterattack. What is unclear is whether the counterattack is against the challenge to tradition or against the new forms of creativity, pleasure, identity, and capitalism that the Crusaders represent.

"Why Don't You Put On Some Music?"

Teorema begins with a false start: a fictitious news report about a factory owner who has turned his factory over to his workers. The reporter asks the puzzled (and very real workers) if this spells the end of class conflict. The film proper then opens as the credits role. The plot revolves around a Milanese family

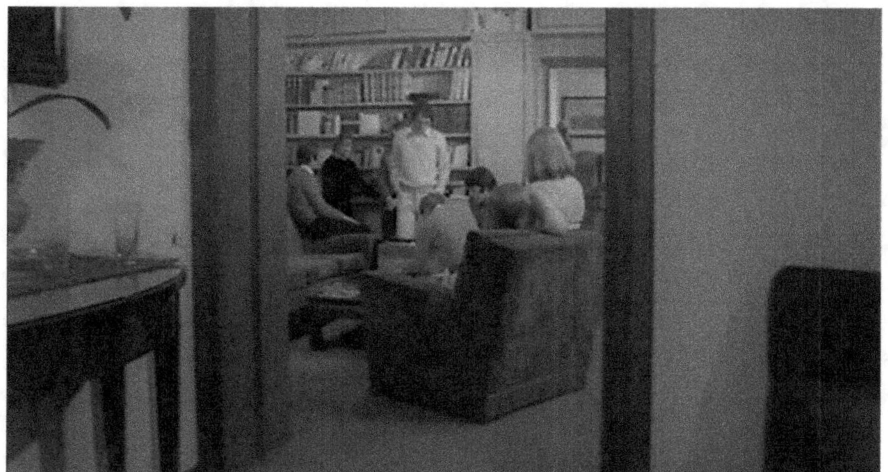

"Why Don't You Put on Some Music?"

that receives a Visitor (Terence Stamp), who has sexual relations with every member of the household, causing each to suffer an existential crisis. The film ends when the father turns his factory over to his workers, strips himself of all his clothes, and wanders into the wastes of Mount Etna; as he approaches the camera, he screams.

In many ways, Pasolini's film, unlike Anderson's, has a more redemptive tone, albeit one that is only made manifest through a series of crises. Given the religious overtones, one would think that it would have a more pointed critique of capitalism and modernity. Here, however, the overall anxiety that opens and closes the film speaks not only to general crises of humanity in the late modern age but also to the years in which it was made. In the opening scene, when the reporter ends by shouting to no one in particular, "Is there anyone here who can answer this question?" what the question actually is, is left open. One way that it could be understood is as an interrogation of the proletariat assembled about what would it mean for them to become bourgeois and for the bourgeoisie to give up its privilege altogether; in the specific case of *Teorema*, it is the example of the father, Paolo (Massimo Girotti), giving his factory over to his workers. Again, a piece of technology might help us to understand the historical juncture that Pasolini attempts to analyze in his film.

A turntable is also of central importance in *Teorema*. Here, as in *If* . . . , it also marks a moment of indistinction between diegetic and nondiegetic sound: what is played on the turntable returns as something short of a leitmotif. Toward the beginning of the film, as the family hosts a small get-together where the Visitor enters into the narrative, Lucia (Silvana Mangano) asks her son Pietro (Andrés José Cruz Soublette) to "put on some music." Pietro moves across the room to where all the young men are talking; he opens up the portable phonograph and puts on a record. What we hear is an untitled piece by Ennio Morricone—a slow jazz-blues shuffle—that, while suggesting American light jazz and cocktail music, speaks more to Morricone's conscious ironic manipulation of popular music within film. Here, the easy repetition of the music refers us back to the revolutions of the turntable. As the music fills the party and, then, the sonoric space of the cinematic text, the young men gather around and admire the turntable. This masculine attention could, following Laurence Rickels, point to the libidinal investment in technology. Such an argument could be extended as we later see the phonograph reappear between Pietro and the Visitor's beds. During this scene the music returns, although it is not played on the phonograph—the continued presence of the phonograph initiates an expectancy that will reach its culmination when Pietro is drawn to the Visitor, crossing the room and entering into his bed.

Unlike the film's other pieces by Morricone or those of Ted Curson, however, this short piece recurs throughout the film with little or no variation. It would be strange to call this a leitmotif, as this would suggest some form of development or variation. If Adorno heard the leitmotif as a form of reductive musical "cueing," what we see in *Teorema* takes this to its logical conclusion: a simple sonoric repetition that signals the Visitor. And, yet, it is not that simple. This particular piece, unlike all others in the film, has a diegetic grounding in that it is actually played on a phonograph within the narrative proper. This marks a return to the materiality of the phonograph as a gadget, a piece of household technology that turns the private sphere into a place of transcendent experience and control. As Friedrich Kittler points out, paraphrasing Klaus Theweleit, "media are always flight apparatuses into the great beyond."[8] If Morricone's music is a leitmotif, it is of a unique kind in that it refers back to the phonograph and the introduction of the Visitor—both objects of desire. What we hear each and every time is the same thing. This repetition is, however, problematic. Unlike the rest of the musical accompaniment, this particular piece of music is rather innocuous as it is light party music, nothing too moving, serious, or somber. This is a reflection, or echo, of the limited sonic capabilities of the phonograph itself. It signals moments of lightness within the film but also the erotic, and then artistic, awakening of Pietro. Here, the question of production is central as Pietro turns to art as part of a larger production of meaning within the world—although not one without frustration and despair. The cheapness of the phonograph is then tied to the Visitor who, in the party scene, is described by Odetta (Anne Wiazemsky) as "No one. Just a boy." Most often read as an angelic form, perhaps he is nothing of the sort.

Turning workers into members of the bourgeoisie allows all to enter into a world of consumption. It will also, in the decades to follow, lead to them losing their jobs as Italy's economic miracle turns into Berlusconi's media empire. The fetish character of the turntable produces only a hollow and formulaic sound that cannot grow or develop. Its repetition does not point beyond itself or suggest a transcendent realm; the transformation to come will be carried out by the banal repetition of sounds and images.

Conclusion: Experimental Cinema?

Pasolini saw *Teorema* as an experiment and as an experimental film. In a most basic sense, he wanted it to offer a set of conditions into which an anarchic element would be interjected within a familiar scenario: the bourgeois family. Moreover, he saw it as a film in which his own theoretical discussions of cinema—the development of the im-sign—would be the guiding philosophy and practice behind the film. Deleuze argued that the film is not so much theorematic as it is problematic. He writes: "A problem lives in the theorem, and gives it life, even when removing its power. The problematic is distinguished from the theorematic (or constructivism from the axiomatic) in that the theorem develops internal relationships from principle to consequences, while the problem introduces an event from the outside."[9] The outside event, the Visitor, does not serve to prove the theorem of capitalism and bourgeois existence but to throw them both into disorder. Much has been said on the melodramatic quality of Pasolini's film,[10] as the family unit is its central focus. I would argue that the larger discussion—the unanswered question that starts the film—of the transformations of Western economies is much more important. The interspersed shots of Mount Etna's[11] desert slopes and the monochromatic images of the factory landscape speak to economies and environments of desolation, offering a larger critical reading of the legacy of Italy's relationship to the land and its resources.[12] If *Teorema* is a reflection on Italy's future at the end of its economic recovery, it should be noted that it reflects in a fashion that is not reductivist or simplistically symbolic; rather, it tries to create a visual language of desire, anxiety, loss, and hope. As Maurizio Viano argues about the close working relationship between Pasolini's cinematic work and his cinema theory:

> And it may be useful to remember that Pasolini had the keenest awareness of etimology [*sic*] and that the title has its roots in theorema, Greek for spectacle, intuition, theorem; from theorein, to look at, to observe; from theoros, spectator. Theory and spectatorship, the theory of looking, are thus implied. And so are the ideas of theory as spectacle and spectacle as theory."[13]

Teorema's speculative nature offers an experimental situation in which the audience is tested. The semiotic paucity of film—in that it creates its own symbolic register and disrupts those from which it borrows—is a challenge to the audience, which is required to serve as an active participant in the deployment and construction of meaning, a construction that echoes the audience's own changing social reality.

In a similar fashion, Anderson's *If*. . . offers a way to analyze the socioeconomic tensions of late 1960s Britain. If the film moves toward the metaphorical, this is not simply a question of style. Instead, it is Anderson and screenwriter David Sherwin's attempt to break open the didactic world of political cinema in the postwar British cinema by creating a film that is driven by affect and emotion and, at the same time, offers a critique of them. Here, the return of the title to the screen at the end of the battle scene reinforces the conditional and hypothetical nature of the narrative; by introducing an anarchic element into the closed environment of the school as allegory for British society, Anderson points to the conflict ahead. If it is in the rather innocuous form of the phonograph that new forms of pleasure and subjectivity are presaged in both films, this is only because the phonograph is one technology with larger systems of consumption, repetition, and control that, in the decades following 1968, would institute new political regimes focused on the desires of the individual.

In *Teorema* and *If . . .* there is a form of resistance to 1968 itself. Given the momentous events of the year within global politics, both films eschew a model of time and the event that would mark their own year of production as singularly monumental. Despite their confrontational endings, their narratives wander off into allegory and speculation. They do not uphold 1968 as a year of failed promise, only a point where we see the transition from discipline to control, from material to immaterial labor, and from an antiquated model of colonialism to the global system in which we still live. Here, our new economic realities are ones driven by the repetition of images and sounds, all made available to us in consumer electronics.

Notes

1. Apart from the elevation of socialist realism as the proper revolutionary form of aesthetic representation under the Comintern, there are larger philosophical and artistic discourses related to the relationship of representation to rational perception and scientific thought. For a thorough and concise reading of these debates, see Fredric Jameson's afterword to the collection *Aesthetics and Politics* (London: Verso, 2010).
2. Angelo Restivo, *The Cinema of Economic Miracles: Visuality and Modernization in the Italian Art Film* (Durham, NC: Duke University Press, 2002), 87.
3. Charles Drazin, "*If*. . . before *If*. . . ," *Journal of British Cinema and Television* 5, no. 2 (2008): 318–34, at 322.
4. *If*. . . is the first of a loose trilogy that also includes *O Lucky Man!* (1973) and *Britannia Hospital* (1982). All three films star Malcolm McDowell as Mick Travis. At the time of *If*. . .'s production, there were no plans on Anderson's part to turn his film into a trilogy.
5. Gilles Deleuze, "Postscript on the Societies of Control," *October* 59 (Winter 1992): 3–7, at 7.
6. The film's questioning of the imperial past is difficult yet productive, but, for the limitations of the present essay, cannot be fully investigated. Suffice it to say, the male fantasies of the Crusaders do not overcome, but rather delight in, the images of colonial politics past and present. Although in his collage Mick has images of Lenin and Geronimo in places of prominence, they serve only as markers of the spirit of violent rebellion, not any ideological stance or affiliation. In a similar fashion, when they launch their attack on the

school, they do so in imitation of British Commandos, donning the outfits and arms of Britain's plucky and cavalier resistance during World War II.

7. Louis Althusser, "Ideology and Ideological State Apparatuses: Notes Toward an Investigation," in *Lenin and Philosophy and Other Essays* (London: NLB, 1971), 127–86, at 155.
8. Friedrich A. Kittler, *Gramophone, Film, Typewriter* (Stanford, CA: Stanford University Press, 1999), 13.
9. Gilles Deleuze, *Cinema 2: The Time Image* (Minneapolis: University of Minnesota Press, 1989), 174.
10. See Restivo, *Cinema of Economic Miracles.*
11. For an allegorical reading of Mount Etna and its status within the Italian imaginary, see Cesare Casarino, "Pasolini in the Desert," *Angelaki*: *Journal of the Theoretical Humanities* 9, no. 1 (2004): 97–102.
12. An extended comparison of *Teorema* with Michelangelo Antonioni's *Red Desert* (1964) would be quite productive for the history of Italian film. A study of the influence of Antonioni's film on Pasolini's thought, writing, and cinematic production would be equally rewarding.
13. Maurizio Sanzio Viano, *A Certain Realism: Making Use of Pasolini's Film Theory and Practice* (Berkeley: University of California Press, 1993), 200.

Bibliography

Adorno, Theodor W. *The Culture Industry*. Edited by J. M. Bernstein. London: Routledge, 1991.

Althusser, Louis. "Ideology and Ideological State Apparatuses: Notes Toward an Investigation." In *Lenin and Philosophy and Other Essays*, 127–86. London: NLB, 1971.

Casarino, Cesare. "Pasolini in the Desert." *Angelaki*: *Journal of the Theoretical Humanities* 9, no. 1 (2004): 97–102.

Deleuze, Gilles. *Cinema 2: The Time Image*. Translated by Hugh Tomlinson and Robert Galeta. Minneapolis: University of Minnesota Press, 1989.

———. "Postscript on the Societies of Control." *October* 59 (Winter 1992): 3–7.

Drazin, Charles. "*If*. . . before *If*. . . ." *Journal of British Cinema and Television* 5, no. 2 (2008): 318–34.

Gourdin-Sangouard, Isabelle. "Creating Authorship? Lindsay Anderson and David Sherwin's Collaboration on *If*. . . ." *Journal of Screenwriting* 1, no. 1 (2010): 131–48.

If. . . . Directed by Lindsay Anderson. 1968. New York: Criterion Collection,

2011.

Kittler, Friedrich A. *Gramophone, Film, Typewriter*. Translated by Geoffrey Winthrop-Young and Michael Wutz. Stanford, CA: Stanford University Press, 1999.

Pasolini, Pier Paolo. "The Cinema of Poetry." In *Heretical Empiricism*, edited by Louise K. Barnett, 167–86. Translated by Ben Lawton and Louise K. Barnett. Bloomington: Indiana University Press, 1988.

———. *Theorem*. Translated by Stuart Hood. London: Quartet Books, 1992.

Restivo, Angelo. *The Cinema of Economic Miracles: Visuality and Modernization in the Italian Art Film*. Durham, NC: Duke University Press, 2002.

Rickels, Laurence. *Nazi Psychoanalysis*. Vol. 3, *Psy Fi*. Minneapolis: University of Minnesota Press, 2002.

Sussex, Elizabeth. *Lindsay Anderson*. New York: Praeger, 1969.

Sutton, Paul. *If* . . . (Turner Classic Movies British Film Guide). London: I. B. Tauris, 2005.

Teorema. Directed by Pier Paolo Pasolini. 1968. New York: Koch-Lorber Films, 2005.

Viano, Maurizio Sanzio. *A Certain Realism: Making Use of Pasolini's Film Theory and Practice*. Berkeley: University of California Press, 1993.

10

Obscurity, Anthologized

Non-Relation and Enjoyment in *Love and Anger* (1969)

Mauro Resmini

> Marxism does not seem to me to be able to pass for a world view [*conception du monde*] . . . Marxism is something else, something I will call a gospel. It is the announcement that history is instating another dimension of discourse and opening up the possibility of completely subverting the function of discourse as such.
>
> —Jacques Lacan, *The Seminar, Book XX: Encore*

Too Much, Not Enough

Amore e rabbia/Love and Anger (Italy/France; dir. Lizzani, Bertolucci, Pasolini, Godard, Bellocchio, 1969) obligingly confirms the critical commonplace about anthology films: they are too much and not enough at the same time, and for this reason they belong to a history that is at once illustrious and marginal.[1] Yes, there is the participation of prominent directors, but the configuration of the whole is amorphous, disjointed—and so the individual segments end up relegated to a footnote in the filmographies of the respective filmmakers. *Love and Anger* is no exception—an Italian and French coproduction where geographical diversity is compounded by generational division (the older Lizzani, one of the driving forces behind the project, belongs to the cohort of directors associated with Neorealism, while the others are representatives of the new waves that swept Europe during the late 1950s and 1960s).

At the time, Italian cinema was certainly accustomed to the anthology form but almost exclusively in its comedic version. Against that tradition, *Love and Anger* was conceived as an explicitly political film. The original idea was to provide a perspective on contemporary society through the prism of five parables from the New Testament—the film's working title, in fact, was *Vangelo '70/Gospel '70*. The thematic coherence of the project began to disintegrate when one of the original participants, Valerio Zurlini, went over the agreed running time and was cut from the project (his segment then became a feature film, *Seduto alla sua destra/Black Jesus* [Italy, 1968]). Bellocchio filled in for Zurlini, but his episode—*Discutiamo, discutiamo/Let's Discuss, Let's Discuss*—bears no connection to the Gospels.

The first segment, Lizzani's *Indifferenza/Indifference*, a take on the Good Samaritan, is set in contemporary Brooklyn and intertwines two narrative strands: the rape and murder of a young woman in the courtyard of a residential building, perpetrated while the residents watch from their windows, and the aftermath of a car accident on a busy highway, where the husband of a gravely injured woman desperately tries to flag down a passing car amid general indifference.[2] Eventually, with the help of two police officers, a reluctant young man—the Good Samaritan of the parable—is convinced to drive the couple to a hospital. But this charitable New Yorker is a wanted criminal, and after dropping off the couple runs away chased by the police. The second segment, Bertolucci's *Agonia/Agony*, is based on the parable of the Barren Fig Tree, which must be cut for not bearing fruit. The episode features a performance by The Living Theater playing a group of damned souls haunting a dying cardinal (Julian Beck), who meditates on the unfruitful life he has led. The third episode, *La sequenza del fiore di carta/The Sequence of the Paper Flower*, directed by Pasolini, is inspired by the Cursing of the Fig Tree, one of Jesus's miracles. It follows Riccetto (Ninetto Davoli) wandering aimlessly through via Nazionale in Rome on a sunny day. Carefree and full of joy, Riccetto is completely oblivious to the horrors of the world, which appear as superimposed photographs and newsreels of contemporary historical events (the Vietnam War, the Cultural Revolution, the death of Ernesto "Che" Guevara, and so forth). God speaks to him and exhorts him to become aware of history, but Riccetto refuses to listen. Eventually, God hands down his punishment and kills him. Godard's episode, *L'amore/Love*, the fourth, chronicles the end of a relationship between a man and a woman on a Parisian terrace, commented on by two *testimoni* ("witnesses," but also "best man" and "maid of honor"—the two lovers are supposed to marry). Spoken in Italian and French, the episode features the musings of the couple until the inevitable end; divided by class and political beliefs, the fiancés break up and return to their respective homes, like the Prodigal Son of the parable. The final episode, Bellocchio's *Let's Discuss, Let's Discuss*, connects most explicitly to the contemporary political climate; it is the farcical rendition of a university sit-in, where student protesters, conservative students, and faculty get into a semiserious political debate, until they are abruptly interrupted by the intervention of the police—with plastic helmets and fake batons.

Even from such a cursory description, it is clear that the links among the episodes are tenuous at best. The biblical references offer only a most general unifying principle, and even disregarding Bellocchio's *Let's Discuss, Let's Discuss*, the rest of the segments reduce their religious sources to little more than vague allusions. In short, the episodes do not seem to be in conversation with one another. They "talk" plenty—they lecture, accuse, mock—but not to each other. And indeed, Godard's segment, rife as it is with translations, repetitions, and thwarted conversations, does not shy away from poking some fun at the anthology film form itself, with its internationalist aspirations and innate lack of cohesion.

Yet, Godard might be onto something. What if the recurring element, the unifying trait of *Love and Anger*, is, in fact, a certain *incommensurability*, a persistence of non-relationality inscribed into each of the episodes in different ways? What if, in other words, the fundamental relation that binds together the five segments is non-relation, in the form of a set of variously configured splits and fissures? The appeal to the gospels in the film would then be a way to give shape to a negation of "religion" in one of its possible etymological senses, as the gesture of binding, of forging connections, of bridging gaps (Lat., *re-ligare*).

This is the line of inquiry that we will pursue here. With this, we are not looking to make a general claim about the insubstantiality of the genre of the anthology film tout court—which would lead us toward a sort of deconstructionist critique of the anthology film form, whose very fragmented existence would testify to the impossibility of a genre that is One. More modestly, we wish to see how one of the most famous—and less investigated—examples of the "cinema of 1968" articulates a perspective on this event through the form of non-relation.[3] By assuming non-relation as its governing principle, *Love and Anger* seems to register a certain difficulty of grasping 1968 as a unitary event—a difficulty, as we will see, that we can interpret in two ways: firstly, as the symptom of a new organization of political desire that emerges in that historical moment; and secondly, as the unresolved dialectics between the local and global dimensions of 1968.

Non-relations

So, what are exactly these "non-relations" in *Love and Anger*? In Lizzani, non-relation belongs to the domain of the social, and it concerns the individual and her neighbor, the fellow human being. In the first scene, Lizzani depicts the breakdown of this relation of human sympathy by separating the murder victim and the indifferent onlookers in a series of shot/reverse shots where the mobility of the woman scrambling around to escape her attackers contrasts with the stillness of the residents peeking down from their windows. Similarly, in the following scene, an extreme close-up of the husband's hand trying to flag down a car is juxtaposed with the heavy, noisy traffic on New York's highways—an incessant flow of metal and smoke that completely obscures the faces of the drivers.

These two scenes are interspersed with images of homeless people on New York City's streets, as if to underline the social fallout of this non-relation between the individual and her neighbor, a neighbor who resembles the Freudian *Nebenmensch*, close to us because similar to us, and yet forever distant, foreign, even menacing. The Good Samaritan—a wanted criminal—becomes thus the exception within a social order that is crumbling under the pressure of individualism. Lizzani frames this non-relation in terms of a humanistic and moral reproach. The juxtaposition of omnipresent modern technology (cars, airplanes, televisions, recording devices, telephones, and so on) and defenseless human bodies (the rape victim, the car crash survivors, the homeless people) speaks to a certain idea of the fundamental dehumanization of contemporary capitalist society, in which "real," compassionate human relations find themselves obliterated amid rampant atomization and alienation.

The Living Theater in Bertolucci's episode embarks on a journey in the opposite direction, leaving behind the domain of the social to undertake a quest for interiority. "I want to be alone," declares the dying cardinal in the opening shot—and alone he is, but his solitary torment immediately assumes a collective shape. Who are the young men and women who visit the cardinal's agony? Phantasmatic projections? Personifications of guilt and regret? Feverish hallucinations? It remains unclear. What is certain is that the segment dramatizes another non-relation—between the individual and himself. The opposition would then be between the individual as a unitary, self-identical projection and the individual as an unruly multiplicity—a non-relation that one could easily read in psychoanalytical terms: the crystallized stillness of the ego versus the chaotic movement of the drives. Bertolucci places Beck center stage, surrounding him with his actors; they approach him menacingly or lovingly, speak to him, carry his body over their shoulders. Beck, however, never acknowledges them. He remains affectless, except for flashes of anguish and playfulness. Beck's frozen, diaphanous body plays in stark contrast to the mobile, contorting bodies of his actors, who explore the boundary between body and signification—they vocalize, retch, gag, moan, scream (more on this later).

In Pasolini's episode, the young lumpenproletarian Riccetto refuses to listen to the voice of God, who urges him not to ignore history. God's effort is to no avail. Formally, non-relation persists; the global plane of history and the local plane of the protagonist never intersect. The images of historical events are spectral presences that quickly fade, superimpositions that do not interrupt the continuity of the long takes that make up the episode. "They are only shadows over his head," explains Pasolini, "of which he knows nothing."[4] The non-relation between Riccetto and the global geopolitical situation is established in the very first shots: an image of the protagonist sitting close to a fountain cuts to a planisphere. The two instances of the present (the individual/local and the collective/global) remain forever incommensurable.

As in Lizzani, the tone here is one of moral condemnation: "innocence," admonishes the voice of God, "is a fault" (*colpa*). The theme of innocence as a fault is a recurrent one in Pasolini's work of the late 1960s, reaching its apotheosis in *Edipo Re/Oedipus Rex* (Italy, 1967). According to the director himself, "there are moments in History when one cannot be innocent, one must be aware; not being aware means being guilty."[5] Hence divine punishment, handed down by a God who borrows the voices of Bertolucci and Pasolini himself, among others. In a further similarity to Lizzani, the non-relation (and the punishment it demands) is historically situated in the present. *Indifference* assumes a more anthropological stance (the shifting costumes of society), while Pasolini's is more properly moral; but the moral judgment stems from the present, or, more precisely, from a certain idea of what being in the present should look like: solidarity between the individual and her neighbor for Lizzani, a self-aware political engagement that bridges the gap between the local and the global for Pasolini.

The political assumes explicit shape in Godard, who centers his episode on the non-relation between revolution and democracy. Godard maps this political antagonism onto a love relationship between a man and a woman whose engagement is doomed. The man speaks (in Italian) like a guevarist *guerrillero*; the woman admits (in French) her bourgeois origins. "The two cannot coexist," claims the man, "even if they love each other." Yet love itself is a response to a more fundamental non-relation—namely, in Lacanian terms, the non-existence of the sexual relation. Love comes to compensate for the lack of sexual relations; it makes up for this radical negativity. And yet non-relation persists; it remains a fundamental, irreducible insistence within love itself. Godard overlooks this aspect and translates non-relation into purely political terms. In a way, what Godard misses with *Love* is precisely love itself, and the fact that it thinks non-relation in a way that is autonomous from politics (according to Badiou, they are to be regarded as two distinct truth procedures).

In the episode, this results in a clear-cut separation, suffused with Godard's habitual misogyny: male/proletarian/revolutionary on one hand; female/bourgeois/democratic on the other. Displaced from sexuality to politics, non-relation loses its problematic insistence and becomes hypostasized in the figures of the betrothed. They have nothing in common, so they simply part ways: the man goes on to make the world a better place; the woman just goes home. The fantasy of the purity of revolution gets to live another day, as politics is substantialized in the struggle between two principles external to each other and eternally opposed. What is missing in this non-relation is the non-relational kernel of politics itself—that is, the possibility that the battle between revolution and democracy might in fact be internal to each of these two terms as well.

The explicitly political content that characterizes *Love* extends to the last episode of the film, Bellocchio's *Let's Discuss, Let's Discuss*. Here, as the title suggests, the proliferation of speech reduces political discussion in a university

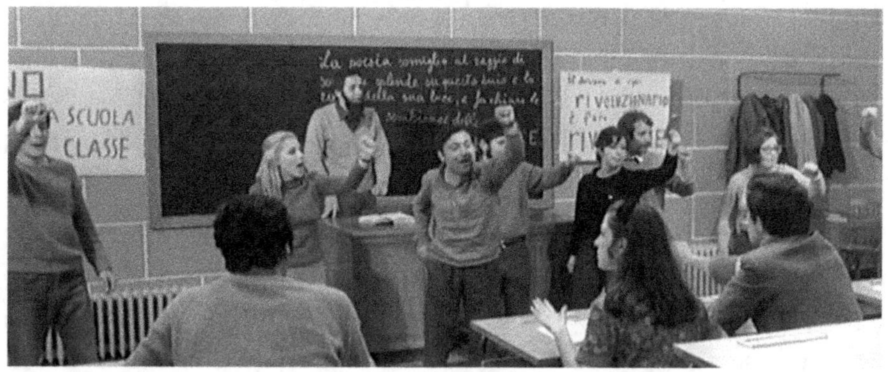

The student protest as farce in *Let's Discuss, Let's Discuss.*

sit-in to pure performance. The parodic hypertrophy of talking is, in fact, the symptom of a dialogue that does not exist, a fundamental non-relation between two of the main actors of 1968—namely, the students and the professors. The theatricality of this nonrelation is conveyed through the formal organization of space: the podium, the audience, and the gap in between are spaces where the characters move freely, defying conventional positions and roles—an apt dramatization of the breakdown of the power relationship between teachers and disciples.

To recapitulate, the fundamental form of non-relation that constitutes the unifying principle of *Love and Anger* takes on different shapes in the various segments: between the individual and her fellow human being (Lizzani); the individual and himself (Bertolucci); the individual and history/God (Pasolini); democracy and revolution, mapped onto love (Godard); and finally, professors and students (Bellocchio). Yet, recognizing and describing the configuration of this set of gaps and fissures does not exhaust the complexity of the problem they pose. Neat as it might seem, this reading remains incomplete at best: something else is at work in these non-relations, something that escapes a simple taxonomy—a repetitive, senseless pleasure that is not quite "pleasurable," a passionate attachment beyond the proper, the useful, or the rational. Lacan calls it a "surplus of enjoyment" ("*plus-de-jouir*"), and if we look at the non-relations in *Love and Anger* from the perspective of this excessive pleasure, we see that there is nothing "innocent" or "neutral" about them. Someone—or something—enjoys in these gaps and fissures.

But looking at non-relation from the perspective of enjoyment might also reveal something about the nature of the event of 1968. Alain Badiou names the period 1965–80 (what is often called the "long 1968") "a series of obscure events," that is, a global historical sequence to which we cannot ascribe a proper unity.[6] We wish to suggest that this obscurity of 1968 is intimately tied to the historical emergence of a new configuration of enjoyment. With its strong antiauthoritarian components, the political desire essential to 1968 is one of liberation of enjoyment, a desire to kill off the master in order to enjoy unreservedly, without limits. This shift produced a discourse in which a condition of free-flowing, unrestrained enjoyment suddenly became not only possible but also desirable. We will return to this later on. For now, we can only suggest that what is indecipherable about 1968—its obscurity, but also its unifying trait—might be precisely enjoyment itself: a dumb, overwhelming intensity that eludes proper representation.[7]

We thus need to take a further step and ask: Who enjoys in the non-relations presented in *Love and Anger*, and how? And what can *Love and Anger* reveal about the intensities of enjoyment that traverse the "obscure event" of 1968?

Enjoyments

For the moment, we will focus on the first four episodes, and return to Bellocchio's *Let's Discuss, Let's Discuss* later on. Let us start with Lizzani's episode. The non-relation between the individual and the *Nebenmensch* that characterizes it is conveyed by way of a certain organization of looking. The indifferent bystanders are cast by Lizzani as spectators of the crimes committed; think for instance about the subjective shots of the courtyard where the rape and murder take place, where the camera scans the space following the victim as she tries to escape, or the blocked view of the shots that depict the violence, with the camera peeking from behind some bushes or through a hole in the wall. The surveillance technology of the police participates, too, in this economy of the desire to look. So the bystanders might be not as indifferent as the segment's title suggests after all; there is enjoyment here, and it is that of the voyeur, who watches from a distance and derives his pleasure from a lack of direct involvement in the scene.

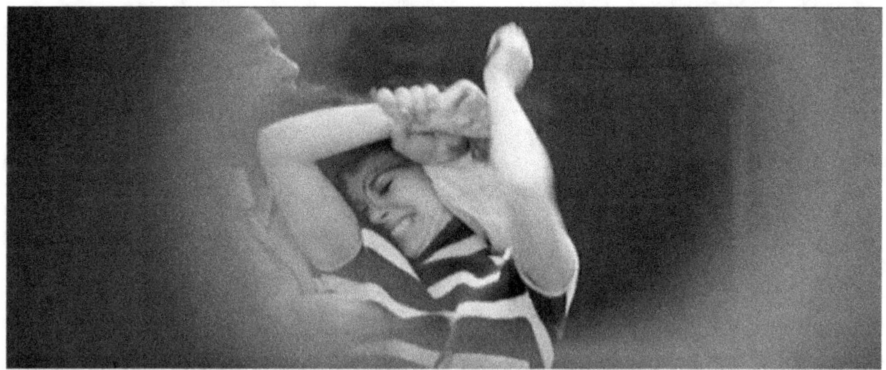

The scopic drive and the spectacle of violence in *Indifference*.

The vicissitudes of the scopic drive portrayed in Lizzani's episode are displaced and reversed in Pasolini's—from the desire to look to the desire not to listen. The radical formal lack of connection among Riccetto's wanderings, the superimposed images, and God's voice emblematizes the protagonist's desire to remain ignorant about the pressing necessity of a conscious political engagement in this historical moment. This sin is ultimately sanctioned by God, and what is God punishing if not Riccetto's enjoyment? He enjoys his ignorance as innocence, and "ignorance is not a sufficient reason for forgiveness since it conveys a hidden dimension of enjoyment. Where one doesn't (want to) know," as Slavoj Žižek puts it, "in the blanks of one's symbolic universe, one enjoys."[8]

Knowing without acting and acting without knowing: indifference and innocence (as ignorance) are two sides of the same coin, two ways of refusing to engage with the present—and of enjoying this non-relation. Within the pedagogical form of the biblical parable, Lizzani and Pasolini are united in their moral condemnation of enjoyment as, respectively, antisocial and antipolitical: the latter assumes—literally—the position of God; the former puts into relief the generosity of the Good Samaritan by contrasting it to the enjoyment of the police's surveilling gaze and the bystanders' voyeurism.

In *Agony*, Bertolucci and The Living Theater take the opposite direction from Lizzani and Pasolini. They wish to unearth in enjoyment an emancipatory potential, and locate it at the intersection of body and language—something that is front and center in Beck and Malina's work. Bertolucci most likely shot his segment in 1968, when The Living Theater was about to complete the European tour it began in 1963. While this five-year period cemented the iconic image of The Living Theater as a wandering anarchist commune, it also influenced their work in very practical ways; as Erika Munk observes, the nomadism from one country (and language) to another forced Beck and Malina to abandon the spoken word as a primary means of expression in their plays.[9] Not incidentally, this phase also marks a shift from the Brechtian influences of the early years to a full embracing of Artaud's theater of cruelty, where the body of the performer becomes a "central source of meaning."[10]

Malina thematizes this shift to corporeality in her diaries, where she writes that "art itself is an externalization of the unspeakable cry."[11] In *Agony*, this "unspeakable cry" takes the form of moans, sighs, screams, vocalizing, and so forth. And in the two exceptions in which this "cry" is articulated into words, the many languages spoken—English, French, German, Italian—only manage to convey the platitude of slogans ("I hope I never do harm to anyone") or the repetition of recitation (Beck recounting the parable). So it is perhaps here, in language, that we can locate the intrusion of enjoyment in *Agony*—not however in the supposedly neutral, communicative language, but in its double, which, like any double, does nothing if not enjoy. Lacan calls it *lalangue*: it is the bodily materiality of the signifier, the nonsensical language that, like in the baby's lallation, produces pleasure in the physicality of its utterance.[12]

The non-relation between the cardinal and his desire that we detected in *Agony* reveals here a further split—namely, the one between desire and enjoyment. As opposed to Lizzani and Pasolini, Bertolucci, Beck, and Malina try to chart the path to a fidelity to the anarcho-pacifist desire through the territory of enjoyment. They wish to deploy *lalangue* as a sort of universal language of emancipation but remain caught in the surplus of non-relational enjoyment it produces. The "unspeakable cry," in its enjoying forms of guttural sounds and screams, remains therefore irremediably disconnected from political desire. Munk criticizes the work of The Living Theater in the late 1960s precisely in these terms, claiming that the group "offered nothing between that cry and the unattainable utopias of nonviolence and anarchy."[13] And what is the recourse to meditation and mysticism (which are such an important part of The Living Theater lore) if not a flawed attempt at bridging the gap between the enjoyment of *lalangue* and political desire—exorcising the fissure by way of its ritualization?

The question of language and its enjoyments is also at the center of Godard's *Love*. The conversations between the two couples in *Love*, abundant with translations and repetitions, emphasize the materiality of the signifiers in a language that is constantly redoubled into a sort of imperfect echo. Indeed, the working title of the episode was the French-Italian mishmash *L'aller et retour andata e ritorno des enfants prodigues dei figli prodighi*, a nod to the bilingualism of the segment, and also an explicit reference to the repetition that every translation implies. But *Love* entertains connections to the enjoyment of *Indifference* as well. The voyeurism stigmatized by Lizzani in his segment is here reintroduced with the figures of the two *testimoni*, who observe the fiancés from a distance, unseen. Their position as voyeurs is reinforced by the bilingual exhortations to look (and to enjoy: "*guardiamo!*," "*regardons!*") that they repeatedly address to each other. As for Pasolini, the refusal to listen in his segment finds its reversal in *Love*, with the *testimoni* who do not just listen, but *listen in* on the couple—the enjoyment of eavesdropping, of hearing unheard and unseen.

Language (and body), gaze, voice: the situation that these terms triangulate in Godard's episode is that of cinema itself, whose name is summoned time and again throughout the episode. The best man and maid of honor, cinephiles at once removed from and involved in the scene, are spectators of the drama of incommunicability between revolution and democracy. But the figure of the spectator hides another one, that of the *witness*. In fact, let us not forget that the best man and maid of honor are also witnesses: "If we're witnesses, we're also observers—we must watch."[14] In *Love*, the incommensurability of democracy and revolution is innervated by the enjoyment of the witness, who wants to see, hear, and speak (through the *lalangue* of repetitions and slogans) this non-relation.

As we have seen, *Love and Anger* is structured on a set of non-relations, gaps in which a certain enjoyment insinuates itself. But if enjoyment permeates the entire film, to what general non-relation is it attached, exactly? To answer this question, we wish to push our argument a little bit further and suggest that the first four segments of the film ultimately define the non-relation (and its enjoyments) as that between the global and the local. *The incommensurability between the local and the global dimensions of the political struggles of 1968 becomes the ultimate non-relation of Love and Anger.*

The international vocation of the film is apparent: the languages spoken, the locations, the participation of artists of various nationalities, and so forth. But on a closer look, the film seems to present the bypassing of local and national boundaries less as a fact than as a horizon of problems and impasses. In *Love*, the couple muses about the global scope of the struggle from a Parisian terrace, so that the non-relation between revolution and democracy is mapped onto an impossible conversation among Italy, France, and the world; Pasolini thematizes precisely this disconnect between the individual and the global historical situation through filmic form, with the superimpositions of newsreel footage onto Riccetto's happy wanderings in via Nazionale; in *Agony*, The Living Theater's invention of a global *lalangue* of emancipation remains confined in the cardinal's narrow quarters; in *Indifference*, finally, the global functions as the erasure of the local: Lizzani travels to the global capital of the world only to look back in nostalgia and mourn the loss of the local as a place of non-alienated existence.

The film and the anthology film form in general stand as witnesses to the non-relation between global and local struggle. In its attempt to address the political struggles of 1968 as a global totality, the anthology film grinds against the difficulty of grasping them as such, of containing them into a coherent form.[15] Badiou's idea of 1968 as a "series of obscure events" finds here a further articulation: not pure multiplicity and heterogeneity (the commonplace of the "many 1968"), but rather a desire for a unitary, "international" grasp that reveals the persistence of the split between the global and local dimensions of the struggle. In this gap, as much as in the recurrence of the failure to bridge it, lies the significance of the anthology film as witness to 1968.

Postscriptum, Postmortem

Let us conclude by returning to *Love and Anger*, and specifically to *Let's Discuss, Let's Discuss*, which is quite literally a postscriptum, an afterthought to the rest of the film, due not only to the lack of Gospel references but also to its uneasy proximity to the actual events of its time. In an interview, Bellocchio looks back at the attempt to work with the student movement while filming, and how this led to a creative impasse: "There was something forced . . . uninspired. It was that use of sarcasm, the mocking of the institution, but without a real or profound conviction . . . as though I had already stopped believing in a certain libertarian dimension of the student protests."[16]

One can see the reasons for Bellocchio's dissatisfaction. The segment stands somewhere between Situationist provocation and Brechtian estrangement but really manages to be nothing more than a poor approximation of both. It is a fully self-conscious farce: "Revolution is not a vaudeville [*varietà*]," a professor quips during the students' sit-in, "and this is not a stage!" Obviously, revolution (this revolution) *is* a vaudeville, and the classroom in the episode is nothing if not a stage. The whole episode is, in fact, a performance—but for whom? Who is watching? Who is enjoying the show?

In a show of his own, the famous "Impromptu at Vincennes," Lacan admonishes the university students of Paris VIII: "You fulfill the role of the helots of this regime. . . . The regime puts you on display; it says: 'Watch them fuck.'"[17] The student protests as antiauthoritarian performances, says Lacan, are a spectacle for the "regime." This regime is not predicated on the old Hegelian master/slave dialectics but on a new set of operations organized into a different discourse—namely, the discourse of the university, which Lacan defines as an "elucidation" of the master's discourse.[18] This shift from the master's discourse to the university discourse lies at the heart of the event of 1968, and *Let's Discuss, Let's Discuss* gives form exactly to this moment of transition. The professors as old masters are shoved aside by the students yet only to make this seemingly subversive gesture into a spectacle for the enjoyment of someone else.

The nature of this enjoyment changes as well: "You are the products of the University," Lacan tells the students, "and you prove that you are surplus value, if only in this: what you not only consent to but actually applaud . . . is that you yourselves emerge from it, equal to more or less credits [*unités de valeur*]. You come here to turn yourselves into units of credit."[19] In the university discourse, enjoyment is *counted*: the surplus becomes quantifiable, and as such it is easily extracted from the subject and integrated into the mass of capital. "Surplus value combines with capital—not a problem, they are homogeneous, we are in the field of values."[20] The demand for an enjoyment without constraints turns therefore into a deadlock: losing enjoyment as an experience of the limit means losing enjoyment altogether. This is where surplus enjoyment coincides with its very opposite, no-more-enjoyment (in French, *plus-de-jouir* means both).[21]

Bellocchio claims that there is "something forced" to the film. Couldn't we read this as the intrusion of the superegoical imperative to enjoy onto the scene of 1968—the "regime" that "puts you on display"? In this sense, as the supplement of *Love and Anger, Let's Discuss, Let's Discuss* would avoid the didactic condemnation of enjoyment (Lizzani, Pasolini), the utopia of its liberating potential (Bertolucci), and the purportedly "neutral" enjoyment of the witness (Godard). Instead, the segment dramatizes a problem: it points to the deadlock of a certain political desire proper to 1968—the desire to liberate enjoyment. In this sense, the postscriptum of *Love and Anger*—a farce—is also a dead-serious postmortem dissection of the libertarian and antiauthoritarian impulses of that event. The student protest reveals its other side: no longer a practice of resistance, but a by-product of the university discourse, like the students themselves. As with the other episodes, the non-relation we first located in *Let's Discuss, Let's Discuss* looks different when observed from the non-neutral perspective of enjoyment: not just an inert division among the professors and the students, but *a fundamental disconnect between the form of the student protest and its political horizon*, a crevice in which the enjoyment of a new master insinuates itself.

As we have seen, the global character of 1968 is constructed by *Love and Anger* as a series of incommensurabilities, so that at the heart of a project that should unify (film movements, political struggles, audiences, and so forth) one only finds irreducible gaps. Non-relation can be, however, politically productive: Alexander Kluge, for one, saw in the non-relations that a film presents to its spectator the possibility to develop an "oppositional public sphere" ("*Gegenöfflichkeit*," a concept that dates back to May 1968). When confronted with discontinuities articulated through montage, the spectator is compelled to intervene and fantasize new relations, and this is where a new collective grasp on reality can emerge. Indeed, Kluge himself explored this idea of oppositional public sphere in another well-known anthology film, *Deutschland im Herbst/Germany in Autumn* (West Germany, 1978).[22] But this utopian aspect of non-relation does not seem to obtain in *Love and Anger*. Rather, the film presents non-relation in all its political ambivalence, with the global emerging as both revolutionary promise and looming defeat.

In fact, one would be tempted to suggest that *Love and Anger* reveals the global as the Other of 1968: on the one hand, the global as Other that is lacking, punctured by discontinuities and non-relations, and yet that stands as a guarantee and support of the political desires of that event. On the other hand, 1968 emerges as the historical turning point at which capitalism managed to radically reinvent itself, letting this global Other become the superegoical imperative to enjoy that characterizes late capitalism. *Love and Anger* inhabits this ambivalence, torn as it is between the desire to provide a unifying horizon for the various geopolitical manifestations of the struggle (a "global 1968"), and, at the same time, the recognition and foregrounding of these nonrelations, together with the enjoyments that permeate them. By thinking the event in terms of desire and enjoyment, *Love and Anger* reactivates for us the latent obscurity of 1968 against so many contemporary discourses that wish to establish once and for all what that event was, what it meant, and what is left of it.

Notes

1. The anthology film form should be distinguished from collective filmmaking: in the anthology film, the directors are individually responsible for their own segments. See David Scott Diffrient, *Omnibus Films: Theorizing Transauthorial Cinema* (Edinburgh: Edinburgh University Press, 2014); and Mark Betz, *Beyond the Subtitle: Remapping European Art Cinema* (Minneapolis: University of Minnesota Press, 2009), 179–244.
2. Lizzani drew inspiration from two news stories: the murder of "Kitty" Genovese in 1964 in Queens, and a car accident on the Brooklyn Bridge that made the cover of *Time* magazine a few years later.
3. Mladen Dolar has addressed the philosophical question of non-relationality from the perspective of psychoanalytical theory. Many aspects of his argument resonate with the present essay. See Mladen Dolar, "Freud and the Political," *Theory and Event* 12, no. 3 (2009). Accessed May 8, 2016, DOI: 10.1353/tae.0.0085.
4. Pier Paolo Pasolini, in *Pasolini on Pasolini: Interviews with Oswald Stack* (London: Thames and Hudson, 1969), 131.
5. Pasolini, *Pasolini on Pasolini*, 131.
6. The expression appears in Alain Badiou, *Manifesto for Philosophy*, ed. and trans. Norman Maradasz (Albany: State University of New York Press, 1999), 89. Badiou comments on it in "Thinking the Emergence of the Event," interview with Emmanuel Burdeau and François Ramone, in Alain Badiou, *Cinema*, trans. Susan Spitzer (Malden, MA: Polity, 2013), 105–28, at 109.

7. See Joan Copjec, "May '68, The Emotional Month," in *Lacan: The Silent Partners*, ed. Slavoj Žižek (New York: Verso, 2006), 90–114.
8. Slavoj Žižek, *For They Know Not What They Do: Enjoyment as a Political Factor* (New York: Verso, 2008), 2.
9. Erika Munk, "Only Connect: The Living Theater and Its Audiences," in *Restaging the Sixties: Radical Theaters and Their Legacies*, ed. James M. Harding and Cindy Rosenthal (Ann Arbor: University of Michigan Press, 2006), 33–55, at 43.
10. Munk, "Only Connect," 43.
11. Judith Malina, "March 17, 1952," in *The Diaries of Judith Malina, 1947–1957* (New York: Grove Press, 1984), 253. Cited in Munk, "Only Connect," 33.
12. See Jacques Lacan, "La Troisième," *Lettres de l'École freudienne* 16 (1975): 177–203; and Jacques Lacan, *Television*, trans. Dennis Hollier, Rosalind Krauss, and Annette Michelson (New York: Norton, 1990). For a critical overview of the concept, see Colette Soler, *Lacan: The Unconscious Reinvented* (London: Karnac, 2014), 25–38. Julia Kristeva has developed—and even anticipated—Lacan's formulations about enjoyment in language. See Julia Kristeva, *Revolution in Poetic Language*, trans. Leon S. Roudiez (New York: Columbia University Press, 1984), 13–106.
13. Munk, "Only Connect," 49.
14. This is a recurring motif in *Love and Anger*: "My name doesn't matter, neither does yours. But I am a witness," declares one the visitors in *Agony*; in Pasolini, the witness is present in its negation, for Riccetto is defined by his staunch refusal to confront history, and what are the bystanders in *Indifference* if not the silent witnesses of the atrocities perpetrated by the *Homo economicus* of late capitalism?
15. A film like *Loin du Vietnam/Far from Vietnam* (France, 1967) offers another example of this dynamic.
16. Interview with Marco Bellocchio in *Behind Love and Anger* (special feature of the DVD of *Love and Anger* released by Noshame in 2005).
17. Jacques Lacan, "Impromptu at Vincennes," in *Television*, 128.
18. Jacques Lacan, *The Seminar, Book XVII: The Other Side of Psychoanalysis*, trans. Russell Grigg (New York: Norton, 2007), 148.
19. Lacan, "Impromptu at Vincennes," 121.
20. Lacan, *Other Side*, 178.
21. See Alenka Zupančič, "When Surplus Enjoyment Meets Surplus Value," in

Jacques Lacan and the Other Side of Psychoanalysis, ed. Justin Clemens and Russell Grigg (Durham, NC: Duke University Press, 2007), 155–78.

22. See Alexander Kluge, Thomas Y. Levin, and Miriam Hansen, "On Film and the Public Sphere," *New German Critique* 24–25 (Autumn 1981–Winter 1982): 206–20; and Miriam Hansen, "Cooperative Auteur Cinema and Oppositional Public Sphere: Alexander Kluge's Contribution to *Germany in Autumn*," *New German Critique* 24–25 (Autumn 1981–Winter 1982): 36–56.

II

Aftershocks

Re-presenting the "Just Image"

Godard-Gorin's *Vent d'est* and the Radical Thwartedness of Maoist Solidarity after May 1968

Man-tat Terence Leung

In the wake of the political watershed of the May '68 movements in France, renowned French-Swiss filmmaker Jean-Luc Godard realized that the proper direction in political cinema was not simply to "make political films" but to "make films politically" as a militant group.[1] Established in the winter of 1968 by Godard, Jean-Pierre Gorin, and an ensemble of young French Maoists, the Groupe Dziga Vertov (Dziga Vertov Group, or DVG) was one of the first pioneering film collectives to practice and experiment with Maoist politics and group authorship in cinema during the long sixties.[2] Unlike another famous film collective during that time, Société pour la lancement des oeuvres nouvelles (Society for the Creation of New Works, or SLON), established by Chris Marker and his Groupe Medvedkine, the DVG endeavored to adopt a formalist approach to cinema with "claims for self-reflexivity, collectivity, and class consciousness."[3]

Although the aesthetic orientation of this rather elusive Maoist period of Godard seems to be radically at odds with his early auteur years and his later metaphysical and metahistorical explorations, it is equally important to keep in mind that his works made between 1968 and 1972 are often unfairly misconstrued and dismissed as either an egalitarian failure or a didactic exercise. Taking one of the most representative works of the DVG, *Vent d'est/The Wind from the East* (1969), as the point of departure, this essay seeks to rehistoricize the Mao-leaning years of Godard in the political aftermath of French May '68, which continues the intense debates over the Sino-Soviet split of the 1950s with certain new and unexpected philosophical twists. In particular, it will show how this collective film produced shortly after May '68, despite carrying a certain irreducible error of its own, may have actually advanced a new kind of dialectical thinking in political filmmaking that radically complicates the classic antidoctrinal aesthetic paradigm of what Peter Wollen called "counter-cinema" a few decades ago. Moreover, this essay will also point out that a critical rereading of *Vent d'est* in relation to the highly heterogeneous and dividing interpretations of "Maoist solidarity" during the European leftist heyday not only is constitutive in helping to resurface many unrealized revolutionary potentialities pertaining to Godard's cinematic radicalism of the 1960s as such but also sheds new light on the continuous problematization of the reigning global capitalist discourse and its allying neoliberal ideology today. Although the discursive construct of neoliberal capitalism becomes increasingly obligatory and predominating in the current scene, there remains much room for our perpetual imaginations of various kinds of utopian possibilities in relation to the profound emancipatory spirit of global 1968 at large.

The Flawed Revolutionary Alliances after May '68

Of all the DVG films, *Vent d'est* is thought to be the most radical experiment in reworking the established relationship between image and sound that characterizes Godard's auteur period. Although Godard's cinema is long distinguished for its deconstructive traits among his other Nouvelle Vague fellows, the filmmaker believed that his works produced prior to 1968 fell radically short of true Marxist-Leninist elements and revolutionary dialectics. Contrary to his early auteur films such as *À bout de soufflé/Breathless* (1960) and *Masculin féminin/Masculine Feminine* (1966), which predominantly relied on the experimentations of jump cuts and other new visual cues, Godard's *Vent d'est* instead makes use of voice-overs, especially female commentaries, to present a dense political discourse and self-criticism on May '68 and its aftermath. Yet no single reading strategy offers a correct or universal formula for the characters' actions. The film presents its political and philosophical concepts in a very lenient and eclectic fashion, thus forcing the audience to evaluate them if they are to "understand" the film at all.

Reducing the storyline to a bare minimum, *Vent d'est* uses typical characters taken from the Western genre, both nominally and visually, to symbolize the essential figures during the uprisings in May '68. A cavalryman symbolically represents "the ruling class" or "a capitalist," while an Indian represents the "working class" or "proletariat"; a pretty young lady and a handsome young man are the equivalents of the "bourgeois student protestors," while a union delegate portrays the "revisionist trade union" in France; finally, an elusive figure named Miss Althusser symbolizes the abject position French Marxist philosopher Louis Althusser experienced shortly after May '68. Divided into several chapters—namely "The Strike," "The Delegate," "The Active Minorities," "The General Assembly," "Repression," "The Active Strike," and "The Police State," *Vent d'est* addresses issues like the various ideological conflicts and debates experienced in May '68, the post-1968 political currents in France, Lenin's commentary on left-wing infantilism, socialist self-management in Yugoslavia during the 1960s, egalitarian medical welfare in Maoist China, the necessity of revolutionary violence, and the relationships and contradictions between European political cinema and Third World cinema.

The opening shot of *Vent d'est* is perhaps the most revealing example of how the DVG's philosophy of image-sound dissociation has found its specific discursive position. In this eight-minute static long take, a young bourgeois couple is lying in a field without any apparent actions or dialogues. While the on-screen images seem to be rather motionless, the parallel soundtrack features mixed opinions from the different perspectives of a manager's family, trade union delegates, and working-class proletariats, who are all commenting on a (fictional) miner's strike that is taking place in France in 1968.[4] Interestingly, the intrusion of the voice-over commentary on the nascent scene can be seen as something like a "strike" that aims at disrupting the apparent visual status quo. The voice-over does not seek to explain the on-screen images; instead, it challenges the stability and consistency of them. James Roy MacBean comments that "in fact, when the voice-over 'commentary' finally breaks in, what we get is not dialogue but a critique of dialogue."[5]

According to the dominant historiography about May '68, the profound failure of the student-worker alliances during the events simply resulted from the fact that the two protesting groups lacked true dialogues and mutual understanding throughout the course of their revolutionary development.

For example, with regard to the failed alliance between the students and the workers during May '68, Marxist philosopher Louis Althusser, one of several left-leaning academic pioneers who introduced systematic Maoist thinking to the European leftist scene during the mid-1960s, argues that "the truth is that the entire working class, and not just its leadership, was not, in general, at all disposed to 'follow' the suggestions of the students, which were based more on a dream-experience than on an understanding of reality."[6] Althusser believes that the students were far too indulged in their spontaneous actions during the "Night of the Barricades" on May 13, 1968, and hence they bypassed the crucial moment of the worker-led insurrections that came afterward. Recuperating Lenin's critique of left-wing infantilism during the early twentieth century, Althusser laments that the bourgeois French students somehow misrecognized themselves as the revolutionary vanguard where "in May it was the working class, and not the students, who, in the final analysis, played the determining role."[7] The so-called student-worker marriage in 1968 became, according to Althusser, a mere "historic encounter" rather than an "organic fusion" insofar as there were no concrete demands and sensible agendas made during the alliance. He succinctly points out that "an encounter may occur or not occur. It can [be] a 'brief encounter,' relatively accidental, in which case it will not lead to any fusion or forces."[8]

What the film *Vent d'est* may have wanted to highlight, however, is that the revolutionary demands between the students and the workers were never preontologically opposed. Rather, the loss of the true revolutionary alliance between these two protesting groups was largely attributed to the idiosyncratic mediation of another left-leaning body—the trade union delegate. In *Vent d'est*, the trade union delegates always speak two languages—French and Italian.[9] On the one hand, this dual linguistic advantage gives them a sort of extra privilege with which to smooth the conflicts between both the insurrectionary class and the ruling authorities, but, on the other hand, this exceptional position also allows the union delegate to manipulate the class interests of the proletariats. As such, the "Italian" language in *Vent d'est* has a highly negative meaning of "promiscuity" and "obscenity," specifically emphasized in a scene featuring the seductive, womanizing "charm" of a handsome young Italian man.[10] The two directors point out that the trade union officials, who are sent from the French Communist Party as a kind of political "translator," not only fail to facilitate concrete dialogues between the students and the workers but also intensify the gulf of misunderstanding between the protestors. Consequently, the trade union does not truly ally with the proletarian subjects but actually stands for the interests of the reigning bourgeoisie. The ideological function of trade-unionism has rendered the true antagonistic edges of the working-class and the proletarian subjects rather obsolete and invisible, thus indirectly facilitating the existing power in maintaining its social status quo.[11]

In order to truly "make films politically," Godard and Gorin realize that it is both important and necessary to make a film that cannot be easily comprehended and translated by typical bourgeois language and its linguistic conventions. Julia Lesage points out that *Vent d'est* is one of the first films from which the educated Western audiences and bourgeoisies can learn nothing except about the fundamental poverty of the language of bourgeois cinema.[12] After the profound political awakening of May '68, renowned critic Peter Wollen argued that Godard-Gorin's *Vent d'est* had actually demonstrated and put forward a new form of counteraesthetics—namely, "counter-cinema" that aims at radically thwarting the cultural taste of the dominant class and bourgeois audiences.[13] The main argument of Wollen's counter-cinema is that Godard and Gorin seek to defamiliarize and estrange the usual conception of Western narrative cinema by means of constant disruptions, digressions, and interventions throughout the process of image building in the film.[14]

Although such counteraesthetics may have upset the bourgeois cinematic paradigm to a certain extent, there is also a highly important aspect of Wollen's argument that has usually been overlooked:

> The cinema cannot show the truth, or reveal it, because the truth is not out there in the real world, waiting to be photographed. What the cinema can do is produce meanings and meanings can only be plotted, not in relation to some abstract yardstick or criterion of truth, but in relation to other meanings. This is why Godard's objective of promoting a counter-cinema is the right objective. But he is mistaken if he thinks that such a counter-cinema can have an absolute existence. It can only exist in relation to the rest of cinema. Its function is to struggle against the fantasies, ideologies and aesthetic devices of one cinema with its antagonistic fantasies, ideologies and aesthetic devices.[15]

Despite the fact that this theoretical remark of Wollen is specifically inserted into the last part of his writing as a sort of alarming supplement, it has traditionally been overshadowed by the same article's mention of seven famous aesthetic traits that radically antagonize classical narrative cinema and counter-cinema.[16] On a closer rereading of such an important component in Wollen's thesis, however, I argue that the sheer oppositional relationship between classical cinema and counter-cinema as such is never totally innocent but is instead inherently leaky and incomplete. That is to say, this very antagonistic posture between these two types of cinema, far from being a self-evident injunction, has to be dialectically juxtaposed with a specific cultural situation. The subversive potential of counter-cinema cannot simply be absolutized or moralized as an uncontested discourse beyond the existing social correspondence. Rather, similar to the classical cinematic narrative, which often brutally truncates the complexity of reality as certain abstract yardsticks within Wollen's aforementioned paradigm, the transgressive aesthetics of counter-cinema are not entirely exempted from giving the same kinds of theoretical abstractions or historical reductions, and are therefore constantly subjected to possible critiques and self-critiques.

Unfortunately, this irreducible aspect of nondialectical abstraction pertaining to countercinema still lingers in many of the DVG films. After 1968, Godard and his allies were very self-conscious about how Western narrative films have long been hijacked to help promote the dominant bourgeois ideology in the form of commercial entertainment and artistic elitism. One major objective of the DVG was, therefore, to transform the bourgeois dimension of cinematic theater into a classroom of revolutionary aspirations and class politics through an overarching use of voice-overs. As such, there is a major paradigm shift in the role of women as a particular type of liberated "educator" or "schoolteacher" in Godardian cinema in the aftermath of 1968. According to Serge Daney, "the master-discourse is, after 1968, somewhat systematically born by the voice of a woman. This means that Godardian pedagogy implies a distribution of roles and discourses by sex. The voice which reprimands, resumes, advises, teaches, explains, theorizes and even terrorizes/theorizes is always a woman's voice."[17] As Julia Lesage argues, to a certain extent, this ubiquitous presence of the female voice-overs as a kind of political "teacher" in *Vent d'est* could have made up for the relative lack of self-agency of women during the uprisings in May '68.[18]

This shift does not necessarily mean, however, that the political appropriation of the "female voice" in *Vent d'est* is totally unproblematic. Indeed, by casually absolutizing and moralizing the female commentary as the ultimate maxim or injunction of the film, these subversive gestures of Godard and Gorin can be fairly annoying from time to time. For example, the tone of the female voices is usually highly repetitive, mechanical, and prescriptive in this Godard-Gorin work, while its speed is so fast that it seems to elude any comprehension. On some occasions, the voice injunctions in *Vent d'est*, instead of simply counterproposing a new aesthetic that allows the audience an alternative viewing position beyond the existing bourgeois conception of art, even conveniently didacticize and universalize the "correct" objective of the two filmmakers as an unshakable revolutionary principle. What is really at stake here is that the latent manipulative position of the directors has been radically concealed by this bold, oversimplistic feminizing gesture. The mediating aspect of the DVG films, which is paradoxically covered up or protected by its overt liberating move, left little room for debates and queries. Daney further describes Godard's vision of woman as "strange feminism": "He puts woman (voice, sound) in the place of what spells out the law (the 'correct thinking' whose phallic character is easily understood) and of what gives life. . . . It is not certain that feminist claims will be contended with this 'place' men want no more, this 'power' they want to abdicate."[19]

In fact, within the textual level of *Vent d'est*, there is a highly idiosyncratic scene orbiting around an elusive female character called "Miss Althusser." Played by the same heroine, Anne Wiazemsky, who resembles a young student revolutionary in a previous part of the film, Miss Althusser is a university lecturer who teaches the doctrines of Marxism-Leninism to young students and workers. In a minor section titled "*Pedagogie*" ("Pedagogy") there are two main characters: one is a trade union delegate, who dresses in a fancy coat, and the other is Miss Althusser, who is responsible for teaching the young intellectuals and the working class the correct Marxist principles. Yet Miss Althusser plays a largely subordinated role compared to the Italian-speaking union official. Each time Miss Althusser distributes her theoretical writings to the workers and the students, she must first submit them to the male trade union delegate for endorsement and comments.

Miss Althusser does not enjoy her teaching position. For example, when she is teaching how the university system has tragically become an ideological state apparatus, she immediately receives a massive negative response from her students. A young male student suddenly comes into view and hijacks her teaching. He occupies the left side of her desk and shouts out sentences that explicitly demand proletarian struggles (for example, "Fiat is our university!"). He immediately receives great and ecstatic support from the audience. Shortly afterward, a peasant holds up a hammer to his chest as a sign to move forward to concrete revolutionary insurrection. Miss Althusser's audience therefore compels her to perform an open "self-criticism." She is transmuted first by the male union official and second by the young students and workers, who are also predominantly men.[20] In this respect, many commentators have questioned whether Godard's cinematic Maoism is just another name for his "Stalinist" mode of filmmaking. Film critic Andrew Britton even comments that *Vent d'est* is arguably "one of the most repressive films ever made."[21] He continues by saying, "The film precisely forbids analysis, or, rather the analysis has been made, and the only positions left are those of unbeliever or proselytizer."[22]

Actually, Godard's potential misogyny and sexism may have been constantly concealed by his overt passion for Maoist politics since the mid-1960s. In his first Mao-leaning film, *La Chinoise/The Chinese Woman* (1967), one of the two female characters, Yvonne, is idiosyncratically cast as a domestic slave who lacks consistent political vision or intellectual clout in a Maoist revolutionary group comprised of several young students. In *La Chinoise*, it is always the two male protagonists, Guillaume and Henri, who lead and initiate the Maoist discussions, whereas the female characters usually serve as a passive backdrop. Unlike the main heroine Véronique (also performed by Anne Wiazemsky), who is eventually bestowed an armed revolutionary mission, the marginal figure, Yvonne, is problematically relegated to almost all of the domestic housework for the Maoist group, like a submissive mother or housewife. She even has to become a prostitute to sustain the daily expenditures of the Maoist cell. Film critic Douglas Morrey notes that "whereas the male figures are both convincing in their roles and come across as articulate exponents of sincerely held political views, the women in *La Chinoise* appear unconvincing and proffer comically inept or dangerously unthought-out opinions."[23] Seen in this light, it is particularly strange to see that while the whole revolutionary group seems to celebrate "Maoist egalitarianism" on the one hand, many of the male members paradoxically spend much time teasing and exploiting Yvonne's weaknesses in reading the political and philosophical texts on the other hand.[24] In short, there may have always been certain self-contradictions silently inhered in Godard's Maoist yearning, which is perpetually caught between proletarian liberation and Stalinist repression, or egalitarianism and sexism, as seen in the pre-1968 making of *La Chinoise*.[25]

The "Sino-Soviet Split" Reloaded

But while the above is true, it is also true that neither "sexism" nor "Stalinism" has proven to be adequate in explaining the profound complexity and ambivalence of this Godard-Gorin film. Those who simply dismiss *Vent d'est* as a repressive cinematic practice may have also overlooked a crucial scene in this work where the two directors seek to overtly question and problematize their latent "Stalinist" implications from the outset. As Colin MacCabe remarks, the key sequence of *Vent d'est* is diegetically structured around a parallel picture of Stalin and Mao taken from an Italian left-wing newspaper with the words "Wanted for Murder" painted on them, as well as a Pepsi advertisement placed right above it.[26] Thematically, this main narrative documents a mass meeting of various Mao-leaning crewmembers debating whether the idiosyncratic image of Stalin should be included in the film. The sequence alternately shows two pictures—one is a Pepsi advertisement and the other is of Stalin (whose face is scored out with heavy black lines) and Mao (whose face remains untouched). Each shot is supplemented by a female voice-over commentary.

The use of this picture of Stalin immediately divides the opinions of the Maoist-libertarian collective. Some members argue that the image of Stalin should not be included because it will remind the audience of the brutal Stalinist repressions that occurred in postwar eastern Europe. The other half of the crew holds the opposite opinion, that Stalin's picture should be included in the film. As for these comrades, the image of Stalin embodies the highly problematic Stalinist legacy that has fervently been debated in Europe since the late 1950s. More specifically, the "Stalinist question" here refers to the "cult of personality" and the extensive bureaucratic network developed by Joseph Stalin during his reign, effectively catalyzing the so-called Sino-Soviet split between Mao's China and Khrushchev's Soviet Union after the onset of the 1960s.[27] Those who support the inclusion of Stalin's picture believe that Stalinism is actually a kind of perversion, rather than a betrayal, of the socialist development prescribed by orthodox Marxism-Leninism. That is to say, regardless of how many controversies and arguments are provoked during that epoch, the so-called Stalinist deviation from the orthodox or teleological pathways of Marxist development is still part of the whole leftist spectrum and trajectory during the long twentieth century. Any premature censure of this Stalinist transgression simply keeps perpetuating the same exclusive mindset of what has been previously excluded and denied by Stalinism per se. Indeed, such a presumptive purification of Stalinist errors of various kinds still confers a form of intellectual "repression" on the founding epistemological questions posed by this problematic issue. That is why one of the anonymous characters laments later in *Vent d'est*: "It's always the same. You are anti-Stalin, but you still make Stalinist images." The female voice-over goes on to discuss the very genesis of this film:

> Why is there an ever-changing relationship between these images and sounds? The intention was to talk about what we experienced in May '68 . . . In May and June '68, the established powers retaliated and repressed these revolutionary groups in France, Italy, Spain and Mexico. The filming of the general assembly was therefore the filming of the general assembly, which debated the following sequence, in which the making of images and sounds of this repression is discussed.

According to Steve Cannon, "the *Groupe Dziga Vertov* were situated at the 'harder' end of French Maoism, more 'M-L' [Marxist-Leninist] than '*Spontex*.'"[28] One has to keep in mind, however, that the sheer "hardline orthodoxy," if not "political didacticism," of the DVG is in fact never preontologically conditioned or inherited. Rather, the "Stalinist" implications of *Vent d'est* as such are always culturally negotiated and historically overdetermined. In the summer of 1969, when Godard and Gorin receive financial support from an Italian tycoon to make their film without traditional institutional constraints, the duo fantasized that they could work perfectly together with several young anarchists and libertarians, including 1968 icon Daniel Cohn-Bendit, in Italy to demonstrate their political solidarity toward the rapid restoration of a capitalist ethos in France shortly after 1968. On the film set, the crew decided to work together as a nonbureaucratic collective throughout the production, filming on the basis of political discussions and collective arguments indebted to Maoist insights on the "mass-line."[29]

Unfortunately, the ideal collaboration between Godard and the other Mao-leaning activists did not entirely work out in making *Vent d'est*, as the cinematic ideas given by Cohn-Bendit were not fully accepted by the group. The original mining strike proposed by Cohn-Bendit is rendered as "just fragments of narrative on the soundtrack in the opening section."[30] The creative voices of the younger libertarian members are therefore radically silenced in the final version of the film. One of the young crewmembers remembers that the shooting of *Vent d'est* sounded "like a comic nightmare in which the collective delusions of '68 were distilled into their purest form."[31] Yet, as Gorin personally recounts, during the making of *Vent d'est*, "there were twenty-nine people doing the script collectively and after two days, three-quarters of those guys were at the beach and Jean-Luc [Godard] and I were alone doing that film, which took us six months to put together."[32] With regard to the inherent predicaments of collective filmmaking, Godard also admits: "To make a film as a political group is very difficult for the moment, because we are more in the position politically of just individuals trying to go on the same road. A group means not only individuals walking side by side on the same road, but walking together politically."[33]

In fact, collective filmmaking was a rather fashionable practice among European leftist art circles between the late 1960s and early 1970s. After the wake of May '68, renowned Maoist documentarian Joris Ivens and several young French militants made a collective film called *Le peuple et ses fusils/The People and Their Guns* (1969) in Laos in order to show the world the marginalized struggles of the Pathet Lao against the feudal tradition of the country as well as the military intervention of the United States. According to Ivens, this collective documentary, however, turned out to be a profound failure; he thereby coined both the so-called democratic environment and egalitarian method advocated by the Laos film collective as an emblem of a "small-minded atmosphere."[34] Produced, like Godard-Gorin's *Vent d'est*, outside of France, the collected work made by Ivens and other young French militants in Laos was originally based on a "democratic" approach, purified of any cinematic hierarchies. Yet as the film shooting proceeded, the excessive creative freedom soon became suffocating and unbearable. The endless debates among the various individuals in the group turned the editing of the film into a protracted and painful process. Recounting the film process in an interview, Ivens recalled that it was actually counterproductive and overbearing to "[have] ten people around the cutting table discussing and then voting where to make the cut."[35]

Interestingly, unlike Ivens's abovementioned discontents about Western nonhierarchical cinematic productions, which he realized after he made his documentary in Laos, the comparable "failure" of collective and self-organized filmmaking was, instead, even self-reflexively placed at the textual level of Godard-Gorin's *Vent d'est*.[36] In one scene in *Vent d'est*, a female voice-over comments on the Soviet policies of the "workers' self-management" in Tito's Yugoslavia. Each line of the critique on the Soviet experiment of self-management in the Eastern Bloc is thereby read over a red freeze frame alternated with a scratched-up image of the film's production crew, along with a chain of on-screen sounds. This sequence features snatches of voices explaining how the film is made, but there is no coherent picture of how the ideas are worked out in the general assembly as a whole. Julia Lesage suggests that the scratched-up image represents the irreducible failure inherent in the idea of Maoist collective filmmaking from scratch.[37] Seen in this light, Godard-Gorin's *Vent d'est* seems to bear witness to the profound deadlock between the two major ideological currents—anarcho-libertarianism and Marxism-Leninism—both of which equally characterized and stigmatized the post-1968 leftist intellectual scene in western Europe.

Coda: The Godardian Phrase-Image

Suffice it to say that both Godard and Gorin are not, strictly speaking, devoted French Maoists like those eloquent members and activists of the popular Maoist group Gauche prolétarienne (Proletarian Left). Although Godard joined Mao-leaning luminary Jean-Paul Sartre several times in distributing the banned Maoist newspaper *La Cause du peuple* (*The Cause of the People*) at railway stations and wrote several articles for a famous Maoist journal, *J'accuse* (*I Accuse*), he did not, unlike most of the French Maoists of the time, simply engage in the proletarian practice of *établissement* (settling down) in the factories or undergo an overt ideological education through farm work and manual labor.[38] Instead, both Godard and Gorin always maintained a rather ambiguous relationship and fraternity with the major currents of French Maoism during this era.[39] In their final DVG film, *Tout va bien/Everything's Fine* (1972), the two directors offer a subtle (self-)critique of the dominant revolutionary tactics of French Maoism. The famous ten-minute-long tracking shot in a large supermarket that is occupied by both "leftists" and "rightists" promoting their goods and ideas in *Tout va bien*, slowly panning to the right and subsequently to the left, perfectly crystallizes the two filmmakers' rising ideological confusion about the reigning Maoist practices during the early 1970s. To Godard and Gorin, rightism and leftism as such may not have always stood in absolute antagonism. Rather, at a certain level, these "isms" may have been just two sides of the same coin. Therefore, it would be far too simplistic to conveniently classify *Vent d'est* as sheer evidence of communal impossibility or leftist failure, as such a pessimistic account would exactly help perpetuate the dominant neoliberal discourse of these days, which usually holds the view that the events of May '68 were nothing more than a thwarted revolutionary episode, an elusive revolt that eventually and inevitably melted into the air.

I argue that the current predominant neoliberal notion, which simply takes the political failure of 1968 for granted, should be critically problematized and rehistoricized so as to truly go beyond the existing dismissive evaluations and judgments on Western political cinema of the 1960s. Although the stigma of egalitarian failure may seem obvious and outstanding in *Vent d'est*, it is equally important to identify the inherent limits pertaining to such a dismissive discourse, which often oversimplistically treats this very literal, particular thwartedness of leftist filmmaking as the structural impasse of radical leftism at large. That is to say, the reigning discursive construct of contemporary neoliberalism, far from being an all-encompassing notion, may have always-already been thwarted and defeated in its very universalization. Similar to the aforementioned "Stalinist" signifier, the existing neoliberal consensus on the leftist failure of the 1960s may also carry an insurmountable level of epistemological limitation from the outset. Thus, it cannot fully repress utopian possibilities from emerging. In fact, although the signifier of "repression" may appear omnipresent and incessant in *Vent d'est*, it has been constantly rendered a radically impotent or generic status by Godard and Gorin. As Peter Wollen remarks, "the sequences in which the image of Stalin is discussed are not simply—or even principally—about Stalin's politics, as much as they are about the problem of finding an image to signify 'repression.'"[40]

In fact, there is a relatively minor yet very important narrative that is elusively attached to the sequence about the problematic "scratched-up image" mentioned in the former part. By inserting an intertitle annotated with the phrase—"*Ce n'est pas une image juste, c'est juste une image*" ("This is not a just image, this is just an image")—into the visual images of the defining "Stalinist debates," the two directors are warning that this kind of "failed image" is not a "just image" per se; it is "just an image" at its most literal level. On closer inspection of this scene, I argue that the two directors may also have wanted to emphasize an even more primordial fact for left-leaning cinematic representation of the 1960s: the very visual message that orients our comprehension of the film, far from being a totally unproblematic image in itself, is, nonetheless, a bare image and nothing more. That is to say, this phrasal expression offered by the filmmakers is not entirely freed or exempted from its inherent failure; the phrase and the image are not totally allied as a self-explanatory couple. Within the textual level of *Vent d'est*, their causal relationship has always-already been short-circuited. Like the "Stalinist image" the film seeks to (re-) present in vain, the Godardian annotation here is never simply a self-evident dictum that forecloses the audience's interpretations. What is precisely lacking in this cinematic work is a metanarrative or a transcendental diegesis that can grant the phrase "*Ce n'est pas une image juste, c'est juste une image*" an absolute authority and unquestionable legitimacy in accounting for the scratched-up image. In this respect, the true profundity of *Vent d'est* may lie in the fact that it has excessively showcased both its emancipatory potentials and epistemological predicaments in relation to the master signifier of "repression" that has historically emerged after the political watershed of 1968. And by doing so, the symbolic consistency of this film may be sharply undermined as a result.

In *The Future of the Image*, Jacques Rancière conceptualizes and defines the "phrase-image" (or "sentence-image") on various occasions, in a variety of discourses and across multiple media and art forms. By phrase-image, Rancière refers to "the combination of two functions that are to be defined aesthetically—that is, by the way in which they undo the representative relationship between text and image."[41] He adds: "It is the unit that divides the chaotic force of the great parataxis into phrasal power of continuity and imaging power of rupture."[42] According to Rancière, "phrase-image" and its analogous term "montage" are understood as immanent responses to the disorder unleashed by the aesthetic regime of post-1968 capitalist societies. They denominate devices of new aesthetic reasoning that not only admit the latent heterogeneity of artistic resources but also help prevent the autonomy of art from collapsing into pure nonsense or convenient doxa.[43]

In this phrase-image, Rancière warns, the phrase or sentence does not simply equal the sayable, nor does the image entirely match the visible. In some sense, the phrase is both the sayable and the visible, and neither. Similarly, to some extent the image is neither the visible nor the sayable, and both. The sayable and the visible are released from their individual form and function, and their distinct qualities are dispersed and distributed over the image's various functions. Instead of harmoniously working together, the disordered materials of the sayable and the visible that "hang together" in the phrase-image manufacture the effects of dissonance while maintaining some semblance of meaningful connectivity or collective "measure" between the different filmic components. In short, the phrase-image is both continuous and ruptured, both an attempt at coherent articulation and a stigma of the impossibility of that articulation.[44] The true liberating potential pertaining to the phrase-image lies in its sheer oscillatory position between the visibility and the audibility with regard to the question of narrative continuity, which gives rise to new and dialectical connections that reopen, rather than foreclose, the initial intensity and expressions of the two primordial elements.

Unlike the Soviet montage school, which tends to hierarchize the eventual, synthesized cinematic connotations over the two primordial visual components, the Godardian phrase-image in *Vent d'est* is, however, unable to fully claim and capture the same kind of transcendental self-presence or self-transparency. Instead, this alternative form of montage is not really an act of ideal balance or suture between the opposite elements. It still bears a striking resemblance to the generic image of "repression" from the outset, yet the phrase-image is not purely a nominal image that fails to exert any influence or interruption over the reigning narrative structure. Rather, by suggesting a residual or paratextual connection between the contrastive images, this elusive combination could even help flesh out a profoundly egalitarian vision that is often overlooked or excluded by the ruling aesthetic distribution and consensual doxa. In retrospect, although the Godardian phrase-image in *Vent d'est* has somewhat materialized the profound ontological failure of bridging post-1968 emancipatory ideas and traditional film authorship, its paratextual dissensus with the intricate historical realities of the time may actually help prevent us from giving a simple dichotomous conclusion between "ideological repression" and "aesthetic liberation" in relation to the very understanding and evaluation of Western political cinema itself. In the meantime, these highly experimental visual and audio compositions pertaining to the DVG films, on closer rereading, may also have prompted contemporary individuals to reconsider the true dialectical relationship between the legacies of global 1968 and the predominant discursive logic of contemporary neoliberalism at large. Although this currently reigning neoliberal system has often retroactively associated the ideas of 1960s left-wing radicalism with some negative moral connotations such as "disastrous errors" and "historical failures," it remains to be seen whether the obligatory discourse as such is fully unproblematic and self-evident throughout its ever-shifting, radically decentered epistemic constructions in the global world.

Notes

1. During the Cannes film festival in May 1968, Godard heavily fumed at one journalist who asked him something about his films' aesthetics instead of the ongoing happenings of 1968. Godard shouted, "I'm talking to you about solidarity, and you talk about tracking shots. You're a bastard!" See Peter Cowie, *Revolution!: The Explosion of World Cinema in the 60s* (London: Faber and Faber, 2004), 202. In a dialogue between Kaja Silverman and Harun Farocki to comment on Godard's *Le gai savoir/The Gay Knowledge* (1968) produced shortly before *Vent d'est*, they both agreed that compared to Stalin's dictatorship of the party, Maoist Cultural Revolution seemed to offer a more authentic revolutionary model to the young intellectuals in France during the 1960s, insofar as "Mao actually provides a much easier access than classical Marxism to a position of untroubled knowledge." See Kaja Silverman and Harun Farocki, *Speaking about Godard* (New York: New York University Press, 1998), 121–22. In particular, there is even a scene in *Le gai savoir* where the camera focuses on a poster with the words: "*Mao sait tout*

(Mao knows everything)."

2. The Groupe Dziga Vertov was named after the Soviet revolutionary documentarian Dziga Vertov. The DVG members believed that Vertov had succeeded in his struggle on two political fronts—the Soviet tradition influenced by "revisionist" filmmaker Sergei Eisenstein and the commercial style of Hollywood cinema.
3. Trevor Stark, "'Cinema in the Hands of the People': Chris Marker, the Medvedkine Group, and the Potential of Militant Film," *October* 139 (Winter 2012): 117–50, at 119.
4. In her important study *May '68 and Its Afterlives*, Kristin Ross argues that the popular historiography and neoliberal consensus on the events of May '68 have been traditionally predominated by a narcissistic, Paris-centric mindset that not only recklessly reduces the temporal activities of 1968 to the two elusive months between May and June 1968 but also brutally confines the spatialities of the whole movement to the city of Paris, particularly the Latin Quarter. According to Ross, May '68 is, first and foremost, a radically heterogeneous, multiregional political event that encompasses both the profound student-worker alliances and the timely anti-imperial struggles occurring in a number of countries, including Vietnam, Italy, Cuba, Algeria, and China, from the early 1960s to the contemporary epoch. See Kristin Ross, *May '68 and Its Afterlives* (Chicago: University of Chicago Press, 2002), 9–10. In fact, there are certain less well-known fiction features and documentaries about the strikes of 1968 that have somewhat problematized the spatiotemporal confines of such dominant historiography on the French May '68. *Classe de lutte/Class of Struggle* (1969) filmed by the Groupe Medvedkine, Chris Marker's *Le fond de l'air est rouge/A Grin without a Cat* (1977) and his collaborative work with Mario Marret, *À bien tôt, j'espère/Be Seeing You* (1968), Romain Goupil's *Mourir à trente ans/Die at Thirty* (1983), and the Zanzibar films like *La revolution n'est qu'un debut: Continuous/The Revolution Is Only a Beginning: Let's Continue* (1968) directed by Pierre Clémenti are among the best examples.
5. James Roy MacBean, *Film and Revolution* (Bloomington: Indiana University Press, 1975), 130.
6. Maria-Antonietta Macciocchi, *Letters from Inside the Italian Communist Party to Louis Althusser*, trans. Stephen M. Hellman (London: NLB, 1973), 309. For a more elaborate reading of Maoist Althusserianism in the 1960s, see Camille Robcis, "China in Our Heads: Althusser, Maoism, and Structuralism," *Social*

Text 30, no. 1 (2012): 51–69; see also Julian Bourg, "The Red Guards of Paris: French Student Maoism of the 1960s," *History of European Ideas* 31, no. 4 (2005): 472–90.

7. Macciocchi, *Letters from Inside the Italian Communist Party to Louis Althusser*, 304.
8. Macciocchi, *Letters from Inside the Italian Communist Party to Louis Althusser*, 306.
9. What is really interesting here is that the word "Italian" also had a specific derogatory meaning of Marxist "revisionism" or liberal "reformism" within French leftist intellectual imaginations during the 1960s. According to Sprinzak, the "Italians," as a younger offshoot of the Parti communiste français (French Communist Party, or PCF), precisely refer to the French "revisionists" who were heavily influenced by Paolo Togliatti's ideas from the Partito Comunista Italiano (Italian Communist Party—PCI) to de-Stalinize and liberalize the Communist Party from within. By accommodating a quasi-democratic ideology, the Sorbonnes-based "Italians" were somehow perceived by the French Maoists as "traitors" in proletarian movements, even prior to May '68. See Ehud Sprinzak, "France: The Radicalisation of the New Left," in *Social and Political Movements in Western Europe*, ed. Martin Kolinsky and William E. Paterson (London: Croom Helm, 1976), 283–84.
10. The voice-over says in the film: "He is in every film and he always plays a Don Juan type. . . . The young man speaks in Italian. . . . The man is young and handsome. When he speaks, he disparages age and ugliness, and glorifies youth and glamor. What he wants is sex, what he offers is sex, inviting the audience to come up on the screen and have sex with him."
11. Alain Badiou defines trade unionism as "a particular piece of the parliamentary State count which comes to complete the one's designate, as a singleton, by the company head. The absolutely singular character of workers' belonging to the factory is rendered invisible through the legal superimposition of a representative excrescence." See Alain Badiou, "The Factory as Event Site: Why Should the Worker Be a Reference in Our Vision of Politics?" trans. Alberto Toscano, *Prelom* 8 (Fall 2006): 171–76, at 174.
12. Julia Lesage, "Godard-Gorin's *Wind from the East*: Looking at a Film Politically," *Jump Cut* 4 (1974): 18–23. http://www.ejumpcut.org/archive/onlinessays/JC04folder/WindfromEast.html, accessed November 6, 2015.
13. See Peter Wollen, "Godard and Counter Cinema: *Vent d'est*," in *Movies and Methods: An Anthology*, vol. 2, ed. Bill Nichols (Berkeley: University of

California Press, 1985), 500–509.

14. Wollen, "Godard and Counter Cinema," 502.
15. Wollen, "Godard and Counter Cinema," 509.
16. Counter-cinema is often self-conscious, constantly bringing critical attention to itself as a textual practice and to the dominant cinematic institutions (especially Hollywood) at large. Wollen thereby proposes seven characteristics: "narrative transitivity-intransitivity," "identification-estrangement," "transparency-foregrounding," "single diegesis-multiple diegesis," "closure-aperture," "pleasure-unpleasure," "fiction-reality," that remarkably differentiate the aesthetics of traditional narrative cinema and counter-cinema. Wollen, "Godard and Counter Cinema," 500–509.
17. See Serge Daney, "Le t(h)errorisé (pédagogie godardienne)" ["Theorize/Terrorize (Godardian Pedagogy)"], *Cahiers du Cinéma* 262–63 (January 1976): 32–39, at 36.
18. Lesage, "Godard-Gorin's *Wind from the East*."
19. Daney, "Le t(h)errorisé (pédagogie godardienne)," 40.
20. Interestingly, this particular abjected fate of Miss Althusser in *Vent d'est* finds its loose resonance in French leftist intelligentsia shortly after the watershed of 1968. Historically, Althusserianism and structural Marxism, which were once so prevalent among those young leftist intellectuals in Paris, became almost entirely outmoded and unpopular shortly after May '68. Due to his steward alliance with the PCF and the leftist trade unions, Althusser was thereby criticized by his Maoist disciples (by Jacques Rancière in particular) at the École normale supérieure for lending support to the revisionist enemy. See François Dosse, *History of Structuralism*, vol. 2, *The Sign Sets, 1967–Present*, trans. Deborah Glassman (Minneapolis: University of Minnesota Press, 1997), 119–20. See also Jacques Rancière, *Althusser's Lesson*, trans. Emiliano Battista (London: Continuum, 2011), xx, 52, 55.
21. See Andrew Britton, "Living Historically: Two Films by Jean-Luc Godard," *Framework* 2, no. 1 (1976): 4–15, at 9.
22. Britton, "Living Historically." Britton adds along the same argument: "It is only because of the unquestioned acceptance of Marxism as The Word that Godard can dismiss 'the Western' as a monstrous weapon in the hands of bourgeois ideology and, at the same time, make a film which violently denounces every political position but its own and elevates a rigid orthodoxy (with its own historical determinations) to the status of a transhistorical heal-all." See Britton, "Living Historically," 9–10. Richard Porton also thinks

that the film could serve only a handful of intellectual audiences. He discredits *Vent d'est* as being politically incoherent and tedious and having no more than an Olympian pseudo-rigor. See Richard Porton, *Film and the Anarchist Imagination* (New York: Verso, 1999), 141.

23. Douglas Morrey, *Jean-Luc Godard* (Manchester: Manchester University Press, 2005), 60. For further discussions of Godard's potential sexism, see also Yosefa Loshitzky, *The Radical Faces of Godard and Bertolucci* (Detroit: Wayne State University Press, 1995), 142.
24. Joan Mellen, in a review in *Film Comment*, argues that neither "China" nor "Mao" was ever rendered visible in *Vent d'est*, and that the so-called wind from the East was just empty rhetoric that could not be taken seriously. See Joan Mellen, "Wind from the East: A Review," *Film Comment* 7, no. 3 (1971): 66.
25. As Colin MacCabe remarks, "If the thought of Mao [Zedong] emphasized contradiction as a principle running through every form of practice, one figure, Mao himself, remained outside contradiction, offering a final resolution." See Colin MacCabe, *Godard: Images, Sounds, Politics* (London: Macmillan, 1980), 56. This self-contradictory nature can be seen in the way that Mao constantly emphasized his revolutionary affinity to the young students during the beginning years of the Cultural Revolution, while he conspicuously resigned from aligning with the masses by simply sending thousands of Red Guards to the countryside for ideological reeducation shortly after the student uprisings had turned sour at the feverish heyday of 1968.
26. Colin MacCabe, *Godard: A Portrait of the Artist at Seventy* (New York: Farrar, Straus and Giroux, 2004), 225.
27. Nikita Khrushchev, the Soviet successor to Stalin in 1956, severely denounced his predecessor for the "cult of personality" he had fostered and the crimes he had perpetrated, including the execution, torture, and imprisonment of "class enemies" in the Gulag labor camps. Khrushchev thereby called for a "peaceful co-existence" with the capitalist West for the sake of moving Soviet Communism forward, a gesture that Chairman Mao and many communists in Europe dismissively saw as a revisionist doctrine and "revolutionary betrayal." The profound dispute between Khrushchev and Mao with regard to the "Stalinist question" is historically known as the "Sino-Soviet split."
28. See Steve Cannon, "Godard, the *Groupe Dziga Vertov* and the Myth of 'Counter-Cinema,'" *Nottingham French Studies* 32, no. 1 (1993): 74–83, at 80.

Gauche prolétarienne (Proletarian Left, or GP) is widely recognized by many critics as a "nonhierarchical" and "anti-Stalinist" Maoist group that bears the label of Mao-spontanex or Les Maos. Established in the fall of 1968, the founding core of the GP was constituted by many members from the former Union des jeunesses communistes marxistes-léninistes (Union of Young Marxist-Leninist Communists, or UJCML) of the Althusserian circles, such as Benny Lévy, André Glucksmann, and a large faction from the anarcho-libertarian current of the "March 22nd Movement." It was also the most popular Maoist organ in France, expressively drawing public sympathies from many intellectual luminaries and celebrities such as Foucault, Beauvoir, Sartre, Clavel, and Montand. Another popular Maoist group during the same epoch in France was the Parti communiste marxiste-léniniste de France (French Marxist-Leninist Communist Party, or PCMLF), which subscribed to what A. Belden Fields has called "hierarchical Maoism" insofar as it "accepted the Leninist concept of a centralized and highly disciplined party and attempted to build organizations along those lines." See A. Belden Fields, *Trotskyism and Maoism: Theory and Practice in France and the United States* (New York: Praeger, 1988), 94.

29. "Mass-line" is an internal people's critique of bureaucracy and the division of labor in revolutionary society. It is founded on the conviction that the eyes of the proletariats always see more justly than those of the bureaucrats and technicians.
30. MacCabe, *Godard: A Portrait*, 225.
31. MacCabe, *Godard: A Portrait*, 223.
32. See Martin Walsh, *The Brechtian Aspect of Radical Cinema* (London: BFI Publishing, 1981), 126.
33. Kent E. Carroll, "Film and Revolution: Interview with the Dziga-Vertov Group," in *Focus on Godard*, ed. Royal S. Brown (Englewood Cliffs, NJ: Prentice-Hall, 1972), 50–51.
34. Joris Ivens and Robert Destanque, *Joris Ivens; ou, la mémoire d'un regard* [Joris Ivens; or, the Memory of a Glance] (Paris: Éditions BFB, 1982), 307.
35. Deborah Shaffer, "Fifty Years of Political Filmmaking: An Interview with Joris Ivens," *Cineaste* 14, no. 1 (1985): 12–15, at 14.
36. Although he is somewhat disillusioned by this kind of "didactic" collective filmmaking, Ivens's passion for communal film practice has not been simply exhausted. Instead, Ivens continues to experiment with egalitarian possibilities in cinematic art in his epic documentary, *Comment Yukong déplaça les*

montagnes?/How the Foolish Old Man Moved the Mountains? (1976), made in Mao's China during the final years of the Cultural Revolution.

37. Lesage, "Godard-Gorin's *Wind from the East*."
38. See Jean-Luc Godard, *Jean-Luc Godard par Jean-Luc Godard* [Jean-Luc Godard on Jean-Luc Godard], ed. Alain Bergala (Paris: Editions de l'Etoile, 1985), 374. See also Michael Witt, "Godard dans la presse d'extrême-gauche," in *Jean-Luc Godard Documents* [Jean-Luc Godard Documents], ed. Nichole Brenez (Paris: Centre Georges Pompidou, 2006), 165–77.
39. See Christian Braad Thomsen, "Jean-Pierre Gorin Interviewed: Filmmaking and History," *Jump Cut* 3 (1974): 17–19. http://www.ejumpcut.org/archive/onlinessays/JC03folder/GorinIntThomson.html, accessed May 7, 2015.
40. Wollen, "Godard and Counter Cinema," 504.
41. Jacques Rancière, *The Future of the Image*, trans. Gregory Elliot (New York: Verso, 2007), 46.
42. Rancière, *The Future of the Image*, 46.
43. Rancière, 46.
44. Rancière, 106.

12

Medium UnCool: Women Shoot Back

Feminism, Film, and 1968—A Curious Documentary

Paula Rabinowitz

I

The movies are a Revolution.

—Taylor Mead

What is there to tell in this story of American feminism, film, and 1968?[1] As Jay Boyer explains, in the *Social Text* volume *The Sixties without Apology*, "You will never read the novel you might like to" about the 1960s because "there is no way to say it."[2]

The 1960s confound representation—or rather narrative—because words fail; image and sound—helicopter blades chopping the air over Vietnam and urban America, rock 'n' roll, nightly body counts from the battles at home and in the jungles of Southeast Asia—are what remain. Todd Gitlin offers a more verbose but essentially similar point: "the years 1967, 1968, 1969, and 1970 were a cyclone in a wind tunnel. . . . When history comes off the leash, when

Versions of this essay have been presented at the 1998 University of Minnesota German Forum "Thirty Years After: The Legacy of 1968 in German and American Culture," the 1998 Barcelona Sixth International Exhibition of Women's Films, and the Fourth Seminar on American Studies in Rome, 1999. It first appeared in the journal *Science and Society* and in an expanded form in my book, *Black & White & Noir: America's Pulp Modernism*.

reality appears illusory and illusions take on lives of their own, the novelist loses the platform on which imagination builds its plausible appearances. . . . Reality was reckless, and so there is the temptation to dismiss it—say with the cliché of compilation, snippets of pure spectacle, in the style of a ticker tape or a clunky documentary."[3] He goes on to reel off the following list:

> draft card burnings . . . the Pentagon . . . Stop the Draft Week . . . the Tet offensive . . . the McCarthy campaign . . . Johnson decides not to run for another term . . . Martin Luther King killed . . . Columbia buildings occupied . . . Paris . . . Prague . . . trips to Hanoi . . . Robert Kennedy killed . . . Democratic Convention riots . . . hundreds of students massacred in Mexico City . . . Miss America protest . . . Nixon elected . . . deserters, flights to Canada and Sweden, mutinies, "fragging" in Vietnam . . . Eldridge Cleaver underground . . . San Francisco State, Berkeley, Stanford, Harvard, etc., etc., besieged . . . People's Park . . . police shootouts with Black Panthers . . . student, freak, black, homosexual riots . . . SDS splits . . . Woodstock . . . women's consciousness-raising . . . the Chicago Conspiracy trial . . . Charles Manson . . . Altamont . . . My Lai . . . Weatherman bombs . . . Cambodia . . . Kent State . . . Jackson State . . . a fatal bombing in Madison . . . trials, bombings, fires, agents provocateurs, and the grand abstractions, "resistance," "liberation," "revolution," "repression"—to name only some of what was swirling."[4]

Of this long litany, only two entries interest me, "Miss America" and "women's consciousness-raising," with "clunky documentary," his visual metaphor describing the whole rapturous, horrible vortex, providing the images. No novel can catalog even the two points relevant to my essay. Alix Kates Shulman's 1978 novel, *Burning Questions*, creates a fictional form of revolutionary autobiography to chart a woman's growing involvement with radical feminism. A clunky documentary edited together from a stockpile of found footage, my essay compiles images from multiple sources of feminism and film culture in 1968.

First Reel:

Bonnie and Clyde (Faye Dunaway) (1967);

Rosemary's Baby (Mia Farrow), *Barbarella* (Jane Fonda), *Funny Girl* (Barbra Streisand), *Vixen, Night of the Living Dead* (1968);

Medium Cool, Butch Cassidy and the Sundance Kid, They Shoot Horses Don't They (Jane Fonda), *Easy Rider, Midnight Cowboy, Once Upon a Time in the West* (Claudia Cardinale) (1969).

Like the long eighteenth century, which stretches for British cultural historians from 1660 to 1832, Restoration to the Reform Act, 1968 is not so much a year as an era.[5] Gitlin runs 1967, 1968, 1969, and 1970 together in his tale of the white male New Left. The long 1968 for the integration in the United States of feminism and film stretches between 1965 and 1972, from Gunvor Nelson's and Dorothy Wiley's *Schmeerguntz* to the founding of Women Make Movies. By 1975, the whole picture of feminist work in film had changed: Laura Mulvey's influential article "Visual Pleasure and Narrative Cinema," signaled the shift. It contributed to what became the emergence of feminist film theory as a discipline by substituting a rigorous semiotics for a simplistic sociological approach to women and film. ("Visual Pleasure and Narrative Cinema" being in some sense Laura Mulvey's answer to Molly Haskell's *From Reverence to Rape* [1974], this British Marxist-feminist Lacanian analysis of the system of desire paralleled the deft theorizing of female subjectivity in *Psychoanalysis and Feminism* [1974], Juliet Mitchell's rib at American feminists' anti-Freudian bent exemplified by Phyllis Chesler's *Women and Madness* [1972].) Women Make Movies supplemented New Day Films and Third World Newsreel as sources of women's documentaries and expanded to include independent films challenging Canyon Cinema and Film-Maker's Coop by distributing only women's films. Thus, by the mid-1970s feminist film practice—spanning filmmaking collectives; narrative, documentary, and experimental films; distribution companies; film festivals; journals; and women's studies courses that tracked "images of women" in Hollywood and European art cinemas or sought to recover lost women's visions by unearthing the feminist subversion of Ida Lupino or Dorothy Arzner—was firmly institutionalized, unleashing an extraordinarily rich field that has been instrumental in refashioning the arts and humanities.

Three tendencies can be traced in US film practices of the long 1968: New Hollywood, a commercial response to the end of the studios and the rise of television (filmmaking as industrial production); documentary, tracking issues within New Left politics (filmmaking as collective activity); and the Underground, celebrating the counterculture (filmmaking as individual art/craft, personal vision). Paralleling this, feminist cultural politics moved against female stereotypes—for example, Miss America (and in so doing got into view through the news media). Feminists documented the politics and history of women and women's struggle—for example, Newsreel's *The Woman's Film* (and in so doing challenged the news media). And they experimented with visions of femininity—for example, the personal films of Marie Mencken, Carolee Schneemann, Gunvor Nelson, and others (and in so doing detailed domesticity—its bliss and horror—the daily life of a female artist, often an artist's wife). Like the projectionist in Robert Coover's "Phantom of the Movie Palace," who splices films, projecting two and three at a time, canting the projector at crazy angles to gather all of film's history into one monument, I need at least three screens for this exhibition of feminist film practice. One confronts popular culture, a concern for radical women since at least the 1930s, but taking on greater urgency in the 1960s; another documents an alternative female culture, a concern for women artists since the 1920s, but assuming new political guises in the 1960s; a third builds an apparatus, both scholarly and institutional (journals, courses, distribution companies, festivals, and such), for its dissemination. Sometimes the images fuse in lap dissolves; sometimes they run separately at competing venues.

Second Reel:

1964 Obscenity cases ban *Scorpio Rising* and *Flaming Creatures* (connected to "clean-up" of New York for World's Fair).

1965 NEA and state arts boards funded; 428 university film courses offered in US.[6]

1967 AFI established; *Cineaste* founded.

1967 Marshall McLuhan's *Mechanical Bride* reprinted.

1968 *Un Chien Andalou* (1929) first screened in US.

1968 Hannah Arendt biography of Walter Benjamin published in *New Yorker*.

II

The publicity of the private

—Roland Barthes

Roland Barthes describes photography's impact as effecting a vast inversion of two reigning terms within modern culture—private/public—by relentlessly bringing the daily and personal into public view, on the one hand, and pushing the historic and political into daily life, on the other hand. "The age of Photography corresponds precisely to the explosion of the private into the public, or rather into the creation of a new social value, which is the publicity of the private: the private is consumed as such, publicly."[7] The snapshot, the news photo, the official portrait, the wedding picture, each a specific genre with a discreet function, begin to merge, and faces and bodies become at once strange and familiar. Barthes speaks of still photography, with its fetishistic quality of a memento mori, at once sacred and disposable in its common place around the homes of the working and middle classes. But moving images, especially in the mass television age of the 1980s, the age of home movies, assume aspects of this eeriness.[8] Stan Brakhage's "amateur" films—home movies of his family life scratched over by hand—Jack Smith's "Baudelarian" films of friends camping in his apartment, Jonas Mekas's diary films, all bring into public view highly erotic, private fantasies of seeing. These early films of the New American Cinema, routinely the object of state censorship, pushed into view a personal cinema, accomplished with minimal funds, cheap equipment, and no crew, actors, or technicians. These films were committed to celebrating the particular, idiosyncratic visions of its maker—"a way shaped . . . by an ever-increasing knowledge of historical aesthetics AND, as is of primary importance, a being true to my senses in all my experiencing of the present," declared Brakhage. In the summer of 1961, twenty-five New York film artists, known as The Group, published their "First Statement of the New American Cinema Group," declaring "official cinema all over the world . . . morally corrupt, esthetically obsolete, thematically superficial, temperamentally boring . . . we know what needs to be destroyed," they continued, "and what we stand for . . . our rebellion against the old, official, corrupt and pretentious is primarily an ethical one. We are concerned with Man . . . with what is happening to Man."[9] Published in Jonas Mekas's journal, The Group signaled that just as *Cahiers du Cinéma* was the organ of the Nouvelle Vague, *Film Culture* gave voice to the New American Cinema.

Film Culture itself is like a family album—hand-typed letters and taped conversations—in which personal and private life of "troublemakers and beatniks" form the public documents of a new age (Aquarius begins in 1962) and art. In a letter to his daughter's principal, after Myrrena's body odor had become a topic of concern to the Rollinsville (Colorado) Elementary School, Brakhage cites his own "life's work, as a film artist" to support her. His claim as an artist "particularly qualifies me to search out and create thru the finest qualities of human vision." Thus he refuses to be shamed into bathing Myrrena, if she is not so inclined.[10] This letter, published with a selection of Brakhage's correspondence in *Film Culture*, journal of the New American Cinema, is preceded by an interview with Kenneth Anger about *Kustom Kar Kommando* and the first screening of *Scorpio Rising* after Anger had won its censorship case. "What *Scorpio* represents is me cluing in to popular American culture after having been away for eight years . . . living in France."[11] His luscious, idiosyncratic observations of American male subcultures obsessed with cars and bike[r]s became a documentary: "I don't see the difference between a symbol and a thing: it's the same."[12] By decade's end, in his "Defense of the 'Amateur' Filmmaker," Brakhage summarizes the move from private to public as New American Cinema became institutionalized: "I have been making films for over 15 years now. . . . Mostly I have worked without title in NO collaboration with others—I have worked alone and at home, on films of seemingly NO commercial value . . . 'at home' with a medium I love, making films I care for as surely as I as a father care for my children. As these 'home movies' have come to be valued, have grown into public life, I as the maker of them have come to be called a 'professional,' an 'artist' and an 'amateur.'"[13]

Anger's "cluing in to popular American culture," like Brakhage's "being true to [his] senses" formed the central tenets of 1960s arts and politics. One can find versions of these declarations everywhere, as in Carolee Schneemann's "Notebooks" for "Round House," her Happening created for the July 1967

International Congress on Dialectics of Liberation. Her notes range among thoughts on quantum physics, the Vietnam War, casual meetings with friends, ideas for the piece: "Happening as basic psycho-social guerilla life-fare," she quips. Then, "expose exposure demystification yes get rid of old deadly mysteries women *our genital and our pronoun* new mysteries waiting for us get it all out tell and show"

the waitress . . . . ?

the airline . . . . ?

the heiress . . . . ?

the hostage . . . . ?

the steward . . . . ?

HOSTESS STEWARDESS. . . ![14]

As in her early 1967 five-screen film/performance, "Snows," which she described as "a work based on Vietnam atrocity images," Schneemann's nude body was central to the politics of her art.[15] In 1960s America, according to Schneemann, both Vietnam and Woman were known through airing "atrocity images," and the struggle against the devastation of each entailed reclaiming those images. In her next piece, "Naked Action Lecture," Schneemann discussed the "Istory" of her work while dressing and undressing. This June 27, 1968, performance asked the questions: "Can an artist be an art istorian? Can an art istorian be a naked woman? Does a woman have intellectual authority? Can she have public authority while naked and speaking? Was the content of the lecture less appreciable when she was naked? What multiple levels of uneasiness, pleasure, curiosity, erotic fascination, acceptance or rejection were activated in an audience"?[16] For the woman "amateur," Schneemann noted in "Istory of a Girl Pornographer," cluing in to popular culture and being true to her senses required a public display of her body, the nude female body—always object of art, retrieved into subjectivity—"to bridge the conventionally public/private areas of experience."[17] By collapsing subject and object, art work and art historian, into one, Schneemann foregrounded her body as a battleground.

Other women artists focused instead on the role the image apparatus itself played in both constructing and violating privacy.

> Third Reel:
>
> Charlotte Moorman arrested in New York for performing "TV Bra" with Nam June Paik (1966);
>
> *Chelsea Girls* cannot be screened at Cannes because it requires two projectors (1966);
>
> "New Documents" exhibition at Museum of Modern Art (1967);
>
> *Portrait of Jason* (1967).

For instance, the only female founding member of the twenty-five film artists composing The Group, Shirley Clarke, whose avant-garde narrative films, *A Cool World* and *The Connection*, explored African American and drug cultures, created the self-mocking cinéma vérité film *Portrait of Jason*. Like Diane Arbus's photographs, on display at the Museum of Modern Art's (MoMA) "New Documents" show, it forced viewers to confront their investments in voyeurism because each accorded the objects of her camera's gaze some element of subjectivity. These two 1967 events—Jason camping at the New York Film Festival and the Jewish Giant hanging in the Museum of Modern Art—are crucial moments in my tale of feminism, film, and 1968. Each woman—wealthy intellectual New York Jewish Bohemian—defiantly took her camera into the world of men and forged a new kind of intimate documentary: Arbus as a street photographer; Clarke in her "fictional documents" of various black male underground cultures. Unlike Schneemann, who was in part responding to Brakhage's lyrical cinepoetics of his families' bodies, these New York women artists chose not to display their own bodies; instead, they foregrounded other culturally marginalized, even disreputable, subjects. Although she rarely got releases, Arbus claimed she developed deep relationships with her subjects—they told her their "secrets" as she clicked away. "I can figure myself into any situation. I choose photography projects that are somehow Mata Harish. I'll not risk my life but I'll risk my reputation or my virtue." Arbus's black-edged photographs of "freaks"—the Jewish giant at home in the Bronx, identical twins, transvestites, nudists, prowar demonstrators with bad acne—fascinated and repelled the MoMA's audience to its major photography show—"New Documents." Arbus herself spent hours hanging around the room with her thirty images eavesdropping on the remarks of those disgusted by her depictions of outlaws and outsiders. As she said of her work style in an interview with Ann Ray in *Newsweek*: "If I stand in front of something instead of arranging it. I arrange myself."[18]

Clarke's relationship with Jason also undercuts her position as filmmaker; she arranged her camera. Shot on an Auricon camera that needed to be reloaded every ten minutes, Clarke set the camera in one position and filmed Jason Holliday talking for twelve straight hours. Clarke observed that "never had anyone [been allowed] to speak for themselves for more than a few minutes at a time" in traditional cinema; thus, she gives Jason license to talk and talk, sometimes responding to the prods of the off-screen voices. Ultimately, Clarke does not succeed in unmasking Jason. Instead, he unmasks the very assumptions of cinéma vérité; it becomes obvious that his stories about black transvestite life are being *performed* for the camera. Most likely they are lies. "For the first time I was able to give up my intense control and allow Jason and the camera to react to each other."[19] Arbus, however, despite her demurring, always maintained control, at least of her shoots, often lying to her subjects to get the pose she wanted. Andy Warhol's Factory Superstar Viva and feminist Ti-Grace Atkinson both claimed to have been violated by Arbus after she photographed them sprawled naked like OD'd junkies for spreads in *New York* and the *London Sunday Times*, respectively.[20] Yet Atkinson had been righteously celebratory of Valerie Solanas's *SCUM Manifesto* and of her actual shooting of Warhol—celebrity filmmaking thief deluxe.[21] In their differing excesses, Arbus and Clarke set the stage for feminist ambivalence toward media, exposure, and a politics of celebrity that would mark post-1968 events.

Fourth Reel:

Valerie Solanas, author of the *SCUM [Society for Cutting Up Men] Manifesto*, shoots Andy Warhol (1968);

Marie Mencken dies (1970);

Diane Arbus commits suicide; a madhouse erupts for possession of her Westbeth studio (1971).

Moving private life, fantasy, and obsession into public life and in so doing challenging economic and political structures—through censorship battles, through distribution and exhibition collectives—is the story of the New American Cinema of the 1960s. Yet, at the same time, the explosion of new filmic forms and images serves paradoxically to reinforce postwar corporate America. As Susan Sontag's synopsis of Walter Benjamin and Guy Debord astutely noted: "A capitalist society requires a culture based on images. . . . Cameras define reality in the two ways essential to the workings of an advanced industrial society: as a spectacle (for masses) and as an object of surveillance (for rulers). The production of images also furnishes a ruling ideology. *Social change is replaced by a change in images.*"[22] Sontag was an early champion of the New American Cinema, penning an important analysis of *Flaming Creatures* in 1963; however, by the mid-1970s she had soured a bit on the radical possibilities of film and photography.

In many ways, The Group, its art and its organization (and Sontag's response to it), provided a model for radical feminism. Through new forms of political organizing, which included the production of new images—consciousness raising, guerilla theater, all-women's actions and speakouts—women's liberation forged a new movement for social and political change; however, the stumbling block to feminist revolution remained ever in the realm of culture and consciousness (or ideology, or psychology, depending on to whom one talked). Because, in a capitalist society, social change is replaced by a change in images, altering images—a struggle to find new ways of representing woman to herself, to women collectively, and to men—became central to every aspect of radical action.

III

The Personal Is Political.

—Carol Hanisch

In her 1970 "Critique of the Miss America Protest," Carole Hanisch recalls how the action, which launched contemporary radical feminism, the Women's Liberation Movement, into the public eye,

> came out of our group method of analyzing women's oppression by recalling our own experiences. We were watching *Schmearguntz* [*sic*], a feminist movie, one night at our meeting. The movie had flashes of

> the Miss America contest in it. I found myself sitting there remembering how I had felt at home with my family watching the pageant as a child, as an adolescent, and a college student. I knew it had evoked powerful feelings. When I proposed the idea to our group, we decided to go around the room with each woman telling how she felt about the pageant. . . . From our communal thinking came the concrete plans for the action.[23]

The process of consciousness-raising, gleaned from Chinese cadre criticism/self-criticism, and speaking bitterness sessions was understood by Hanisch as "a political action," not a therapeutic one because, as Kathie Sarachild later noted, "the importance of listening to a woman's feelings was collectively to analyze the situation of women. . . . The idea was not to change the woman . . . it's male supremacy we want to change."[24] It was out of talk that theory, then action, proceeded to build mass female solidarity.

Hanisch and Sarachild, proponents of the "pro-woman line" within radical feminism, sought to support women in their limited choices. Alice Echols contrasts the radical feminists concerned with organizing women as women to those "politicos," who advocated organizing separate women's contingents to antiwar demonstrations. Like *Schmeerguntz* as a catalyst for the Miss America action, these, too, often took their inspiration from the movies. For instance, "at Florika's suggestion, a number of NYRW (New York Radical Women) members participated in an April 1968 anti-war demonstration as a contingent from NYRW. They dressed like Vietnamese women, handed out leaflets about women's liberation to women only, and ran through the crowd ululating like the Algerian women in Gillo Pontecorvo's 1966 film *The Battle of Algiers*."[25] Echols relates these two incidents to distinguish between the actions of feminists and politicos. These two films—one lyrically documenting two women's experiences of daily life in the postwar United States; the other fictionalizing a documentary about Algerian anticolonialist struggle, featuring militant women setting bombs and amassing in the streets—to some degree charted the range of feminist political action in 1968. Public feminist action made tangible Guy Debord's "Society of the Spectacle," in which seeing obscure films, talking about them, demonstrating, and then seeing the political actions eventually broadcast on network TV become steps in mass political organization. All that's needed to complete the picture is Newsreel's first all-woman documentary of the all-women's Jeannette Rankin Brigade's 1968 action at the Capitol—from critiques of popular culture, to celebrations of revolution, to documents of women's mobilization, radical feminism and alternative film trailed each other.

Tellingly, none of these films was part of the dominant film culture of the American 1960s: Hollywood's unraveling studio system and European art cinemas. Arguably these two film practices, being more pervasive, should have been instrumental in forming a feminist film culture; however, feminist responses to Hollywood and its Other, European art cinema, were not central to the critiques of mass culture mounted by feminists. Mostly the edgy rebellion or outright camp typical of 1960s films gave them an air of the counterculture, what Ethan Mordden called Hollywood's "own apocalypse."[26] Dominant cinema came in for attack for its unreal depictions of women (Jeanne Moreau as Catherine in François Truffaut's *Jules et Jim* was universally denounced) and for its exploitation of the star system, while poems by lyn lifshin reimagining Marilyn or by Karen Lindsey mourning Jayne Mansfield spoke to the ambivalence feminists felt toward the culture industry's use of female bodies. Lindsey's "Elegy for Jayne Mansfield, July 1967" reads:

> she was a
> sunday news centerfold
> bosoms thrust toward subway—
> rush men leaning on the
> legs of pretty secretaries
> always a bleeding
> divorcé or a beaten child,
> she had a pink voice, and lived in a pink house.
> no hints of a self
> cringing away from sticky headlines
> or an art groping beyond
> barebreasted titters.
> we used to have fun laughing at her.
> when she lost her head, the joke turned sick.[27]

The joke turned sick—Jayne Mansfield, Marilyn Monroe, Miss America—tested the limits of radical feminist analyses of culture and its industry.[28] How to come to terms with women who used the system of male supremacy to make it? Hanisch ultimately condemned the Miss America action, with its free-for-all theatrics admitting slogans such as "Up Against the Wall Miss America," because she felt these alienated women and blamed those participating in sexist institutions—including marriage—for their self-contributions to victimization. A "pro-woman" line would celebrate women's many subversive responses to her oppression. Thus, even Jayne Mansfield needed to be reassessed, perhaps rehabilitated, or more accurately, feminist response to Jayne Mansfield needed revising. Solidarity among women required recognition of the underground submerged stream of women's culture within a sexist world, including its most ludicrous and debased extremes. Ever attentive to the Zeitgeist, new stars in updated, hip, genre films commercialized dissent, furthering complicating the relationships among popular culture, public life, and private desire.

A smile stretches across the ashen face of platinum-blonde, spit-curled Faye Dunaway as she strokes Warren Beatty's pistol in the opening sequence of *Bonnie and Clyde*. The graphic violence of Arthur Penn's film came to be seen as a touchstone for the New Left, especially media speculations about it. Bonnie's beret, echoing Che's, was the dress code of the Black Panthers, eventually hitting the fashion pages. *Bonnie and Clyde* retrofitted America's past, showing how the body counts racking up on the nightly news were not aberrations but a key aspect of United States history. In a key scene, Bonnie sits engrossed in a motion picture theater watching the Busby Berkeley musical *Golddiggers of 1933* for fashion tips. Despite this, Albert Johnson noted Penn's "flaw" of "Bonnie's persistent 1967 look [as] disturbing."[29] Bosley Crowther of the *New York Times* lambasted the "slap-stick" of *Bonnie and Clyde*, its romance of guns and gangs. His dismissal was mild compared to Page Cook's denunciation in *Films in Review*: "One final word," Cook appended to his August 14, 1967, review of the opening night of the Montreal Film Festival, "there is *evil* in the *tone* of the writing, acting, and direction of this film, the calculated effect of which is to incite in the young the delusions that armed robbery and murder are mere 'happenings.'"[30] The period dress and antique cars never for a moment masked the contemporary feel of the images *Bonnie and Clyde* purveyed, as

Richard Shickel noted in his October 13, 1967, *Life* magazine review: "Bonnie and Clyde are the products of the rootlessness of ill-taught youth growing up absurd in a period of historical transition. The parallel between the middle 1930s and the middle 1960s is never too far from the minds of the movie's creators."[31] As Hollywood's studio system increasingly fell apart, independent productions mainstreamed radical critiques of America. *Bonnie and Clyde*'s resurrection of the 1930s, the era of America's Old Left, aestheticized violence by politicizing style according to these mainstream critics.[32] Radicals flocked to the film, however, boosting its flagging attendance after Warner Brothers rereleased it in the wake of 1968 assassinations, civil unrest, and Democratic Convention police riot.[33]

Film as just such a system of contradictory thought and experience—not only as a source of negative and positive images—was crucial to at least one feminist theorist. Shulamith Firestone's 1970 manifesto *The Dialectic of Sex* found in film the precursor to her ideal postrevolutionary "anti-culture": "the young art of film, based on a true synthesis of the Aesthetic and Technological Modes (as Empiricism itself had been) carried on the vital realistic tradition. . . . It broke down the very division between the artificial and the real, between culture and life itself," she exclaimed ecstatically.[34] Much like Maya Deren, Firestone, a painting student at the Chicago Institute of Art (where Stan Brakhage later taught) during the mid-1960s and "star" of a cinéma vérité documentary about her, saw film as a philosophic system.[35] In this, she paraphrased the conclusion to The Group's "First Statement": "we are not only for the new cinema, we are also for the New Man . . . we are for art, but not at the expense of life. We don't want false, polished, slick films—we prefer them rough, unpolished, but alive; we don't want rosy films—we want them the color of blood."[36] Few feminist theorists, however, took up Firestone's line on cinema as prefigurative. Instead, more often they, like Sherry Sonnett Trumbo, asked, "where is the movie that shows us what alternatives and possibilities are open to us as women?" In her *New York Times* article, Trumbo noted that "for women, there are very few relevant models offered by movies or the rest of culture that will help ease the fear and pain of liberation."[37] If "A Woman's Place Is in the Oven" rather than behind the camera, how was a feminist film vision to be expressed? In these minor nods toward film criticism, so-called second wave feminists were rehashing debates among Popular Front feminists.

Muriel Rukeyser's poem, "Movie," skewered the nascent fascism in Hollywood fantasies of female stars:

> Spotlight her face her face has no light in it
> . . . We focus on the screen: look they tell us
> you are a nation of similar whores remember the Maine
> remember you have a democracy of champagne—
>
> And slowly the female face kisses the young man,
> over his face the twelve-foot female head
> the yard-long mouth enlarges and yawns
>
> The End.[38]

Like Trumbo, Joy Davidman, film critic for the *New Masses* during the 1940s, challenged the commercial culture and female objectification endemic to Hollywood and America yet relished the possibilities mass culture offered radical organizing.

IV

The revolution will not be televised.

—Gil Scott-Heron

If "movies and the rest of culture" offered little of use to feminists, notwithstanding Firestone's attempt to argue otherwise, movies, even alternative cinema, and the rest of culture were still central to maintaining women's oppression. In the "Fourth World Manifesto," Barbara Burris, writing on behalf of her collective, declares: "A Female culture exists." The emphasis on finding and nurturing that submerged female culture became the genesis of what Alice Echols calls "cultural feminism" because "male culture, which is the dominant culture in every nation, i.e., is synonymous with the national culture, cannot accept a female view of things as expressed by female writers, artists and philosophers."[39] Burris based her conclusions on a dissection of the Algerian revolution's betrayal of NLF women, evidenced in part by Pontecorvo's film, *The Battle of Algiers*, offering a thoroughgoing critique of Frantz Fanon's emphasis on male identity formation through anti-imperialist struggle. Her ideas had resonances among black feminists, many of whom had been active in the

Black Arts Movement. For instance, Francee Covington writing in Toni Cade's influential 1970 anthology, *The Black Woman*, also uses *The Battle of Algiers* as a source for analyzing the revolutionary potential of US movements—anti-imperialist, black nationalist, or feminist.[40] Because, as Sontag would argue in "The Third World of Women," "all women live in an 'imperialist' situation in which men are the colonialists and women are the natives . . . the same basic relations of inferiority and superiority, of powerlessness and power, or cultural underdevelopment and cultural privilege, prevail between men and women in all countries."[41] Thus a film, such as *The Battle of Algiers*, which offered a blueprint for anticolonial struggle, moved from the realm of representation to that of strategic manual. It is a virtual given that the film is a documentary, because, if film in general "broke down the very division between the artificial and the real, between culture and life itself," then this one did so in a powerfully self-conscious way. The impact of the film turned many feminists to documentary to secure the truth of women's lives within a liberated women's cinema.

Newsreel's films opened with their trademark film projector and machine gun staccato, resurrecting the 1930s Film and Photo League's assertion that "the camera is a weapon." In December 1967, the collective announced its birth in the *Village Voice*: "Films made by the Newsreel are not to be seen once and forgotten. Once a print goes out, it becomes a tool to be used by others in their own work. . . . We intend to cover demonstrations; to interview figures like LeRoi Jones and [Jim] Garrison; we want to show what is at stake in a housing eviction or in consumer abuses in Harlem; we should provide information on how to deal with the police or on the geography of Chicago."[42] The logic behind Newsreel's perceived need was, in part, "documented" by Haskell Wexler's extraordinary 1969 film, *Medium Cool*, which follows a television news cameraman as he shoots scenes of Chicago life leading up to the 1968 Democratic National Convention. *Medium Cool* earned an X rating (no one under eighteen admitted) under the Motion Picture Association of America (MPAA)'s newly instituted rating system. A clear move to censor a political film, branding it "pornography," the MPAA appeared to be doing to commercial cinema what the cops had done to underground film a few years earlier, and the television networks were doing to the Vietnam War and domestic resistance. According to Newsreel: "The news that we feel is significant—any event that suggests the changes and redefinitions taking place in America today, or that underlines the necessity for such changes—has been consistently undermined and suppressed by the media."[43]

For all its radical form and content—intercutting actual black-and-white documentary footage into the color narrative, improvisational acting, hand-held camera, highly self-reflexive commentary on filmmaking—*Medium Cool* was predictably sexist. It still featured a man shooting footage of men shooting guns (camera as weapon) and of women who may or may not want to be looked at (camera as voyeur). In one of the key scenes, white cameraman and journalist Robert Forster has gone to a South Side Chicago apartment to interview a black cab driver who found a wallet containing $10,000, turned it in, and then was arrested. As Forster exits, he is challenged by a black actress who demands he put her on television because "the tube is life," as someone remarks. Delivering images, perhaps the cameraman is obstetrician, but he is nevertheless cut off from real life. The hot everyday life of summer 1968 is antidote to that cool medium, the tube, and it is embodied in the earth mother: a young Vietnam War widow serving canned tomato soup to her teenaged son. She challenges Forster to take responsibility for the pictures he takes that end up on her television, invading her life. But, in Wexler's quotation of Jean-Luc Godard's *Contempt*, she ends up dead in a car smash-up as the two vainly search for her missing boy during the chaos of the convention and police riot. The final credits mimic the opening sequence: a passing car slows as someone snaps a photo of the dead couple. The question remained, especially for women, how to "serve the needs of people who want to get hold of news that is relevant to their own activity and thought"? How to film in a medium uncool?

The women active in New York Newsreel offered one answer: demand that the white men who were already filmmakers, in effect, the ringleaders of the collective, cede their power by spreading their knowledge to those working crew. Rather than lecture the cameraman about his complicity in the violence of the shot, women demanded access to the cameras themselves. They wanted to shoot back. Newsreel collective's female members felt that by making films about black male radicalism, like *Black Panther Party*, the white male filmmakers were either honing in on another's vital revolutionary culture (a form of imperialism) or in making films of *The Columbia Revolt* were celebrating their own struggles as if they constituted the revolution (another form of imperialism). In one of their first actions in January 1968, Lynn Phillips and an all-women crew from Newsreel's original thirty members filmed the Jeannette Rankin Brigade, an all-women antiwar organization, in its attempt to petition Congress to end the war.[44] However, a year later, Christine Choy was filming the Newsreel footage of the Attica prison uprising as a complete novice after Robert Kramer and other founders, including Phillips, had left New York Newsreel.[45] Explaining her early departure, Phillips concluded that "preciousness and pandering are the Scylla and Charybdis of left culture. Newsreel, to avoid the pandering of 1930s nice-guy sentimentality, lapsed into a muscular kind of French intellectualism; and for all our trashy surface and rough posturing, I think we got as precious as well, Waiting for Godot, or Godard, Waiting for Godard. . . . Besides the women's movement had grown a great deal by then, and there was too much in the feminist critique of the left leadership that was too true and too slow to change."[46]

The slippage between "real life" revolution or struggle—say Algeria or Chicago—and filmic ones—say *Battle of Algiers* or *Medium Cool*—"Waiting for Godard," is precisely what sutured Miss America to revolutionary ululations. That *The Battle of Algiers* recreates the feel of documentary—using techniques *Medium Cool* mimicked—points to the conventions of truth-telling so important to 1960s political investments in cinema. But, as Mekas pointed out, the true documentary work in cinema had been going on in New American Cinema; for Mekas, Carolee Schneemann's investigation of her sexuality and her active handling of the film itself offered more real cinema than anything coded as "real" including cinéma vérité documentary.[47] Parker Tyler argued that underground films were always "curiously 'documentary'" because they "document the traditional social activity of making life itself into a work of art."[48] According to David James's assessment, "By far the majority of underground films were essentially documentaries of these [homosexual, women's, Bohemian, drug, antiwar] subcultures . . . instances of minority social groups representing themselves." Moreover, "the radical innovation of the underground . . . invent[ed] film as practice rather than as manufacture.[49] Art of life, practice of art, life as art—this was the aesthetic flowering of Firestone's dream of "anti-culture," the cinematic dispersion of Hanisch's "personal is political."

V

IF YOU'RE GOING TO CHANGE THINGS YOU'RE GOING TO MAKE A MESS every housewife knows that!

—Carolee Schneemann

Cheap, lightweight equipment and the "cinema of an effortless (as much as it can be) self-expression, which culminated in *Blonde Cobra* and *Flaming Creatures* and 8 mm" had made possible a new wave of "women . . . coming to cinema," commented Jonas Mekas in 1963 after viewing new work by Naomi Levine, Storm de Hirsch, and Barbara Rubin. "Now," he declares, "Marie Mencken is no longer alone."[50] In 1966, Marie Mencken, heiress to Maya Deren as mother of the avant-garde, appears as Gerard Malanga's mother in *The Chelsea Girls*. Mencken's career as a filmmaker, like that of her many avant-gardist sisters, began in collaboration with her husband, Willard Maas. The "istory" of women in art features a litany of wives, lovers, and models tagged on as afterthoughts. For instance, Sheldon Renan concludes his profile of Robert Nelson in the Gallery of Film-Makers with the following sentence: "His wife Guvnor (sic) has, with Bill Wiley's wife, Dorothy, made a film called *Schmeerguntz* (1965), which satirizes the modern woman."[51] Both Gunvor and Dorothy, who rarely appear in accounts of underground film, can claim a decent pedigree—the history of modernist women artist is an "istory" of wives and lovers serving as footnotes to greater male visionaries.[52] Jane Brakhage—her body a central image and her camera work a central element of "Brakhage"—is incorporated within the final title of the films shot in Colorado: "By Brakhage" flickers at the end of *Thigh Line Lyre Triangular* and *Dog Star Man*. These homemade movies of birth and wood chopping are family productions, but celebrating whose personal metaphors on vision?

In a 1971 interview with Brenda Richardson, titled "Women, Wives, Film-Makers," which ironizes on, but cannot fully escape, the legacy of belittling artists' wives as second-class artists, Nelson and Wiley described the beginning of their collaboration: "Dorothy and I made two little 8 mm movies, and Bob went with Bill Wiley, Bob Hudson, and Ron Davis and made *Plastic Haircut*, and that was more like a professional thing—Dorothy and I just fiddled around with little stuff."[53] Four years before, in a conversation recorded in 1967 and transcribed in *Film Culture*, Shirley Clarke and Storm de Hirsch had pointed out that despite being acclaimed filmmakers, "we are both little women" patronized constantly as women artists. Clarke begins their conversation with the tongue-in-cheek question: "Do you think that lady film-makers are mechanically equipped to handle their field?" She compares their status to female trolley drivers in the Soviet Union as the two proceed to circle the woman question in the history of independent cinema.[54] Both of these conversations shy away from declaring women's experimental filmmaking as a form of "women's liberation," yet each emphasizes the different treatments male and female artists receive from journalists, other artists, and friends. Nelson and Wiley remember bitterly how after *Schmeerguntz* received first prize at the 1966 Ann Arbor Film Festival, male artist friends started speaking to them; Clarke notes that journalists always comment first on her demure appearance.[55]

These pre–Women's Liberation Movement underground cinematic revisions of home movies paved the way for a new radical feminist cinema, even for radical feminism itself. Carolee Schneemann's film, *Fuses*, got a rave from Mekas when it screened in 1968 as heir(ess) apparent to his pantheon; it too was the object of a censorship battle.[56] In production for three years, *Fuses* features long sequences of Schneemann and her lover James Tenney's sex seen from the point of view of her cat, Kitch. She then scratched the film, baked it in the oven, left it out in the rain, until bodies and film fused. "With *Schmeerguntz*," notes Nelson, "we wanted to make a 16 mm movie, I think. But we had no subject. And one day I was looking at all the gunk in the sink and thought of the contrast between what we do, and what we see that we 'should' be [doing]—in ads and things—and that was the idea right from there, from the sink."[57] Joyce Weiland's *Rat Life and Diet in North America*—premiering in 1968 at the Jewish Museum—uses close-ups of rodents and cats scurrying amid food left out on her kitchen table to allegorize resistance to imperialism, war, and the violence of daily life. Domesticity continued to be the focus of Dorothy Wiley's later 8 mm works, such as the 1972 *Cabbage*, about which she says: "while watching film, I can abandon myself to the event. I don't find that so easy to do in the kitchen in the morning. I still don't understand that part."[58] Unsettling domestic settings, by turns inviting and erotic and violent and repulsive—domesticity with a vengeance, something Arbus accomplished in her 1963 portraits of New Jersey nudists—is part of the complicated interrelationship of photography and image under capitalism, as much an aspect of the publicity of the private, as of a "personal politics," which women's film work and feminist politics highlighted.[59] "*Schmeerguntz* is one long raucous belch in the face of the American Home. A society that hides its animal functions beneath a shiny public surface deserves to have such films as *Schmeerguntz* shown everywhere—in every PTA, every Rotary Club, every club in the land. For it is brash enough, brazen enough and funny enough to purge the soul of every harried American married woman," declared Ernest Callenbach in its sole review.[60] Following the leads of Mencken, Wiley, Nelson, Schneemann, and Weiland, domesticating cinema—home movies, sex, ordinary objects—forged a key to women's filmmaking in the 1970s. Homey images eventually became a way to entice women into filmmaking, as Liane Burton explained in a 1972 radio interview on WBUR: "If you can thread a sewing machine, you can thread a projector, and if you can follow a recipe, you can do still photography developing."[61] Women reshot underground home movies and documented women's struggles for private audiences—the cognoscenti of the New American Cinema and those committed to the New Left.

VI

Free in the dusty beam of the projector

—Adrienne Rich

Looking back through the *Notes from the First, Second, and Third Years,* it becomes clear, as Fredric Jameson remarks in "Periodizing the 60s," that "an immense and inflationary issuing of superstructural credit; a universal abandonment of the referential gold standard; an extraordinary printing up of ever more devalued signifiers" were part of the decade's legacy. If the 1960s marked the emergence of late capitalism, in Ernst Mandel's term, then the long 1968 of feminism and film hints at a brief triumph of its cultural revolution. The woman question had been lurking beneath Marxism for more than a hundred years, popping its head out at various times only to be pushed back from view. But the late 1960s' reorganization of capital and desire opened the floodgates as public space became the site of private conscience, freeing the imagination in Paris and Prague, declaring sisterhood is powerful in the United States. "The superstructural movement and play enabled by the transition from one infrastructural or systemic stage of capitalism to another" mitigated, for a time, class-based analyses of social and political change by unleashing "social energies" in the form of new cultural movements.[62] Viewed from today's perspective, in which the distinction between culture, consciousness, and commodity is increasingly elided, the struggles of feminists to "name the system" that oppressed women, as Paul Potter had exhorted the New Left at the 1965 antiwar March on Washington, was exceedingly prescient; Potter later recounted that he had purposely evaded naming the system, capitalism, "because capitalism was for me and my generation an inadequate description of the evils of America—a hollow, dead word tied to the thirties."[63] In part, this explains why guerilla theater actions inspired by film and television became a key form of feminist political organizing. It appeared certain that women's liberation, understood by radical feminists as freedom from men's control, individual men as well as systems of male chauvinism, would never be achieved solely by structural changes in the economic relationships between classes; only a fundamental change in consciousness, and in its public expression, culture, would accomplish a feminist revolution.

With its dual struggle against censorship (to gain visibility) and for revolution (to change the world), the work of the underground, both cultural and political, was lodged, in part, within film. Censorship crucially acts as an official refusal to circulate knowledge publicly, by, on the one hand, insisting that the hidden remain private (inhibiting sex), and, on the other, hiding state secrets (waging war). Politics and culture in the 1960s unraveled and tangled these threads—underground films and Happenings, often public displays of private love and friendship, were raided by the police, while the nightly news brought the brutality of state-sponsored death in Vietnam into middle-class American living rooms. Thus, it makes sense that *Medium Cool* would be given an X rating by the MPAA; it was deemed pornographic for pointing out how obscene war is.

Revolution demands the public demonstration of a refusal, bringing the masses into the streets because their solely private existence as individuals becomes untenable and they seek power collectively. Women's work in film during the long 1968 united, as radical feminism did, the struggles to fight censorship and make revolution. It located woman's body—its private spaces and its public consumption—as the site of a new kind of politics—a politics of the image and of the personal. Fighting censorship meant bringing into view the vomiting pregnant woman, the sink full of dirty dishes, the shitty diapers, as much as it meant revealing women's erotic desires. Making revolution meant refuting the culture of images that depended on the female body and documenting the long history of women's presence yet invisibility in politics. Exposure, expression, exploitation, excess: the cinema as metaphor for daily life (a theme prevalent in much twentieth-century literature and criticism) became cinema as a paradigm for living—a clunky, curious documentary. Cinema structured politics and its poetics. Adrienne Rich's 1970 poem, "Images for Godard" concludes:

> the mind of the poet is the only poem
> the poet is at the movies
> dreaming the film-maker's dream but differently
> free in the dark as if asleep
> free in the dusty beam of the projector
> the mind of the poet is changing
> the moment of change is the only poem.[64]

The long 1968 offers a prehistory to feminist film work. First generation feminist films may not have made the revolution, but they did project the moment of change.

Fifth Reel:

"Women's Cinema as Counter Cinema" (Claire Johnston, 1973);

Legend of Maya Deren Project (begun in 1973, first edition appeared in 1988);

Popcorn Venus (Marjorie Rosen, 1973);

Women in Film and Video Conference, Buffalo 1974;

From Reverence to Rape (Molly Haskell, 1974);

Jeanne Dielman, 23 quai du Commerce, 1080 Bruxelles (Chantal Akerman, 1975);

"Visual Pleasure and Narrative Cinema (Laura Mulvey, 1975);

Women and Film (1975);

Camera Obscura (1977);

Telluride Film Festival, 1977—includes Agnès Varda's *L'Opera Mouffe,* Marie Marie Menken's *Orgia,* Gunvor Nelson and Dorothy Wiley's *Schmeerguntz,* Anne Severson's *Near the Big Chakra,* Carolee Schneemann's *Fuses* and *Plumb Line* in a program titled The Erotic Woman;

Soft Fiction (Chick Strand, 1980);

Women's Pictures: Feminism and Cinema (Annette Kuhn, 1982);

Thelma and Louise (1991);

Shirley Clarke dies (1997).

Notes

1. For an excellent detailed account of France, film, and 1968, but one that has nothing about women, much less feminism, see Sylvia Harvey, *May '68 and Film Culture* (London: BFI, 1978).
2. Jay Boyer, "You Will Never Read the Novel You Might Like To," in *The Sixties without Apology*, ed. Sohnya Sayres et al. (Minneapolis: University of Minnesota Press, 1984), 309–10.
3. Todd Gitlin, *The Sixties: Years of Hope, Days of Rage* (New York: Bantam, 1987), 242–43.
4. Gitlin, *The Sixties,* 243.
5. See Henry Abelove, "Some Speculations on the History of Sexual Intercourse during the Long Eighteenth Century in England," *Genders* 6 (November 1989): 125–30.
6. Lauren Rabinovitz, *Points of Resistance: Women, Power and Politics in the New York Avant-Garde Cinema, 1943–71* (Bloomington: Indiana University Press, 1991), 134. Jonas Mekas estimates over forty venues to view non-Hollywood cinema in New York alone in 1965.
7. Roland Barthes, *Camera Lucida: Reflections on Photography*, trans. Richard Howard (New York: Hill and Wang, 1981), 98.
8. See Patricia Zimmerman, *Reel Families: A Social History of Amateur Film* (Bloomington: Indiana University Press, 1995).
9. The Group, "The First Statement of the New American Cinema Group," *Film Culture* 22–23 (Summer 1961): 130–33, at 131.
10. Stan Brakhage, "Letter to Dolores Daniels," *Film Culture* 40 (Spring 1966): 73–75.
11. Kenneth Anger, "An Interview with Kenneth Anger, Conducted by *Spider*

Magazine," *Film Culture* 40 (Spring 1966): 68.

12. Anger, "An Interview with Kenneth Anger, Conducted by *Spider Magazine*," 68.
13. Stan Brakhage, "Defense of the 'Amateur' Filmmaker," *Filmmakers Newsletter* (Summer 1971): 20.
14. Carolee Schneemann, *More Than Meat Joy: Complete Performance Works and Selected Writings*, ed. Bruce McPherson (New York: Documentext, 1979), 122–27.
15. "Vietnam a vegetable culture which leaves no garbage." Notes about "Snows" (Schneemann, *More Than Meat Joy*, 120).
16. Schneemann, *More Than Meat Joy*, 180.
17. Schneemann, *More Than Meat Joy*, 192.
18. In Patricia Bosworth, *Diane Arbus: A Biography* (New York: Knopf, 1984), 248.
19. John Wakeman, "Shirley Clarke," in *World Film Directors*, vol. 2, *1945–1985* (New York: H. W. Wilson, 1988), 219–24, at 222.
20. See Bosworth, *Diane Arbus: A Biography*.
21. On violence, see Ti-Grace Atkinson, *Amazon Odyssey* (New York: Links Books, 1974).
22. Susan Sontag, *On Photography* (New York: Farrar, Straus and Giroux, 1977), 178, emphasis added.
23. Carole Hanisch, "Critique," in *Notes from the Second Year: Women's Liberation* (New York: New York Radical Women, 1970), 86–87.
24. Alice Echols, *Daring to Be Bad: Radical Feminism in America, 1967–1975* (Minneapolis: University of Minnesota Press, 1989), 86–87.
25. Echols, *Daring to Be Bad*, 86.
26. For a history of 1960s Hollywood's "own apocalypse," see Ethan Mordeen, *Medium Cool: The Movies of the 1960s* (New York: Knopf, 1990), 287.
27. Reprinted from *Women: A Journal of Liberation* (1970). Also: Robin Morgan, ed., *Sisterhood Is Powerful: An Anthology of Writings from the Women's Liberation Movement* (New York: Vintage, 1970), 496.
28. See Gloria Steinem and George Barris, *Marilyn* (New York: New American Library, 1986).
29. Albert Johnson, "Review of Bonnie and Clyde," *Film Quarterly* 21, no. 2 (1967–68): 44–48, at 46.
30. John Cawelti, ed., *Focus on Bonnie and Clyde* (Englewood Cliffs, NJ: Prentice-Hall, 1973), 22–25.

31. Cawelti, *Focus on Bonnie and Clyde*, 22–25.
32. Violence and its almost slapstick visualization propelled the renaissance of the genre film: *Bonnie and Clyde* an update of the late 1930s rural gangster film, *Butch Cassidy and the Sundance Kid* of the westerns Sergio Leone had already resurrected, and *Rosemary's Baby*, Roman Polanski's eerily contemporary monster movie. But the genres had been feminized; Faye Dunaway, Claudia Cardinale, and Mia Farrow figure centrally in these films.
33. Peter Biskind, *Easy Riders, Raging Bulls: How the Sex, Drugs, and Rock 'n' Roll Generation Saved Hollywood* (New York: Simon and Schuster, 1998), 46.
34. Shulamith Firestone, *The Dialectic of Sex: The Case for Feminist Revolution* (New York: Bantam, 1970), 188.
35. This 1967 film, *Shulie*, by Jerry Blumenthal, Sheppard Ferguson, James Leahy, and Allan Rettig, was "adapted" as a shot-by-shot, line-by-line re-creation in 1997 by Elizabeth Subrin. Elizabeth Subrin, "Director's Statement," program notes for "Fakes/Remakes: Stretching the Truth," March 20, 1999, Minneapolis, Walker Art Center.
36. The Group, "First Statement of the New American Cinema Group," 133.
37. Sherry Sonnett Trumbo, "A Woman's Place Is in the Oven," in *Notes from the Third Year: Women's Liberation* (New York: New York Radical Women, 1971), 91.
38. Muriel Rukeyser, *Theory of Flight* (New Haven, CT: Yale University Press, 1935), 87. See Rebecca Hill ("Fosterites and Feminists; or, 1950s Ultra-Leftists and the Invention of AmeriKKKa," *New Left Review* 228 [March/April 1998], 66–90) for an argument that these critiques of Hollywood are central to left-wing feminism in the postwar years and so offer a continuity between the two periods.
39. Barbara Burris, "Fourth World Manifesto," *Notes from the Third Year* (New York: New York Radical Women, 1971), 109.
40. Francee Covington, "Are the Revolutionary Techniques Employed in *The Battle of Algiers* Applicable to Harlem?," in *The Black Woman: An Anthology*, ed. Toni Cade (New York: Signet, 1970), 244–54.
41. Susan Sontag, "The Third World of Women," *Partisan Review* 60 (1973): 180–206, at 184–85.
42. The Newsreel Manifesto was reprinted by Mekas in the January 25, 1968, *Village Voice* column. See Jonas Mekas, *Movie Journal: The Rise of a New American Cinema, 1959–1971* (New York: Collier Books, 1972), 305–6.
43. Mekas, *Movie Journal*, 305.

44. For descriptions of these actions, see Charlotte Bunch, *Passionate Politics: Feminist Theory and Action, Essays 1968–1986* (New York: St. Martin's Press, 1987), 5–6, and Alice Echols, *Daring to Be Bad: Radical Feminism in America, 1967–1975* (Minneapolis: University of Minnesota Press, 1989), 45–59.
45. David James, *Allegories of Cinema: American Film in the Sixties* (Princeton, NJ: Princeton University Press, 1991), 217.
46. David Talbot and Barbara Zheutlin, *Creative Differences: Profiles of Hollywood Dissidents* (Boston: South End Press, 1978), 362. Ironically, both Kramer and Phillips, who also parted ways, became interested in narrative forms: Kramer, who died in 1999, made a number of feature-length narrative films with European financing, among them *Milestones*, which traced the demise of the 1960s New Left; Phillips moved into soap opera, seeing it as a popular female form whose never-ending storyline appeared to undo classic Hollywood cinema and mobilize a female mass audience. She and friends produced an alternative radio soap opera, "Winds of Change," in Saint Louis; eventually she became a scriptwriter for the satirical television soap, "Mary Hartman, Mary Hartman."
47. Mekas, *Movie Journal*. For a devastating critique of *Battle of Algiers*'s "cloying" fakery, see Nancy Ellen Dowd, "Popular Conventions," *Film Quarterly* 22, no. 3 (1969): 26–31. David James makes this point over and over, esp., in the chapter on Brakhage: David James, *Allegories of Cinema*.
48. Parker Tyler, *Underground Film: A Critical History* (New York: Grove Press, 1969), 69.
49. David James, *Allegories of Cinema*, 119–20.
50. Mekas, *Movie Journal*, 89–90.
51. Sheldon Renan, *An Introduction to the American Underground Film* (New York: Dutton, 1967), 174.
52. With the exception of the *Film Quarterly* review and interview and Renan's offhand remark, I can find no mention of this germinal film in any accounts of underground, experimental, expanded or avant-garde cinema, until a brief mention in Wheeler Winston Dixon, *The Exploding Eye: A Re-Visionary History of 1960s American Experimental Cinema* (Albany: State University of New York Press, 1997). Even Patricia Mellencamp's *Indiscretions* (Bloomington: Indiana University Press, 1990), whose subtitle is "Avant-Garde Film, Video, and Feminism," fails to mention this momentous event. Of the mini-industry of memoirs and histories about the 1960s, only Alice Echol's careful re-creation of those "Daring to Be Bad" mentions this

film. See Alice Echol's, *Daring to Be Bad.*

53. Brenda Richardson, "Women, Wives, Film-Makers: An Interview with Gunvor Nelson and Dorothy Wiley," *Film Quarterly* 25, no. 1 (1971): 34–41, at 34.
54. Shirley Clarke and Storm de Hirsch, "A Conversation," *Film Culture* 46 (Autumn 1967): 44–54.
55. Richardson, "Women, Wives, Film-Makers," 36; and Clarke and De Hirsch, "A Conversation," 50.
56. See Kate Haug ("Femme Experimentale: Interviews with Carolee Schneemann, Barbara Hammer, and Chick Strand," *Wide Angle* 20 [1998]: 1–19, at 18), in which she reprints a letter from Adrienne Mancia on MoMA stationery dated August 1968 that "regret[s] that Carolee Schneemann's film, FUSES, is confronted with problems of censorship."
57. Richardson, "Women, Wives, Film-Makers," 35.
58. Dorothy Wiley, *Canyon Cinema Catalogue #6* (1988), 247.
59. The phrase is taken from Sara Evans's book of the same name.
60. Ernest Callenbach, "Review of *Schmeerguntz*," *Film Quarterly* 19, no. 4 (1966): 67.
61. Maureen McCue, "Filmmaking," *Second Wave* 2, no. 3 (1973): 32–34, at 32.
62. Fredric Jameson, "Periodizing the 60s," in *The Sixties without Apology*, ed. Sohnya Sayres et al. (Minneapolis: University of Minnesota Press, 1984), 208.
63. Gitlin, *The Sixties*, 185, is quoting from Paul Potter's reminiscence, *A Name for Ourselves*; however, as David Bernstein, who was present at the speech, suggests, underlying this sensibility were two others: McCarthyism had successfully indoctrinated even those radicals into suspicion of anything that smacked of Communism, on the one hand, and "the system" was at the same time tacitly understood by everyone to be capitalism, on the other hand. Thus, self-censorship served, paradoxically, to open up new metaphors. Personal communication.
64. Adrienne Rich, *Poems: Selected and New, 1950–1974* (New York: Norton, 1975), 169–72.

Bibliography

Abelove, Henry. “Some Speculations on the History of Sexual Intercourse during the Long Eighteenth Century in England.” *Genders* 6 (November 1989): 125–30.

Anger, Kenneth. “An Interview with Kenneth Anger, Conducted by *Spider Magazine*.” *Film Culture* 40 (Spring 1966): 68.

Atkinson, Ti-Grace. *Amazon Odyssey*. New York: Links Books, 1974.

Barthes, Roland. *Camera Lucida: Reflections on Photography*. Translated by Richard Howard. New York: Hill and Wang, 1981.

Biskind, Peter. *Easy Riders, Raging Bulls: How the Sex, Drugs, and Rock 'n' Roll Generation Saved Hollywood*. New York: Simon and Schuster, 1998.

Bosworth, Patricia. *Diane Arbus: A Biography*. New York: Knopf, 1984.

Boyer, Jay. “You Will Never Read the Novel You Might Like To.” In *The Sixties without Apology*, edited by Sohnya Sayres et al. Minneapolis: University of Minnesota Press, 1984.

Brakhage, Stan. “Defense of the 'Amateur' Filmmaker.” *Filmmakers Newsletter* (Summer 1971): 20.

———. “Letter to Dolores Daniels.” *Film Culture* 40 (Spring 1966): 73–75.

Bunch, Charlotte. *Passionate Politics: Feminist Theory and Action, Essays 1968–1986*. New York: St. Martin's Press, 1987.

Burris, Barbara. “Fourth World Manifesto.” *Notes from the Third Year: Women's Liberation*. New York: New York Radical Women, 1971.

Callenbach, Ernest. “Review of *Schmeerguntz*.” *Film Quarterly* 19, no. 4 (1966): 67.

Canyon Cinema Catalogue #6. 1988.

Cawelti, John, ed. *Focus on Bonnie and Clyde*. Englewood Cliffs, NJ: Prentice-Hall, 1973.

Clarke, Shirley, and Storm de Hirsch. “A Conversation.” *Film Culture* 46 (Autumn 1967): 44–54.

Covington, Francee. “Are the Revolutionary Techniques Employed in *The Battle of Algiers* Applicable to Harlem?” In *The Black Woman: An Anthology*, edited by Toni Cade, 244–54. New York: Signet, 1970.

Dixon, Wheeler Winston. *The Exploding Eye: A Re-Visionary History of 1960s*

American Experimental Cinema. Albany: State University of New York Press, 1997.

Dowd, Nancy Ellen. "Popular Conventions." *Film Quarterly* 22, no. 3 (1969): 26–31.

Echols, Alice. *Daring to Be Bad: Radical Feminism in America, 1967–1975*. Minneapolis: University of Minnesota Press, 1989.

Evans, Sara. *Personal Politics*. New York: Knopf, 1979.

Firestone, Shulamith. *The Dialectic of Sex: The Case for Feminist Revolution*. New York: Bantam, 1970.

Gitlin, Todd. *The Sixties: Years of Hope, Days of Rage*. New York: Bantam, 1987.

Hanisch, Carole. "Critique." In *Notes from the Second Year: Women's Liberation*. New York: New York Radical Women, 1970.

Harvey, Sylvia. *May '68 and Film Culture*. London: BFI, 1978.

Haug, Kate. "Femme Experimentale: Interviews with Carolee Schneemann, Barbara Hammer, and Chick Strand." *Wide Angle* 20 (1998): 1–19.

Hill, Rebecca. "Fosterites and Feminists; or, 1950s Ultra-Leftists and the Invention of AmeriKKKa." *New Left Review* 228 (March/April 1998): 66–90.

James, David. *Allegories of Cinema: American Film in the Sixties*. Princeton, NJ: Princeton University Press, 1991.

Jameson, Fredric. "Periodizing the 60s." In *The Sixties without Apology*, edited by Sohnya Sayres et al. Minneapolis: University of Minnesota Press, 1984.

Johnson, Albert. "Review of *Bonnie and Clyde*." *Film Quarterly* 21, no. 2 (1967–68): 44–48.

Leon, Barbara. "Separate to Integrate." In *Feminist Revolution*, edited by Redstockings, 60–63. New Paltz, NY: Redstockings, 1975.

McCue, Maureen. "Filmmaking." *Second Wave* 2, no. 3 (1973): 32–34.

Mekas, Jonas. *Movie Journal: The Rise of a New American Cinema, 1959–1971*. New York: Collier Books, 1972.

Mellencamp, Patricia. *Indiscretions: Avant-Garde Film, Video, and Feminism*. Bloomington: Indiana University Press, 1990.

Mordden, Ethan. *Medium Cool: The Movies of the 1960s*. New York: Knopf, 1990.

Morgan, Robin, ed. *Sisterhood Is Powerful: An Anthology of Writings from the Women's Liberation Movement*. New York: Vintage, 1970.

Rabinovitz, Lauren. *Points of Resistance: Women, Power and Politics in the New York Avant-Garde Cinema, 1943–71*. Bloomington: Indiana University Press, 1991.

Renan, Sheldon. *An Introduction to the American Underground Film*. New York: Dutton, 1967.

Rich, Adrienne. *Poems: Selected and New, 1950–1974*. New York: Norton, 1975.

Richardson, Brenda. "Women, Wives, Film-Makers: An Interview with Gunvor Nelson and Dorothy Wiley." *Film Quarterly* 25, no. 1 (1971): 34–41.

Rukeyser, Muriel. *Theory of Flight*. New Haven, CT: Yale University Press, 1935.

Schneemann, Carolee. *More Than Meat Joy: Complete Performance Works and Selected Writings*. Edited by Bruce McPherson. New York: Documentext, 1979.

Subrin, Elizabeth. "Director's Statement." Program Notes for "Fakes/Remakes: Stretching the Truth." March 20, 1999. Minneapolis: Walker Art Center.

Sontag, Susan. *On Photography*. New York: Farrar, Strauss and Giroux, 1977.

———. "The Third World of Women." *Partisan Review* 60 (1973): 180–206.

Steinem, Gloria, and George Barris. *Marilyn*. New York: New American Library, 1986.

Talbot, David, and Barbara Zheutlin. *Creative Differences: Profiles of Hollywood Dissidents*. Boston: South End Press, 1978.

The Group. "The First Statement of the New American Cinema Group." *Film Culture* 22–23 (Summer 1961): 130–33.

Trumbo, Sherry Sonnett. "A Woman's Place Is in the Oven." In *Notes from the Third Year: Women's Liberation*, 91. New York: New York Radical Women, 1971.

Tyler, Parker. *Underground Film: A Critical History*. New York: Grove Press, 1969.

Wakeman, John. "Shirley Clarke." In *World Film Directors*. Vol. 2, *1945–1985*, 219–24. New York: H. W. Wilson, 1988.

Wiley, Dorothy. *Canyon Cinema Catalogue #6* (1988).

Zimmerman, Patricia. *Reel Families: A Social History of Amateur Film*. Bloomington: Indiana University Press, 1995.

13

Third Cinema in the First World

L.A. Rebellion and the Aesthetics of Confrontation

Allyson Nadia Field

for Teshome

Third Cinema theories and practices comprised some of the most significant of global engagements with the politics and aesthetics of film around 1968. In its basic definition, the idea of Third Cinema was a concept meant to apply to revolutionary situations in countries outside dominant modes of production. Nonetheless, the idea has always retained a hold on the minds of politically inclined filmmakers operating outside of a Third World context. One such group is the L.A. Rebellion, a group of African and African American filmmakers who came together as film students at the University of California, Los Angeles, from the late 1960s to the early 1980s.[1] The L.A. Rebellion has also been termed the "L.A. School" of black filmmakers, and we can think of them as a "school" in the sense of being a collective, however loosely associated.[2] But we should also take the notion of "school" seriously; that is, as demarcating a site of learning. This also means thinking about how being film *students* at

Early versions of this essay were presented at the University of California, Santa Barbara, and at Cornell University. I am grateful to the audiences at both institutions for their very helpful comments and suggestions as well as to feedback from Daniel Morgan, Samantha Sheppard, Christina Gerhardt, and Sara Saljoughi. Many thanks as well to the filmmakers of the L.A. Rebellion whose work I engage with here, in particular Larry Clark, Haile Gerima, Alile Sharon Larkin, and Bernard Nicolas. Ben Caldwell remains an inspiration. With deep gratitude and affection, this essay is dedicated to my former colleague Teshome H. Gabriel (1939–2010).

UCLA shaped their approach to filmmaking. In *L.A. Rebellion: Creating a New Black Cinema*, I argued that the pedagogical training of the students' first film project, the "Project One" film, had a significant impact on their subsequent work and their understanding of themselves as a collective or movement, however loosely defined.[3] In this essay, I turn to their film *studies* training, formal and informal, to consider the ways in which the L.A. Rebellion filmmakers adapted and transformed the aspects of Third Cinema theory and practice that were taught to them and with which they engaged in extracurricular reading groups, applying lessons learned from critical discourses of film and politics to their own work, and, ultimately, demonstrating the flexibility of Third Cinema concepts.[4] In this translation of Third Cinema into black American cinema—a cinema specific to Los Angeles from the 1970s to 1980s—what Teshome Gabriel termed the "aesthetics of liberation" takes on new valences and investments, becoming what I call an "aesthetics of confrontation."[5] Producing an activist cinema, the filmmakers of the L.A. Rebellion applied the strategies of Third Cinema to the situation of the mostly urban black American underclass. Put another way, they produced Third Cinema in the First World. The goal of this essay, therefore, is twofold: first, to contextualize the aesthetic choices of L.A. Rebellion filmmakers in a broader rubric of politically committed film practice; and second, to reconsider the category of Third Cinema as a conceptual, analytical, and practical framework, one that is rooted in specific geographical and political contexts but nonetheless has broader applicability and greater elasticity than critical assessments have allowed.

As with many movements named by critics and historians, the L.A. Rebellion describes not a self-defined group but a conjunction of forces and voices, varied in thrust and emphasis but united in purpose. The filmmakers may have represented widely diverse origins, experiences, and points of view, yet they shared a common goal that constituted them as a whole greater than the sum of its parts. They aimed, that is, to create an alternative cinema—alternative in narrative, style, and practice—to the dominant American model, which they deemed an unwelcoming and virtually impenetrable space for minority filmmakers, and which routinely displayed insensitivity, ignorance, and defamation in its on-screen depictions of people of color. While my focus here is not on the production culture of the L.A. Rebellion, it is important to note that their production practices are central to understanding the group as a loose collective. L.A. Rebellion filmmakers employed guerilla production practices, emphasized collaboration, and worked collectively. Crewing on one another's films created a sense of camaraderie among the black filmmakers and their friends who shared perspectives and sensibilities.

The common purpose shared by L.A. Rebellion filmmakers did not, however, result in a common aesthetic. While Charles Burnett's *Killer of Sheep* (1977) and Julie Dash's *Daughters of the Dust* (1991), probably the two most prominent films to come out of the movement, gained traction on the international film festival circuit and were seen as art films with aesthetic ties to Neorealism and European art cinema more generally, another subset of L.A. Rebellion films evinced a different kind of formal experimentation that relied on a more direct confrontation with issues of injustice. Ben Caldwell, Haile Gerima, Larry Clark, and Alile Sharon Larkin, for example, made films that heed the spirit of the Dziga Vertov Group's objective, stated in 1968, "not to make *political* films but to make films *politically*."[6] We might characterize this other tendency as "radical" in the sense that they overtly, and (arguably) self-consciously, aligned with countercinema practices and global liberation movements. This was especially true with the movement known as Third Cinema, a term initiated with the Argentine filmmakers Fernando Solanas and Octavio Getino but which quickly spread throughout the region.[7] Third Cinema was a concept meant to apply to revolutionary situations in which films were being made outside the dominant modes of production (principally in Africa and Latin America). As Solanas and Getino argued in 1969, all aspects of cinema—production, aesthetics, distribution, and exhibition—were to be revolutionary. They write, "The anti-imperialist struggle of the peoples of the Third World and of their equivalents inside the imperialist countries constitutes today the axis of the world revolution. *Third cinema* is, in our opinion, the cinema that *recognises in that struggle the most gigantic cultural, scientific, and artistic manifestation of our time*, the great possibility of constructing a liberated personality with each people as the starting point—in a word, the *decolonization of culture*."[8]

Given these terms, the United States seems a strange place to welcome the concept of Third Cinema. And yet, to varying degrees, as students, a number of L.A. Rebellion filmmakers self-identified as Third World filmmakers (Barbara McCullough and Julie Dash explicitly articulated this allegiance in a circa

1977 interview for the UCLA student-run cable TV show *Convergence*).[9] This was not simply a declaration of affinity or liking. As these politically inclined filmmakers refigured concepts and strategies of Third Cinema to their own situation, they aligned the condition of black Americans with global liberation struggles and positioned filmmaking as first and foremost a form of activism, a tool in broader struggles for social justice. In a sense, they posited their practice as a kind of Third Cinema that could arise in an internal colony within a First World country. Their application and adaptation of the principles and strategies of Third Cinema followed two strands—modes of production on the one hand and narrative and formal investments on the other hand—highlighting a direct concern with the issues of black representation on screen and the mechanisms of film form appropriate to counterhegemonic representation.

Both of these aspects relating L.A. Rebellion filmmaking to Third Cinema pivot on the climate of and possibilities afforded by UCLA—and Los Angeles more generally—in this period. When Clyde Taylor dubbed this group the "L.A. Rebellion" for a 1986 exhibition at the Whitney Museum, he was consciously mobilizing the associative values of the 1965 Watts Rebellion, and so explicitly linked the group of filmmakers to the urban revolt.[10] The Watts Rebellion directly led to institutional changes across Los Angeles, and at UCLA it led to a series of opportunity programs that enabled underrepresented students to enroll in increasing numbers. It brought about changes to the film school as well, most notably with the hiring of Professor Elyseo Taylor, who coordinated the early initiatives to recruit and train students of color. Taylor's importance for the L.A. Rebellion filmmakers is hard to overestimate. He was the first black faculty member in UCLA's film school and was the founding director of a program called Media Urban Crisis Committee (MUCC for short—affectionately dubbed the "mother muckers" by students), which brought black, Chicano, Asian, and Native American students into the department. Taylor used his position in the school to educate the students, and the department as a whole, about what he took to be the political possibilities of cinema. He brought African filmmakers to the UCLA campus to connect this emerging cinema with the struggles of the "mother muckers" as US "minorities." He also created the long-standing course Film and Social Change in which he screened works by emerging African and Latin American filmmakers. Although he had a tremendous impact on the filmmaking students of color, Taylor's case for tenure was denied—a controversial and deeply politicized case whose outcome was protested by the students of color in the film school. (The closing credits of Ben Caldwell's thesis film, *I&I: An African Allegory* [1979] dedicated the film to Taylor, "who was fired for racist reasons.")

Even without his presence in Westwood, Taylor's impact on UCLA's film students continued through the course he created, which was taught by his successor, renowned Third World film theorist Teshome Gabriel. Gabriel, who had been a graduate student at UCLA, picked up Taylor's mantle by recruiting and mentoring students of color at UCLA and inspiring them in an ongoing exploration of the relationships among cinema, identity, history, and politics. In addition to teaching courses on Third Cinema and on Film and Social Change, Gabriel also led the joint student and faculty Third World Film Club, which screened a wide range of international films on campus. The intellectual and political ambitions of these projects coalesced in his book, *Third Cinema in the Third World: The Aesthetics of Liberation*, revised from his 1979 dissertation and published in 1982. In it, Gabriel emphasized a "new cinematic language" of a "cinema of decolonization and for liberation."[11] To show this, he traced the contours of a film practice that aligns with the plight and struggle of a Third World people against imperialism and class oppression, even if from the relatively privileged position of the United States. Taking up Gabriel's call for "politicizing cinema," the L.A. Rebellion filmmakers sought to align their work with global anti-imperialist fights, while also using it to inform an approach to domestic concerns, with local issues presented as part of a larger international struggle against systemic oppression. Their filmmaking sought to visualize these concerns and put them in terms that would be relatable and transformative for black audiences.

Third Cinema here is not simply dropped intact into a new setting. As L.A. Rebellion filmmakers drew on it, the concepts and strategies of global liberation cinema shifted and transformed to suit the African American context. Their appropriation of Third Cinema thus raises a set of questions. Some are speculative: what does it mean to speak of a Third Cinema practice in the so-called First World? How would a "cinema of decolonization" look in the United States in the late twentieth century? Others are more historical: what are the elements of a Third Cinema practice found in the United States? How did the concepts of Third Cinema translate through the film school experience to generate the kind of work that came out of the L.A. Rebellion? It is not my purpose to reduce Third Cinema to a set of prescriptive tenets; rather, it is to demonstrate the influence of this strand of thought—namely, UCLA's Third Worldism—on the L.A. Rebellion and to suggest the critical value of this approach for explicating black independent film practices in the United States at this particular time as well as beyond. Indeed, this is in keeping with Solanas and Getino's belief that Third Cinema could and should emerge from anywhere in the world. As Mike Wayne notes of Gabriel's theoretical and pedagogical interventions in understanding Third Cinema practices, it "is not a cinema defined by geography; it is a cinema primarily defined by its socialist politics."[12]

In *Third Cinema in the Third World*, Gabriel posits four main purposes of an aesthetics of liberation: to decolonize minds, to contribute to the development of a radical consciousness, to lead to a revolutionary transformation of society, and to develop new film language with which to accomplish these tasks. Characterized by Gabriel as a "cinema of subversion," Third Cinema is a cinema of both "destruction" and "construction": "a destruction of the images of colonial or neo-colonial cinema and a construction of another cinema that captures the revolutionary impulse of the peoples of the Third World."[13] He applied this directly to the UCLA film school: the "destruction" manifested as what I have termed as "rebellious unlearning," a dismantling of the tools of classical Hollywood cinema in order to "construct" a film form that would be more suitable to the investments of African American life.[14] Third Cinema also offered a means of accessing a notion of authenticity with its grounding in "folk culture"—harnessed in the fight for political *and* cultural liberation—something that would crop up repeatedly in the work of the L.A. Rebellion filmmakers. Charles Burnett's *To Sleep with Anger* (1990), Julie Dash's *Diary of an African Nun* (1977) and *Daughters of the Dust*, and Carroll Parrott Blue's *Varnette's World: A Study of a Young Artist* (1979) are a select few that employ this notion. This was one way that Third Cinema not only gave L.A. Rebellion filmmakers a critique of dominant cinema but also a pathway to alternative expressive strategies.

As a way of getting at the relationship between L.A. Rebellion filmmaking and Third Cinema, we can take the central elements that Gabriel labels as the goals of Third Cinema practices and trace how they appear in the work of these filmmakers. First, what does it mean "to decolonize minds" through cinema? Drawing on Frantz Fanon, Gabriel posits the central subject position in Third Cinema as "a historical perspective on radical social change."[15] In L.A. Rebellion films, the concerns of global liberation struggles are applied to the situation faced by many African Americans across the country, primarily in urban environments. In terms of the project of decolonizing minds, this takes two tracks: first, to align the diaspora with struggles in Africa (and other peoples engaged in anti-imperialist fights); and second, to call attention to the cultural impoverishment generated by assimilation. These same concerns resonate across a number of L.A. Rebellion films, especially in those centered on the lives of the underemployed residents of Watts in South Central Los Angeles. Perhaps the most famous example of this in L.A. Rebellion filmmaking is Haile Gerima's 1975 *Bush Mama*, in which the protagonist Dorothy, a pregnant welfare recipient being harassed by the government to get an abortion, comes to an awakened political consciousness, understanding her situation in relation to broader global systemic oppressive mechanisms. Gerima directly aligns Dorothy's plight, and her political awakening, with the anti-imperialist struggles in places like Angola, emphasizing common class-based struggles across national borders. In this internationalist vein, Cynthia Young has argued that while Dorothy "has arrived at a radical subjectivity . . . it is one contained by state forces."[16] For Young, the film is pessimistic, showing how "liberation is delayed." (Indeed, Young sees the L.A. Rebellion on the whole as deeply pessimistic about the possibilities for social transformation.) I disagree with this assessment. Gerima treats Dorothy's trajectory of coming into political consciousness as a success even if the conditions of her environment remain unchanged, and even though she faces imprisonment (the concluding monologue is in the form of a letter from prison). Indeed, one of the arguments I hope to make here is that by reconsidering the L.A. Rebellion movement, not least by expanding the scope of films that constitute it—factoring in recent rediscoveries and rounding out the filmography—we find an important and committed optimism for the possibility of individual and collective engagement. This is especially evident in the more "radical" films of the movement like *Bush Mama*. These films tend to posit the trajectory of politicization and radicalization, a coming into consciousness, as itself a form of liberation—a familiar move in radical narrative art that Gabriel emphasizes. Other examples of this tendency within the L.A. Rebellion include the fashion model's journey back in time in *Sankofa* (dir. Haile Gerima, 1993), the student's political awakening in *Hour Glass* (dir. Haile Gerima, 1971), and the young boy's refusal to sing "My Country 'Tis of Thee" in school at the conclusion of *Fragrance* (dir. Gay Abel-Bey, 1985). Decolonizing the mind is not just the first step in an anti-imperialist struggle; in the case of the "internal colony" inhabited by a nonwhite underclass, it is perhaps the most radical gesture.

This form of liberation finds a more extensive dramatization in Alile Sharon Larkin's *Your Children Come Back to You* (1979), a film that focuses on the consciousness of a child to suggest that the success of a pan-African struggle hinges on the education of the next generation into a new mindset. Made in 1979, the film centers on the conflict between resistance and assimilation, broadly understood. Tovi (played by Charles Burnett's niece Angela who also acted in *Killer of Sheep* and *Bless Their Little Hearts* [Billy Woodberry, 1984]) lives with her father's partner Lani while he is in Africa fighting in an unnamed liberation movement. (The film shows flashbacks of the father helping Tovi spell "MPLA," implying that he has joined the Marxist People's Movement for the Liberation of Angola.) The father's sister, Chris, is a middle-class woman who doesn't approve of how Tovi is being raised and continually reminds Lani that she has "more than enough" and can take care of her niece in ways that Lani cannot. Struck by the differences between her immediate family (Lani emphasizes pride and heritage) and Chris (who brags about traveling to Europe many times and being the "only Negro in the group"), Tovi asks Chris if she's "adopted"—a perspective that is explained by Tovi's recounting of a story told at her progressive, Afrocentric school (a school similar to the school captured in Don Amis's *Ujamii Uhuru Schule Community Freedom School* [1974]), which promotes a collective consciousness of nonwhite people against white hegemonic oppression (economic, political, and cultural).

Tovi recounts the fable of a mother whose children are stolen from her, allegorizing the cultural displacement of slavery and imperialism. From the perspective of a child, the assimilated black woman has been "adopted" by the white "strangers." At the end of the film, Tovi rejects the idea of moving in with Chris and confronts her, saying: "You're adopted. You're like the strangers. We'll never get home with you." Larkin posits the child's growing cultural and political consciousness—a specifically pan-African consciousness—as the solution to the damage perpetuated by generations of increasing alienation from an African heritage. As a child, Tovi represents the fantasy of a blank slate, the untaught mind of a person who, because of age or lack of experience, can escape all previous assumptions, permitting the inscription of a new, revolutionary consciousness. The film ends with a series of shots of Lani and Tovi embracing; after Tovi rejects Chris, Lani gives a very subtle smile suggesting that the immediate tragedy—Tovi's father's death fighting in Africa—has nonetheless yielded a domestic victory in the next generation's rejection of assimilation and political compromise.

Following this kind of idea, Gabriel's second definition of "a film in a Third World context" is one that seeks to contribute to the development of a radical consciousness.[17] The obvious exemplar of this tendency is Haile Gerima, whose films, like *Bush Mama* and *Sankofa*, aim to take their audiences on a journey along with the protagonists so that the characters' coming into awakened consciousness is a motivating model for the possible spectator. But Gerima was not alone in this goal. As a student at UCLA, Bernard Nicolas set out to learn Hollywood techniques in order to use them to convey a counternarrative. Motivated to learn the methods by which Hollywood films captivated people, Nicolas explained: "I wanted to learn how they do it and then reverse the message and . . . have a revolutionary message."[18] The subject of Nicolas's Project Two film, *Gidget Meets Hondo* (1980), is "Gidget," a self-absorbed young white woman living in Marina del Rey, an affluent coastal community in Los Angeles, who is oblivious to the outside world and the violence erupting around her. She becomes an accidental victim of police brutality when a SWAT team mistakes her home for a terrorist haven. The film opens with still photography taken by Nicolas of a demonstration in downtown Los Angeles against the LAPD's murder of Eula Love in 1979. (Eula Love, a thirty-nine-year-old widow and mother of three with a delinquent gas bill, was shot eight times in her front yard by the LAPD for brandishing a knife. The police's actions were deemed appropriate and the officers were not indicted despite public outcry and mass protests.)

As a critique of white complacency toward the LAPD's treatment of African Americans, *Gidget Meets Hondo* pointedly asks whether such police brutality would be tolerated if the victim were a middle-class white woman. The narrative that follows this prologue plays out this premise, suggesting that no one is safe from police misconduct—not even "Gidget"—in a society where the police wage violence on the poor. *Gidget Meets Hondo*, though, is not just designed to shift perspectives and challenge received narratives; it is to produce revolution. In this, *Gidget Meets Hondo*, along with many other L.A. Rebellion films, corresponds to Gabriel's third definition of Third Cinema, that the goal in filmmaking is to catalyze a revolutionary transformation of society.[19] From the desire to develop a radical consciousness in spectators, these films seek to participate in and even instigate social transformation. Typically, this happens on two fronts. First, the films enact a shift in representational paradigms organized around the centering of black subjects and subjectivities (already a radical gesture in American cinema). Second, the films model strategies of resistance for their viewers.

Larry Clark's *As Above, So Below* (1973) comprises a powerful political and social critique in its portrayal of black insurgency. The film centers on Jita-Hadi, a disillusioned Marine who returns from Vietnam with heightened political consciousness and becomes involved with an underground black insurgency. Like *The Spook Who Sat by the Door* (dir. Ivan Dixon) and *Gordon's War* (dir. Ossie Davis), which were both also released in 1973, *As Above, So Below* imagines a post–Watts Rebellion state of siege and an organized black underground plotting revolution. With sound excerpts adapted from the 1968 House Un-American Activities Committee report "Guerrilla Warfare Advocates in the United States," *As Above, So Below* is one of the more overtly politically radical films of the L.A. Rebellion.

Although similar to the work of Gerima in its concern with decolonizing the mind and condemning black complicity with social inequities, Clark extends this critique to picture an organized, armed insurgency. Throughout the film, Clark destabilizes expectations, revealing that the characters coded as compromised might in fact be insurgents, and those who aren't will get their comeuppance. The climax of the film bears this out. Pee Wee, a character presented as the epitome of a "colonized mind"—someone who blames social inequities on the disenfranchised—attempts to aid the police in catching the guerillas. What happens to him is predictable; the police turn their weapons on him, not differentiating between an informant and a threat. Bea, who was introduced earlier in the film as a numbers-playing devout Christian, is in fact one of the leaders of the insurgency and provides the explosives to the insurgents (Clark includes a brief freeze frame to draw attention to this subterfuge).[20]

At once a cautionary tale—a kind of warning—against those who would try to get in the way of the revolutionaries, the film also demonstrates the kind of organization and cooperation necessary for real change. Like *Gordon's War* and *The Spook Who Sat by the Door*, Clark's *As Above, So Below* speculates that the military training provided to young men of color by the government (especially from the Vietnam War) could be applied to a domestic liberation struggle and anti-imperialist insurgency within the United States.

As countercinema movements asserted from the start, transformative film practices must be coupled with transformative film language. In Gabriel's schema, the fourth purpose of Third Cinema is to develop a new film language with which to accomplish the political tasks undertaken by the films.[21] In practice, this kept the L.A. Rebellion closely affiliated with the radical aesthetics of Solanas and Getino's conception of Third Cinema, while still adapting it to the specifics of the African American context. As I have been arguing, part of this—recuperated from earlier black filmmaking practices (such as race films produced explicitly for black audiences)—involves the centering of black subjects and subjectivities. It also applies, however, to more overt experimentation with film form as L.A. Rebellion filmmakers sought to break from the formal hegemony of classical Hollywood cinema. To varying degrees, these filmmakers challenged representational norms and sought a kind of cinema that would be more "authentic" to their subject, one that broke from the ideological implications of traditional Western film.

Haile Gerima's films represent perhaps the most systematic instance of this tendency. The ways in which he subverts formal tenets of classical Hollywood cinema ask critical questions of the assumptions inherent to film form. *Bush Mama* is a case in point. The liberation struggle that Gerima presents is primarily one of the mind, and the mechanisms by which he represents that struggle reflect a radical rethinking of narrative form—the refusal of narrative expediency in favor of a confronting meditation on systemic injustice, especially the role of incarceration as a means of controlling black mobility, and police brutality.

Fairly early in the film, Dorothy's partner T.C. goes out for a job interview. As Dorothy and her daughter wave to him out of the window, the scene abruptly cuts to T.C. entering prison. Gerima has commented on this radical cut, saying: "one of the experiences of being black in America is not going where you want to go, being stopped. . . . It is a truthful representation to cut from him leaving for the job interview to a prison scene without justifying how he got in jail. . . . That one cut in *Bush Mama* satisfies a truthfulness to a black experience."[22] Defying the logic of classical continuity editing, Gerima refuses narrative explanation for how T.C. landed in jail. There is no need to show the alleged crime, he suggests, when the very system itself is predicated on the presumption of guilt as a means to justify the surveillance of black bodies. Indeed, the scene of a black man being arrested is all too familiar in popular visual culture and, for Gerima, an unnecessary component of T.C.'s trajectory. But this does not mean he elides police interference with black mobility. In fact, the first image in the film is of a group of black men being stopped by the LAPD. In a film about state surveillance of black bodies (Dorothy by the welfare system, her daughter Luanne by the LAPD, and T.C. by the penal system), it is unsurprising that the first image functions as an establishing shot of South Los Angeles from the point of view of a surveillance lens.

Gerima subverts the surveillance gaze, however, as it is actually *his* camera capturing—and being captured by—the scene. Instead of a random arrest, what is shown is actually documentary footage of him and his crew being stopped by the LAPD, surreptitiously (and serendipitously) captured by his cameraman. Suspicious of a group of black men with expensive film equipment, the LAPD questioned the UCLA students during the shooting of *Bush Mama*—an encounter that Gerima recalls almost cost him his life.[23] This shot is often cited as emblematic of what the UCLA black filmmakers were up against in their filmmaking practice and of the kinds of harassment typical of the LAPD. In the context of the film, though, the footage functions as a kind of found footage inserted into the fictional narrative that destabilizes the diegesis. As an index of the production process, we are shown the guerilla filmmakers at work. Positioning this footage at the opening of the film, Gerima foreshadows T.C.'s trajectory from work to custody with his own work as a filmmaker being met with suspicion. Seen against the subsequent scene of T.C.'s incarceration, Gerima's reality serves as a stand-in for the fictional T.C.'s plight. The opening confronts the spectator with the unwarranted harassment of the crew, as Gerima presents the problem of "not going where you want to go" at the very outset.[24]

What follows from the cut of T.C. heading to a job interview to winding up in jail is an even stronger break from narrative expectations. Gerima films T.C. arriving in jail in one continuous shot that lasts over two minutes, accompanied by a song by Onaje Kareem Kenyatta that narrates T.C.'s subject position: "Why does it seem like the real criminals go free? Talkin' bout Nixon." In this sequence shot, Gerima inverts points of narrative significance; where the cut elided the presumed crime, arrest, trial, and sentencing, here we get an extended sequence of T.C.'s incarceration. We are shown the long walk to his cell, in the deep recesses of the jail, shot from both inside its halls and then through its bars—the camera remains free while T.C. (and the unindividuated black men in adjacent cells) are locked up. The inversion of narrative expectations and an insistence on attending to the processing of the black man as he is incarcerated—the duration of him losing the already tenuous mobility that he had—confront the spectator with facts without justification. It makes the very question, "what did he do to deserve imprisonment?" vulgar and irresponsible—and, according to the logic of the film, irrelevant. So Gerima not only refuses classical narrative continuity but also deploys filmic devices that more effectively communicate a different logic. This long single tracking shot affords a meditation on incarceration as a fact of life for too many black men and precludes a narrative logic that would justify it. Discontinuity of form reflects the discontinuity of T.C.'s joblessness to incarceration trajectory, a destabilizing gesture central to Gerima's politicized mobilization of film form. Seen this way, Gerima's formal experimentation calls into question the stakes of narrative conventions and points to the insufficiency of these conventions to the urgent tasks of the day: (1) representing black urban struggles, and (2) modeling a means of consciousness-raising if not a mechanism for direct action.

In these ways, what Third Cinema offered the filmmakers of the L.A. Rebellion was a compelling framework with which to critique the dominant media and to imagine forms of resistance. But to take it up they had to adapt its strategies to a very different situation, not just cinematically but in terms of their geopolitical context. First, these filmmakers were working in Los Angeles, and so the dominant cinema was not an imperialist force from outside—it was the very environment of the city and the educational structure in which they were trained. Second, and more importantly, these films run against a tendency to think of Third Cinema (and Political Modernism more generally) as having a set of shared aesthetic criteria (overt reflexivity, explicitly theoretical investments, destroying the power of illusion, and so forth). One of the distinctive and compelling features of the L.A. Rebellion filmmakers is that they offer a set of differing yet overlapping accounts of what constitutes resistant cinematic practices. This is born out of the very nebulousness of what it means to define them as a "movement." The L.A. Rebellion is not a group because they all went to UCLA (though they did) or because they declared themselves a movement (which they did not). They are a group because it is only in considering them together that we are able to see how the disparate strategies—films made in different decades and for different ends—nonetheless share a set of aesthetic and political concerns. These overlapping strategies are related but not identical to Third Cinema; they involve several large-scale transpositions—if they endorse film's role in combatting state violence and promoting resistance (from raising political consciousness to engaging in direct guerilla warfare), they modify it with a new interest in confrontation in and through film itself—its possibilities for resisting dominant paradigms of misrepresenting people of color and its abilities to respond to the need for an alternative image. Seen this way, the L.A. Rebellion is a *cinematic* rebellion that sought its political goals in the medium itself. Perhaps the personalization of confrontation, the positioning of themselves as filmmakers within the world they were showing, is necessary because they were living side by side with those they wished to confront. Regardless, this kind of shift is what defines the L.A. Rebellion as Third Cinema in the First World: an attempt to bring a set of aesthetic and political ambitions into a radically different situation, the promotion of an aesthetics of confrontation for the very purpose of liberation from the internal colony of an unrealized democracy.

Notes

1. For more on the L.A. Rebellion, see Allyson Nadia Field, Jan-Christopher Horak, and Jacqueline Najuma Stewart, eds., *L.A. Rebellion: Creating a New Black Cinema* (Berkeley: University of California Press, 2015). The UCLA

Film and Television Archive has a website dedicated to the films and filmmakers of the L.A. Rebellion: https://www.cinema.ucla.edu/la-rebellion.

2. Ntongela Masilela, "The Los Angeles School of Black Filmmakers," in *Black American Cinema*, ed. Manthia Diawara (New York: Routledge, 1993), 107–117.
3. See Field, "Rebellious Unlearning: UCLA Project One Films (1967–1978)," in Field, Horak, and Stewart, *L.A. Rebellion: Creating a New Black Cinema*, 83–118.
4. As students, the L.A. Rebellion filmmakers met frequently for informal discussions and debates about art, politics, and aesthetics. See Field, Horak, and Stewart, *L.A. Rebellion: Creating a New Black Cinema*, and the L.A. Rebellion Oral History Project for more on these engagements.
5. Teshome H. Gabriel, *Third Cinema in the Third World: The Aesthetics of Liberation* (Ann Arbor, MI: UMI Research Press, 1982).
6. Quoted in Colin McCabe, *Godard: Image, Sound, Politics* (London: Macmillan, 1980), 19.
7. Fernando Solanas and Octavio Getino, "Towards a Third Cinema: Notes and Experiences for the Development of a Cinema of Liberation in the Third World" (1969), in *New Latin American Cinema*, vol. 1, *Theory, Practices, and Transcontinental Articulations*, ed. Michael T. Martin (Detroit: Wayne State University Press, 1997), 33–58.
8. Solanas and Getino, "Towards a Third Cinema," 37.
9. In the conversation, McCullough interviews Dash about her adaptation of Alice Walker's short story *The Diary of an African Nun* (1977).
10. Clyde Taylor, "The L.A. Rebellion: A Turning Point in Black Cinema," in *Whitney Museum of American Art: The New American Filmmakers Series* 26 (New York: Whitney Museum of Art, 1986), 1–2.
11. Gabriel, *Third Cinema in the Third World*, 1. While some differences exist between Gabriel's dissertation and the resulting book, for the purposes of this essay the differences are negligible, and I have chosen to cite the version of the text that is more readily available to current readers.
12. Mike Wayne, *Political Film: The Dialectics of Third Cinema* (London: Pluto Press, 2001), 1.
13. Gabriel, *Third Cinema in the Third World*, 95.
14. Field, "Rebellious Unlearning," 83–118.
15. Gabriel, *Third Cinema in the Third World*, 7.
16. Cynthia Young, *Soul Power: Culture, Radicalism, and the Making of a U.S.*

Third World Left (Durham, NC: Duke University Press, 2006), 239.

17. Gabriel, *Third Cinema in the Third World*, 3.
18. Bernard Nicolas, oral history interview by Jacqueline Najuma Stewart, Allyson Nadia Field, and Jan-Christopher Horak, June 17, 2010, L.A. Rebellion Oral History Project, UCLA Film and Television Archive.
19. Gabriel, *Third Cinema in the Third World*, 3.
20. The male insurgents are played by Nathaniel Taylor, who will go on to star in *Passing Through* (Larry Clark, 1977), and by Haile Gerima, who was an actor before he was a filmmaker. The leader of their unit is played by Johnny Withers, the same actor who will go on to play T.C., Dorothy's politically aware partner in *Bush Mama*.
21. Gabriel, *Third Cinema in the Third World*, 3.
22. "Haile Gerima: Radical Departures to a New Black Cinema." Interview by Tony Safford and William Triplett, *Journal of the University Film and Video Association* 35, no. 2 (1983): 59–65, at 62. For a discussion of this cut, see Mike Murashige, "Haile Gerima and the Political Economy of Cinematic Resistance," in *Representing Blackness: Issues in Film and Video*, ed. Valerie Smith (New Brunswick, NJ: Rutgers University Press, 1997), 183–203, at 192.
23. Haile Gerima, oral history interview by Jacqueline Najuma Stewart, Allyson Nadia Field, and Zeinabu irene Davis, September 13, 2010, L.A. Rebellion Oral History Project, UCLA Film and Television Archive.
24. The theme of immobility is one that runs through L.A. Rebellion films, most notably in *Several Friends* (dir. Charles Burnett, 1969) and *Killer of Sheep*, for example.

14

The Politics of (In)Action

Humanism, Violence, and Revolution in Satyajit Ray's *Pratidwandi/The Adversary*

Sarah Hamblin

From the release of his groundbreaking first film, *Pather Panchali/Songs of the Road* in 1955, Satyajit Ray has been a constituent figure in postwar global art cinema and is without doubt the most celebrated Indian filmmaker in the West. Ray is credited with forging the Indian parallel cinema movement and thus with transforming the landscape of a national industry. At the same time, his cosmopolitan perspective and engagement with a rich international film history have been central to expanding the conventionally European borders of the art cinema tradition. For a collection on the cinemas of 1968, however, Ray might seem like an odd choice. He is typically identified as the least radical of the Bengali filmmakers at work during the politically tumultuous years of the late 1960s and 1970s, and unlike the more overtly marxist cinema of his contemporaries Mirnal Sen and Rhitwik Ghatak, Ray's films are thought to favor broad humanist ideals over a specific political program. Given the Bengali poet Rabindranath Tagore's influence on Ray, his films are celebrated for their lyricism and naturalism, not for their penetrating ideological critiques. As such, humanism and radical politics are largely placed in opposition to each other, and Ray is located firmly on the side of the former; he is the "gentle humanist,"[1] whose films remain "timeless and international,"[2] not the radical revolutionary.

This is not to say that Ray's humanism is apolitical. Indeed, for critics attentive to the larger historical context of Ray's work, his films are profoundly tied to Prime Minister Jawaharlal Nehru's liberal nationalism. Ray's earlier realist films are typically seen as manifestations of this Nehruvian vision of a cosmopolitan India capable of uniting tradition with modernization and their humanist sensibility as an expression of the ethical framework that underscored this project.[3] The shifting political landscape of the 1960s, however, reflected the failures of Nehru's modernizing program and a turn away from the liberal humanism that propelled it. As India's political climate became increasingly unstable, the film society movement with which Ray was intimately connected moved away from aesthetics toward political radicalism as an indicator of quality.[4] Ray became increasingly reviled as an aesthete whose films fell far short of this new standard. Unlike the work of his contemporaries, which positioned revolutionary socialism against such bourgeois liberalism, Ray films, by either affirming the liberal faith in modernization or lamenting its failures, were seen as "conservative or at best . . . reformist."[5]

Recently, critics have begun to challenge this paradigm, with Keya Ganguly's *Cinema, Emergence, and the Films of Satyajit Ray* going a long way toward overturning this assumption of political reformism. Ganguly positions Ray's films within the internationalist avant-garde and its larger investment in art as a means of questioning the historical and social conditions that govern its production. For Ganguly, Ray's is "'an ideational cinema'—a conceptualization of the world rather than a representational reaction to it."[6] This chapter builds on Ganguly's reconsideration of Ray's politics through a discussion of *Pratidwandi/The Adversary* (1970), the first film of Ray's Calcutta trilogy.[7] These three films were made between 1969 and 1975, a period of increasing economic instability, political corruption, and social unrest, and they explore the conditions of labor and unemployment in contemporary Calcutta.[8] Taken together, they examine what Ray describes as "the new breed that has grown up in India since Independence,"[9] that is, the new capitalist class that maintained strict control over the economy and dominated an increasingly disenfranchised youth that struggled to find employment. *Pratidwandi* focuses on Siddhartha, a young man who, after his father dies, leaves medical school in a half-hearted attempt to assume the position of head of the family. Despite several interviews, however, the intensely competitive nature of the job market and Siddhartha's own ambivalence about securing employment renders this attempt futile. After attacking an interview panel for their inhumane treatment of the candidates, Siddhartha leaves Calcutta to take up work as a medical salesman in a small town 250 miles north of the city. This narrative unfolds against a backdrop of Naxalite violence and revolutionary uprisings that render the Calcutta of this time an urban war zone.

Pratidwandi is of particular interest because this more explicit engagement with politics accompanies an aesthetic shift away from the realist style of Ray's earlier films toward the stylizations of the new wave cinemas that swept the globe in the previous decade. As such, this chapter turns to this film to deepen Ganguly's argument about the political commitment of Ray's cinema. Despite challenging the assumption that his films are reformist or conservative, Ganguly concedes that they may not "avow a socialist or programmatically revolutionary perspective."[10] While claims for a sustained revolutionary standpoint across Ray's career would be hard to support, I want to position *Pratidwandi* as a revolutionary film that is part of the international wave of radical political modernist cinema that emerged in tandem with the political upheavals of the long 1968. Specifically, *Pratidwandi* intervenes in debates about the role of violence in revolutionary struggle. While Gandhi's nonviolence is taken to be the oppositional strategy compatible with a humanist philosophy, *Pratidwandi* positions humanism not as the antithesis of radical commitment but as the necessary supplement to revolutionary ideology, one that prevents the violence of revolutionary struggle from ossifying into its own oppressive dogma. *Pratidwandi* makes this argument in relation to Naxalism, a radical peasant movement that in advocating for the complete annihilation of class enemies became intimately connected with extreme violence. Situating *Pratidwandi* within the political turn of the film society movement and thus within the larger mode of filmmaking allied with the politics of the long 1968 highlights its contribution to debates about the role of violence in revolutionary struggle, thus demonstrating how this film, in terms of form and content, shapes and is shaped by the period's revolutionary politics. At stake in this move, then, is both a further politicization of Ray's cinema and a deeper understanding of the politics and form of the cinema of 1968 as a global film practice.

Political Modernism and Third World Marxism

Reading *Pratidwandi* as an engagement with the larger political ideas of the long 1968 concerns the film's style as well as its content. Alongside its intervention into debates concerning revolutionary violence, *Pratidwandi*'s more explicitly avant-garde film style mounts a challenge to the Eurocentric parameters of political modernism, as critics like David Rodowick and András Kovács have characterized it, and expands the international lines of influence that cut across the politics and form of this cinema. Ray is already understood as a key figure in postwar art cinema, a mode of film practice that Keya Ganguly situates within the larger context of the internationalist New Wave.[11] In establishing its global contours, Ganguly argues that this New Wave was more than the "youthful revolt of modern European subjects."[12] Rather, it developed in concert with various anticolonial movements around the world and in mutual opposition to the discourses of modernization in both Europe and the Third World. While the effects of these global forces registered differently in Europe and its former colonies, they were "nonetheless perceived as a common plight and shared predicament to be contested by artists and intellectuals worldwide."[13] Although France is often taken to be the epicenter of 1968, this global political framework rests at the heart of the radical ends of political modernist cinema. To acknowledge this is to do more than point out that student and worker uprisings occurred the world over or to emphasize Godard's international popularity; it is also to recognize that Third World marxism and anti-imperialism stood at the very center of the long 1968. Indeed, the politics of 1968 were influenced as much by the tricontinental revolutionary philosophies of Che, Fanon, and Mao as much as they were by Marcuse, Althusser, and Debord. Moreover, filmmakers both inside and outside of Europe were questioning European aesthetic ideology and searching for new political-aesthetic paradigms. In India, as Rochona Majumdar argues, the film society movement's increasing investment in radical political commitment as the mark of quality was directly linked to the rise of radical leftist movements both domestic and international and resonated with both post-1968 French film and Third Cinema as well as other left-oriented cultural movements in India, including the Progressive Writers and the Indian People's Theater Associations.[14]

Third World marxism was particularly important for its theorization of revolutionary violence, a question that took on increasing weight as the war in Vietnam persisted and student protests morphed into armed insurrections and terror campaigns. With the development of militant left-wing groups across Europe, Asia, and the Americas, violence became central to the idea of revolution, and militants as well as filmmakers turned to the anticolonial and anti-imperialist liberation struggles in Africa, Asia, and Latin America to justify violent insurrection in the name of revolution. It is at this level that *Pratidwandi* makes a significant contribution to the political discourse of the long 1968 through its theorization of violence and the need for a humanist supplement to revolutionary ideology.

Autogestion and Refusal

If the Apu trilogy articulated an optimistic faith in Nehru's nation-building project, the Calcutta trilogy is taken to represent the loss of this social promise by revealing how pervasive corruption, bureaucratic inefficiency, and increasing economic precarity plague the city, the symbol of Nehru's modern, cosmopolitan India. This sense of disillusionment led to widespread unrest and an increasingly volatile political climate that Ray himself said could be felt at "every moment of the day in Calcutta: not just the bombs and the explosions, but meeting people and walking the streets with the posters on the walls."[15] This explosive political atmosphere was tied to the influx of refugees from East Pakistan and the Bengali Independence Movement but mostly, in 1969–70 at least, to Naxalite violence. Naxalism emerged in 1967 from conflicts within India's two established communist parties with the aim of overthrowing the current government via armed insurrection. Spreading from the villages to the city and capturing the imagination of students and disenfranchised young men, this Maoist-inspired group launched a campaign of left-wing terror that included violent confrontations with police, bombings, kidnappings, and murder. At the time of filming, Calcutta was a battleground between the Naxalites and the police, the latter responding to the uprisings with equal brutality. This increase in radical political activity, rather than acting as a deterrent to filming in the city as it had done previously, now motivated Ray to return to Calcutta and explore these tensions. Indeed, it seemed unavoidable. As Ray put it, "I made [*Pratidwandi*] because the situation in Calcutta was politically so tense. The students were very active, there was a lot of violence in the city, and if I was going to make another film it seemed it had to be about Calcutta and the young people there."[16]

Pratidwandi is immersed in this turbulent political climate. Siddhartha spends large portions of the film debating his engagement, or lack thereof, with the uprisings taking place around him. This is in contrast to his

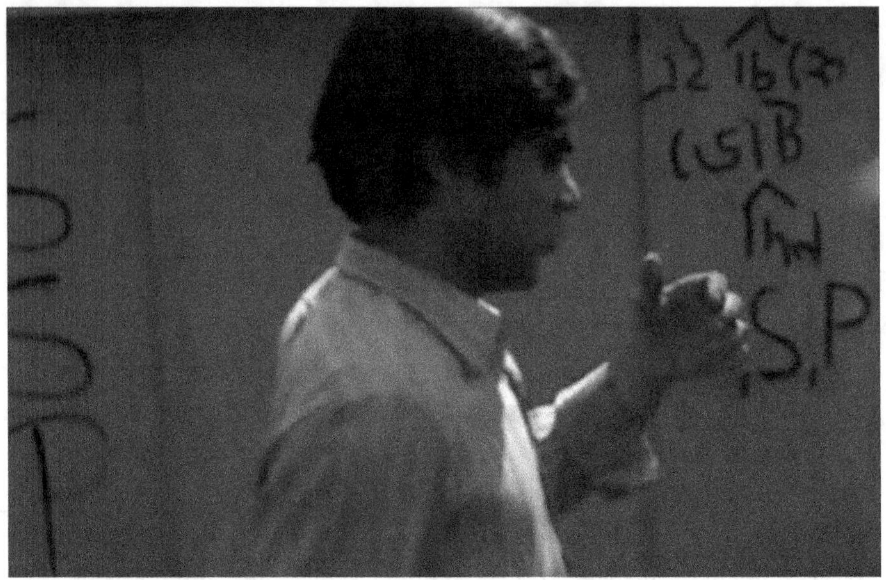

Siddhartha walks past a wall covered with authentic political graffiti telling people to vote for the Samyukta Socialist Party (*Pratidwandi* 1970).

brother Tunu, a committed Naxalite who plants bombs across the city and is forced to flee under threat of police retaliation. Naxalite violence permeates the film, with Siddhartha at one point having to evacuate a movie theater after a bomb explodes. Beyond the narrative though, this history is documented in the film's mise-en-scène; wherever Siddhartha goes in Calcutta the walls are plastered with authentic political graffiti and agitational posters, and one scene captures in the background the mass public rally at the announcement of the formation of the Marxist-Leninist Communist Party of India (CPI), which became the official party of the Naxalite movement. The mise-en-scène thereby demonstrates the inescapability of this revolutionary atmosphere and anchors the film to this larger radical political context.

In line with this political climate, the anticapitalist politics of *Pratidwandi* are fairly clear cut. The film focuses on the ways in which the new bureaucratic business class in Calcutta perpetuates the disenfranchisement of the increasingly large number of unemployed young men in the city. At each interview, throngs of applicants are forced to wait for hours in miserable conditions before being subjected to a litany of bizarre questions that have nothing to do with the position. The interview panel then sits in arbitrary judgment, threatening to cancel interviews if anyone dares complain. *Pratidwandi* thus exposes the systems of power that control the city's economy and the ways by which this elite perpetuates its own authority and privilege at the callous expense of a marginalized younger generation.

Pratidwandi combines this political critique with a stylistic shift toward what András Kovács refers to as political modernism's "more self conscious, ideologically based filmmaking style," this new style providing the formal complement to its engagement with radical politics at the level of content.[17] If we accept that the realist aesthetic of Ray's previous films was bound, at least in part, to the post-Independence ideology of nation-building, it accords that *Pratidwandi*, as a film that exposes the failures of this earlier vision, would require a new style to communicate this new politics. Indeed, Ray explained his formal turn in this way: "I wanted it to be apparent also in the style that this was my first political film: a different film from what I had done before, so let it be different."[18] As a result, *Pratidwandi* moves away from the linear, progressive narrative of the Apu trilogy toward a more episodic and elliptical structure, this lack of coherence marking the fragmented nature of contemporary experience where the narratives of development and progress have broken down.

Despite this political critique, however, *Pratidwandi* has not been considered a revolutionary film. Indeed, rather than referring to the subjects of revolution, the adversary of the film's title is taken to be the modern city and the new comprador class to which the film fails to present a viable challenge. This interpretation frames Tunu as a "simplistic stereotype"[19] whose Naxalite violence accomplishes nothing, and Siddhartha, despite being politically active as a student, as a disaffected dropout who refuses to commit to any cause or to take any decisive action, preferring instead to wander aimlessly through the city and to daydream about the past. As such, Siddhartha is seen to reflect the "larger paralysis of will" that characterizes his disenfranchised generation[20] rather than a possible oppositional stance.

If we compare Siddhartha to the other marginalized groups in the film, however, his attitude appears distinct from this larger malaise. In a telling scene, Siddhartha sits under a pavilion between a ragged beggar and a group of American hippies. In this moment, Siddhartha's difference from these other two marginal groups is profound—he is neither the destitute beggar who lacks agency nor is he the hippie dropout whose privilege is thinly cloaked by countercultural politics. Moreover, Siddhartha maintains vestiges of a commitment to radical politics; throughout the film he remains sympathetic to his brother's cause, at one point commenting that the city is so corrupt that the only viable response is "a machine gun to clean it all up." At times, Siddhartha appears in awe of his brother's revolutionary commitment as he imagines himself as Che Guevara and wonders if, like Tunu, he would have the courage to die for a cause. In a similar expression of radical political sensibility, at his first interview, when asked what he thinks is the most significant event of the last decade, Siddhartha replies that it is the "plain human courage" shown by the Vietnamese, though he knows the response will provoke the panel. Even when given the opportunity to correct his answer to the moon landing, which one interviewer suggests instead, Siddhartha doubles down on his original response, arguing that the moon landing was predictable, whereas "no one knew they [the Vietnamese] had it in them." Labeled by the panel as a communist for an answer that betrays his admiration for anti-imperialist, anticapitalist resistance over the Western, techno-scientific power of the moon landing, Siddhartha does not get the job.

In the context of these broad revolutionary sympathies, Siddhartha's inaction takes on a different valence, one that is profoundly in line with the autogestive politics of 1968.[21] Significantly, Siddhartha's gestures of refusal are generally directed at three oppressive institutional structures: the state and workforce (his refusal to behave as required at his interviews); the family (his failure to become the provider and patriarch, as evidenced by his inability to get a job or "protect" his sister's virtue); and the party (his rejection of an offer to work in the CPI offices and his refusal to help his brother procure explosives). Rather than attacking these structures directly, Siddhartha refuses the symbolic identifications they offer. The rejection of Naxalite affiliation is particularly significant, for although the movement emerged partly in response to the entrenched bureaucracy and conservatism of the various factions of the CPI, Naxalism soon developed its own rigid infrastructure and ideological orthodoxy.

Ray commented on the repressive power of party politics numerous times, arguing that total identification with a cause erases individual thought and the possibility of autonomy: "Anybody who identifies himself with a movement is depending on directives from higher figures who are dictating, controlling their movement."[22] As such, "revolutionaries don't think for themselves";[23] rather, they become extensions of an abstract ideology determined from without. Siddhartha's rejection of any social institution that would control his behavior accords with the principles of self-determination and the broad advocacy of individual freedom over collective repression that underscore the politics of 1968. While there are certainly differences across the various national articulations of this politics, taken as a whole they all share some degree of opposition to institutionalized hierarchy, including the competitive class logic of capitalism, the repressive morality of the bourgeois family, and the authoritarian control of party orthodoxy. Understood through this larger political framework, Siddhartha's refusals are autogestive, springing, as Ray himself puts it, not from "the dictates of ideology" but his "own, human experiences."[24]

It is easy to see this emphasis on self-determination as an expression of bourgeois individualism, as is the case in most critical discussions of the film. Ray's own comments on Indian politics seemingly affirm this interpretation: "I still believe in the individual and in personal concepts rather than in a broad ideology."[25] Taking Ray at his word, critics who are willing to entertain the idea that Siddhartha is, in fact, the adversary of the film's title understand Siddhartha's refusals as the affirmation of a "personal life vision,"[26] as his attempt to "remain true to himself"[27] and "retain what is intrinsically [his] own" in the face of the dehumanizing impulses of the office and the crowd.[28] As Tom Milne argues, "an inborn and sternly cultivated sense of honor . . . mean[s] that [Siddhartha's] revolutionary impulses are always blocked by his desire to preserve the status quo of humanity."[29] Humanism, it seems, is both counter and preferable to revolutionary ideology.

Yet these ideas only stand in opposition if we accept that *Pratidwandi* rejects Naxalite ideology tout court, and as I have argued, Siddhartha is significantly more sympathetic to its politics than this interpretation would allow. As such, it is my contention that Siddhartha's humanism is not a critique of or replacement for revolutionary commitment but a necessary supplement to it. For Ray, as for many other radicals, the sticking point with Naxalism was the extreme brutality of its methods, which became hard to reconcile with its larger emancipatory project. The violence of Naxalite ideology thus needs tempering or else it becomes its own oppressive regime, and in *Pratidwandi* it is Siddhartha's humanist impulses that provide this necessary counterbalance. This claim, then, takes seriously a different comment that Ray made about the film. In a letter to Marie Seton about the release of *Pratidwandi*, Ray comments, "the present EXPLOSIVE atmosphere here—anarchy and revolution and violent anti-American feeling—make me pretty tense about the possible reaction to my new film. It's certainly the first truly contemporary film made here and basically, though not blatantly, pro-revolution—because I feel nothing else can set the country up on its feet."[30] If revolution is the only answer, Siddhartha's humanist impulse is vital as it is precisely that which prevents the violence of revolution from becoming a reactionary and oppressive gesture.

Violence and Humanism

Throughout the film, Siddhartha's refusals stem from his humanist impulses. What stops him from committing is his concern over the effects his actions will have on others; in his refusals of Naxalite insurrection in particular, his apprehension is grounded in the human cost of this violence. In a key scene, Siddhartha watches a Naxalite mob pull a driver from his car after he knocks down a pedestrian. Seeing that the man drives a Mercedes, Siddhartha joins in the group assault until he spots the driver's daughter sitting petrified in the back seat. Immediately, Siddhartha disengages and runs away. In this moment, Siddhartha is spurred into action by a vague sense of revolutionary solidarity; the driver is rich, and even though Siddhartha did not witness the accident he feels the driver deserves to be punished for his wealth and privilege. On seeing his daughter, however, this ideologically driven violence is tempered by concern about its impact. "Facing him," as Milne puts it, "is not the abstract mask of oppression, but another frightened, helpless child."[31] Ray's humanist investment in the shared capacity of all beings to suffer takes on a radical political valence, and Siddhartha's indecision—what has typically been characterized as a mark of Ray's humanist preoccupation with flawed yet sympathetic individuals—is recast as revolutionary strategy.

Revolutionary strategy in *Pratidwandi* is thus bound to the tension between the abstract violence of revolution and humanist compassion for the suffering of others that this scene establishes. As Raymond Williams explains, revolution is inevitably a time of violence and suffering, but the revolutionary ideologies of the twentieth century recast this violence as the expression of dialectical historical forces, thus disavowing the suffering that it causes as the necessary precursor to revolutionary triumph. Building on this logic, Karla Oeler argues, "In the strictest extreme of class struggle, murder cannot take place because killing an oppressor is not murder, but rather the creation of a new social order, and killing the oppressed is always a matter of class violence in which the individual is irrelevant."[32] The historical determinism of marxist teleology transforms human beings into objects in a class relation that, in turn, enables and justifies violence. As Williams continues, "Real suffering is then at once non-human: [it] is a class swept away by history. . . . The more general and abstract, the more truly mechanical, the process of human liberation is ordinarily conceived to be, the less any actual suffering really counts, until even death is a paper currency."[33]

The question of revolutionary violence was (and still is) central to Naxalite ideology. Naxalism adopted the same teleological revolutionary logic of orthodox marxism, proclaiming its triumph as historical inevitability, even going so far as to posit 1975 as the year of final victory. This teleology was supplemented by a vulgar marxist fixation on violence as the principle political currency. Naxalism advanced two tactical campaigns: guerilla warfare and *khatam*—the unequivocal extermination of all class enemies. While the former involved violent clashes with landlords and businessmen, seizing land, torching buses, and bombing public buildings, the latter meant the assault and execution of anyone in a position of bourgeois authority, from businessmen and government officials, to traffic police, doctors, academics, and other middle-class professionals. Details of this annihilation line were published in the February 1970 edition of the Naxalite journal *Liberation*, which quickly became known as the "murder manual."[34] This violence was particularly gruesome, with many bloodthirsty Naxalites taking all too literally Charu Majumdar's comment that, "he who has not dipped his hand in the blood of class enemies can hardly be called a communist."[35] As Suranjan Ganguly points out, Naxalism "redefined masculinity in violent terms," thus firmly establishing violence as fundamental to revolutionary strategy.[36]

If the abstract tenets of Naxalism legitimize violence in the name of revolution, Siddhartha's humanist deliberation becomes a key means of preventing this ideology from hardening into its own oppressive culture of violence where even the worst atrocities are excused in the name of Tomorrow. Unlike

Tunu's ideological commitment, which obscures the human cost of violence, Siddhartha's preoccupation with the effect of his actions on the lives and desires of individual subjects opens up a space for contemplation that forces engagement with this cost, thereby undermining the blind assurance of ideological commitment and its faith in a justifying future-to-come. Reinserting the question of human suffering into potential acts of violence destabilizes such convictions and opens up the possibility of inaction that nonetheless remains consistent with revolutionary commitment.

In emphasizing the capacity of others to suffer and thereby highlighting the shared humanity of both oppressor and oppressed, *Pratidwandi*'s humanism may appear to echo Gandhi's philosophy of nonviolence. As Colin Wright argues, the logic of liberal humanism typically considers politics and violence as absolute antonyms,[37] and at first glance it may seem that Siddhartha's own rejection of violence in favor of a more passive mode of resistance affirms the incompatibility of these ideologies. Siddhartha's violent response to the inhumane conditions of his last job interview, however, demonstrates that this humanist supplement does not undermine violence as a political strategy in and of itself. After one of the applicants passes out from heat stroke, Siddhartha storms past the guard into the interview room and demands the board provide more seats and water. When the board dismisses his claims as weakness, Siddhartha acts out violently, punching the interviewers and overturning their desks.

Significantly, Siddhartha's expression of violence is predicated not on an abstract ideological principle but on a humanist deliberation over the experience of collective suffering. *Pratidwandi* establishes this humanist conception of suffering through the flashbacks to Siddhartha's time in medical school, which underscore the shared physiology of all individuals, despite what Siddhartha refers to as a few surface "abnormalities." The film couples this emphasis on common anatomy with a preoccupation with suffering bodies, from the discomfort of interviewees to scenes of crowded city buses where people jostle for space in similarly uncomfortable conditions, from malnourished and injured vagrants to wounded Naxalites and bomb victims. As Supriya Chaudhuri notes, Siddhartha is constantly aware of these bodies,[38] and the film repeatedly foregrounds a sense of physical discomfort as well as sympathy for bodies in pain.

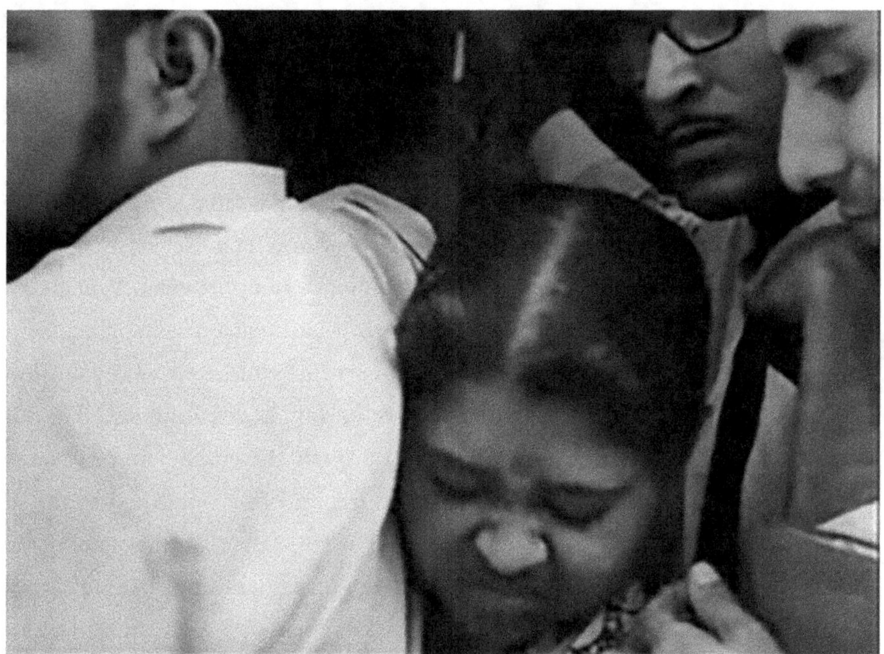

City residents ride an overcrowded bus, the close-up shot highlighting their physical discomfort (*Pratidwandi* 1970).

During his last interview, this link between a shared anatomy and concomitant capacity for suffering becomes explicit. While waiting to be called, Siddhartha stands with the other applicants in a stifling corridor when the body position of one man leaning against the wall reminds him of a lecture on the human skeleton. The camera seamlessly pans from the memory of this lecture to the men standing in the corridor, but they are all now skeletons. The flashback to medical school once again highlights how all bodies have the same basic physiological structure, but through Siddhartha's present-time hallucination it is tied to a humanist recognition that this shared physiology indicates a similarly shared capacity for suffering; not only are all the men in this corridor the same, they are all equally at risk of dying under an oppressive and impersonal economic system. This recognition of suffering and its potentially lethal consequences, both physical and psychological, results in Siddhartha's violent insurrection, albeit on a significantly smaller scale than Tunu's. The possibility of violence as a revolutionary strategy remains, however; Siddhartha's humanist deliberation this time leads to action rather than withdrawal.

If we return to Ray's comment that *Pratidwandi* endorses a revolutionary message because "nothing else can set the country up on its feet," Siddhartha's violent response at the end of the film, his only moment of action, seems inevitable, as violence is embedded within the very situation that the film addresses. As Fanon does in his analysis of anticolonial violence, *Pratidwandi* "begins from the fact of existing violence,"[39] assuming its presence within revolutionary struggle as the inversion of the violence of oppression. Violence is not grafted onto the situation but intrinsic to it and hence inescapable. Only violence tempered by humanist deliberation, however, maintains a revolutionary potential. What the film proposes has something in common with Fanon's critique of spontaneous violence, which, although triumphant in the initial phase of insurrection, is cultlike in its thinking and thus "destined to fail as a doctrine."[40] According to Fanon, spontaneous violence is reactionary and uncritical; it is opposition driven by "hatred, resentment, and the legitimate desire for revenge" that, while understandable, lacks the "control and guidance" necessary to sustain the larger struggle.[41] While for Fanon the uncritical nature of spontaneous violence is due to the lumpenproletariat's lack of political consciousness,[42] in the case of 1970s Naxalism it resulted from the revolutionaries' overidentification with Majumdar's annihilation line. Both conditions lead to the same result—a violent mass whose brutal opposition is unmoored from critical reason. As Fanon states, "hatred is not an agenda," and unless it can be harnessed to a larger organizational structure, it is not enough to sustain a movement.[43]

This decoupling of class rage from larger organizational forms of opposition was precisely what happened to the Naxalite movement under Majumdar's leadership. His focus on the twin tactics of guerilla warfare and the annihilation of class enemies meant that Naxalism deemphasized organizational politics; as Sanjay Seth illustrates, in response to what they saw as the reformist policies of the two Indian communist parties, Naxalism placed a reduced importance on "organizational forms such as trade unions, peasant organizations and student unions," instead according increasing significance to violent forms of opposition.[44] In consequence, class hatred became the driving force behind the escalating excesses of Naxalite violence, something that the pages of *Liberation* regularly fueled with inflammatory statements like, "The people's hatred and anger found expression when they painted slogans with his blood and hung his head from the roof of his house."[45]

In *Pratidwandi*, the snap actions of the Naxalites, driven as they are by blind class hatred, lack the critical thought necessary to maintain their revolutionary potential and instead take on the feverish cultlike mindset that Fanon warns of. In place of this uncritical spontaneity, the film posits Siddhartha's humanist deliberation as a means of reestablishing a critical relationship to violence without discounting it as a potentially viable mode of insurrection. In this way, the film attempts to square the circle of class hatred and humanist compassion to produce a revolutionary humanism, one that undermines the strict and unwavering logic of class opposition but still allows it to persist in a more strategic register, that is, as a sociohistorical relation rather than an ontology. In this way, the blind rage of class hatred that fueled and excused any and all acts of Naxalite bloodlust is untenable in the face of humanist compassion, but that very same awareness of human suffering can be the grounds for violent uprising. This rejection of blind class hatred explains the difference between Siddhartha's inaction with the Mercedes driver and his response to the interview panel. In the first scene, Siddhartha has no proof that the driver is at fault; he reacts purely out of class hatred. In the second, however, he is confronted with concrete, experiential evidence of the panel's involvement in systemic oppression. The distinction is thus between a reified, purely objectifying ontology of class hatred that inhibits any acknowledgment of suffering and a nonreified, humanist understanding of class as a sociohistorical relation that entails identifying those who actively perpetuate class inequality and the violence of the system itself. *Pratidwandi* thereby refuses the binary opposition of humanism and violence and the concomitant requirement to privilege one philosophy over and against the other. Instead, the film recasts them as antinomies—both valid and fundamental yet seemingly unresolvable—and attempts to imagine a way to navigate this tension.

In staving off the cultlike adherence to ideology that enables violence detached from critical reflection, humanist deliberation encourages an ethical relationship to violence as any action must be undertaken in full consciousness of its consequences. Naxalism's reliance on the teleologically determined certainty of victory routinized violence and absolved revolutionaries from responsibility for the suffering they caused. Conversely, Siddhartha's violent outburst carries with it no clear revolutionary outcome. Instead, the film jump-cuts from Siddhartha attacking the interview panel to him riding a bus out to the country where he has taken a job. The fact that Siddhartha's actions are "fruitless in the outcomes"[46] undermines the faith in the future that would a priori rationalize revolutionary violence, the jump cut between these scenes underscoring our inability to know the future and thus invalidating the vindicating logic of historical determinism. As both Jacques Derrida and Alain Badiou have argued, the undecidability of change is a fundamental element of revolutionary process, as knowledge of outcomes cannot be calculated in advance. To accept this is to accept the risk involved in any action and therefore accept responsibility for it, knowing that there is no assurance of victory. This undecidability does not mean the perpetual deferment of action, nor does it invalidate the use of violence—Siddhartha both acts and acts violently—but it does require a careful consideration of violence as a revolutionary strategy as there is no recourse to the future as a means of justification. Humanist deliberation requires careful and critical reflection on any use of violence and the conscious choice to act with full awareness of the suffering that it will cause; one must face this suffering as such, not disavow it as the enactment of an abstract class relation or historical inevitability. Siddhartha's humanist deliberation thus maintains an ethical relationship to violence and takes responsibility for it. He remains sensitive to the suffering of others and compelled to act against it but simultaneously aware of the dehumanizing and destructive effects of violence and, most importantly, capable of judging when and if violence is warranted.

Film Style and the Deliberative Revolutionary Subject

In replacing the logic of teleological determinism with a humanist deliberation over violence and suffering, *Pratidwandi* tries to imagine a revolutionary subject from *within* the processes of revolution. That is, the film does not posit a postrevolutionary utopia where violence is no longer necessary and from which a new humanist subject can emerge. Instead, it attempts to envision a new self-materializing from within the act of struggle, a reasoned humanist revolutionary whose actions are grounded in critical thought, not simply reactionary class hatred. Indeed, in refusing the future anterior of revolutionary victory, *Pratidwandi* implies the fundamental incompleteability of struggle and advances through Siddhartha a revolutionary strategy that incorporates the values of a universal humanism that would structure utopia without presuming its arrival. In this way, *Pratidwandi* allows for the oppositional logic of class antagonism that drives violence, but it inserts humanist deliberation to prevent this oppositional logic from ossifying into a deterministic and totalizing relation that evacuates human suffering in the name of a tomorrow that can never be known. Siddhartha's humanism supplements Naxalism with an ethical relation that, rather than undermining its potential violence, renders it a more viable revolutionary strategy.

Pratidwandi's stylistic innovations reinforce this larger investment in humanist deliberation as a supplement to abstract revolutionary violence. The film incorporates multiple strategies of disorientation and aesthetic estrangement that emphasize the irreal and irrational; freeze frames, jump cuts, and ellipses disrupt the viewers' experience of time and distort the logic of cause and effect. Similarly, the narrative slides seamlessly between past and present as Siddhartha's memories intertwine with present-day action and between reality and fantasy as we move in and out of his dreams, fantasies, and anxieties. This slippage blurs the distinction between objective reality and subjective desire. Such emphasis on the irrational can be understood in opposition to the instrumental rationality of ideological dogma where the reduction of human beings to abstractions in a calculation (be it of profit or revolutionary strategy) justifies horrific violence and exploitation. In opposition to the dangers of this instrumentalizing rationality, *Pratidwandi* promotes a sense of irrationality, one that lines up with Siddhartha's experience and thus his humanism. At the same time, the film's aesthetic estrangement makes it somewhat more challenging to follow, and in this way, it requires of its audience a mode of contemplation somewhat akin to Siddhartha's own deliberative mindset. Just as Siddhartha refuses to give himself over to an ideology that would prohibit independent thought, the audience, too, is unable to be swept along by the narrative. More than simply marking a shift in political orientation or the expression of the lived experience of modernity, then, *Pratidwandi*'s new wave style works to foster a new mode of consciousness, one that is grounded in contemplation and the irrationality of feeling and sympathy, as opposed to a seductive and ruthless rationality.

This emphasis on the irrationality of dream and desire challenges the logic of a totalizing ideology and provides the space for humanist deliberation. If the ideologies of the party, the family, and the workforce have become rigidly inflexible, dreaming becomes the space where antireified, autogestive thought can happen. Following Herbert Marcuse, the realms of fantasy and the imagination operate as key spaces of negation where the possibility of something radically new and different remains thinkable. Rather than marking his separateness from the political events surrounding him, then, Siddhartha's revolutionary dreams and hallucinations supply the utopian supplement necessary to prevent revolutionary ideology from ossifying into an oppressive ontology. The seamless integration of dreams into the narrative is more than disorienting; it undermines the strict opposition between reality and fantasy, thereby suggesting the necessity of the imaginative when attempting to transform the present. Indeed, Siddhartha's moment of rebellion is prompted by precisely this slippage between reality and the imagination. In this way, these dreams and fantasies link up with *Pratidwandi*'s formal innovations to create a space of humanist deliberation. The strategies of aesthetic estrangement that the film employs all generate a kind of break or gap, be it between times, places, or levels of reality. These gaps are bridged by the imaginative as Siddhartha or the audience reflect on these discontinuities and imagine a series of possible causes and effects. As such, they do the work of humanist deliberation as they represent the possibility of thinking and thus acting differently, which is fundamental to an autogestive revolutionary imagination that aims to function outside the disciplinary norms of orthodox revolutionary thought.

Positioning *Pratidwandi* within the political and aesthetic framework of political modernism opens up this mode of film practice beyond its European borders and traces more complex global connections between the politics and the cinemas of the long 1968. As such, it requires us to rethink the lines of influence and replace what Keya Ganguly refers to as the current "directional imperative" that positions Ray's politics and style as "borrowed" from the European tradition.[47] In its place we can begin to develop a more complex dialectical relationship between the various international films that comprise the cinemas of 1968, one that recognizes their mutual influence on each other and affords each their own unique stylistic and political contribution within this larger global network. Ray's critique of Calcutta's business class and his turn to avant-garde techniques does not, therefore, suggest that his experience of modernity had finally caught up with that of his European counterparts. Instead, it identifies *Pratidwandi* as Ray's contribution to the radical ends of political modernist filmmaking around the 1968 conjuncture and recognizes the film as a part of a larger international mode of film practice invested in using cinema as a means of political engagement. Perhaps most importantly, it illuminates the dialectic between Third World and European revolutionary discourse and cinema, the contributions of these "darker nations" moving from the periphery to the core.

Notes

1. Chandak Sengoopta, "Satyajit Ray: Liberalism and Its Vicissitudes," *Cineaste* 34, no. 4 (2009): 16–22, at 16.
2. Ashish Rajadhyaksha, "Satyajit Ray, Ray's Films, and Ray-Movie," *Journal of Arts and Ideas* 23, no. 4 (1993): 7–16, at 8.
3. Sharmistha Gooptu, *Bengali Cinema: An Other Nation* (New York: Routledge, 2011), 141.
4. Rochona Majumdar, "Debating Radical Cinema: A History of the Film Society Movement in India," *Modern Asian Studies* 46, no. 3 (2012): 731–67, at 735.
5. Geeta Kapur, "Cultural Creativity in the First Decade: The Example of Satyajit Ray," *Journal of Arts and Ideas* 23–34 (1993): 181–89.
6. Keya Ganguly, *Cinema, Emergence, and the Films of Satyajit Ray* (Berkeley: University of California Press, 2010), 26.
7. The other two films in the trilogy are *Seemabaddha/Company Limited* (1971) and *Jana Aranya/The Middleman* (1975).
8. Although Calcutta officially became Kolkata in 2001, for the sake of historical accuracy and consistency I have elected to use the former name throughout this essay.
9. Christian Braad Thomsen, "Ray's New Trilogy," in *Satyajit Ray: Interviews*, ed. Bert Cardullo (Jackson: University Press of Mississippi, 2007), 53–60, at 54.
10. Ganguly, *Cinema, Emergence*, 194.
11. Ganguly, *Cinema, Emergence*, 19.
12. Ganguly, 3.
13. Ganguly, 3.
14. Majumdar, "Debating Radical Cinema," 754.
15. Thomsen, "Ray's New Trilogy," 54.

16. Thomsen, "Ray's New Trilogy," 53.
17. András Bálint Kovács, *Screening Political Modernism: European Art Cinema, 1950–1980* (Chicago: University of Chicago Press, 2007), 355.
18. Thomsen, "Ray's New Trilogy," 57.
19. Sengoopta, "Satyajit Ray," 19.
20. Suranjan Ganguly, "Becoming Father: The Politics of Succession in Satyajit Ray's *Pratidwandi* (*The Adversary*)," *Quarterly Review of Film and Video* 29, no. 4 (2012): 320–28, at 321.
21. For more on the politics of autogestion, see Henri Lefebvre, "Theoretical Problems of Autogestion," in *State, Space, World: Selected Essays*, ed. Neil Brenner and Stuart Elden, trans. Gerald Moore, Neil Brenner, and Stuart Elden (Minneapolis: University of Minnesota Press, 2009), 138–52.
22. Udayan Gupta, "The Politics of Humanism: An Interview with Satyajit Ray," in *Satyajit Ray: Interviews*, 122–32, at 129.
23. Thomsen, "Ray's New Trilogy," 57.
24. Thomsen, "Ray's New Trilogy," 58.
25. Thomsen, 58.
26. K. G. T. Mahavidyalaya, "The Portrait of an Agonist: A Reading of Ray's *Pratidwandi/The Adversary*," *Studies in South Asian Film and Media* 3, no. 2 (2011): 87–96, at 88.
27. Tom Milne, "The Adversary," *Sight and Sound* (Spring 1973). *CineFiles Database*, University of California, Berkeley Art Museum and Pacific Film Archive. https://cinefiles.bampfa.berkeley.edu/cinefiles/DocDetail?docId=1921.
28. Suranjan Ganguly, *Satyajit Ray: In Search of the Modern* (Lanham, MD: Scarecrow Press, 2000), 125.
29. Milne, "The Adversary."
30. Andrew Robinson, *Satyajit Ray: The Inner Eye; The Biography of a Master Film-Maker* (New York: I. B. Tauris, 2001), 204.
31. Milne, "The Adversary."
32. Karla Oeler, *A Grammar of Murder: Violent Scenes and Film Form* (Chicago: University of Chicago Press, 2009), 12.
33. Raymond Williams, *Modern Tragedy* (Stanford, CA: Stanford University Press, 1966), 75.
34. Srila Roy, *Remembering Revolution: Gender, Violence, and Subjectivity in India's Naxalbari Movement* (New Delhi: Oxford University Press, 2012), 23.
35. Satya Prakash Dash, *Naxal Movement and State Power* (New Delhi: Sarup and Sons, 2006), 22.

36. Ganguly, "Becoming Father," 322.
37. Colin Wright, "The Violence of the New: Badiou's Subtractive Destruction and Gandhi's *Satyagraha*," *Subjectivity* 4, no. 1 (2011): 9–28, at 10.
38. Supriya Chaudhuri, "In the City," in *Apu and After: Re-visiting Ray's Cinema*, ed. Moinak Biswas (New York, Seagull, 2006), 251–76, at 264.
39. Wright, "Violence of the New," 12.
40. Frantz Fanon, *The Wretched of the Earth*, trans. Richard Philcox (New York: Grove Press, 2004), 82, 85.
41. Fanon, *Wretched of the Earth*, 89, 86.
42. Fanon, 87.
43. Fanon, 89.
44. Sanjay Seth, "From Maoism to Postcolonialism? The Indian 'Sixties,' and Beyond," *Inter-Asia Cultural Studies* 7, no. 4 (2006): 598–605, at 593.
45. Quoted in Seth, "From Maoism to Postcolonialism, 594.
46. Chidananda Das Gupta, *The Cinema of Satyajit Ray* (New Delhi: National Book Trust, 1994), 96.
47. Ganguly, *Cinema, Emergence*, 17.

15

Maysles Films

Some Paradoxes of Direct Cinema in the 1960s and 1970s

J. M. Tyree

The political turn in filmmaking and criticism after 1968 offered formal radicalism as an antidote to a politically suspect entertainment culture; cinematic realism was attacked as naive. Direct Cinema's rhetoric about itself, as a noninterventionist documentary filmmaking style with some supposedly unique access point to the truth about its subjects, can be viewed in retrospect as either logically impossible or else as a utopian dream of the 1960s. Yet the Anglophone films produced under the aegis of Direct Cinema by Robert Drew, D. A. Pennebaker, Richard Leacock, and Maysles Films remain richly complex classics. As recent scholarship has demonstrated, this is true not in spite of their internal contradictions or paradoxes but rather because of them. Jonathan B. Vogels, for example, has influenced later criticism on Maysles Films by highlighting the tensions between theory and practice not as fatal flaws but as durable sources of interest in the films.[1]

Nevertheless, the larger shift in sensibilities exposed Direct Cinema to the linked charges of being politically disengaged, remaining focused on individual lives rather than larger-scale systems and institutions, and following a dubious formal strategy of pretending to offer unmediated contact with its documentary subjects. This critique, though powerful, takes insufficient account of the historical complexities and paradoxes of Maysles Films from the mid-1960s to the mid-1970s, including *What's Happening? The Beatles in the USA* (1964), *Meet Marlon Brando* (1965), *Salesman* (1966–69), *Gimme Shelter* (1970), and

Grey Gardens (1975). Maysles Films—a corporate name suggesting the multifaceted authorship on its productions—presaged many of the formally radical moves that would be deployed later by more politically motivated filmmakers. Yet while Maysles Films strongly resisted a more overtly political mode of filmmaking, many of these productions contained criticism of American myths and norms. The refusal of Maysles Films to abandon its realist style and its humanist mode of inquiry for a more rhetorical and argumentative cinema, meanwhile, forms a challenge to the core idea developed in the post-1968 context that radical formalism and political critique inevitably must go hand in hand.

Bill Nichols is one documentary theorist who frames his analysis of Maysles Films in terms that articulate an overtly political reading of cinema grounded in post-1968 intellectual culture. Vogels notes that Nichols's line of attack follows earlier complaints against Direct Cinema, by Brian Winston and others, as exploitative, and also that this is an "opinion that continues to hold sway in film studies."[2] A case in point, worth exploring in greater detail, is Nichols's interpretation of *Grey Gardens* (1975), the Maysles's portrait of the Beales, poor relations of the Kennedy family living in a decrepit Long Island mansion. Nichols first establishes a general argument that documentaries partake of a greater social realm, "an ideological arena that establishes our commitment to or detachment from the dominant practices and values of our culture."[3] The realm of rhetoric, for Nichols, is the proper lens for assessing the value of documentary in general. The "ethical considerations" of observational documentaries involve particular problems of voyeurism and the potential exploitation of the filmmakers' subjects.

Using this theoretical framework, Nichols assesses *Grey Gardens* critically:

> This position, "at the keyhole," can feel uncomfortable if a pleasure in looking seems to take priority over the chance to acknowledge and interact with the one seen. This discomfort can be even more acute when the person is not an actor who has willingly agreed to be observed playing a part in a fiction. . . . How can the filmmakers simply observe and pass along what they see if what we now see becomes fodder for diagnoses of illness or judgments of dysfunction? Did they have no ethical obligation to confront these concerns more directly?[4]

One of Nichols's potential remedies for these ethical problems involves the introduction of various estranging effects that make documentaries more reflexive. By breaking down the supposed realism and illusory transparency he strongly associates with observational documentary, Nichols suggests that filmmakers can question the "dominant ideology" of their culture, "a process of political engagement based on *ostranenie*, or in somewhat more familiar, Brechtian terms, on the experience of alienation effects."[5] He praises "the bipolarity of reflexive strategies" for "calling attention to form itself or to the 'other side' of ideology where we can locate a utopian dimension of alternative modes of material practice, consciousness, and action."[6] Putting together these two strands of Nichols's argument, it would seem that *Grey Gardens* fails to sufficiently alienate its audiences in order to provide any ideological critique. This reading is based on the assumptions that the film is nonreflexive and deceptively illusionistic, that the former always implies the latter, and that this combination is ethically (and therefore politically) problematic.

Nichols's theory of reflexive documentary film in turn resembles the critique of realist cinematic techniques made in the post-1968 context. Laura Hubner summarizes the post-1968 zeitgeist as one in which "the theory questioning traditional narrative evolved towards the end of the 1960s, nourished by May 1968," and was "politically motivated towards liberating the spectator from the ideology associated with mainstream cinema."[7] Hubner quotes Richard Allen's description of the era:

> Mass culture—classical Hollywood cinema—was deemed illusionistic and manipulative, and an alternative film-making practice was celebrated in which cinematic illusionism and the pleasures of narrative involvement it afforded were eschewed in favor of the cerebral pleasures of films that sought to foreground the manner of their construction and undermine the effect of cinematic illusion.[8]

The problem with this interpretation, for Allen, is that "film theorists construe the film spectator as a passive observer of the image who is duped into believing that it is real."[9] In fact, spectators are capable of understanding films—including documentaries—as constructed artifacts, and the works themselves often often contain aspects that highlight this facet.

Nichols reproduces this difficulty in his reading of *Grey Gardens*. He views the film with suspicion because he interprets the formal strategies of Direct Cinema, rather than the content of *Grey Gardens*, as being largely determinative of its ethics. And that reading aligns with the post-1968 Marxian modernist preference in favor of reflexive artworks.

I follow Vogels in challenging Nichols through exploring the "humanistic means of encountering the world" in Maysles Films.[10] More specifically, I propose revisiting Maysles Films by adopting Edward W. Said's humanist conception of art. Said's wider argument in favor of a more open, inclusive, engaged, and self-critical humanism does not attempt to deny the importance of historical or political context, but instead offers "overlapping yet irreconcilable experiences," an "exilic realm" rife with paradoxes: "the intellectual's provisional home is the domain of an exigent, resistant, intransigent art in which, alas, one can neither retreat nor search for solutions."[11] Said notes that after successive waves of thought driven by the work of Marx, Nietzsche, Freud, Saussure, Lévi-Strauss, Barthes, and Foucault, by the 1960s and 1970s antihumanism had a powerful and definable intellectual shape:

> Groups of systems of thinking and perceiving transcended the powers of individual subjects, individual humans who were inside those systems (systems such as Freud's "unconscious" or Marx's "capital") and therefore had no power over them, only the choice to use or be used by them. This of course flatly contradicts the core of humanistic thought, and hence the individual *cogito* was displaced, or demoted, to the status of illusory autonomy or fiction.[12]

By contrast, Said's self-critical humanist method seeks to establish, in the mode of R. S. Crane, a realm of study that views humanism as "an achievement of form by human will and agency; it is neither system nor impersonal force like the market or the unconscious, however much one may believe in the workings of both."[13] Akeel Bilgrami glosses humanism's tendency to emphasize "the yearning to show regard for *all* that is human, for what is human *wherever* it may be found," according to the anthropological dictum "Nothing human is alien to me."[14] This humanist mode of inquiry is never free from rhetoric or blinders; for Said, however, there is a baby in the bathwater.

A flawed but potentially illuminating analogy between Maysles Films and the cinema of Ingmar Bergman suggests a linked historical trajectory for 1960s humanist cinema whose value is difficult to grasp within the Marxian modernist framework. Maysles Films, like the pictures of Bergman, innovated early on with film form while remaining committed to a filmmaking ethos lacking in any specific political agenda. Bergman had pioneered the use of radical frame-smashing cinematic strategies, such as the appearance of the film and the projector at the beginning and the end of *Persona* (1966), as well as the famous sequence in which the film itself breaks down and the faces of his protagonists, Liv Ullmann and Bibi Andersson, appear spliced together. As radical as these moves are, according to Hubner, they are not "a distancing effect in a Godardian or Brechtian sense"; instead, the ripping apart of the film "in some ways adds to the psychological breakdown of the characters."[15] Bergman's projects asserted cinematic self-consciousness and self-reflexive filmmaking, certainly, but did so in an attempt to bring audiences closer to the narrative and the characters, not further away. Maysles Films in the 1960s and 1970s arguably feel more "Bergmanesque" than "Godardian," at least in the specific sense that their shared formal radicalism serves a humanist sensibility. (Vogels calls this aspect of Maysles Films a "modernist/humanist aesthetic."[16]) Maysles Films and Bergman's productions presaged many of the techniques associated with post-1968 cinema while remaining outliers to its overtly political drift.

The textbook ideals of Direct Cinema supposedly involved an absolutist doctrine of noninterventionism—"photographing people without intruding."[17] In practice the productions of Maysles Films were much more complicated. Vogels argues: "Condemning direct cinema for its blind allegiance to the tenets of a naive objectivity does not allow for the countless examples in films like *Grey Gardens* that, at least in part, contradict those tenets."[18] Matthew Tinkcom also notes the paradoxical position of Direct Cinema regarding its self-professed ideals. He argues that *Grey Gardens*

> heralded, in its making and in its subsequent lives with audiences, the reinvention of documentary cinema from an activity of scientific objective recording of natural and human phenomena to a new and dynamic set of relations among the film's subjects, the film-makers

and its audiences, all of whom come to have a stake in making sense of what exactly it is that the Beales are getting at.[19]

Tinkcom argues that Maysles Films innovated by accepting the "observer's paradox": "the film-maker could not assume that his presence was irrelevant as a motivation for the action that unfolded before his camera because he participated in the film's events."[20] Building on the work of Michael Renov, Tinkcom argues that the cultural and political events of the 1960s acted to erode the illusion of Direct Cinema's "heroic" self-conception regarding its supposed exemption from identity politics through its self-defined quest for "objectivity," which had been founded on the deeply problematic picture of a "white male 'universal' observer/film-maker."[21] Tinkcom describes the results in *Grey Gardens* far more positively than Nichols, however, because he reexamines the role of its feminist female film editors—Ellen Hovde, Muffie Meyer, and Susan Froemke, cocredited as codirectors on the film—in emphasizing interactivity between the Maysles brothers and the Beales and in championing the female gaze of Little Edie in particular.

Tinkcom's conclusion that "*Grey Gardens* as a Direct Cinema project is always under siege by the Beales"[22] is difficult to square with Nichols's impression that it operates "at the keyhole" as a problematic example of the observational mode of documentary. Allen's work on film spectatorship provides one way to explain the disparity between these two interpretations of *Grey Gardens*. Allen notes that it is up to the *viewer* to decide how to think about the image: a "spectator may equally experience the image illusionistically and hence 'ideologically,' or not illusionistically and hence as a critique of ideology."[23] *Grey Gardens* contains so many ambiguities on this front that sophisticated viewers can form seemingly incompatible interpretations.

Further complicating these issues is evidence that self-awareness regarding the "observer's paradox" emerged at Maysles Films far earlier than *Grey Gardens*. *What's Happening? The Beatles in the USA*, about the Beatles' first visit to the United States, already provides early hints in this direction. The film was shot in 1964, but to date it only has been released on DVD by Apple Records in a form substantially different from the version produced by Maysles Films. Joe McElhaney, who studied both films and published a detailed summary of the differences between them, emphasizes the dramatic difference in length between the two versions' scene of the band frolicking on a train from New York to Washington, DC. The episodes cut out of Apple's DVD release (titled *The Beatles: The First U.S. Visit*) reveal the band interacting with members of the public, with Paul McCartney discussing the differences between American and British television with a group of reporters, and Ringo Starr goofing around with the camera bags of the photographers who are following them.[24] The filmmakers' version contains more moments in which the film foregrounds the actual apparatus of the media itself, in the form of the reporters and the camera bags.

Outtakes offered as DVD Supplements on *The Beatles: The First U.S. Visit* go even further in a reflexive direction, showing the Beatles playing with the sound equipment of David Maysles, delighting in the immediacy of feedback the Nagra recorders produced, and taking an intellectual interest in the conceptual basis of synced sound. The film, which also features footage of a Manhattan family watching the Beatles on television only a few blocks away from where the music was being recorded live, displays a sophisticated determination to emphasize and question the various means by which the mass media mediates. The outtakes might not count as integral to the feature film, but they reveal a playful reflexive side out of keeping with the textbook conception of Direct Cinema's ideal of noninterventionism.

What's Happening?, as originally conceived by Maysles Films, already contained gestures toward the problems of voyeurism and mediation. Anne S. Lewis links together *What's Happening?* with *Meet Marlon Brando* as two early Maysles Films that are marked by many "conceptual paradoxes."[25] A short film released in 1965, *Meet Marlon Brando* presents an even larger problem for the standard definition (and critique) of Direct Cinema as an observational cinema lacking in reflexive strategies and adhering to doctrines of objectivity, transparency, and noninterventionism among artist, medium, and subject. The film is a portrait of a performer who teases, mocks, and flirts uncomfortably with some of the women reporters covering him. "Every time we get in front of the television, everyone starts hustling," Brando complains, testing the agreed conventions of the press conference. He goes on to argue that "news is hawked in the same way as shoes are, or toothpaste or lipstick." When a reporter confesses that she hasn't seen the film Brando is supposed to be selling (*Morituri*, 1965), he denies her claim that it must be "wonderful," noting that "we mustn't believe propaganda." He then continues his media appearance pointedly by walking out into the streets of New York and himself interviewing a black passerby about the politics of race relations in the United States. He asks her if she thinks the government can claim credit for some of the advances in civil rights, and she denies it; the film then cuts to them shaking hands.

While it's true that the camera is never turned back on the filmmakers themselves, it is difficult to view *Meet Marlon Brando* as anything other than a wry and self-conscious send-up of a specific format of nonfiction film, and one that inevitably encourages its viewers to reconsider who controls what is visible inside the frame. Allen's film spectator has little difficulty in reading *Meet Marlon Brando* both as a puncturing of the bubble of cinematic illusionism (on multiple levels, given that its subject matter is an actor promoting a movie!) and as a critique of ideology, or what Brando calls "propaganda," regarding the wider cultural effects of those selfsame illusions manufactured in Hollywood.

Meet Marlon Brando foregrounded the powerful stamp of a new author on the core collaborative ethos of Maysles Films, the vision of film editor Charlotte Zwerin. The Maysles brothers, at Zwerin's urging, began to credit her as a codirector on their films together, including *Salesman* (shot in 1966–67 and released in 1968–69) and *Gimme Shelter* (shot in 1969 and released in 1970). In Zwerin's commentary track on the DVD of *Gimme Shelter*, she reveals that she suggested structuring the narrative around the footage of the Rolling Stones watching the film of themselves and their disastrous concert at Altamont on Zwerin's editing board in her cramped hotel room in London. This reflexive move electrified the final film in narrative terms while simultaneously revealing the cinematic apparatus. The deconstruction of media contained in *Meet Marlon Brando* had its full flowering in *Gimme Shelter*, suggesting Zwerin's powerful role as an author within the collaborative bundle of Maysles Films. But this larger process of inquiry regarding reflexivity continued—albeit in different and complicated ways—in *Grey Gardens*, transcending the agenda of any single editor or group of editors. However difficult it remains to forensically describe the authorship on Maysles Films across time, recovering its historical complexity means acknowledging that this ongoing navigation of the core paradoxes of Direct Cinema was itself an enduring concern.

That Maysles Films tended to modify the ideals of Direct Cinema in favor of hybrid forms and a looser, more open, and more practical filmmaking ethos is a paradox that critics have often noted. Keith Beattie, for example, glosses this problem by noting that "a strict adherence to an observational Direct Cinema is not the sole or exclusive characteristic of the films."[26] The process began much earlier than is generally recognized. In 1964, Albert Maysles compared his camera to a "non-directive therapist" and a "real person listening," explaining that the observer is "a kind of participant" and that a "bounce-back" existed between the subject and the camera, which is "not a wall."[27] These intriguing comments, although admittedly against the grain of Albert Maysles's many other remarks, may be read as an indication of self-consciousness about the paradoxes of Direct Cinema at Maysles Films. Direct Cinema was supposed to be noninterventionist on every level, but the observer-participant paradoxes of anthropological filmmaking could not be escaped so easily. And the three masterpieces of Maysles Films arrayed around the end of the 1960s and the early 1970s—*Salesman*, *Gimme Shelter*, and *Grey Gardens*—became more open to reflexivity, especially concerning the presence of the filmmakers in the frame, rather than less so, over time.

As Vogels and Tinkcom emphasize, *Grey Gardens* contains many reflexive moments: the Beales attempting to elicit comments from Albert and David Maysles; the recording of interactions between subjects and filmmakers; Little Edie flirting with and performing for David; the camera turning away to film the filmmakers in a bedroom mirror when the fighting between the Beales becomes particularly intense, and so on. These aspects of the film are not accidental overlays or flaws in an unsuccessful film designed to be purely observational. Rather, these disruptions, caesuras, lacuna, and even blunders are integral to the film. *Grey Gardens*, then, is a form of portraiture made up of a carefully edited, open-ended set of performances by two brilliantly self-scripting women. In sum, the reflexive filmmaking strategies suggested by Nichols as a potential remedy to the pitfalls of the observational style of films like *Grey Gardens* are already present on some level in *Grey Gardens* itself. Therefore, one might wonder whether *Grey Gardens* is really the best example of a purely observational documentary in which the filmmakers wholeheartedly "retire to the position of observer."[28] In fact, *Grey Gardens* takes more full advantage of reflexive strategies than Nichols is prepared to recognize, and these strategies, in turn, offer alternative interpretations of *Grey Gardens* as a more open-ended film. As Vogels summarizes his defense of the film, "the humanistic side of the enterprise superseded the artistic or philosophical issues."[29]

The most obvious and challenging paradox identified by Vogels and Tinkcom involves the problem that *Grey Gardens*, like *Gimme Shelter*, fails in significant ways to conform to the ideals of nonintervention expressed by the tenets of Direct Cinema. In *Grey Gardens*, this paradox deepens when one considers Albert Maysles's notes on his camerawork as containing a "bounce-back" of meaning created from the perspective of a "non-directive therapist" who participates as well as observes. The Beales's specific mode of authorship on the film often takes the form of their refusal to allow the filmmakers to record them passively, and their persistent thwarting of the supposed objectivity of the camera remains one of the film's key sources of enduring interest, as Tinkcom argues. It would be exaggerating to offer *Grey Gardens* as a self-deconstructing account of Direct Cinema, in which the entire concept of noninterventionist documentary is put through the wringer. And yet, as Tinkcom notes, it is one of the film's sources of amusement and joy to watch its subjects breaking rules and confounding conventions, with the filmmakers remaining savvy enough as portrait painters to incorporate this very tendency into the frame. Far from simply observing the Beales, it might be argued instead that Maysles Films stretched its own conceptions of documentary practice to the breaking point in order to prioritize the Beales's pointedly reflexive performances.

On one level, Maysles Films failed to live up to its ideals, and, like Direct Cinema more generally, its theories about its own mode of operation continually ran aground on the paradoxes endemic to its own practices. It has long been accepted, following the research of Jeanne Hall, that Direct Cinema set out to discover reality but in fact formulated and contributed to the cinema a durable filmmaking *style*.[30] It constantly championed itself, wrongly, as a style with unique access to the truth, rather than as a style with many blind spots of its own.

Yet Maysles Films *did* call attention to form itself and, equally, Maysles Films *did* offer in the Beales a politically resonant example of a lifestyle that, while far from utopian, represented tolerance for values outside of the mainstream. The film's reflexivity goes beyond simple voyeurism and instead provokes questions about authorship and control as well as about the differences between celebrity and obscurity—who gets noticed and why, the different ways the media pay attention to the rich and the poor, or to the "normal" versus the queer-seeming outliers and outsiders. If *Grey Gardens* is asking its viewers to consider why the poorer relations of the Kennedys should be passed over and ignored, it appears to contain a subtle but persistent critique of the mass media and poses insistent questions about American culture. In fact, Maysles Films from 1965 to 1975 often contained a critical stance toward bourgeois mythologies: *Meet Marlon Brando*'s skepticism about mass media "propaganda" and advertising culture, *Salesman*'s searing exposé of the failed rhetoric of entrepreneurial capitalism, *Gimme Shelter*'s illumination of commodified dissent, and *Grey Gardens*' exploration of normality. The notion that Maysles Films was apolitical seems untenable, despite the double irony that its own claims on this front have been echoed by its most stringent critics. Dave Saunders has argued against the assertion that Direct Cinema more generally was "an uncommitted aesthetic mode" that inevitably leads to a "craven, politically purposeless vacuum."[31] While Saunders's work focuses on D. A. Pennebaker and Frederick Wiseman, his remarks can also be applied to the critiques of American national myths contained in Maysles Films.

Maysles Films—*Salesman* and *Grey Gardens* in particular—seem to offer its subjects as synecdoches of various American problems, allowing its viewers to extrapolate into the wider culture despite leaving political systems resolutely outside of the frame. This deployment of the rhetorical technique of synecdoche further complicates the cultural and political resonance of these films, since Allen's film spectator is welcome to notice that these individuals are somehow speaking to larger issues beyond their own individual lives.

Yet Maysles Films never offered a political account of its filmmaking practices in general or of its inconsistent use of reflexive formal strategies in particular. I have analogized this drift as a more "Bergmanesque" mode of 1960s self-conscious humanist filmmaking in order to distinguish it from the more "Godardian" turn toward overt politicization in the context of post-1968. While Maysles Films often seemed to presage or reflect the philosophical, cultural, formal, and even some of the political concerns of post-1968 filmmaking, the humanism of these productions remained at odds with more radical concerns. The post-1968 critique of mass entertainment culture was based on its concern that viewers bathed without worry in a seamless dream. Another paradox is that Maysles Films productions *did* "foreground the manner of their construction and undermine the effect of cinematic illusion" (as Allen puts it[32]), but in ways that actually made them *more* immersive, made the viewer trust the filmmakers *more* rather than less, and created a closer bond between the viewer and the subject rather than causing a politically motivated alienation effect. Instead of feeling distanced, the viewer is disarmed and perhaps even more trusting than before. If the illusion of realism is only deepened by revealing the cinematic apparatus, then it could be argued that the alienation effect is not fit for purpose. Yet the realism of Maysles Films often encoded critiques of society that remain powerful, insistent, and at odds with American national myths. Stylistic realism is not logically incompatible with social critique unless one accepts the Marxian modernist model.[33]

Taken together, all of these paradoxes leave Maysles Films productions in a peculiar place vis-à-vis their own era, as innovators and outliers, precursors to be emulated and cinematic antecedents to be criticized for their self-defeating notions of a noninterventionist cinema, a set of very "early to mid-1960s" ideals about heroic art that presents obvious theoretical impasses. Maysles Films embodied the optimistic mood connected with self-conscious cinema that sought to film human intimacy in ways that new technologies of the late 1950s and early 1960s, such as sophisticated hand-held cameras and lightweight sound recording rigs, led its filmmakers to believe had never been attempted before. In Maysles Films, radical style operates paradoxically to heighten the sense of psychological realism. The problem with the self-definition of Direct Cinema as a noninterventionist cinema was that it contained rhetoric without acknowledging it or understanding how rhetoric links up with ideology. As James Naremore has argued in a different context, "some form of rhetoricality always underlies our words and representational arts; rhetoric could in fact be defined as any technique that transforms poetics and philosophy into ideology."[34] From the perspective of humanist inquiry, however, another problem lies in the jump between these two statements. The first statement contains undeniable truths that Direct Cinema sought to suppress or deny, while the second statement risks an unnecessary limitation on the function of art. A similar limitation is placed on the paradoxical resonances of *Grey Gardens*—and, by implication, of Direct Cinema as an observational form of filmmaking—by Nichols's reading of the proper sphere of documentary as participating in the ideological arena.

An alternative reading of Maysles Films from a humanist perspective might acknowledge art's rhetoricality while also noting paradoxes that induce doubt about the certainty of its own truth-claims. To paraphrase and adopt Montaigne for this alternative reading of *Grey Gardens*, we might well ask: What do we know? About the Beales, or the filmmakers, or any person? What do we know about what it means to be normal, healthy, happy, productive, or successful in America? What do we know about how documentaries change their subjects' behavior in front of the camera? About the complex relationships, if any obtain, between film and reality, art and truth, fiction and nonfiction, portrait and person? These questions do not exist in a realm outside of rhetoric. But they serve to un-limit the functions of rhetoric and to challenge the unwarranted expectation that consonance should exist between art and ideology. Even within the ideological realm, however, the notion of Marxian modernism may be challenged on its own grounds, insofar as realist art may prove highly critical of the dominant ideology of its culture.

One of the key elements of Said's reading of humanism is that, while making clear that art can never be viewed in a sanitized apolitical realm that is separate from ideology and history, his position rejects the conception of art as the solely owned property of "politics" writ large. Said draws a direct comparison between his own criticism and "the way Adorno has throughout his work on music insisted that modern music can never be reconciled with the society that produced it, but in its intensity and often despairingly crafted form and content, music can act as a silent witness to the inhumanity all around."[35] Said's critique of antihumanism engages with the problem of politics and art directly. "I do not believe that, like the social sciences," he argues, "the humanities must address or somehow solve the problems of the contemporary world."[36] Said's position is at odds with Hubner's summary of the post-1968 "turn" to being more "politically motivated towards liberating the spectator from the ideology associated with mainstream cinema."[37] This emerging theory of cinema described historically by Hubner, in turn, resonates with Nichols's theoretical belief that documentary must be interpreted as operating in "an ideological arena that establishes our commitment to or detachment from the dominant practices and values of our culture."[38] From the humanist perspective, this theory of documentary does not describe the full range of what Said calls "the achievement of form by human will and agency."[39] As regards the cinema, ignoring this aspect risks treating an art form in ways that both deflate its historical complexity and deny its less controllable effects on its spectators. *What's Happening?*, *Meet Marlon Brando*, *Salesman*, *Gimme Shelter*, and *Grey Gardens* do not seek to solve the problems of the contemporary world. They do contain subtle but insistent resonances with wider cultural phenomena and social problems—mass media manipulation, the failed dreams of entrepreneurship, the co-option of 1960s utopianism, and the invisibility of the poor—but these resonances are not designed to "address" these problems, to use Said's loaded word.

Maysles Films productions from 1964 to 1975 occupy a paradoxical place within Direct Cinema and also within the debates about the politics of cinema that came to a boil in the post-1968 context. If these filmmakers do not fit comfortably into Nichols's theory of documentary as part of a larger ideological arena, they do, however, reflect with marked consistency on the contradictions of the American success myth, and, therefore, seem to carry a strong, if untheorized, complaint about its dominant cultural values. If these productions deploy radically reflexive filmmaking strategies much earlier and much more frequently than has been assumed, however, it is not because they intend to break the spell of cinematic realism for any deliberatively political purpose.

It is intriguing to note that *Gimme Shelter* had been preceded by Godard's own highly rhetorical film about the Rolling Stones, *Sympathy for the Devil* (a.k.a. *One Plus One*, 1968). Godard's film attempts to dissociate itself from the values of the dominant culture on the level of both form and content, cramming in interludes about Black Panthers, revolutionaries scrawling Maoist graffiti, and other radical moves. But it is difficult to avoid the conclusion that *Sympathy for the Devil* is hampered in a significant way *because* it follows the political guidance of art to the letter. *Gimme Shelter* has proved more durable and culturally resonant *despite* its lack of overt political signposts. Godard's abandonment of his own early New Wave strategies, in fact, took many forms, revealing the durability of his shift to Marxian modernism, a facet of his work that remains essential to the formally disruptive pictures *Film Socialisme* (2010) and *Goodbye to Language* (2014). Clearly, Marxian modernism remains a valuable weapon for challenging commercial conventions and mainstream ideology, both theoretically and practically.

Direct Cinema, meanwhile, had its greatest influence on the cinema of the 1970s through its stylistic adoption by the New Hollywood. Martin Scorsese, who worked as a lighting man for Albert Maysles and collaborated on the editing of Michael Wadleigh's Pennebaker-like concert documentary *Woodstock* (1970), used a trick from *Salesman* when he introduced his characters one by one and printed their names on the screen in *Mean Streets* (1973).[40] This reflexive tactic, in turn, recapitulated one of the core paradoxes of Maysles Films. Its productions "broke the rules" of Direct Cinema by drawing attention to their own framing, but did so in ways that sought to establish intimacy with their subjects/characters. The complex fate of the New Hollywood, by contrast, offers a final paradox. While skepticism certainly may be directed toward its drift into apolitical commercialization, the realism of the New Hollywood—its self-conscious stylistic inheritance from both the early New Wave and from Direct Cinema—arguably bolstered the radical potential for socially critical content to be contained within commercial cinema itself.

Notes

1. Jonathan B. Vogels, *The Direct Cinema of David and Albert Maysles* (Carbondale: Southern Illinois University Press, 2005), 150–51.
2. Vogels, *The Direct Cinema of David and Albert Maysles*, 147.
3. Bill Nichols, *Introduction to Documentary* (Bloomington: Indiana University Press, 2010), 139.
4. Nichols, *Introduction to Documentary*, 195.
5. Nichols, *Representing Reality: Issues and Concepts in Documentary* (Bloomington: Indiana University Press, 1991), 65.
6. Nichols, *Representing Reality*, 65.
7. Laura Hubner, *The Films of Ingmar Bergman: Illusions of Light and Darkness* (New York: Palgrave, 2007), 74.
8. Richard Allen, *Projecting Illusion: Film Spectatorship and the Impression of Reality* (Cambridge: Cambridge University Press, 1995), 9. Allen is quoted in Hubner, *Films of Ingmar Bergman*, 74.
9. Allen, *Projecting Illusion*, 3.
10. Vogels, *The Direct Cinema of David and Albert Maysles*, xi.
11. Edward W. Said, *Humanism and Democratic Criticism* (New York: Columbia University Press, 2004), 143, 144.
12. Said, *Humanism and Democratic Criticism*, 9–10.

13. Said, 15.
14. Akeel Bilgrami, foreword to *Humanism and Democratic Criticism* by Edward W. Said (New York: Columbia University Press, 2004), ix–xiii, at x.
15. Hubner, *Films of Ingmar Bergman*, 76.
16. Vogels, *The Direct Cinema of David and Albert Maysles*, xii.
17. Jack C. Ellis and Betsy McLane, *A New History of Documentary* (New York: Continuum, 2006), 217.
18. Vogels, *The Direct Cinema of David and Albert Maysles*, 150.
19. Matthew Tinkcom, *BFI Film Classics: Grey Gardens* (London: BFI Publishing and Palgrave Macmillan, 2011), 13–14.
20. Tinkcom, *BFI Film Classics*, 16.
21. Tinkcom, 16.
22. Tinkcom, 64.
23. Allen, *Projecting Illusion*, 23.
24. Joe McElhaney, *Albert Maysles* (Bloomington: Indiana University Press, 2009), 177.
25. Anne S. Lewis, "Stories That Tell Themselves," *Austin Chronicle*, February 11, 2000. Reprinted in Keith Beattie, ed., *Albert and David Maysles: Interviews*, Conversations with Filmmakers Series (Jackson: University Press of Mississippi, 2010), 119–23, at 120.
26. Keith Beattie, introduction to Beattie, *Albert and David Maysles: Interviews*, vii–xi, at vii.
27. Maxine Haleff, "The Maysles Brothers and 'Direct Cinema,'" *Film Comment* 2, no. 2 (1964): 19–23. Reprinted in Beattie, *Albert and David Maysles: Interviews*, 6–16, at 15.
28. Nichols, *Introduction to Documentary*, 195.
29. Vogels, *The Direct Cinema of David and Albert Maysles*, 152.
30. See Jeanne Hall, "Realism as a Style in Cinema Verite: A Critical Analysis of *Primary*," *Cinema Journal* 30, no. 4 (1991): 24–50.
31. Dave Saunders, *Direct Cinema: Observational Documentary and the Politics of the Sixties* (New York: Wallflower Press, 2007), 2.
32. Allen, quoted in Hubner, *Films of Ingmar Bergman*, 74.
33. I follow Allen in using the term "Marxian modernism" instead of "Marxist modernism" to denote a larger cultural influence rather than a specific economic program.
34. James Naremore, *An Invention without a Future: Essays on Cinema* (Berkeley: University of California Press, 2014), 84.

35. Said, *Humanism and Democratic Criticism*, 143.
36. Said, *Humanism and Democratic Criticism*, 53.
37. Hubner, *Films of Ingmar Bergman*, 74.
38. Nichols, *Introduction to Documentary*, 139.
39. Said, *Humanism and Democratic Criticism*, 15.
40. McElhaney, *Albert Maysles*, 51.

16

The Rhetoric of Parapraxis

The 1967 Riots and Hong Kong Film Theory

Victor Fan

The "May Days" in Hong Kong took place in 1967, a year before similar Marxism-inspired students, workers, and intellectuals took to the street in North American, European, and other Asian cities. That year, twenty-one workers from the Hong Kong Artificial Flower Works went on strike. Inspired by the Cultural Revolution that started in mainland China in 1966, factory workers, students, cultural workers, and intellectuals quickly broadened the strike into a mass anticolonial protest. Acting governor of the British colonial government Jack Cater (1922–2006) reacted with police brutality, unconstitutional arrests, and prolonged detention of not only the rioters but also politically inactive writers, publishers, film producers, and actors who were considered "left wing." On August 25, radio host Lam Bun (1926–1967), who spoke openly against the rioters, was burned alive in his car on his way to work. The riots lasted eight months with fifty-one deaths, eight hundred sustained injuries, and two thousand criminal convictions. It ended with an injunction issued by the premier of the People's Republic of China Zhou Enlai (1898–1976), who ordered the rioters to stop all Cultural-Revolution-styled activities in Hong Kong and assured the British government that China had no interest in exercising its sovereign authority over the city.[1] Since then, academic and public discussions of the 1967 riots have been banned by the Hong Kong government by means of the Public Order Ordinance of 1967, which is still considered good law today.[2]

The 1967 leftist riots had certainly made an impact on Hong Kong film theory and criticism, in a way different from the one made on Euro-American and Japanese film theories by similar protests and mass movements in those regions.[3] The leftist protests in many urban centers in the aforementioned areas were symptomatic of the class, generational, and racial tensions actively produced and repressed by Cold War capitalism, which sought to exteriorize communism as a threat and align the socially othered with it.[4] By exteriorizing communism as a threat, the "First World" could then be defined as a polis with its own interiority and exteriority. Such a strategy of exteriorization/interiorization had the effect of constructing a political binary between right (interior) and left (exterior), which remained pertinent in the First World sociocultural discourses into the 1970s. Meanwhile, the leftist riots in Hong Kong emerged out of a colonial condition where contesting notions of juridical rights, linguistic practices, and sociopolitical identities competed with each other and occupied one's consciousness in a fragmented and incoherent manner.[5]

Between 1842 and 1898, Hong Kong was ceded to Great Britain in a series of treaties. Even though the Island of Hong Kong and later on the rest of the city were named a crowned colony, the understanding in these treaties was that the Qing Empire (1644–1911) retained the sovereign authority over these territories, while Great Britain had the rights to governance. Juridically and judicially, Hong Kong had therefore always been under contesting claimants to sovereign authority—the People's Republic of China (PRC), the Republic of China (ROC), and Great Britain. In this sense, Hong Kong is best understood not as a *colony* in the classical sense but as a zone of exception or an *extraterritorial* space where no effective sovereign intervention was present. After 1949, it became a site of contestation between colonial capitalism (of Great Britain), national capitalism (of the ROC), and communism (of the PRC).[6] During the 1967 riots, Hong Kongers witnessed the fact that both the colonial power and the revolutionary power exercised the same form of violence in order to assert authority. In the eyes of many Hong Kongers, both capitalism and communism had failed to perform what they promised to deliver—socioeconomic stability and prosperity.

In this chapter, I first introduce the historical background of Cold War Hong Kong as a site of contestation between conflicting sovereign claims and political powers, that is, its *extraterritoriality*. I then illustrate how the 1967 riots could be understood as a symptom of Hong Kong's extraterritorial position. After that, I analyze how Hong Kong film criticism negotiates the structure of difference between Hong Kong and China, a geopolitical divide that emerged during the 1970s. I argue that the 1967 riots triggered a sense of failure, among a group of Hong Kong film critics, to make sense of their extraterritorial status.

This sense of failure, I propose, is the key to understanding the impact of the 1967 riots on Hong Kong film theory. Unlike European film critics, who openly turned to Althusserian Marxism and Lacanian psychoanalysis to critique cinema as an ideological apparatus, Hong Kong filmmakers and critics had to confront the question: What if both capitalism and socialism have already failed?[7] In order to address this question, they employed what I would call a rhetoric of parapraxis in their writings. The term *parapraxis* is popularly known as a Freudian slip, defined by Thomas Elsaesser as a double (para) performance (praxis). For example, if I invite you for coffee in my house and end up serving you whiskey, I fail to perform what I promised to deliver (to bring you coffee). At the same time, my act of failure performs my failure to address a deeper trauma I have repressed all along (for example, I have always desired to have whiskey with my father, since he always enjoyed a glass of whiskey with his dates before he abandoned me to go out with them). In this sense, a failure of performance is always a performance of failure.[8]

Cold War Hong Kong

During the 1930s, Hong Kong was gradually transformed into a battleground of conflicting political beliefs, as the political struggle between the ruling Kuomintang (KMT or Nationalist Party) and the Chinese Communist Party (CCP) emerged in the mainland, and as the Japanese military began to invade Manchuria, Shanghai, and other coastal cities. During that period, migrant workers from the southern provinces of China including Guangdong (Kwangtung), Guangxi (Kwangsi), and Fujian (Fukien) moved to Hong Kong to escape the political turmoil. They brought with them not only contesting political affiliations (the KMT, the CCP, or even the Japanese military), but also different understandings of what "China" meant to them.[9] For example, while some subscribed to KMT's notion of the Chinese nation as a centralized polis managed by the state, others took pride in what they would call *Guangdong jingshen* (*Gwongdung zingsan* or Cantonese spirit), and understood the nation as an assemblage of mutually dependent regional communities with conflicting cultural, linguistic, or even political identities and affiliations.[10] After the Japanese occupation of the eastern seaboard in 1937, many workers, merchants, industrialists, and financiers from Shanghai took refuge in Hong Kong. Many of them considered themselves patriotic and pragmatic. They supported the national course on the one hand, and collaborated with the KMT, CCP, and the Japanese for survival on the other.[11] After the Sino-Japanese War (1937–45), many Shanghai expatriates stayed in Hong Kong. Some of them did so because they were in fear of political persecution; others resigned themselves to a life of self-exile, as the continued political conflict between the KMT and the CCP had failed to provide any sense of political coherence.[12] China therefore became an imaginary home that they had once abandoned, and that, since the war, had abandoned them.[13]

Many leftists from Shanghai or the Guangzhou (Canton) region also ended up staying in Hong Kong. Even though most of them sympathized with the CCP, they chose to remain because their political beliefs were not entirely in line with the party's. Between 1949 and 1950, leftists in Hong Kong hoped that the Red Army would cross the Shenzhen (Shumchun) River and take over its sovereignty. Nonetheless, by mid-1950, it was clear that the Beijing (Peking) government intended to respect Hong Kong's colonial status, and the colonial government began to expel union leaders from the territory.[14] In addition, the Sino-British border was officially closed in 1951. Many leftists found themselves "stranded" in Hong Kong and were caught in a double bind. On the one hand, they failed to return to the "motherland" to contribute their effort to the revolution. On the other hand, they would not have done so had they been given a chance, since they would have been considered "rightists" and persecuted by the CCP.[15]

Hong Kong was, however, far from being an anticommunist base in the 1950s. The British government recognized the PRC in 1949 as the legitimate Chinese government. It was primarily done out of an interest in protecting its colonial trade in India and Malaya, which formed the financial backbone of Great Britain. Meanwhile, the US government recognized the ROC as a Cold War ally. And during the Malayan Emergency (1948–60), it was crucial for

Great Britain to keep CCP's interference in Southeast Asia under control by falling in line with US policy.[16] Hong Kong therefore became a zone of exception where the sociopolitical and economic interests of the PRC, the ROC, Great Britain, and the United States were negotiated. Economically, it served as an entrepôt where Chinese products could be shipped to Great Britain and the United States under the label "Made in Hong Kong." Politically, it remained a "neutral" space where contesting sociopolitical values and ideologies could be freely expressed and discussed.

Extraterritoriality and the 1967 Riots

Elsewhere, I called this state of exception extraterritoriality: the mode of colonialism and semicolonialism practiced in the coastal cities of China between 1844 and 1945.[17] The concept emerged in sixteenth-century Europe. As Europeans believed that "Oriental" law in the Ottoman Empire was fundamentally incompatible with European law, they demanded that they be judged in accordance with their own law even outside their juridical territory. Interestingly, according to the Qing code, subjects from different ethnic groups were to be judged in accordance with their own laws. As a result, when the concept of extraterritorial rights was first introduced in the Treaty of Wangxia (Wanghia) by the United States, the Qing court considered it in accordance with the imperial law. Not until the signing of the Treaty of Shimonoseki did the Qing officials adopt the Japanese term *sagai hōken* (*zhiwai faquan*, the rights to exercise one's law outside one's own sovereign territory) to mark it as a colonial privilege.[18]

The result of colonizing China's trading ports as extraterritorial zones effectively put sovereign authority "under erasure."[19] On the one hand, these zones were under double sovereign authorities, as European trade administrations, courts, police forces, and business associations were set up in Chinese territories. On the other hand, having double or even multiple sovereign authorities that were constantly in contestation with each other led to the absence of any juridical center. As a result, conflicting laws, linguistic systems, cultural values, and political beliefs coexisted, which were severed from their geopolitical *territories*, yet their constant negotiation and mutual dependency made them resistant against any reterritorialization. Thus, Hong Kong as an extraterritorial zone was geopolitically and symbolically occupied by contesting sovereign authorities, yet it stood in an *extra*-territorial position: being *exceptional of* the sociopolitical and economic intervention of these state powers.

The difficulty with defining and understanding the 1967 riots precisely lies in the extraterritorial conditions in which it took place. As Jon D. Solomon argues, extraterritoriality has the effect of severing sovereignty from the apparatus of governance.[20] In so doing, lives under the governance of such an apparatus became hyper aware that they were depoliticized (without any sovereign affiliation) and desubjectivized (not constituted as political subjects). Rather, they were biological or bare lives that were instrumentalized as expendable laborers and consumers.[21] As the pro-British administrators and historians claimed, the 1967 riots emerged out of a discontent of a growing working-class population who lived in subhuman housing conditions and suffered from an impoverished education system.[22] In other words, by 1967, the deterritorialized and desubjectivized status of working-class and lower-middle-class Hong Kongers became literally and symbolically unlivable.

According to the study of Gary Cheung, the riots began on May 6, 1967, when twenty-one workers, who were dismissed from the Hong Kong Artificial Flower Works, tried to stop their colleagues from loading the truck because of harsh working conditions and unfair payment. The unions, which were supported by the CCP, decided to go on strike.[23] What turned a labor dispute into riots that lasted until January 1968 was a series of mismanagements. In mainland China, the Cultural Revolution commenced in 1966, which inspired some Hong Kong workers and left-wing intellectuals to broaden the strike to an anticolonial movement. Nonetheless, the Beijing government was in a state of disarray. Hence, bureaucrats who worked for the Chinese representative body in Hong Kong, the Xinhua (New China) agency, were in danger of being called back to Beijing and persecuted. Despite Zhou Enlai's mandate not to instigate any Cultural-Revolution-styled social movement in Hong Kong, the Xinhua bureaucrats gave instructions to union leaders to do so. The results were a citywide strike and a food strike in June, and as the events escalated, protesters began to plant bombs around the city.[24] Meanwhile, the colonial government under Acting Governor Jack Cater advocated the use of police violence. They set up a detention camp to detain left-wing intellectuals, filmmakers, editors, and actors.[25] The riots eventually ended when Zhou issued an executive injunction to the New China Agency.[26]

As I have argued elsewhere, the riots "lasted [eight] months with fifty-one casualties (including the brutal killing of radio host Lam Bun), eight hundred sustained injuries and two thousand criminal convictions, [and] traumatized many Hong Kongers as they witnessed the instantiation of these contesting sovereign claims in the form of animal violence."[27] Those who were arrested and permanently injured found themselves being used as political tools by the Xinhua bureaucrats, but at the same time, they deeply resented the colonial government that unconstitutionally violated their human rights. The image of the CCP, which gained increasing acceptance among Hong Kongers in the 1950s, was irreparably tarnished.[28] The effect was that Hong Kongers were left in a juridical void in which no sovereign authority could be considered trustworthy and reliable.

Hong Kong Cinema as a Difference and Deferral

In this light, film criticism after the riots was seen as a public sphere where Hong Kong's relationship with China and Chineseness could be negotiated. After 1949, the Hong Kong film industry was divided linguistically into Mandarin and dialect cinemas. The former was produced and directed by filmmakers migrated from the Shanghai film industry, initially for an audience of their fellow expatriates. The latter were dominated by the Cantonese film industry, which produced Cantonese-speaking films for a local, primarily working-class audience. Politically, each industry was further divided by the pro-CCP (left-wing) camp and the pro-KMT (right-wing) camp. Filmmakers in each camp swore allegiance to their respective political parties, and in some cases, received direct financial support from their respective governments. Many of the left-wing filmmakers--both Mandarin and Cantonese--considered themselves as direct descendants of the left-wing filmmaking tradition in Shanghai in the 1930s (and arguably, the 1940s).[29]

In the 1960s, the most influential forum of cultural criticism was the *Zhongguo xuesheng zhoubao* (*Zunggwok hoksaang zaubou* or *Chinese Students Weekly*, 1952–74).[30] Although film-related articles appeared in the newspaper as early as its first issue, its special column "Dianying quan" ("Dinjing hyun" or "Cinema Circle") was first published in 1960. While film theory and criticism gathered momentum with the apparatus theory in Europe, their Hong Kong counterparts retreated to a mode of self-reflection between 1967 and 1969.[31]

Retrospectively, one can see that the apparatus theory was constructed on the assumption that a strong nation-state acts as a constituting and constitutive power, which was precisely missing in Hong Kong during the 1960s. On the contrary, revolutionary violence became an unchecked and preconstitutive *force of law*, which was the same form of violence exercised by the political powers that claimed themselves as a *law of force*.[32] In other words, for Hong Kongers, colonialism and communism uncannily shared the same juridical principle--animal violence--as a means to execute them as bare lives.

In film theory, therefore, the period between 1967 and 1969 was one in which critics felt compelled to reexamine the relationship between Hong Kong and China and reexamine the term *Chinese cinema* as a failed experiment. This was considered an especially urgent issue by the contributors to the *Chinese Students Weekly*, as the newspaper claimed itself to be "Established by Chinese students; Operated by Chinese students." As Zhang Weihong (Cheung Wai-hung) argues:

> The name *Chinese Student Weekly* demonstrates a self-awareness that identity is a learning process. It encompasses an imagined response and continuation of the idealism of the May-Fourth period [ca. 1919–21]. Yet, one can also see it as a self-nomination given by the artistic and literary workers of Hong Kong. At first glance, such a nomination seems to be self-assertive. Upon a closer look, however, it is a premature act of naming that is caught between [sociopolitical] phases: a lack of clarity of one's actual identity between the past and the future. It is a projection of an active yet submissive present as a will of being.[33]

Therefore, the word *Chinese* in the name *Chinese Students Weekly* is best considered a placeholder of a liminal identity that is neither Chinese nor non-Chinese (for example, Hong Konger or British), which film critics struggled to define. It signifies one's difference from China and Chineseness, and one's deferral to become Chinese in a foreseeable yet unfathomable future.

The first effort to wrestle with this question was made by Gu Er (Ku Yee). As Ku points out in "*Songhuajiang shang* de kusheng" ("*Cungfaagong soeng* dik huksing" or "Crying in *Along the Sungari River*"), many Hong Kong critics complained that "Mandarin cinema does not have any tradition, that it is only a filmed theater."[34] Nonetheless, on seeing the 1947 film *Cungfaagong soeng/ Along the Sungari River* (Jin Shan, Changchun Film Studio), Ku realized that Chinese filmmakers in the 1930s and 1940s had already laid down a solid cinematic style. In his article, Ku analyzes the use of crying in the film, and argues that: (1) "the appearance of crying" in *Along the Sungari River* is "natural" to its narrative structure; (2) crying in the film is not conveyed simply in close-ups that would have severed it from its narrative continuity and be presented as an effect on its own; rather, it is embedded in the mise-en-scène in order to enhance effects that have already been produced by other cinematic devices.[35]

For Ku, what constitutes the cinematic is the director's successful deployment of the mise-en-scène in order to allow the spectators to approach the image as a *natural* experience, a position borrowed from *Cahiers du Cinéma*.[36] Unfortunately, Ku argues that Mandarin filmmakers in Hong Kong and Taiwan after 1949 failed to carry on with such tradition:

> The roaring waves of political struggle swept away the foundation of Chinese cinema. As a result, the special political environment interrupted our tradition. Our misfortune is that almost all the excellent early filmmakers had left-wing tendencies [i.e., the left-wing filmmakers in 1930s Shanghai]. They were all deceived by the political myth of communism. Therefore, their talent had been unconsciously buried by themselves in the red earth of authoritarianism. It had no chance to be conveyed to the free world overseas.[37]

Ku's search for a Chinese cinematic tradition may seem nationalistic at first. However, in this passage, he deliberately connects--and unconsciously disconnects--the left-wing Shanghai filmmakers in the 1930s and 1940s, who laid down what he calls the Chinese tradition, and the Hong Kong and Taiwanese filmmakers in the 1960s, who made Mandarin films in the "free world overseas."[38] The interruption of tradition was therefore treated as a matter of geopolitical displacement—a failure to successfully transfer such tradition geographically from China to overseas (Hong Kong and Taiwan) and politically from the left to the right. Most importantly, Ku's mourning for a failed displacement of Chinese tradition is in itself a performance of failure to define his epistemic and geopolitical difference from China and Chineseness as a critical framework.

The idea that Hong Kong Mandarin cinema was not only a geopolitical difference but also a displaced and misplaced deferral of a Chinese cinematic tradition was raised in 1966 by Shi Qi (Shek Kei). In "Gangchan zuopai dianying ji qi xiao zichan jieji xing" ("Gongcaan zopaai dinjing kap kei siu zicaan gaaikap sing" or "The petit bourgeois sensibility in the Hong Kong left-wing film"), Shek argues that the Hong Kong left-wing Mandarin cinema was not a continuation of the Shanghai left-wing tradition in the 1930s. For him, the Hong Kong productions were considered left wing not because they conveyed socialist ideas. Rather, they were simply funded by left-wing financiers, who were expatriates from Shanghai or representatives from the Beijing government. These films were ultimately made by petit bourgeois filmmakers for a petit bourgeois audience. They manage to critique certain superficial problems in a capitalist society, but they do so by simply displacing the source of the problem to an imaginary "feudal power" that no longer existed in the 1960s:

> The petit bourgeoisie is the foundation of a capitalist society. Its members have certain intellectual cultivation. They have a stable foothold in the society, and they have a certain connoisseurship regarding the arts, that is, they understand what it means by having a "taste of life." Therefore, what a petit bourgeois film represents is the harmonious surface of the quotidian, and it pays attention to describing those minute details in human affections, feelings, and emotions. Since the petit bourgeois is socially observant, its films often make harmless fun of those cosmopolitan characters in the capitalist society. Yet since it is satisfied by its status quo, its films never confront any deep-structural traumas. Hence, no matter how hard it tries, its works always seem to be realistic, but at the same time highly unrealistic; they often critique an imaginary "feudal power" that has ceased to exist since the end of the May-Fourth era.[39]

In one register, Shek's criticism and methodology are both similar to the *Cahiers* editors' criticism and methodology on John Ford's *Young Mr. Lincoln* (Fox, 1939).[40] He seeks to make visible the ideological apparatus at work on the industrial and textual levels. In another register, Shek suggests that the Hong Kong filmmakers' and spectators' understanding of left-wing cinema was a displaced notion from Shanghai cinema in the 1930s. Its political concerns were entirely detached from the actual lived conditions of the working class in Hong Kong.

As Po Fung suggests, what Ku and Shek consider a Chinese tradition was in fact a projection of the notion *dianying gan* (*dinjing gam* or *cinématique*), a critical framework largely borrowed from *Cahiers du Cinéma*.[41] The fact that a Chinese cinematic tradition has to be constructed out of the European notion of the *cinématique* betrays the fact that China or Chineseness was merely a placeholder of a geopolitical difference and historical deferral. The idea of China and a sense of sociopolitical affiliation with it, seen from both the political right and the political left, is a potentiality that could never be actualized. This problem was eventually addressed by film theorist Lin Niantong (Lam Nin-tung) in 1969. As I summarized elsewhere, for Lam:

> Cantonese cinema could not be considered a national-language cinema because in their imagination, China's national cinema is the Putonghua (common language or Mandarin). Yet, the Putonghua is in fact a language constructed academically and politically based on the Beijing and Northeast dialects, which not only sounds different from the way Mandarin is spoken on the street, but also detached from the lived experience of the working class in these regions. Meanwhile, the term "Chinese cinema" ignores the contesting sovereign claims between the PRC and the ROC, and Hong Kong's in-between-ness as a colony. Finally, the term "Chinese-language cinema" overlooks the linguistic divide between *yu* (spoken languages, including dialects, which have been historically diverse) and *wen* (written languages, including classical and modern written Chinese, which have been historically standardized) by imposing the Euro-American concept of a linguistic system onto the Chinese case.[42]

If we posit Lam's understanding of the Hong Kong Cantonese cinema of the 1950s as a site where China and Chineseness are put into question, we can consider such cinema as a "minor cinema"—a cinema that uses a variation of a major language to rewrite its codes from *within*.[43] Yet, Lam's notion also tests the edges of the notion of minor cinema. First, Mandarin as a major language is a linguistic and historical construction. Thus, from the perspective of a Hong Konger, Cantonese is not a minor language but a language that has struggled since the Ming dynasty (1368–1644) as one of the major languages. Second, the "minor" language does not really rewrite a system from within. The fact that it manages to rewrite, and potentially reauthors, a major language means that it occupies a zone of exception between a state of territorialization and deterritorialization. In other words, the "minor" language draws its potential to authenticate itself by recognizing its status of being *extra*-territorial to a mythological authority, with which it maintains a geopolitical and cultural difference, as well as a historical deferral.

Conclusion

The theoretical discourse of the cinema in Hong Kong between 1967 and 1969 therefore focuses on an aporia: that film productions in Hong Kong could no longer be understood simply as *Chinese* or part of the larger notion of *Chinese cinema*. This notion that Hong Kong was somehow both part of and outside of the larger *Chinese* cultural and sociopolitical imaginary and practice is symptomatic of its historical status as an extraterritorial space. During this period, however, Hong Kong film critics did not immediately make sense of this sociopolitically liminal space. Rather, by struggling to negotiate Hong Kong cinema's relationship to *China as the Other*, their writings become a failure to perform their political subjectivity––and at the same time, they serve as a performance of their failure to perform any kind of subjectivity. In other words, while European, North American, and Japanese film theorists and critics after 1968 actively critiqued and resisted the power of the state and its ideological apparatus to constitute their subjectivity, Hong Kong film theorists and critics came face to face with the fact that under their extraterritorial conditions, they have always been desubjectivized in the first place. In a way, sociopolitical and ideological apparatuses are built on a process of actively stripping political lives of their subjectivity.

Notes

1. Gary Ka-wai Cheung, *Hong Kong's Watershed: The 1967 Riots* (Hong Kong:

Hong Kong University Press, 2009).

2. See Article 43c of Public Order Ordinance of 1967, Laws of Hong Kong, Chapter 245, *Historical Laws of Hong Kong Online*, accessed August 8, 2016, http://oelawhk.lib.hku.hk/items/show/2969; Cheung, *Hong Kong's Watershed,* 6.
3. See Robert Bickers and Ray Yep, "Studying the 1967 Riots: An Overdue Project," in *May Days in Hong Kong: Riot and Emergency in 1967*, ed. Bickers and Yep (Hong Kong: Hong Kong University Press, 2009), 1–18.
4. This rhetoric was analyzed in Aijaz Ahmad, "Jameson's Rhetoric of Otherness and the 'National Allegory,'" (1986), in *The Post-Colonial Studies Reader*, ed. Bill Ashcroft, Gareth Griffiths, and Helen Tiffin (Abingdon: Routledge, 2006), 84–85.
5. Victor Fan, "Cultural Extraterritoriality: Intra-regional Politics in Contemporary Hong Kong Cinema," *East Asian Journal of Popular Culture* 1, no. 3 (2015): 389–402, at 392; Fan, "Extraterritorial Cinema: Shanghai Jazz and Post-War Hong Kong Mandarin Musicals," *The Soundtrack* 6, nos. 1 and 2 (2014 [2015]): 33–52, at 39.
6. Fan, "Mirroring-Drifting—Lam Lin-tung and Film Aesthetics," *Asian Cinema* 27, no. 1 (2016): 29–42, at 31; Fan, "Poetics of Parapraxis and Reeducation: The Hong Kong Cantonese Cinema in the 1950s," in *The Poetics of Chinese Cinema*, ed. Gary Bettinson and James Udden (London: Palgrave Macmillan, 2016), 167–83, at 175.
7. See David Rodowick, *Crisis of Political Modernism* (Urbana: University of Illinois Press, 1998).
8. Thomas Elsaesser, *Hollywood heute: Geschichte, Gender und Nation im postklassischen Kino* (Berlin: Bertz + Fischer, 2009), 190–92; Fan, "Poetics of Parapraxis and Reeducation," 169; Fan, "The Unanswered Question of *Forrest Gump*," *Screen* 49, no. 4 (2008): 450–61, 454.
9. Lin Niantong (Lam Nin-tung), "Wushi niandai yueyu pian yanjiu zhong de jige wenti" ["Ngsap nindoi jyutjyu pin jingau zung dik geigo mantai" or "Several Questions on the Study of Cantonese Cinema in the 1950s"], *Da texie* [*Daai dakse* or *Close-up*] 59, no. 48 (1978).
10. Song Wanli (Sung Manlei), "Huanan dianying yu Guangdong jingshen" ["Waanaam dingjing jyu Gwongdung zingsan" or "South China Cinema and Its Kwantung Spirit"], *Yilin* [*Ngailam* or *Art Lane*] 35 (August 1, 1938): n.p.
11. Poshek Fu, *Passivity, Resistance, and Collaboration: Intellectual Choices in Occupied Shanghai, 1937–1945* (Stanford, CA: Stanford University Press,

1993), xv.

12. Fan, "Extraterritorial Cinema," 40.
13. Jean Ma, *Sounding the Modern Woman: The Songstress in Chinese Cinema* (Durham, NC: Duke University Press, 2015), 149–60.
14. Zhong Baoxian (Chung Po-yin), Xianggang yingshi ye bainian [Hoenggong jingsijip baaknin or One Hundred Years of Hong Kong Film and Television Industry] (2004; repr., Hong Kong: Joint Publishing, 2007), 111–19.
15. Fan, "Poetics of Parapraxis and Reeducation," 169.
16. Andrew Mumford, "The Malayan Emergency and America's Asian Cold War," and Nicholas J. White, "'Ungentlemanly Capitalism': John Hay and Malaya, 1904–64," papers presented at the conference "Emergency Cultures: New Approaches to the Study of Late Colonialism and the Cold War in Malaya, Singapore and Hong Kong," University of Nottingham, Nottingham, July 8, 2016.
17. Fan, "Cultural Extraterritoriality," 392, "Extraterritorial Cinema," 39, "Mirroring-Drifting," 31.
18. Pär Kristoffer Cassel, *Grounds of Judgment: Extraterritoriality and Imperial Power in Nineteenth-Century China and Japan* (New York: Oxford University Press, 2012), 39–62 and 184–85; Teemu Ruskola, *Legal Orientalism: China, the United States, and Modern Law* (Cambridge, MA: Harvard University Press, 2013), 152–235.
19. According to Jacques Derrida, as one text puts another "under erasure," the trace of erasure foregrounds the difference between the two texts as an in-between text. See Derrida, *Of Grammatology*, trans. Gayatri Spivak (Baltimore: Johns Hopkins University Press, 1976).
20. Jon D. Solomon, "Taiwan Incorporated: A Survey of Biopolitics in the Sovereign Police's East Asian Theater of Operations," in *Traces: A Multilingual Series of Cultural Theory*, vol. 3, ed. Thomas LaMarre and Kang Naei-hui (Hong Kong: Hong Kong University Press, 2004), 230–35.
21. See Giorgio Agamben, *Homo Sacer: Sovereign Power and Bare Life*, trans. Daniel Heller-Roazen (Stanford, CA: Stanford University Press, 1998), 1–2.
22. See the interview of Jack Cater, acting governor of Hong Kong during the riots, in Cheung, *Hong Kong's Watershed*, 149; John Cooper, *Colony in Conflict: The Hong Kong Disturbances May 1967–January 1968* (Hong Kong: Swindon Book, 1970); see also Frank Welsh, *A Borrowed Place: The History of Hong Kong* (New York: Kodansha International, 1993), 459–73.
23. Cheung, *Hong Kong's Watershed*, 23–42.

24. See the interview of Liang Shangyuan, director of the Hong Kong branch of the New China Agency during the riots, in Cheung, *Hong Kong's Watershed*, 149–54.
25. See the interviews of Tsang Tak-sing, in Cheung, *Hong Kong's Watershed*, 154–61; of Wu Tai-chow, in Cheung, *Hong Kong's Watershed*, 168–80; and of Chak Nuen-fai, in Cheung, *Hong Kong's Watershed*, 180–87.
26. Cheung, *Hong Kong's Watershed*, 127–30.
27. Fan, "Mirroring-Drifting," 32; the figures can be found in Cheung, *Hong Kong's Watershed*, 223.
28. Fan, "Mirroring-Drifting," 32; the figures can be found in Cheung, *Hong Kong's Watershed*, 223.
29. Zhou Chengren, "Glory Be with Cantonese Films: Ng Cho-fan and Union Film," trans. Tam King-fai, in *One for All: The Union Film Spirit*, ed. Grace Ng (Hong Kong: Hong Kong Film Archive, 2011), 9–18.
30. Fan, "Mirroring-Drifting," 29–30.
31. Luo Ka (Law Kar), "Qianyan • Ganyan" ["Cinjin • gamjin" or "Foreword; words of thought"], in 60 fengshang: Zhongguo xuesheng zhoubao yingping shinian [60 fungsoeng: Zunggwok hoksaang zaubou jingping sapnin or *The 60s Style: Ten Years of Film Criticism in the Chinese Students Weekly*], 2–3.
32. Giorgio Agamben, *State of Exception*, trans. Kevin Attell (Chicago: University of Chicago Press, 2005), 38–39.
33. Zhang Weihong (Cheung Wai-hung), "Zhongguo shenfen de tansuo" ["Zunggwok sanfan dik taamsok" or "An exploration of Chinese identity"], in Law, *The 60s Style*, 152.
34. Gu Er (Ku Yee), "Songhuajiang shang de kusheng" ["Cungfaagong soeng dik huksing" or "Crying in Along the Sungari River"], in Zhongguo xuesheng zhoubao [Zunggwok hoksaang zaubou or Chinese Students Weekly] 787 (August 18, 1967), repr. in Law, *The 60s Style*, 179–80.
35. Ku, "Crying in Along the Sungari River."
36. See Jim Hillier, "Introduction: *Cahiers du Cinéma* in the 1960s," in *Cahiers du Cinéma, 1960–1968: New Wave, New Cinema, Reevaluating Hollywood*, ed. Jim Hillier (Cambridge, MA: Harvard University Press, 1986), 3–18.
37. Ku, "Crying in Along the Sungari River," 179.
38. Ku, "Crying in Along the Sungari River," 179.
39. Shi Qi (Shek Kei), "Gangchan zuopai dianying ji qi xiao zichan jieji xing" ["Gongcaan zopaai dinjing kap kei siu zicaan gaaikap sing" or "The petit bourgeois sensibility in the Hong Kong left-wing film"], *Chinese Students*

Weekly 740 (September 23, 1966): 11.

40. Editors of *Cahiers du Cinéma*, "John Ford's *Young Mr. Lincoln*," trans. Helen Lackner and Diana Matias, *Screen* 13, no. 3 (1972): 5–44.
41. Po Fung, "Zhongguo jianshi he dianyinggan" ["Zunggwok ginsik wo dinjing-gam" or "Chinese sight and understanding and the *cinématique*"], in Law, *The 60s Style*, 155.
42. Lin Niantong [Lam Nin-tung], "You guoqing xiangqi de Hanyu dianying, fangyan dianying" ["Jau gwokhing soenghei dik Honjyu dinjing, fongjin dingjing" or "From National day to Chinese-language cinema, dialect cinema"], *Chinese Students Weekly* 794 (October 10, 1969): 10.
43. Gilles Deleuze and Félix Guattari, *Kafka: Toward a Minor Literature*, trans. Dana Polan (Minneapolis: University of Minnesota Press, 1986), 16–27. Here, I would also like to thank my PhD student George Crosthwait for his inspiration.

17

Cultural Revolution Models on Film

The Third World Politics of Self-Reflexivity in *On the Docks* (1972)

Laurence Coderre

The Hong Kong International Film Festival premiere of Chen Kaige's *Huang tudi/Yellow Earth* on April 12, 1985, is typically understood to have inaugurated "New Chinese Cinema." Part of what marked the film as distinctly "new" in this context was the extent to which Chen and his cinematographer Zhang Yimou—both then-recent graduates of the Beijing Film Academy—apparently broke with the narratological and aesthetic conventions of the Mao period (1949–76).[1] Gone were the meditative gazes into the utopian future; gone, too, the melodramatic declarations of love for the leader of the Chinese Communist Party (CCP). Instead, Chen and Zhang drew heavily on a cinematic vocabulary much more familiar and palatable to international "art" film audiences, emphasizing ambiguity, ellipsis, and polysemy. Ironic, then, that—as the essays in this volume make clear—this vocabulary was intimately tied to the legacy of May '68 and therefore, by extension, to the global love affair with Mao and the Chinese Cultural Revolution (1966–76). Unbeknownst to them, in turning away from the long-prescribed aesthetic of the People's Republic of China (PRC), these so-called Fifth Generation filmmakers smuggled Mao in by the back door. In the spirit of the revolutionary agent provocateur, in fact, one might argue that such conventions had and have, in some sense, been both Maoist and Chinese all along.

I confess, I am not so bold as to see this argument through in the pages that follow, not least because doing so would reassert the very naturalized categories—of nation and national cinema—to which this collection of essays gives the lie. Still, there is something to be said here for the undeniably critical role of Maoist discourse, circulating internationally, in the global 1960s. The aphorisms of "The Little Red Book," among other texts, produced a shared frame of reference and ideological affinity among thinkers and filmmakers both inside and outside the PRC, while images of Red Guard throngs on Tiananmen Square captured many an imagination.[2] Fittingly enough, one of the areas of emphasis within this discourse was precisely revolutionary internationalism and a Third-Worldist sense of responsibility toward those fighting against imperialism and colonialism in all their forms. This endeared Mao to many leftists in the West who shared his anticolonial vision of the future, while at home in the People's Republic, declarations of solidarity with one's Latin American, African, and Asian brothers—to say nothing of black power activists in the United States—became a touchstone of Cultural Revolution rhetoric in newspapers and posters.

This chapter considers how this Third-Worldist orientation manifested itself in the Chinese cinema of the Cultural Revolution. I focus primarily on the 1972 film version of *Haigang/On the Docks* (dirs. Xie Tieli and Xie Jin), a Beijing opera about class struggle—and the international aid caught in the middle—in the Shanghai dockyard, set in 1963. *On the Docks* is overtly Third Worldist in its plot, but rather than analyzing these narratological themes in isolation, I employ them as a springboard in order to investigate the ways in which they are present aesthetically as well. As one of eight original "*yangbanxi*" or "model performances," *On the Docks*, the opera, was actively overseen by Mao's wife, Jiang Qing, and officially promoted as an exemplar of the new socialist performing arts. The work's model status guaranteed its endless reproduction in a panoply of media forms, including cinema. The "remediation" of the stage opera into an opera film, in Weihong Bao's sense,[3] proved especially complex aesthetically—many of the model performances, including *On the Docks*, were filmed more than once for this very reason. My contention in this essay is ultimately that *On the Docks*' explicit narrative engagement with Third Worldism is reproduced in the particularities of this remediative effort: the film version's self-conscious rejection of realism, its insistent aesthetic of self-reflexivity, particularly in its depiction of technology and mechanized labor, also enacts a Third-Worldist geopolitics whose implications extend far beyond this single, cinematic text.

Mao Goes Global

In China today, as in most quarters around the world, the Cultural Revolution is officially remembered as a time of misguided violence and chaos. The CCP Central Committee's 1981 resolution on Party history deems the 1966–76 decade a mistake to be disavowed.[4] Blamed for the destruction of Chinese cultural heritage, the brutal treatment of "counterrevolutionaries," a suicide epidemic, the breakdown of the Party-state, and the mass displacement of urban youth, for many, the Cultural Revolution has become difficult to imagine as anything short of an unmitigated disaster. How easy it now is to discount the passion the movement first instilled in its early participants—the devotion of millions upon millions of Red Guards to the furtherance of "Mao Zedong Thought" and the pursuit of continuous revolution. How easy now to forget, too, that the outbreak of the Cultural Revolution in 1966 was positively received in many foreign enclaves, including, and perhaps especially, among French intellectuals. Consider the fault lines that emerged within the French Left in advance of the events of May '68, with some, including a group of self-proclaimed Maoists at the École normale supérieure, drawing on Mao to critique the French Communist Party's ties to the Soviet Union.[5] It is no accident, in fact, that Julian Bourg refers to this group of students as the "Red Guards of Paris," for they and their many French compatriots—both students and not—found, in the Cultural Revolution, inspiration on a great number of fronts.[6]

One wonders what the Great Helmsman himself thought of his cachet on the Rive Gauche, so far removed were many French appropriations of his words and likeness from their Chinese origins. Indeed, it has become something of a truism that the reality of the Chinese socialist experiment differed widely from the utopian imagination of leftist activists in the developed world. That is to say, Paris's Red Guard contingent, for one, might be forgiven their (some would say naive) turn to Chairman Mao; they were not alone in cleaving the man and his thought from his real-world surround. By virtue of China's isolation during this period, foreign Maoists often operated with limited to no information about what was happening on the ground in the People's Republic—they were mostly on their own. French Maoism, the argument therefore goes, may tell us a great deal about France in the 1960s but very little about the Chinese Cultural Revolution proper.[7] Arif Dirlik, for instance, identifies a "Third Worldist fantasy" motivating many leftist appropriations of Mao "as a Chinese reincarnation of Marx who fulfilled the Marxist promise that had been betrayed in the West," the Soviet Union, and its revisionist satellites.[8] The notion that Mao Zedong's actions might also be construed as a betrayal of Marxist promise was seldom on the table, at least until Nixon's game-changing visit to the PRC in 1972.

Rather than focusing on the ways in which French Maoists and their confrères "got the Cultural Revolution wrong," however, as this position maintains, I am more interested in what they ostensibly got right; for whatever the flaws of their "Third Worldist fantasy," there is little doubt that Mao was, in fact, immensely concerned with positioning himself and the PRC as enemies of both capitalist imperialism and Soviet revisionism. Whether motivated by a realpolitik desire for allies outside the USSR and the Eastern Bloc in the wake of the Sino-Soviet split or an internationalist dream of revolutionary solidarity, China loudly and repeatedly committed itself to its brothers in Latin America, Africa, and Asia. Consider, for example, the poster in figure 17.1. The audience for these declarations was twofold: on the one hand, they elevated the PRC's standing among like-minded individuals around the world, from left-leaning First World youth to anticolonial guerillas, while, on the other hand, these pledges of support also impressed on Chinese citizens just how lucky they themselves were—thanks to Mao and the CCP—to be in a position to help those less fortunate. Aid projects in newly independent countries were particularly effective in conveying this twin sense of Chinese solidarity and superiority. China was instrumental in the construction of TAZARA, for example, a new railroad line linking Tanzania and Zambia, for which the PRC provided funding, equipment, and personnel in the early 1970s.[9] Internationally, this project greatly endeared Mao's China to American black radicals, among others.[10] Domestically, TAZARA was promoted as a manifestation of China's privileged status in the Third World, as in comedian Ma Ji's crosstalk performance *Youyi song* (Ode to Friendship).[11]

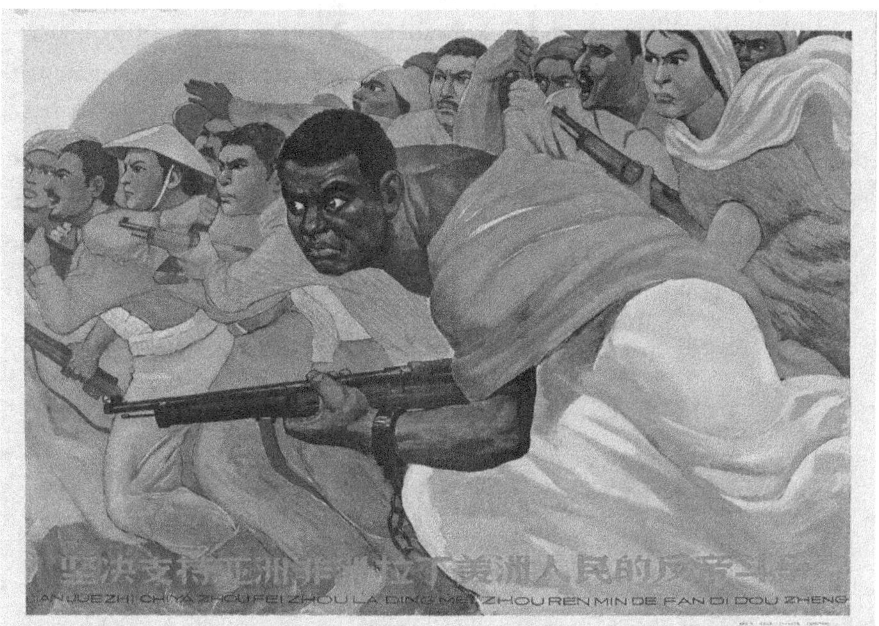

Zhou Ruizhuang, "Jianjue zhichi Yazhou Feizhou Ladingmeizhou renmin de fandi douzheng" (Resolutely Support the Anti-Imperialist Struggle of the Asian, African, and Latin American Peoples) (Shanghai: Shanghai renmin meishu chubanshe, ca. 1967). Poster image courtesy of the C. V. Starr East Asian Library, University of California, Berkeley.

It is precisely this complex internationalist move that underlies the story of *On the Docks*, in which the timely shipping of aid to anticolonialist "Africa" becomes an opportunity for counterrevolutionary sabotage, proletarian consciousness raising, and class struggle. Two shipments are meant to be loaded and go out from Shanghai: one filled with rice seed bound for some unspecified African locale, that is, aid for China's brothers in revolution, the other full of fiberglass headed to Scandinavia, that is, goods purchased by the capitalist First World. An incoming typhoon forces the dockworkers to prioritize their tasks; only one ship will make it out as scheduled. In truth, this is not much of a dilemma. The "correct" choice for the dockworkers is painfully clear: not only is the aid the revolutionary option, but it alone is deemed time sensitive. Still, this choice begets disagreement between Fang Haizhen, the paradigmatic revolutionary hero, and Qian Shouwei, the nefarious class enemy. Fang's forces carry the day—the shipment of agricultural aid will be dealt with first—but Qian is only getting warmed up. He begins to corrupt a young, impressionable dockworker, Han Xiaoqiang, who learns to belittle manual labor and ultimately turns his back on his comrades. When Han's inattention causes a bag of rice seed to tear, Qian decides to contaminate the bag's contents with some spilled fiberglass. Qian's sabotage is discovered before the aid can leave port, though not before the punctured bag has been mixed in with all the others. The workers quickly band together and vow to find the offending sack. They toil through the night, checking and reloading every individual bag, until their mission is complete, the Africans are safe to plant the seed, and the counterrevolutionary element among the proletarian ranks is ferreted out.

Even by Cultural Revolution standards, *On the Docks* seems contrived. Whereas the other seven original model works are set in wartime and rely heavily on foreign, and/or foreign-backed, enemies (the Japanese, the Americans, the Guomindang, and the South Koreans), *On the Docks* takes place in postrevolutionary, peacetime Shanghai. This setting creates a rather peculiar situation in which the piece's central political struggle—the heart of any work of the era—must be serious enough to propel the narrative forward but not so serious as to undermine the audience's faith in the fundamental soundness of the Communist project. *On the Docks* arguably fails to accomplish this tricky two-step convincingly. Qian's grand act of sabotage—mixing fiberglass into one bag of seed among thousands—for example, is met with a response so wildly out of proportion with the scale of the damage caused that the work as a whole scarcely holds together. And while one could argue that this "problem," as I describe it here, has more to do with my own "bourgeois" approach to the text than with the text itself—indeed, my belittling of the opera's stakes echoes Qian Shouwei's objection to the bag-by-bag search of the rice seed shipment—I would still like to suggest that even a fleeting alignment between viewer and counterrevolutionary has the potential to unsettle the work's overarching system of signification. In effect, the revolution has lost so much of its motivation on the home front in *On the Docks* that the opera essentially reproduces one of the "real world" PRC problems it was intended to address: complacency, especially among the young, and the flagging of revolutionary ardor. Within this context, the reliance on the unspecified "Africans" as both recipients of aid—read: worse off than the PRC—and a proxy actively engaged in pitched ideological, if not actual military, battles with a veritable and formidable imperialist foe provides a structurally necessary workaround for the temporal stasis simultaneously required of and denied by socialism as a stage of historical development: on the one hand, history must always be moving forward toward a communist utopia, while, on the other hand, state-socialist regimes depend for their survival on a notion that this utopia has, in a sense, already arrived.[12] In this regard, Third World internationalism, as articulated in *On the Docks* and more broadly in Cultural Revolution discourse, might best be understood as a way to deal with this paradox, by diverting attention from China's own historical development to that of another region or nation.

While important, this analysis of *On the Docks* as a Third-Worldist text—that is, as a text that espouses the very internationalist worldview that made Mao so appealing to many First World leftists—is notable for its restriction to the realm of narrative and narratology. In the remainder of this chapter, however, I am interested in the ways in which the film version of *On the Docks* aesthetically engages with the geopolitics of Third Worldism as well.

An Aesthetic Education

My turn to aesthetics is motivated by the priorities of the Cultural Revolution itself as well as the circumstances of its many appropriations abroad, including those in France, which took on cultural and cinematic forms in addition to those of mass politics. That is to say, the Cultural Revolution was as much a battle waged over and through aesthetics as anything else—more on this in a moment—a fact that seems to have been implicitly recognized in the Mao manias of the late 1960s and early 1970s. Consider the 1967 Parisian fad for "*les cols Maos*" (Mao-collared suits), the publication of a Cultural Revolution–themed spread in *Lui* (the French *Playboy* of sorts), and Jean-Luc Godard's 1967 film *La chinoise*.[13] From West German debates over the Mao "brand" to Andy Warhol's 1972 series of Mao portraits,[14] the Sinophilia that took much of the world by storm during this time was deeply preoccupied with looks *and* politics. In other words, it was not only the philosophy of Mao Zedong that resonated around the world; the arresting visuals of the Cultural Revolution struck a significant chord as well. This turn of events was as it should be, perhaps, for a movement concerned with the revolutionary remaking of culture and the aesthetic education of the masses.

The Marxist and Maoist notion that politics and aesthetics are inextricably linked was, of course, not new or unique to the Cultural Revolution. In the PRC context, the locus classicus for this principle is Mao's so-called "Yan'an

Talks" on literature and art of 1942. Not precisely concerned with aesthetics per se, the text nonetheless articulates the role of artistic production in the time of revolution: art for art's sake was deemed a bourgeois fallacy—artistic production was rooted in class struggle. And henceforth, it would explicitly be put in the service of the masses and the dictatorship of the proletariat.

> Literature and art are subordinate to politics, but in their turn exert a great influence on politics. Revolutionary literature and art are part of the whole revolutionary cause, they are cogs and wheels in it, and although in comparison with certain other and more important parts they may be less significant and less urgent and may occupy a secondary position, nevertheless they are indispensable cogs and wheels in the whole machine, an indispensable part of the entire revolutionary cause. If we had no literature and art, even in the broadest and most ordinary sense, we could not carry on the revolutionary movement.[15]

Even in this seemingly straightforward passage, however—with its famous Leninist image of cogs in a machine—we see signs of a considerably more complex relationship between art and politics than initially meets the eye. That is, the subordination of art to politics is nowhere near as categorical or instrumental as the mechanistic metaphor implies. Indeed, the rhetorical figure seems rather more trouble than it is worth in these few tortured sentences, for there is decidedly a tension here between a would-be (institutional) hierarchy—artists must not act against the interests of the Party—and a much more abstract dialectic in which politics requires art to function. I would like to suggest that part of what renders this tension so palpable in the above passage is the repeated invocation of literature and art as opposed to a suppler notion of aesthetics. Literature and art, as cultural products, may be subordinated to a political cause or agenda, but aesthetics are not so easily harnessed. If we take literature and art "in the broadest and most ordinary sense" to imply an aestheticization of the quotidian, then not only must aesthetics, like art and literature, be political by definition, but also politics, both of the everyday and of the unfurling of history, must likewise be bound up with a notion of aesthetics.

Lest this seem like a willful over-reading of the "Yan'an Talks," I hasten to add that this understanding of the complex relationship between aesthetics and politics, though dating back to the Party's time in Yan'an, arguably did not come to its ultimate fruition until the mid-1960s. It was at this time that, through the concerted efforts of Jiang Qing, among others, the revamping of the revolutionary arts took center stage. By the time of the Cultural Revolution, the vast majority of the literature and art of the so-called Seventeen Years (1949–66), despite having been considered politically correct at the time of its creation, now found itself under attack for being insufficiently socialist. The promise of revolutionary culture had, by these accounts, been forsaken—and with dire consequences—for one of the great underlying claims of the Cultural Revolution was that art and literature were not simply reflections of economic social relations. In Marxist terms, the superstructure was now understood to impact the base. A revolutionary opera could therefore push history forward just as a revisionist film could pull it backward—to the era of capitalism or worse. Thus, the stakes of cultural production as a revolutionary enterprise, its tedious and laborious revision, and the ideological overdetermination of its every minor detail were incredibly high.

But this is only part of the story: "The Cultural Revolution created not only its own art, as in the numerous paintings and portraits of Mao and in the revolutionary model plays (*yangban xi*), but also an 'artistic' way of life, an elaborate pattern of daily living that [put an] enormous premium on forms—forms of speech, behavior, bearing, and countless other ritualistic details."[16] Fully understanding the Cultural Revolution is therefore not simply a matter of grappling with the politicization of everyday life, as is still the customary approach. It is also a question of the aestheticization of that quotidian politics. After all, as the so-called Shiliu tiao (Sixteen Points), issued by the Central Committee on August 8, 1966, put it, the movement as a whole was meant to be "a new period of socialist revolution" that would "touch people's souls."[17] The desire to reach and mold the individual at this most intimate of levels translated into much more than simply overt political engagement; rather, it required of everyone "a life that was aesthetically driven."[18] It is within this context that we begin to see revolutionary culture as part of an aesthetic education in this particular sense, an aesthetic education that was also always already deeply political.

A film like *On the Docks*, with its explicitly internationalist plot, pushes us to consider how this aesthetic-political nexus produced itself in relation not only to the Chinese everyday but also to the positioning of China within the Third World. In other words, it invites us to ask how the film enacts and promotes both an ethical *and* aesthetic Third Worldism. The latter half of this query has been studied surprisingly little with regard to the Cultural Revolution as a whole. Ban Wang's recent engagement with the Third Worldism of this period, for example, has heavily relied on film readings largely restricted to the realm of plot and narratology.[19] In the case of *On the Docks*, one wonders whether this reluctance to venture into the field of aesthetics stems from its position in the model repertoire, a repertoire with which it seems aesthetically consistent, despite being its only overtly Third-Worldist piece. One might easily argue, then, that *On the Docks*' most salient formal characteristics have little if anything to do with its major themes and that its particular form is simply the result of adhering to the conventions established by other model work films. I want to flip this line of reasoning on its head and suggest that, as a model outlier in many respects—including its post-1949 setting—*On the Docks* constitutes an opportunity to examine the ways in which the film versions of the other model works also engage with Third Worldism. That is, *On the Docks* gives us an "in" to a conversation we can and should be having much more broadly. The key to doing this, I believe, is to focus on *On the Docks*' obsessive self-reflexivity—the multiple ways in which it repeatedly highlights its own status not only as a film but also as a demonstrably and identifiably *Chinese* film—as an articulation of what we might call, riffing off Weihong Bao, the "geopolitics of remediation."

What Not to Show

Much of what I want to file under self-reflexivity in *On the Docks* consists of a marked turn away from film's realist potential as a medium, that is, in the repeated act of not showing or of only showing indirectly or in a highly stylized way that which realism would show "as is." In part, we can ascribe this aesthetic mode to the work's status as a filmic remediation of the opera stage, that is, to its positioning vis-à-vis and within the Chinese generic tradition of the opera film. As a genre, opera film has grappled with bridging the gap between realist cinema's purported Real and Chinese sung-drama's heavy reliance on the realm of the "as if," since its very inception—more on this in a moment. This has led to efforts to pinpoint and perform the medium specificity of film and sung-drama, which, crucially, have always been heavily laden with nationalistic and geopolitical concerns.[20] The production of a distinctly "Chinese" cinema aesthetic, in contradistinction to Hollywood and the USSR, in the wake of the Sino-Soviet split was, in this sense, the continuation of a deeply political endeavor that required the careful negotiation of the "as is" and the "as if"—the former a testament to cinema as a powerful, modern technology and the latter taken as an emblem of "Chineseness" and, by extension, a Third-Worldist stance.

We can see the traces of this negotiation in *On the Docks*' marked emphasis on mechanization and mechanized labor. Indeed, my invocation of "self-reflexivity," as opposed to a concept much more closely associated with opera film discourse, stems precisely from this overt engagement with, and fetishization of, the mechanical (stand-in for the ever-present apparatus of the camera) as an avatar of historical progress. Ma Hongliang, a retired dockworker recently returned from a trip to the countryside, for example, is forever marveling at all the newfangled equipment on the docks and the resulting improvement in labor conditions. In one of the film's most tedious sections, Ma, together with the infallible Fang Haizhen, attempts to convey this sense of wonder and appreciation to young Han Xiaoqiang by contrasting the lives of dockworkers in the Old Society with the dockworkers of today. They used to labor like "beasts" (*niuma*), Han is told, but now, thanks to socialism, with its forklifts and cranes, workers can finally—paradoxically—labor like men. Marxist humanism aside, this lesson is most notable because of what it is paired with: not realist shots of this much-lauded machinery, but rather, the repeated visual caress of a bamboo carrying pole, precisely that which heavy machinery rendered obsolete. I ultimately want to suggest that the importance of technology, here and elsewhere in *On the Docks*, needs to be understood in relation to this formal bait and switch. In other words, the central role of the mechanical is in large part a function of its filmic absence, that is, by its not being shown, in flagrant violation of realist conventions.

The specter of realism—born of a familiarity with how the Real is typically depicted—is crucial to this meaning-making mode, since it so clearly hinges on a form of implicit negation. To that end, it is important to note that *On the*

Docks itself directly invokes and denunciates a (socialist) realist film. One of the ways Qian Shouwei tries to corrupt the impressionable Han Xiaoqiang is through the movies. Specifically, he provides Han with a ticket to see *Chengfeng polang/Brave the Wind and Waves* (1957; hereafter referred to as *Brave*), a film directed by Sun Yu, who is best known as the writer/director of *Wu Xun zhuan/The Life of Wu Xun* (1950), which became the subject of a mass criticism campaign—the first aimed at a film in PRC history. *Brave*, though originally released to positive reviews in 1957, predictably also ran afoul of the Anti-Rightist Movement, only to be rereleased in 1962. (*On the Docks* is ostensibly set in 1963, that is, after *Brave*'s return to the screen.) The film's rehabilitation did not last long; by the standards of the Cultural Revolution, *Brave* could only be considered a first-rate "poisonous weed." In addition to Sun Yu's past political problems, the work itself is far too concerned with romance and adventure and far too flip about the proletariat to be anything else. Moreover, it is these aspects of the movie that most appeal to and, temporarily at least, corrupt *On the Docks*' young Han: Han Xiaoqiang longs to leave the docks and its workers behind to sail the seven seas, and *Brave* turns on the intrepid spirit of three female mariners' quest for love and glory in a male-dominated profession. *Brave* thus testifies to all that was wrong with pre–Cultural Revolution Chinese cinema. In other words, it is meant to stand for all that *On the Docks* is most emphatically not—both politically/ideologically and, as we shall now see, aesthetically.

The key here is that, as part of its role as internalized counterpoint to *On the Docks*, *Brave* offers us not only an alternative politics, but also an alternative, yet strikingly parallel, cinematic vision, for it too depicts the Shanghai shipyard. That is to say, the two films' many emphatic differences are grounded by a marked similarity of setting and purpose: whatever else they may be, both are deeply invested in promoting the Shanghai docks of the socialist era as modern and mechanized. Which sets up, for example, the possibility of a one-to-one comparison between the two works' dockyard establishment sequences. In *Brave*, our initial exposure to the docks, experienced alongside the film's three female protagonists, is clearly meant to emphasize and actively illustrate the massive scale of the site. A low-angle shot, with the camera situated immediately behind the characters, engages their upward gaze toward a huge scaffold; nondiegetic music is replaced by diegetic engine noises, as the young women and their male comrade are corralled by machinery left and right; the camera now perched high off the ground, human actors cede the upper two-thirds of the screen to the forklifts dancing around them; shifting behind one of these vehicles, a point-of-view shot captures two female drivers as they turn back and smile at the group of trespassers; one of the girls notices a female crane operator, and the camera tilts upward, tracking her movements as she takes her seat. Everything in this sequence glorifies the mechanical, rooted as it is in the repeated juxtaposition and realist visualization of human and machine. By contrast, the opening sequence of *On the Docks* emphasizes an elaborate, bodily choreography—men pulling ropes and carrying bags. What little machinery is seen at all is rendered toylike prop. A mammoth ship is flattened out onto the painted backdrop, the docks a wondrous but ultimately manageable setting on which a drama can unfold.

My contention is that *Brave* deploys the very aesthetics of showing required to make *On the Docks*' proclivity not to show meaningful. I want to go further, however, and couch this difference as a disagreement over realism—socialist or otherwise—and its political implications. To that end, Jason McGrath, who has situated the model work films as a group within the broader history of revolutionary Chinese cinema, posits the existence of a "formalist drift," in which a concern with ideological forms usurps an earlier interest in realist aesthetics.[21] This move usefully breaks down often-naturalized distinctions between cinematic genres, and I echo it here. For what has hitherto gone unremarked in my comparison of *On the Docks* and *Brave* is that while the former is an opera film, the latter is a narrative feature. This, in turn, brings us back to the notion of an exceptional, nationalist aesthetic of not showing attributed to Chinese sung-drama's defining "suppositionality," to use Haiping Yan's influential term—the fact that "its workings prevent both the performers and audiences from forgetting that what they enact and behold is consciously *made*."[22] Given that Chinese operatic practices are consistently rooted in a notion of "as if," it makes sense that Chinese opera films would be as well. And yet, while there is little doubt that *On the Docks*, for one, fits quite neatly within a long lineage of attempts to translate the suppositional opera stage to the silver screen, we must be careful not to assume that this was a self-evident and easy process. Much like the many debates over opera film of the late 1950s and early 1960s, the "correct" approach to model opera filmmaking as a form of remediation was the subject of great contestation.[23]

In contemporary published accounts of the filmmaking process, this contestation tends to assume a dialectical narrative in which initial attempts to capitalize on cinema's realist potential—always understood as antithetical to opera's suppositionality—inevitably fail. The guiding principle of remediation is eventually understood within this narrative as "*huanyuan wutai gao yu wutai*" (returning to the stage and surpassing the stage), which itself also operated as a prescriptive dialectic.[24] In practice, this seems to have meant developing a slightly stagier version of the opera film aesthetic Weihong Bao dubs "rhythmic mise-en-scène," in which camera movements are determined in relation to the actor's movements, ultimately creating a kind of kinetic, virtual—suppositional—body.[25] We therefore once again find ourselves in the realm of human-machine interactions, whose hybridity facilitates a new cinematic mode in which the opera stage is paradoxically more stagelike than ever before. Much like the dockworkers, who are never more human than when they labor alongside machines—even, and perhaps especially, when those machines are not actually seen—according to the operative Cultural Revolution understanding of remediation, the correct collaboration of actor and camera can render opera ever-more operatic. Fitting, then, that the camera, like the crane, should be continuously, if indirectly, referenced, but nowhere seen; we look through it, never at it.

Much more could be said about the articulation of this aesthetic—both in *On the Docks* and the model work films as a group. But for reasons of space, as I draw to a close, I want to return to another aspect of pre–Cultural Revolution opera film debates—namely, that the push and pull of remediation has always been burdened with political implications.[26] The development of a "Chinese" cinema aesthetic is part of a much larger set of concerns. It is in this regard that we might speak of a "geopolitics of remediation" at the very heart of McGrath's "formalist drift" and, therefore, of a Third-Worldist aesthetic project, more generally. *On the Docks* allows us to make this leap and, in the process, reveals itself to be a much more intriguing filmic text than it at first appeared, one that is notably Third Worldist in more than plot alone. Moreover, it reminds us that the model repertoire films as a group—and the project out of which they arose—must also be understood in relation to Chinese cinematic history as well as in the context of contemporary geopolitics, that is, as a product of and participant in the global 1960s.

Notes

1. My thanks to the anonymous reviewers as well as the editors of this volume, Christina Gerhardt and Sara Saljoughi, for their suggestions and support. My thanks also to the University of Michigan's Lieberthal-Rogel Center for Chinese Studies for its support, in the form of a postdoctoral fellowship for the 2015/16 academic year, without which this essay would not have been possible.
2. Alexander C. Cook, ed., *Mao's Little Red Book: A Global History* (Cambridge: Cambridge University Press, 2014).
3. Weihong Bao, "The Politics of Remediation: Mise-en-scène and the Subjunctive Body in Chinese Opera Film," *The Opera Quarterly* 26, no. 2–3 (2010): 256–90.
4. CCP Central Committee, "The Cultural Revolution—Excerpt from 'Resolution on Certain Questions in the History of Our Party Since the Founding of the People's Republic of China,'" in *China's Cultural Revolution, 1966–69: Not a Dinner Party*, ed. Michael Schoenhals (Armonk, NY: M. E. Sharpe, 1996), 296–303.
5. Julian Bourg, "The Red Guards of Paris: French Student Maoism of the 1960s," *History of European Ideas* 31, no. 4 (2005): 472–90.
6. For many examples of this, see, among others, Bourg, "The Red Guards of Paris"; Julian Bourg, "Principally Contradiction: The Flourishing of French Maoism," in Cook, *Mao's Little Red Book*, 225–44; Richard Wolin, *The Wind from the East: French Intellectuals, the Cultural Revolution, and the Legacy of the 1960s* (Princeton, NJ: Princeton University Press, 2010).
7. For a recent example of this take, see Julia Lovell, "The Cultural Revolution and Its Legacies in International Perspective," *China Quarterly* 227 (2016): 632–52, at 635. For a rebuttal slightly different from my own, see Fabio Lanza, *The End of Concern: Maoist China, Activism, and Asian Studies* (Durham, NC: Duke University Press, 2017), 6–10.
8. Arif Dirlik, "The Predicament of Marxist Revolutionary Consciousness: Mao Zedong, Antonio Gramsci, and the Reformulation of Marxist Revolutionary Theory," *Modern China* 9, no. 2 (1983): 182–211, at 186.
9. Priya Lal, "Maoism in Tanzania: Material Connections and Shared Imaginaries," in Cook, *Mao's Little Red Book*, 96–116.

10. Robeson Taj Frazier, *The East Is Black: Cold War China in the Black Radical Imagination* (Durham, NC: Duke University Press, 2014), 203.
11. Ma Ji, *Youyi song* (Ode to Friendship), performed by Ma Ji and Tang Jiezhong, crosstalk, Zhongguo changpian (China Records), BM-406/7, 1973, 2 flexi-discs.
12. For more on the peculiarities of socialist time, see Susan Buck-Morss, *Dreamworld and Catastrophe: The Passing of Mass Utopia in East and West* (Cambridge, MA: MIT Press, 2000); Laurence Coderre, "Socialist Commodities: Consuming *Yangbanxi* in the Cultural Revolution" (PhD diss., University of California, Berkeley, 2015); Alexei Yurchak, *Everything Was Forever, Until It Was No More: The Last Soviet Generation* (Princeton, NJ: Princeton University Press, 2006).
13. Wolin, *The Wind from the East*, 114.
14. For the former, see Quinn Slobodian, "Badge Books and Brand Books: The Mao Bible in East and West Germany," in Cook, *Mao's Little Red Book*, 206–24.
15. Mao Zedong, "Talks at the Yan'an Forum on Literature and Art," in *Modern Chinese Literary Thought: Writings on Literature 1893–1945*, ed. Kirk A. Denton (Stanford, CA: Stanford University Press, 1996), 474–75.
16. Ban Wang, *The Sublime Figure of History: Aesthetics and Politics in Twentieth-Century China* (Stanford, CA: Stanford University Press, 1997), 208.
17. "Zhongguo gongchandang zhongyang weiyuanhui guanyu wuchanjieji wenhua da geming de jueding" (The CCP Central Committee's Decision concerning the Great Proletarian Cultural Revolution), *Renmin ribao* (People's Daily), August 9, 1966, 1.
18. Wang, *Sublime Figure of History*, 209.
19. Ban Wang, "Third World Internationalism: Films and Operas in the Chinese Cultural Revolution," in *Listening to the Cultural Revolution: Music, Politics, and Cultural Continuities*, ed. Paul Clark, Laikwan Pang, and Tsan-Huang Tsai (London: Palgrave Macmillan, 2016), 85–106.
20. Weihong Bao, "The Trouble with Theater: Cinema and the Geopolitics of Medium Specificity," *Framework: The Journal of Cinema and Media* 56, no. 2 (2015): 350–67.
21. Jason McGrath, "Cultural Revolution Model Opera Films and the Realist Tradition in Chinese Cinema," *The Opera Quarterly* 26, no. 2–3 (2010): 343–76.
22. Haiping Yan, "Theatricality in Classical Chinese Drama," in *Theatricality*, ed.

Tracy C. Davis and Thomas Postlewait (Cambridge: Cambridge University Press, 2003), 65–89, at 67. Original emphasis.

23. Bao, "Politics of Remediation."
24. Many of these accounts are brought together in *Huanyuan wutai gao yu wutai* [Returning to the Stage and Surpassing the Stage] (Beijing: Renmin wenxue chubanshe, 1976).
25. Bao, "Politics of Remediation."
26. Bao, "Trouble with Theater."

Bibliography

Bao, Weihong. "The Politics of Remediation: Mise-en-scène and the Subjunctive Body in Chinese Opera Film." *Opera Quarterly* 26, no. 2–3 (2010): 256–90.

———. "The Trouble with Theater: Cinema and the Geopolitics of Medium Specificity." *Framework: The Journal of Cinema and Media* 56, no. 2 (2015): 350–67.

Bourg, Julian. "Principally Contradiction: The Flourishing of French Maoism." In Cook, *Mao's Little Red Book*, 225–44.

———. "The Red Guards of Paris: French Student Maoism of the 1960s." *History of European Ideas* 31, no. 4 (2005): 472–90.

Buck-Morss, Susan. *Dreamworld and Catastrophe: The Passing of Mass Utopia in East and West*. Cambridge, MA: MIT Press, 2000.

CCP Central Committee. "The Cultural Revolution—Excerpt from 'Resolution on Certain Questions in the History of Our Party since the Founding of the People's Republic of China.'" In *China's Cultural Revolution, 1966–69: Not a Dinner Party*, edited by Michael Schoenhals, 296–303. Armonk, NY: M. E. Sharpe, 1996.

Coderre, Laurence. "Socialist Commodities: Consuming *Yangbanxi* in the Cultural Revolution." PhD diss., University of California, Berkeley, 2015.

Cook, Alexander C., ed. *Mao's Little Red Book: A Global History*. Cambridge: Cambridge University Press, 2014.

Dirlik, Arif. "The Predicament of Marxist Revolutionary Consciousness: Mao Zedong, Antonio Gramsci, and the Reformulation of Marxist Revolutionary Theory." *Modern China* 9, no. 2 (1983): 182–211.

Frazier, Robeson Taj. *The East Is Black: Cold War China in the Black Radical Imagination*. Durham, NC: Duke University Press, 2014.

Huanyuan wutai gao yu wutai (Returning to the Stage and Surpassing the Stage). Beijing: Renmin wenxue chubanshe, 1976.

Lal, Priya. "Maoism in Tanzania: Material Connections and Shared Imaginaries." In Cook, *Mao's Little Red Book*, 96–116.

Lanza, Fabio. *The End of Concern: Maoist China, Activism, and Asian Studies.* Durham, NC: Duke University Press, 2017.

Lovell, Julia. "The Cultural Revolution and Its Legacies in International Perspective." *China Quarterly* 227 (2016): 632–52.

Ma, Ji. *Youyi song* (Ode to Friendship). Performed by Ma Ji and Tang Jiezhong. Zhongguo changpian (China Records), BM-406/7, 1973. Crosstalk, 2 flexi-discs.

Mao Zedong. "Talks at the Yan'an Forum on Literature and Art." In *Modern Chinese Literary Thought: Writings on Literature, 1893–1945*, edited by Kirk A. Denton, 458–84. Stanford, CA: Stanford University Press, 1996.

McGrath, Jason. "Cultural Revolution Model Opera Films and the Realist Tradition in Chinese Cinema." *Opera Quarterly* 26, no. 2–3 (2010): 343–76.

Slobodian, Quinn. "Badge Books and Brand Books: The Mao Bible in East and West Germany." In Cook, *Mao's Little Red Book*, 206–24.

Wang, Ban. *The Sublime Figure of History: Aesthetics and Politics in Twentieth-Century China*. Stanford, CA: Stanford University Press, 1997.

———. "Third World Internationalism: Films and Operas in the Chinese Cultural Revolution." In *Listening to the Cultural Revolution: Music, Politics, and Cultural Continuities*, edited by Paul Clark, Laikwan Pang, and Tsan-Huang Tsai, 85–106. London: Palgrave Macmillan, 2016.

Wolin, Richard. *The Wind from the East: French Intellectuals, the Cultural Revolution, and the Legacy of the 1960s*. Princeton, NJ: Princeton University Press, 2010.

Yan, Haiping. "Theatricality in Classical Chinese Drama." In *Theatricality*, edited by Tracy C. Davis and Thomas Postlewait, 65–89. Cambridge: Cambridge University Press, 2003.

Yurchak, Alexei. *Everything Was Forever, Until It Was No More: The Last Soviet Generation*. Princeton, NJ: Princeton University Press, 2006.

"Zhongguo gongchandang zhongyang weiyuanhui guanyu wuchanjieji wenhua da geming de jueding" (The CCP Central Committee's Decision concerning the Great Proletarian Cultural Revolution). *Renmin ribao* (People's Daily), August 9, 1966.

18

Workers Interrupting the Factory

Helena Lumbreras's Militant Factory Films between Italy and Spain (1968–78)

Pablo La Parra-Pérez

> Hey, let the readers know that we are not simpletons. We are making a new cinema, also in terms of film language, even if it is rather didactic. . . . We are advancing forms of radically democratic and collective work. And we have a professional background. . . . I think we know something about cinema. But in Spain, to have the chance to fully develop what we want to do in cinema, let alone the TV, we will need time and things to happen.
>
> Helena Lumbreras, 1977[1]

Introduction: The Internationalized Gaze

One of the most unknown chapters of the international cycle of struggles of the long 1968 took place in Spain throughout the last years of the Franco dictatorship and the transition to democracy. Although the hypothesis of a "Spanish 1968" has received some attention in recent academic literature,[2]

This essay was made possible by support from the Social Science Research Council's International Dissertation Research Fellowship, with funds provided by the Andrew W. Mellon Foundation. Thanks to Enrique Fibla-Gutiérrez, Sonia García López, Jo Labanyi, Jordana Mendelson, Lur Olaizola, Kristin Ross, Masha Salazkina, and the editors of the volume, Christina Gerhardt and Sara Saljoughi, for helpful comments and support. I also thank Rosa Cardona, Isabel Felguera, and Rosa Saz at Filmoteca de Catalunya for their help with accessing their collection and providing visual materials. Special thanks to Mariano Lisa for his generosity and commitment to keep Lumbreras's legacy alive.

the Spanish case has mostly been understood as an exception: nothing like "a 1968" happened there or, if something happened, it was a subsidiary, mimetic reminiscence of the "real 1968" taking place elsewhere. And yet, while it has often been said that General Francisco Franco peacefully died in his bed in 1975, the last years of his four-decade-long dictatorship were defined by the intensification of a heterogeneous cycle of struggles in universities, popular neighborhoods, and factories. Likewise, the transition that followed his death until the gradual stabilization of parliamentary democracy in the early 1980s was anything but peaceful: it saw massive popular mobilizations, and its violent repression by official and semiofficial means. Eventually, a series of institutional pacts between some remnants of the Franco regime and oppositional parties and unions in the late 1970s co-opted these movements from above, taking away any subversive edge. The electoral victory of the Spanish Socialist Party in 1982 and its gradual drift toward neoliberalism completed a historical sequence that unmistakably recalled the way other cycles of struggles of 1968 were closed down in Europe.

Amid these social upheavals, a considerable number of radical militant films were produced, distributed, and exhibited outside of any institutional or industrial structure.[3] In this essay, I focus on the role played in this militant film formation by one particular filmmaker: Helena Lumbreras (Cuenca 1935–Barcelona 1995). Specifically, I will examine her last two films: *O todos o ninguno/Everybody or Nobody* (1976), and *A la vuelta del grito/After the Call to Action* (1978). These "factory films" create a dynamic portrait of the radicalization of the Spanish working class in the late 1970s. *Everybody or Nobody* analyzes the long strike of the Laforsa factory in Cornellà de Llobregat (Barcelona) in the context of massive proletarian struggles that fought for a radical break with the Francoist past. *After the Call to Action* focuses on the workers' occupation and self-management of bankrupt factories in Barcelona, Bilbao, and Seville, evidencing the first signs of proletarian mistrust of the new democratic regime in the making. While both films were based on radically collective modes of production, and presented as the work of the Colectivo de Cine de Clase (Class Cinema Collective, CCC), they undoubtedly were the result of Lumbreras's initiative.

Lumbreras has remained a largely understudied figure until very recently.[4] Her filmography is a compelling case study, not only because of her careful rethinking of film production in terms of class and gender but also on account of the productive dialogues her films create with the theory and practice of Italian militant cinema. Lumbreras's unconventional trajectory was inextricably intertwined with Italy: after working as a rural schoolteacher in the late 1950s, she decided to study fine arts, moved to the state-run Madrid Institute for Film Research and Experiences, and finally, in 1962, received a scholarship from the Italian government to study film direction in the Centro Sperimentale di Cinematografia in Rome. She graduated in 1964, worked as an assistant director for Nanni Loy (*Il padre di famiglia/The Head of Family*, Italy, 1967), Federico Fellini (*Satyricon*, Italy, 1969), and Gillo Pontecorvo (*Queimada/Burn!*, Italy-France, 1969), and as a producer for Radiotelevisione Italiana (RAI), where she became familiar with lightweight film equipment. But, above all, these years led to her political radicalization; she not only was involved in the Italian film milieu of the 1960s, which was a hotbed of radical filmic-political proposals, but also was a friend of feminist activists, such as poetess Sandra Mangini, and had firsthand knowledge of unorthodox communist experiences, such as the Il Manifesto group.[5]

Thus, when Lumbreras came back to Spain in 1968 she was no longer the apolitical film student she had been when she left the country. She returned to clandestinely shoot a militant film about the anti-Franco struggles: *Spagna 68: El hoy es malo pero el mañana es mío/Spagna 68: Today Is Bad but Tomorrow Is Mine* (1968). This film, produced by Unitelefilm (the production and distribution company of the Italian CP), inaugurated Lumbreras's militant filmography, which comprises six pieces shot in Spain between 1968 and 1978 and several uncompleted works.[6] Moreover, she also made accessible an international network of references crucial for understanding the emergence of some of the most interesting militant film experiences in Spain. As filmmaker Llorenç Soler points out, his encounter with Lumbreras contributed to the "internationalization of [his] gaze."[7] After working as director of photography on *Spagna 68*, Soler accompanied Lumbreras to the Leipzig Film Festival.[8] And he adds: "until 1968 I couldn't see how to frame the films I wanted to make. Then I learnt that there was a compelling international movement of filmmakers that had decided to put their images at the service of the exploited. . . . I felt I was morally part of that collective without borders."[9]

Soler's words point to a fundamental observation. While Lumbreras undoubtedly aimed to intervene with her films in local contexts of struggle in Spain, she perceived her activities as part of an international militant film movement. Thus, to approach her films, we also need to internationalize our gaze. This means combining an examination of the specific Spanish context with an analysis of a larger international circuit of influences of which her films were a part. In what follows, my study of Lumbreras's factory films will try to develop this twofold strategy. On the one hand, I will disentangle the specific meaning that shooting these pieces had in the post-Franco social context. On the other hand, I will interlace these observations with a comparative analysis that situates Lumbreras's film practice in a productive dialogue with certain theoretical and practical experiences of Italian militant film culture.

Interrupting the Factory

In 1975, during the third week of their strike, the Laforsa metalworkers received an unexpected visit: Helena Lumbreras and her partner Mariano Lisa came to the factory and proposed to shoot a film about their strike *with them*. The workers were astonished: "we listened to the proposal somewhat suspiciously: this was such a new thing that our first reaction was to be hesitant."[10] A series of similar scenes were repeated between 1976 and 1978, when various film crews coordinated by Lumbreras and Lisa presented themselves at the gates of occupied factories in Seville, Barcelona, and Bilbao.

The camera at the doors of the factory inevitably points to a paradox noted by German director Harun Farocki: "the first camera in the history of cinema was pointed at a factory but a century later it can be said that film is hardly drawn to the factory and even repelled by it."[11] As a space delimited by the industrialist's rule, filming the factory is only possible when its proper working order (the pure logic of production) has been interrupted.[12] In this case not only were the factories interrupted—by the strike in *Everybody or Nobody*, by the occupations in *After the Call to Action*—but also the workers ceased to function as disciplined workers so as to join the film crews.

That filmmakers and unruly workers were working hand in hand in militant film projects within the factories is a good example of the "polemical relations and impossible identifications" that, according to Kristin Ross, defined the disruptive politics of equality of the 1968 years.[13] Until quite recently, the

Spanish factories were subject to a rigid regime of visibility and class segregation. Protected by Francoist laws, industrialists had extraordinary powers of surveillance, punishment, and control over the factory space.[14] A space that, to use Nicholas Mirzoeff's idiom, relied on its own "complex of visuality."[15] Behind the factory doors it was a panoptic-like space of control supervised by foremen or, when the workers' disobedience went too far, even by the police.[16] From the outside, however, the factory was an impenetrable space of invisibility, even for the most daring militant cameras. Take, for instance, the film *La lucha obrera en España/Workers' Struggles in Spain*, made in 1973 by the Grupo de Madrid (GM), a clandestine film collective in the Spanish CP's orbit.[17] It was easier for the GM to enter a prison than a factory. In this film, factories are seen only from afar, shot with telephoto lenses from hidden places (resulting in a perplexing clandestine aesthetics, with plants and fences constantly in the foreground, as material reminders of the absolute boundary separating the factory from the external world). By contrast, the GM managed to smuggle their camera into Carabanchel prison, where the government had incarcerated a number of leaders of the Workers' Commissions, then an illegal trade union. While the film included some unusual scenes of the trade unionists in their prison cells, the interior of the factory remained an inscrutable blind spot.

When Lumbreras and Lisa arrived at the gates of the Laforsa factory in 1975, immediately after Franco's death, factories nationwide were openly on the warpath. As an internal government report anxiously observed, the uncontrolled proliferation of "illegal strikes" resulted in a situation of "complete anarchy, much worse than the announced constituent process."[18] The workers' struggle, crucially, was a struggle for visibility; the strikes, occupations, demonstrations, and open assemblies but also the countless leaflets, periodicals, banners, and graffiti were attempts to make their struggle visible and to consolidate a social support network. To use Georges Didi-Huberman's nuanced term, the workers were "exposing" themselves.[19] They exposed themselves in a complex terrain where social visibility intertwined with the struggle for recognition and the dispute over public space. But, in doing so, they were also exposing themselves to a risk, since the state did not hesitate to use brutal police violence to regain control over industrial areas.

Everybody or Nobody operated at the heart of this struggle for the "right to the image"; it exposed the workers as full political subjects—and therefore took risks. Some Laforsa workers recall "the film crew working tirelessly, often risking their integrity to get good images."[20] Later on, the police seized a negative of the film in a developing lab in Barcelona and confiscated a copy during a screening in Alcoi. And yet, with this film Lumbreras had made a crucial decision: "to break the circle of clandestinity in which power has enclosed us during too many years."[21] This meant publicly announcing and distributing her films in an attempt to keep pace with the workers' struggle: "our cinema wants to be a vehicle of expression for the working class. And if the working class exposes itself to make its struggles public, we must undergo the same fate."[22] Lumbreras's factory films, thus, were something more than mere "filmic mirrors" of already existent oppositional movements. Paraphrasing Ross's remarks about the role of the arts in 1968, Lumbreras did not aspire "to a level of 'representing' what was occurring; the goal, rather [was] to be at one with—at the same time with, contemporary with—whatever *was* occurring."[23] To achieve this radical imbrication with events, Lumbreras developed a complex filmic-political practice that echoed, and expanded, the legacy of some particular episodes of Italian militant film culture.

Making History with Cinema

Bringing cinematic representation so close to events that filmmaking becomes a system of historical inscription—that is exactly how Lumbreras and Lisa defined the activity of the CCC in 1978: "we don't make cinema history; we make history with cinema."[24] It was not the first time that such a striking claim was heard in Europe. In 1969, Daniele Protti outlined his enthusiastic participation in a series of Italian film collectives that had decided "to actively employ the camera in the contemporary political struggle, using it as an instrument to produce political history."[25] Protti was describing the emergence of the Cinegiornali Liberi (Free Newsreels), a militant film experience that, as I wish to argue, entailed a crucial relationship to Lumbreras's practices.

The Free Newsreels originated with a proposal launched by Cesare Zavattini in 1967. It called for "an open, direct, and immediate cinema," shot in substandard formats by professional and non-professional filmmakers, in the hope that cinema could become a disruptive "political practice."[26] It resulted from what Stefania Parigi terms "the most incandescent" phase of Zavattinian thought.[27] From the early 1950s onward, Zavattini radicalized the principles of Neorealism with a series of proposals that anticipated Direct Cinema, also articulating some striking remarks on television's revolutionary potential.[28] These years of critical reflection on the political potential of the cinematic medium are at odds with conventional readings that misrepresent Zavattini by assigning him to a bland art/national cinema discourse. The years 1968 and 1969 saw the shooting of various Free Newsreels around Italy. Among them, the *Cinegiornali* number 2, titled *Apollon, una fabbrica occupata/Apollon, an Occupied Factory* (1969), became a milestone for militant film history. Directed by Ugo Gregoretti, it reenacted, starring the workers' themselves, the occupation of the Apollon factory in Rome. Either perceived as a major achievement (in the milieux of the Italian CP) or branded as a deceitful "emblem of revisionism" (by the "extra-parliamentary" left) *Apollon* undoubtedly haunted the imagination of radical filmmakers and theorists in Italy and abroad.[29] *Apollon*'s impact even led to a proposal to shoot a series of "Free Proletarian Newsreels" aiming to bring Free Newsreels into "direct collaboration with the working class."[30] This proposal, however, was unsuccessful; not a single of these Cinegiornali Liberi del Proletariato was shot in Italy, and the Free Newsreels project declined in the early 1970s.[31]

This fact leads me to a fundamental working hypothesis: can the factory films shot by Lumbreras in Spain between 1976 and 1978 be considered a belated, and displaced, derivation of the Free Proletarian Newsreels' unfulfilled project? First, as Soler has often recalled, Lumbreras knew Zavattini personally, and it is hardly conceivable that she was unfamiliar with his ideas.[32] Moreover, Free Newsreels were known, and discussed, in the Spanish context. A copy of *Apollon* arrived early on in Barcelona via the illegal communist distribution company El Volti,[33] then becoming part of the catalog of La Central del Curt—an independent film cooperative that, indeed, often programmed Lumbreras's factory films together with Gregoretti's piece.[34] Nonetheless, the most compelling evidence rests in Lumbreras's films themselves; as I hope to show in what follows, a close inspection of her factory films reveals a thorough understanding of the principles envisioned by Zavattini, their practical development in the Free Newsreels project, and their subsequent critical revision by other Italian militant film experiences.

Dangerous Practices

Instead of a conventional credits sequence, the opening scene of *Everybody or Nobody* shows Manuel González, one of the Laforsa workers, presented in close-up. While the camera slowly zooms out, revealing that he is accompanied by Lumbreras and Lisa, González presents the film as an example for other workers. He then gives the floor to "comrade Lumbreras," who directly addresses the spectator: "the film you are about to see is the result of a discussion with the Laforsa comrades and other workers." Finally, Lisa lists the role played by the workers and other collaborators in the film crew.

This scene provides a veritable declaration of intent. The CCC's fundamental point of departure was to challenge "the social division of labor, considering everybody who participates in its [film] products as equals."[35] In Lumbreras's factory films the workers not only operated the camera and the recorders but also participated in a series of assembly meetings to discuss the films' structure and editing.[36]

This collectivist mode of production echoes a fundamental debate that permeates the international history of militant film culture, one that Trevor Stark summarizes as follows: "how to translate the workers' struggle into cinema such that the filmmaker would not simply reinscribe the relations of domination between those . . . who have the power to represent and those who are simply represented?"[37] Zavattini's response to this question was a vague refusal of "the figure of the intellectual as exegete and 'foreseer' of society,"[38] proposing instead a nonhierarchical collaboration between filmmakers and workers.[39] For radical authors such as Pio Baldelli or Goffredo Fofi, this ideal was not achieved in Free Newsreels such as *Apollon*, where Gregoretti's authorial role still was perceived in hierarchical terms as standing above the workers.[40] Thus, the idea of "putting the camera into the hands of the workers" would keep hovering over the theory and practice of Italian militant cinema, becoming the point of departure for radical film formations such as the Collettivo Cinema Militante of Turin (CCMT).[41]

Some Spanish communist directors and critics perceived Lumbreras's reception and development of these debates with distrust, as a 1977 roundtable on militant cinema makes clear. Lumbreras's position was extraordinary, not only because she was the only woman (and this was not a minor matter in the

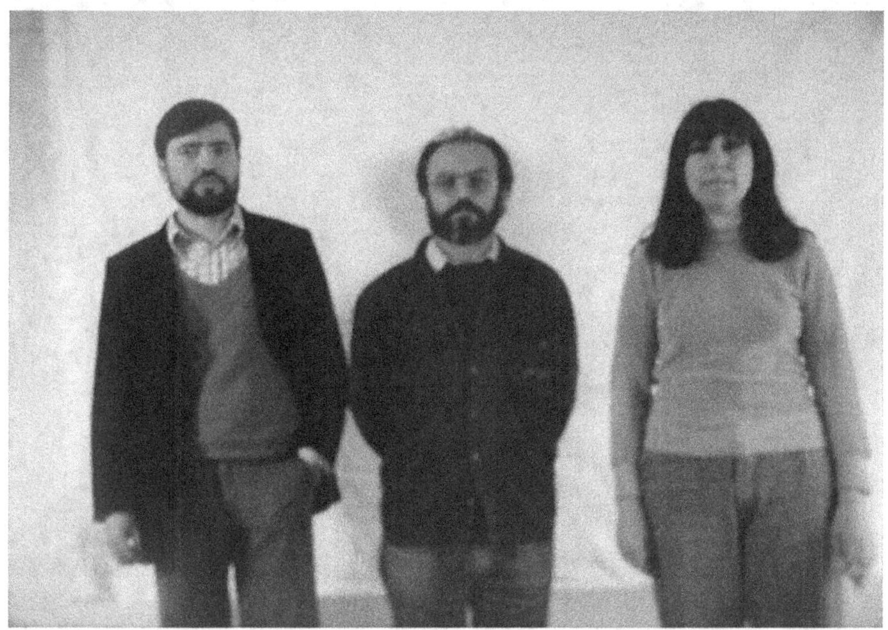

From left to right: Mariano Lisa, Manuel González, and Helena Lumbreras. Opening scene of *Everybody or Nobody* (Colectivo de Cine de Clase, 1976). Courtesy of Mariano Lisa and Filmoteca de Catalunya.

patriarchal milieu of the Spanish left) but also for the singularity of her positions. As Manuel Esteban put it: "Lumbreras's idea of giving the camera to the workers seems unconvincing to me . . . a scene shot by a worker can transmit the feeling of an amateur film, its imperfection may show the fascination of the camera, seen as a magic object . . . but creating a new aesthetics from that is going too far! I think it is dangerous to glorify things this way."[42] Although the debate's moderators subscribed to Esteban's remark, Lumbreras responded with conviction: "Of course it is dangerous! When you try to give the working class an autonomy and strengthen its culture, you are doing something really dangerous."[43] This discussion points to a larger ideological debate: while Esteban (a member of the PSUC, the Catalan branch of the Spanish CP) evidenced the classical, strongly hierarchical position of the Leninist party avant-garde, Lumbreras was closer to a "new, more corrosive communism" that had formed outside the structures of the "old Left" parties in the 1968 years.[44] Her "corrosive" conception of the political, which refused any representative hierarchy in the name of direct democracy, produced in her films an antihierarchical

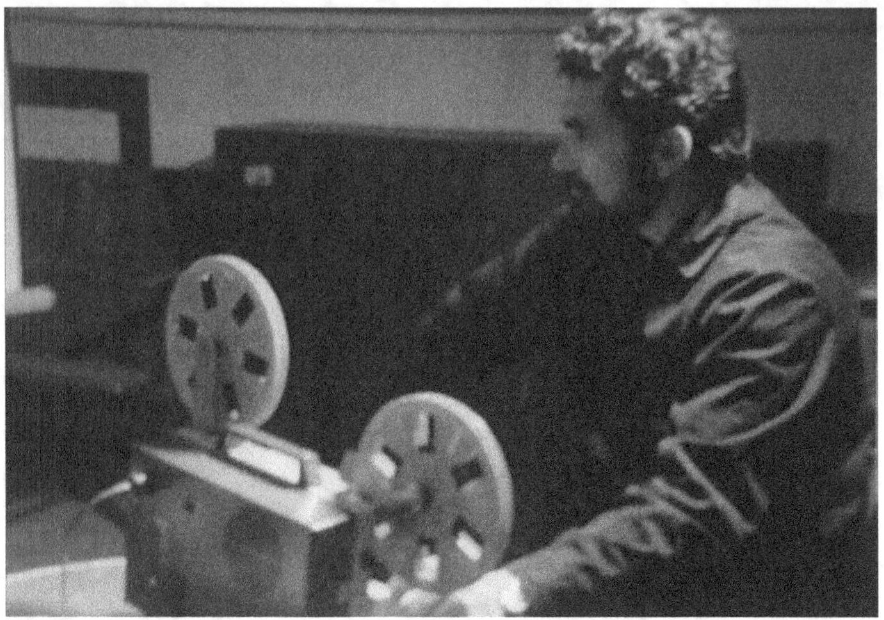

Worker Ramón Rulo operates a Super-8 projector to screen his own footage. *Everybody or Nobody* (Colectivo de Cine de Clase, 1976). Courtesy of Mariano Lisa and Filmoteca de Catalunya.

narrative of dense complexity. This "radical horizontality" emerges in at least four aspects of her factory films: their *voice*, their gender perspective, their logic of equal aesthetic rights, and their politics of reception.

Radical Horizontality

The contrast of Lumbreras's factory films' voice with the abovementioned *Workers' Struggles in Spain*, a much more traditional militant film, is revealing.[45] While the GM's piece is articulated by an omniscient voice-over that speaks with ultimate authority, one that remains faithful to the official line of the Spanish CP, Lumbreras's factory films never resort to an external narrator. Instead, we find a polyphony that diffuses authority. For instance, in a sequence of *Everybody or Nobody*, Laforsa worker Ramón Rulo operates a Super 8 mm projector to show the sequences he shot during some episodes of the strike. When Rulo's footage occupies the entire screen, we hear him discussing his own images, as if the film had suddenly morphed into a metacinematic reflection, in first person narration, on the unexpected figure of the worker/filmmaker.

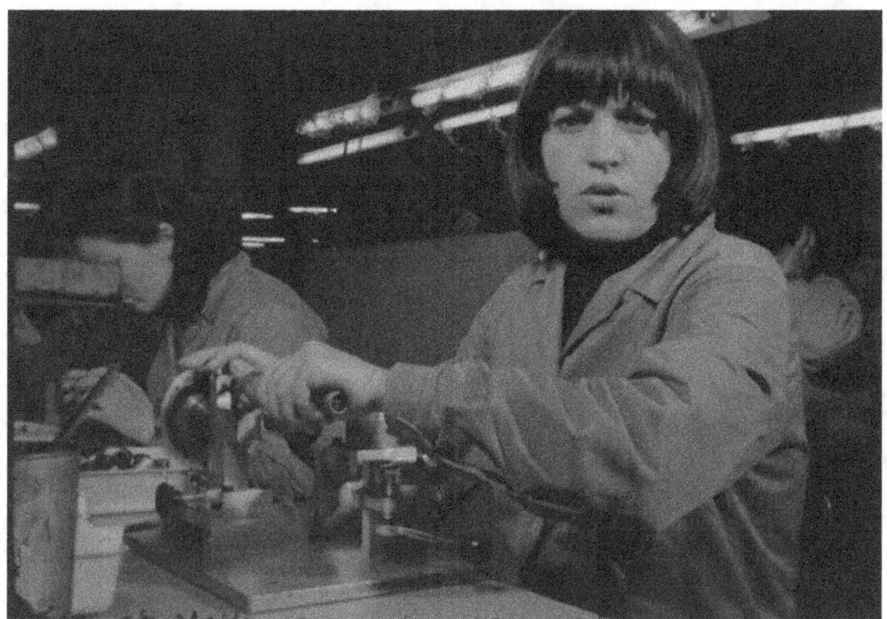

Worker at the self-managed factory Roselson (Barcelona). *After the Call to Action* (Colectivo de Cine de Clase, 1978). Courtesy of Mariano Lisa and Filmoteca de Catalunya.

Likewise, Lumbreras's films frequently allow space for the irruption of discrepancy, as happens in a scene of *After the Call to Action* where a young female worker regrets in front of the camera that the unions are "manipulating" their assemblies, only to be immediately interrupted by another out-of-frame woman, who disagrees with this observation, triggering a dissonant discussion that does not provide a univocal or "correct" reading of events but that actually reflects a heterogeneity of political subjectivities.

This scene, in which a group of female workers engages in political debate, is not an exception in Lumbreras's films. Nonetheless, the appearance of women as workers or militants in their own right is rare in the Spanish militant film archive as a whole. Take, for instance, Pere Portabella's *Informe General/General Report* (1976), a monumental synthesis-film that aimed to comprehensively portray the social forces struggling for democracy immediately after Franco's death. Only men appear in its chapter devoted to proletarian struggles, as is the case in most of the interviews included in its 154-minute-long footage. By contrast, Lumbreras's films carefully pay attention to the voice of female militant workers, who in turn did not hesitate to denounce the patriarchal bias of the labor movement. As one of the abovementioned workers declares in *After the Call to Action*, "as we are women, it seems that our presence at the factory gates is seen as a joke . . . but if you are a male worker everybody views you with a respect that is totally different."

Lumbreras's feminist perspective reached a more nuanced and incisive level, well beyond the mere depiction of female industrial workers. In her films we see, and hear, a succession of housewives who cook, take care of children, and participate in the mobilizations. These women are not there as a "decoration" to the real struggles taking place in the factory; on the contrary, their exposition *decenters* the relevance of the factory. Not by chance, one of the most decisive contributions of Italian feminism in the 1960s and 1970s was the challenge to "the socialist movement's myopic fixation on wage labor in the factory," calling for consideration to be given to the feminized activities of "social reproduction" that made productive work possible in the first place.[46] Many scenes in Lumbreras's factory films point to this issue. For instance, in *Everybody or Nobody* a group of wives of Laforsa workers reenact one of the assemblies they organized to coordinate their involvement in the strike. The staged scene is spontaneously interrupted by a child reclaiming his mother's attention. The fact that the scene was kept as such in the final cut has a particular meaning: militancy and carework appear on screen *on the same level*, that is, as necessarily imbricated aspects of the struggle.[47]

This staged sequence provides a good example of the "logic of equal aesthetic rights" that prevails in Lumbreras's films.[48] According to her, the refusal of the separation of manual and intellectual labor must be accompanied by a radical equality between different aesthetic forms and genres: "[CCC's films] are not mere documents or mere fictions, but integrate documents, fictions, direct testimonies, reenactments, and explicative graphic elements, drawings, songs."[49] This fundamental intermediality led, for example, to the insertion of extrafilmic elements into filmed actions; while in *Everybody or Nobody* the narration of the Laforsa conflict is articulated by a series of vignettes painted by children from Cornellà, *After the Call to Action* incorporates a series of intertitles designed by the "El Cubri" collective.[50]

As for the systematic use of reenactments, a strategy that unmistakably adheres to one of the most valuable lessons of *Apollon*, Lumbreras once again demonstrates her distinctive conception of militant filmmaking. This is particularly clear if we take into account the simplistic points of view defended by other coetaneous alternative Spanish filmmakers. In a comment on *Apollon*'s reenactments, Andrés Linares drew the following conclusion: "militant cinema must think about how to do without this rudimentary *mise-en-scène* that pretends to pass itself off as real events."[51] Besides his overly simplified understanding of filmic mediation, Linares fails to understand that neither Gregoretti nor Lumbreras tried to "pass off" reenactments as "real events." On the contrary, they were based on a much more nuanced understanding that, yet again, brings us back to Zavattini. For the Italian thinker, filmic reenactments were *specific acts of knowledge*: "the immediate repetition, controlled by its own protagonists, of a gesture that had already happened is . . . an almost scientific *ritual* for the search and revelation of sense."[52] From this point of view, reenacted scenes accomplished a precise twofold function in Lumbreras's films. On the one hand, they are addressed to the participants themselves, who participate in a performative self-analysis of their own struggle. One can perfectly imagine, for example, that the presence of the child in the aforementioned reenacted scene triggered a reflection about the combination of these women's roles as activists, mothers, and housewives. On the other hand, these "specific acts of knowledge" captured by the camera are addressed as a "functional example" to the film's potential receivers, which were intended to be working-class audiences involved in similar contexts of struggle.

Only with this potential working-class audience in mind can we fully understand González's words in the opening scene of *Everybody or Nobody*: "in the name of my comrades, may I present to you the film about our strike. . . . We offer you our experience so that the struggle may spread and so that we may thus achieve our goals as a people and as a class." Lumbreras's factory films, then, aim to open up an analytical conversation among equals, a logic that in Italy came to be known as "horizontal communication." Loosely inspired by the Maoist motto "from the masses, to the masses," this blanket term described different initiatives that aimed to create independent circuits of political knowledge and analysis produced by and addressed to working-class populations.[53] Militant films have often been caricatured as formulaic political images that could only produce their desired effects on people sympathetic with the films' cause in advance.[54] This analytical premise cannot sufficiently account for the peculiarities of some of the most complex expressions of militant filmmaking, such as Lumbreras's. Her pieces were not mere "campaign films" trying to raise the spectator awareness but cinematic attempts to open a dialogue and an exchange of experiences among *active* scenarios of struggle, in the hope that cinema could not only generate grassroots historical and political narrations but also spread working-class mobilization.[55]

Conclusion

The diverse cultural-political experiences of the international cycle of struggles of 1968 demand an analytical framework that recognizes a periodicity constituted by uneven temporalities. Consequently, I have integrated Lumbreras's practice into an international sequence of transmissions and interruptions whereby her factory films, shot in the specific social and historical context of Spain in the mid- and late 1970s, are understood as belated derivations of projects and discussions developed in Italy around 1968.

In the opening quotation, Lumbreras asked for time and radical changes to fully develop the revolutionary film culture she had in mind. Nevertheless, her history, and the history of the unruly workers with whom she worked, would be a history of defeat. The access of leftist parties to power in Spain in the early 1980s did not lead to the support for militant film collectives; indeed, it resulted in their isolation and dissolution. Lumbreras was not an exception: *Everybody or Nobody* and *After the Call to Action* would be her last two films. The extinction of Spanish militant film culture has often been analyzed from a simplistic point of view, which assumes that its sole raison d'être was to oppose the dictatorship, thus being redundant after the consolidation of institutional democracy. I strongly reject this interpretation. Lumbreras's film practices were inextricably intertwined with the radical grassroots mobilizations that sprang up in Spain in the late 1960s and 1970s. Their political neutralization necessarily meant the extinction of a film culture that aspired to be "at one with" episodes of social unrest. A comprehensive account of this historical sequence would, of course, demand the examination of complementary case studies. I am thinking in particular of Joaquín Jordá, a filmmaker who also spent some crucial years in Italy before coming back to Spain to shoot *Numax presenta . . . /Numax Presents . . .* (1979). Jordà's piece portrays a group of workers whose "interruption of the factory" took its most radical form: in an absolute refusal of industrial discipline, they no longer wanted to be workers.

In many senses, *Numax . . .* represents a closure of the project for a revolutionary filmic encounter with the industrial working class that Lumbreras actively pursued.

Nevertheless, I have deliberately avoided foregrounding the idea of defeat. As has happened with other expressions of the long 1968, militant film culture has too often been evaluated as a failed project. This judgmental attitude not only obscures the richness of militant film formations (turning them into unintelligible artifacts in both filmic and political terms) but also neglects figures such as Lumbreras, whose role in the history of international film practices deserves to be revisited. My approach has therefore eschewed the moralizing logic of assessing failures and achievements, instead exploring the *living experience* of Lumbreras's film practice: the social scenario in which she intervened, the referents she had in mind, the international discussions she developed, the horizons of social transformation she envisioned. Only through this "archaeology of the experience" can the power of Lumbreras's films be recognized today, as Benjaminian dialectical images, brushing film history against the grain.

Notes

1. In Rosa María Pereda, "Helena Lumbreras: Un nuevo cine político en España," *El País*, July 2, 1977. http://elpais.com/diario/1977/07/02/cultura/236642404_850215.html. All translations are my own except where otherwise indicated.
2. Konstantinos Kornetis, "¿Un 68 periférico? Reflexiones sobre un análisis comparativo de la resistencia estudiantil en los regímenes autoritarios de la Grecia de los coroneles y de la España tardofranquista," *Studia historica: Historia contemporánea* 21 (2010): 83–112.
3. Miguel Fernández Labayen and Xose Prieto Souto, "Film Workshops in Spain: Oppositional Practices, Alternative Film Cultures and the Transition to Democracy," *Studies in European Cinema* 8, no. 3 (2011): 227–42.
4. As Martin-Márquez reminds us, only recently have a series of contributions rescued Lumbreras "from almost complete critical oblivion." Susan Martin-Márquez, "Editing in the Woman Auteur," in *A Companion to Spanish Cinema*, ed. Jo Labanyi and Tatjana Pavlović (Chichester, West Sussex: Wiley-Blackwell, 2015), 152–89, at 183. A nonexhaustive bibliography would include: Eduardo Ledesma, "Helena Lumbreras' *Field for Men*

(1973): Midway between Latin American Third Cinema and the Barcelona School," *Studies in Spanish and Latin American Cinemas* 11, no. 3 (2004): 271–88; María Camí-Vela, "Entre la esperanza y el desencanto: El cine militante de Helena Lumbreras," in *Plan Rosebud: Sobre imágenes, lugares y políticas de memoria*, ed. María Ruido (Santiago de Compostela: Xunta de Galicia, 2009), 543–54; Isadora Guardia, "La escritura de la realidad a través de la mirada de Helena Lumbreras: Participación política y estética desde la cámara cinematográfica," *Quaderns de filologia: Estudis literaris* 17 (2014): 77–99. On completion of this essay, another paper on Lumbreras was published: Miguel Fernández Labayen and Xose Prieto Souto, "A Network of Affinities: Helena Lumbreras's Collective Films and Social Struggle in Spain," *Modern Language Review* 112, no. 2 (2017): 397–412.

5. Lumbreras's biographical details are based on an interview with Mariano Lisa (Barcelona, January 18, 2014). See also Joaquim Romaguera and Llorenç Soler, *Historia crítica y documentada del cine independiente en España (1955–1975)* (Barcelona: Laertes, 2006), 234–35; and Isabel Felguera, "Proposta de conservació i restauració de l'obra fílmica d'Helena Lumbreras" (Grade thesis, Universitat de Barcelona, 2014), 22–31.
6. Felguera, "Proposta de conservació i restauració de l'obra fílmica d'Helena Lumbreras," 33–39.
7. Llorenç Soler, *Los hilos secretos de mis documentales* (Barcelona: CIMS, 2002), 39.
8. See J. M. García Ferrer and Josep Miquel Martí Rom, *Llorenç Soler* (Barcelona: Associació d'Enginyers Industrials de Catalunya), 41, and Caroline Moine, *Cinéma et Guerre froide: Histoire du festival de films documentaires de Leipzig (1955–1990)* (Paris: Sorbonne, 2014), 178–87.
9. Soler, *Hilos secretos de mis documentales*, 40.
10. Esteban Cerdán, Manuel González, and Simón Ródenas, *O tots o cap: Laforsa, una vaga que va fer història* (Manresa: Tigre de Paper, 2015), 88.
11. Harun Farocki, "Workers Leaving the Factory," in *Nachdruck: Texte, Imprint; Writings*, ed. Susanne Gaensheimer and Nicolaus Schafhausen, trans. Laurent Faasch-Ibrahim (New York: Lukas and Sternberg, 2001), 230–46, at 232.
12. See Bernard Benoliel, "Le cinéma à la porte de l'usine," *Cahiers du Cinéma* HS-23 (1998): 20–23. "Industrial films" commissioned by industrialists or corporations would be an exception. There are rare examples of clandestine sabotages of these official representations of the factory in Spain: filmmakers, such as Llorenç Soler or Lluís Rivera *détourned* outtakes of industrial

films with critical soundtracks.

13. Kristin Ross, *May '68 and Its Afterlives* (Chicago: University of Chicago Press, 2002), 10.
14. Carme Molinero and Pere Ysàs, *Productores disciplinados y minorías subversivas: Clase obrera y conflictividad laboral en la España franquista* (Madrid: Siglo XXI, 1998), 72–77.
15. Nicholas Mirzoeff, *The Right to Look: A Counterhistory of Visuality* (Durham, NC: Duke University Press, 2011), 4–22.
16. Molinero and Ysàs, *Productores disciplinados y minorías subversivas*, 225.
17. The film is available online at *Ciné-Archives: Fonds Audiovisuel du PCF-Mouvement Ouvrier et Démocratique.*
18. In Molinero and Ysàs, *Productores disciplinados y minorías subversivas*, 236.
19. Georges Didi-Huberman, *Peuples exposés, Peuples figurants* (Paris: Minuit, 2012), 11–16.
20. Cerdán, González, and Ródenas, *O tots o cap*, 132.
21. Manuel Esteban et al., "Cine militante," *El Viejo Topo* 7 (1977): 59.
22. M. Goicoechea, "El cine político como revulsivo," *Vindicación feminista* 6 (1976): 5.
23. Ross, *May '68 and Its Afterlives*, 15.
24. In Matías Antolín, *Cine marginal en España* (Valladolid: Seminci, 1979), 167.
25. Daniele Protti, "Letter from Italy," *Cineaste* 3, no. 3 (1969–70): 26 and 28, at 26.
26. Cesare Zavattini, "Free Newsreels," *Cinema Journal* 54, no. 3 (2015): 9–11.
27. Stefania Parigi, *Fisiologia dell'immagine: Il pensiero di Cesare Zavattini* (Turin: Lindau, 2006), 289.
28. Cesare Zavattini, interview by Arturo Gismondi, "Proposals for a Television Open to Reality and Democracy," *Cinema Journal* 54, no. 3 (2015): 7–9.
29. Christian Uva, *L'immagine politica: Forme del contropotere tra cinema, video e fotografia nell'Italia degli anni Settanta* (Milan: Mimesis, 2015), 42–45.
30. Cesare Zavattini, "Estratto dal documento di presentazione del Cinegiornale Libero del Proletariato," *Bollettino dei Cinegiornali Liberi* 3 (1970), 3.
31. Faliero Rosati, ed., *1968–1972: Esperienze di Cinema Militante* (Rome: Società Gestioni Editoriali, 1973), 10.
32. In García Ferrer and Martí Rom, *Llorenç Soler*, 42 and 148.
33. Mariano Aragón and Joan Martí Valls, interview by Josep Torrell. "El Volti, Informe 35 y la vocalía de cine-clubs," *El Viejo Topo* 32 (2013): 44.
34. In fact, a founding member of La Central explicitly proposed a genealogy

connecting *Apollon* with Lumbreras's factory films. Josep Miquel Martí Rom, "*Numax* de Joaquín Jordá (Los problemas de autogestión en un contexto capitalista)," *Dirigido por . . .* 80 (1981): 7.

35. Antolín, *Cine marginal en España*, 167.
36. Esteban et al., "Cine militante," 56.
37. Trevor Stark, "'Cinema in the Hands of the People': Chris Marker, the Medvedkin Group, and the Potential of Militant Film," *October* 118 (2012): 117–50, at 126. As Stark analyzes, this problem triggered interesting filmic experiences in France, although I do not have the space to develop that side of the argument here.
38. Rosati, *1968–1972*, 7.
39. Rosati, *1968–1972*, 7–8.
40. See Uva, *L'immagine politica*, 43–45, and Rosati, *1968–1972*, 8.
41. Indeed, in 1970 the CCMT organized a screening of a film codirected by Lumbreras and Soler, *El cuarto poder/The Fourth Power* (1970). Armando Ceste et al., *Collettivo cinema militante: Torino, 1968/1975*. Turin: 2o Festival Internazionale Cinema Giovani, 1984, 32.
42. Esteban et al., "Cine militante," 57.
43. Esteban et al., "Cine militante," 57. The similarity between the line of argument of Lumbreras and the CCMT is striking. See Ceste et al., *Collettivo cinema militante*, 22.
44. Ross, *May '68 and Its Afterlives*, 68. Paradoxically, as already noted, Zavattini was despised by the Italian "extra-parliamentary" Left as a "revisionist" at the service of the Italian CP. The fact that his ideas were influential for Lumbreras (whose film practice developed to the left of the Spanish CP) points to a *décalage* characteristic of the transnational circulation of referents in the long 1968: practices that appeared as moderate in one part of the world were perceived as radical in another region.
45. My understanding of film's "voice" largely draws on Bill Nichols, "The Voice of Documentary," *Film Quarterly* 36, no. 3 (1983): 17–30.
46. Asad Haider and Salar Mohandesi, "Making a Living," *Viewpoint Magazine* 5 (2015). https://viewpointmag.com/2015/10/28/making-a-living.
47. The same scene is analyzed, in slightly different terms, in Guardia, "Escritura de la realidad a través de la mirada de Helena Lumbreras," 89–90.
48. I borrow this term from Boris Groys, "The Logic of Equal Aesthetic Rights," in *Art Power* (Cambridge, MA: MIT Press, 2008), 13–22.
49. In Antolín, *Cine marginal en España*, 167.

50. On the intermediality in other film by Lumbreras, see Ledesma, "Helena Lumbreras' *Field for Men* (1973)."
51. Andrés Linares, *El cine militante* (Madrid: Castellote, 1976), 80.
52. In Parigi, *Fisiologia dell'immagine*, 283–84.
53. Uva, *L'immagine politica*, 33. See also "Il cinema militante," *Ombre Rosse* 3, no. 4 (1972): 9–10.
54. This idea has been largely shaped after Jean-Luc Godard's dictum that militant cinema could only "preach to the choir." Jean-Luc Godard, "Le groupe 'Dziga Vertov,'" in *Jean-Luc Godard par Jean-Luc Godard*, ed. Alain Bergala (Paris: Cahiers du Cinéma—L'Étoile, 1985), 342–50, at 346. This aphorism has been recurrently used, explicitly or not, as a point of departure for many critical discourses. See, for example, Jean-Louis Comolli, "Le miroir à deux faces," in *Arrêt sur histoire* (Paris: Centre Georges Pompidou, 1997), 14–18.
55. Once again, *Apollon* set a haunting precedent: in 1969, a group of workers in Brugherio occupied their own factory after watching the film. Uva, *L'immagine politica*, 46–47.

Bibliography

Antolín, Matías. *Cine marginal en España (. . . experimental, paralelo, clandestino, independiente, marginal, marginado, corto, pobre, undergrund, militante, alternativo, substandard, subversivo . . . los "Cines Nacionales" y la Crítica "Nacional" . . .)*. Valladolid: Semana Internacional de Cine de Valladolid, 1979.

Aragón, Mariano, and Joan Martí Valls, interview by Josep Torrell. "El Volti, Informe 35 y la vocalía de cine-clubs." *El Viejo Topo* 32 (2013): 42–51.

Benoliel, Bernard. "Le cinéma à la porte de l'usine." *Cahiers du Cinéma* HS-23 (1998): 20–23.

Camí-Vela, Maria. "Entre la esperanza y el desencanto: El cine militante de Helena Lumbreras." In *Plan Rosebud: Sobre imágenes, lugares y políticas de memoria*, edited by María Ruido, 543–54. Santiago de Compostela: Xunta de Galicia, 2009.

Cerdán, Esteban, Manuel González, and Simón Ródenas. *O tots o cap: Laforsa, una vaga que va fer història*. Manresa: Tigre de Paper, 2015.

Ceste, Armando, Stefano Della Casa, Franca Manuele, and Gianfranco Torri, eds. *Collettivo cinema militante: Torino, 1968/1975*. Turin: 2o Festival Internazionale Cinema Giovani, 1984.

"Il cinema militante." *Ombre Rosse* 3–4 (1972): 3–21.

Comolli, Jean-Louis. "Le miroir à deux faces." In *Arrêt sur histoire*. Paris: Centre Georges Pompidou, 1997.

Didi-Huberman, Georges. *Peuples exposés, Peuples figurants*. Paris: Minuit, 2012.

Esteban, Manuel, Jesús Garay, Jaime Larrain, Helena Lumbreras, Joan Puig, Llorenç Soler, Pere Joan Ventura, Gustau Hernàndez, Ernest Blasi, Tomás Declós, Fèlix Fanés, and Octavi Martí. "Cine militante." *El Viejo Topo* 7 (1977): 55–59.

Farocki, Harun. "Workers Leaving the Factory." In *Nachdruck: Texte, Imprint; Writings*, 230–46. Edited by Susanne Gaensheimer and Nicolaus Schafhausen. Translated by Laurent Faasch-Ibrahim. New York: Lukas and Sternberg, 2001.

Felguera, Isabel. "Proposta de conservació i restauració de l'obra fílmica d'Helena Lumbreras." Grade thesis, Universitat de Barcelona, 2014.

Fernández Labayen, Miguel, and Xose Prieto Souto. "Film Workshops in Spain: Oppositional Practices, Alternative Film Cultures and the Transition to Democracy." *Studies in European Cinema* 8, no. 3 (2011): 227–42.

______. "A Network of Affinities: Helena Lumbreras's Collective Films and Social Struggle in Spain." *Modern Language Review* 112, no. 2 (2017): 397–412.

García Ferrer, J. M., and Josep Miquel Martí Rom. *Llorenç Soler*. Barcelona: Associació d'Enginyers Industrials de Catalunya, 1996.

Godard, Jean-Luc. "Le groupe 'Dziga Vertov.'" In *Jean-Luc Godard par Jean-Luc Godard*, edited by Alain Bergala, 342–50. Paris: Cahiers du Cinéma—L'Étoile, 1985.

Goicoechea, M. "El cine político como revulsivo." *Vindicación feminista* 6 (1976): 5.

Groys, Boris. "The Logic of Equal Aesthetic Rights." In *Art Power*, 13–22. Cambridge, MA: MIT Press, 2008.

Guardia, Isadora. "La escritura de la realidad a través de la mirada de Helena Lumbreras: Participación política y estética desde la cámara cinematográfica." *Quaderns de filologia: Estudis literaris* 17 (2014): 77–99.

Haider, Asad, and Salar Mohandesi. "Making a Living." *Viewpoint Magazine* 5 (2015). https://viewpointmag.com/2015/10/28/making-a-living.

Kornetis, Konstantinos. "¿Un 68 periférico? Reflexiones sobre un análisis comparativo de la resistencia estudiantil en los regímenes autoritarios de la Grecia de los coroneles y de la España tardofranquista." *Studia historica: Historia contemporánea* 21 (2010): 83–112.

Ledesma, Eduardo. "Helena Lumbreras' *Field for Men* (1973): Midway between

Latin American Third Cinema and the Barcelona School." *Studies in Spanish and Latin American Cinemas* 11–3 (2004): 271–88.

Linares, Andrés. *El cine militante*. Madrid: Castellote, 1976.

Lisa, Mariano. Interview by Pablo La Parra-Pérez. Personal interview. Barcelona, January 18, 2014.

Martín-Márquez, Susan. "Editing in the Woman Auteur." In *A Companion to Spanish Cinema*, edited by Jo Labanyi and Tatjana Pavlović, 176–89. Chichester, West Sussex: Wiley-Blackwell, 2015.

Martí Rom, Josep Miquel. "*Numax* de Joaquín Jordá (Los problemas de autogestión en un contexto capitalista)." *Dirigido por . . .* 80 (1981): 6–7.

Mirzoeff, Nicholas. *The Right to Look: A Counterhistory of Visuality*. Durham, NC: Duke University Press, 2011.

Moine, Caroline. *Cinéma et Guerre froide: Histoire du festival de films documentaires de Leipzig (1955–1990)*. Paris: Publications de la Sorbonne, 2014.

Molinero, Carme, and Pere Ysàs. *Productores disciplinados y minorías subversivas: Clase obrera y conflictividad laboral en la España franquista*. Madrid: Siglo XXI, 1998.

Nichols, Bill. "The Voice of Documentary." *Film Quarterly* 36, no. 3 (1983): 17–30.

Parigi, Stefania. *Fisiologia dell'immagine: Il pensiero di Cesare Zavattini*. Turin: Lindau, 2006.

Pereda, Rosa María. "Helena Lumbreras: Un nuevo cine político en España." *El País*, July 2, 1977. http://elpais.com/diario/1977/07/02/cultura/236642404_850215.html.

Protti, Daniele. "Letter from Italy." *Cineaste* 3, no. 3 (1969–70): 26 and 28.

Romaguera, Joaquim, and Llorenç Soler. *Historia crítica y documentada del cine independiente en España (1955–1975)*. Barcelona: Laertes, 2006.

Rosati, Faliero, ed. *1968–1972: Esperienze di Cinema Militante*. Rome: Società Gestioni Editoriali, 1973.

Ross, Kristin. *May '68 and Its Afterlives*. Chicago: University of Chicago Press, 2002.

Stark, Trevor. "'Cinema in the Hands of the People': Chris Marker, the Medvedkin Group, and the Potential of Militant Film." *October* 118 (2012): 117–50.

Uva, Christian. *L'immagine politica: Forme del contropotere tra cinema, video e fotografia nell'Italia degli anni Settanta*. Milan: Mimesis, 2015.

Zavattini, Cesare. "Estratto dal documento di presentazione del Cinegiornale Libero del Proletariato." *Bollettino dei Cinegiornali Liberi* 3 (1970): 3–4.

———. "Free Newsreels." *Cinema Journal* 54, no. 3 (2015): 9–11.
———. Interview by Arturo Gismondi. "Proposals for a Television Open to Reality and Democracy." *Cinema Journal* 54, no. 3 (2015): 7–9.

Political Cinema, Revolution, and Failure

The Iranian New Wave, 1962–79

Sara Saljoughi

In thinking about the global 1960s, Iran is often left out of the picture. This omission is especially the case when it comes to thinking about cinema during the 1960s. One can imagine that Iran's relatively isolated position regionally in the Arab-dominated Middle East, as well as in international politics, is partly responsible for this dynamic. But Iran was hardly an underdog in the international cultural scene during this period. Events such as the Shiraz Festival of Arts (1967–77) and the Tehran International Film Festival both promoted and participated in creating a network of exchange between Iranian and foreign artists, intellectuals, filmmakers, and musicians.

The government of monarch Mohammad Reza Shah Pahlavi (in power from 1941 to 1979) sponsored state-led initiatives to put Iran on the global stage in terms of cultural production. It is the association of the 1960s with the Pahlavi regime's totalitarian governance of Iran that is more likely the cause of dissociation between 1960s Iran and the revolutionary spirit. It is, of course, the Iranian Revolution of 1979—known to many as the Islamic Revolution—that is imprinted on Western cultural memory as Iran's revolutionary moment. Not only has the memory of the Iranian Revolution overshadowed the persistence of the people's struggle against the state throughout the first half of the twentieth century, but it has also cast a veneer of failure on the film movements that undertook, with similar struggle, an attempt to forge an Iranian countercinema.

This essay takes as its starting point a rethinking of filmmaking in Iran during the 1960s and 1970s.[1] It posits that while the outcome of the 1979 Revolution—a theocratic state that continued and expanded the pure execution of power under the Pahlavi regime—was not desired by many and thus understood as the failure of left politics in Iran, the afterlife of the Revolution should not determine how we understand the political cinema of the preceding period. Mirroring anticolonial film movements around the globe, in 1970s Iran, cinema was intricately connected with the politics of the Revolution in part due to its status as a technology of imperialist ideology. Events such as the infamous burning of the Cinema Rex in Abadan (and over one hundred subsequent theater fires) in 1978 fixed cinema as a target of nativist appeals to return to a "pure," traditional Iranian identity.[2] Perceptions of cinema in Iran during the final years of the Pahlavi period, however, have been overdetermined by the religious-nationalist reaction to cinema. The discourse that suggests cinema in Iran was purely an imported form that weakened national culture dismisses the complex ways in which Iranian filmmakers were painfully articulating a new aesthetics of cinema, one that was tied to a utopian hope for new social and political dynamics.

This essay offers an overview of the dynamic film practice of the Iranian New Wave. I will focus on three dimensions of the movement: (1) an experimental documentary practice, much of which incorporated modern Persian poetry into a new film language; (2) a series of neorealist-influenced feature films, many of which were adaptations of contemporary dissident literature; and (3) a countercinema using modernist strategies of estrangement. I argue that all three of these examples of Iranian New Wave filmmaking were forms of political cinema that aimed, in part, at critiquing the existing ideologies of the state. In order to elucidate this new aesthetics and politics, I will examine the different ways in which Iranian filmmakers attempted to create a countercinema during the 1960s and 1970s. In examining these different facets of the Iranian New Wave, the essay will discuss the documentaries of Kamran Shirdel, Iranian New Wave feature films such as Dariush Mehrjui's *Gav/The Cow* (1968), and feminist experiments with form as seen in the work of Forough Farrokhzad and Marva Nabili.

Iran in the 1960s and 1970s

The relationship of cinema to radical politics in Iran must be understood beyond the framework of the 1979 Revolution. Since its dawn in Iran at the turn of the nineteenth century, the politics of moving image culture in Iran have been intricately linked with changes in Iranian society. The first half of the twentieth century saw the emergence of a national arena that made it newly possible for social actors to make political claims toward the nation and the nation-state.[3] Films such as *Haji Agha Aktor Cinema/Haji Agha, the Cinema Actor* (1933, dir. Ovanes Ohanian) exhibited a dynamic awareness of the ways in which the moving image put pressure on traditional notions of art, propriety, and the politics of looking. These issues, particularly the matter of looking, continue to puzzle Iranian films in productive and innovative ways, with Abbas Kiarostami's *Shirin* (2008) as a particularly compelling recent example. It is beyond the scope of this essay to chart the ways in which Iranian cinema was both reflective and constitutive of key political debates throughout the twentieth century. Despite this limitation, it is necessary to briefly examine the ways in which the politics of the early 1960s factored into the articulation of a new film language during this period.

The national politics of 1960s Iran are haunted by the specter of the coup d'état against Prime Minister Mohammad Mossadegh in 1953.[4] The demise of a certain confidence in national politics weakened the optimism attached to the Mossadegh era. As Nikki Keddie demonstrates, this atmosphere prompted the Shah to respond in a recuperative manner, first rather feebly and eventually, at the beginning of the 1960s with what became his *Enghelab-e sefid*, or White Revolution.[5] The White Revolution consisted of a series of reforms that were formulated in the late 1950s and early 1960s and officially adopted as policy from 1963 to 1978. The reforms ranged from land programs to education missions (*Sepah-e danesh* or Literacy Corps) that attempted to modernize Iran according to Western standards. Ali M. Ansari notes the paradox of a monarchical attempt to modernize along "revolutionary" grounds, arguing that the White Revolution "can be interpreted as an attempt by the Shah and his supporters to provide a legitimating myth for the Pahlavi monarchy by reconciling the contradictions implicit in these various ideologies in the person of the monarch."[6] The result of these efforts was one of the most turbulent periods in Iranian history, running parallel with anti-imperial and decolonization movements worldwide. The Shah's modernization program was based largely on plans to westernize and to create a monolithic notion of "pure" Iranian-ness that created "an official culture of spectacle that depended both on Westernizing Iran and on revitalizing a partly fabricated monarchic and chauvinistic ideology and history that predated Islam."[7]

The official arts culture of the Pahlavi regime had limits that were typical of a dictatorial style of governing. The era produced some remarkable and long-lasting initiatives, such as Kanoon, or the Institute for the Intellectual Development of Children and Young Adults (*Kanoon-e Parvaresh-e Fekri-e Koodakan va Nojavanan*), where many prominent filmmakers such as Abbas Kiarostami, Bahram Beyzai, and Amir Naderi made their first films. But the state's sponsorship of the cultural sector was accompanied by a heavy-handed control of any potentially dissident action. The institutions that supported the production of films, such as the Ministry of Culture and Art (MCA), were often prompt to ban those same films for political and social reasons. However, these arms of the state paid careful attention to the reception of Iranian films abroad, often allowing the exhibition of films that attained a degree of international success.[8]

Iranian New Wave films were produced in the same media landscape as commercial films, and it is crucial to understand how that relationship manifested in both the aesthetics and politics of new wave films. During the period following World War II, a commercial cinema known as *film farsi* ("Persian [language] film") dominated the Iranian film industry. First appearing in the 1940s and produced consistently throughout the next thirty years under Pahlavi rule, *film farsi* occupies a paradoxical position in the national imaginary. On the one hand, it has been disparaged for the crudeness of its narratives and its shameless mimicking of Hollywood, Egyptian, and Indian commercial cinema. On the other hand, it is a properly popular cinema insofar as it constituted, along with foreign imports, the bulk of what was shown on Iranian screens for much of the twentieth century. *Film farsi* has been held largely responsible for the ways in which cinema came to signify only as a source of cheap entertainment, one that was the cause of national embarrassment. It provided obvious evidence for the nativist claim that imported technologies and their attendant forms had diluted national traditions.[9] Consequently, assessments of cinema during the Pahlavi era, as well as perceptions of the conservative backlash against cinema, have tended to take *film farsi* as symptomatic of cinema tout court. As I will demonstrate in this essay, although the alternative forms of cinema were marginal relative to *film farsi* in terms of their domestic reach, a wide-ranging and heterogeneous set of filmmakers were prolific in their search for new models of cinematic language.

Not only was the Iranian New Wave challenging the aesthetics and reception of *film farsi* as the dominant cinematic discourse, it also had to contend with critics who employed a troubling narrative in order to suggest that new wave films were too highbrow for Iranian audiences. The inability of audiences to understand new wave films was often conflated with the notion that cinema should be above all a realist representation of the world. Attributing this desire for realism to a deep rift within Iranian society between so-called intellectual culture and "traditional society," Parviz Jahed cites an astonishing domestic response to Ebrahim Golestan's new wave film *Khesht va Ayneh/Brick and Mirror* (1965) from the film critic Parviz Davai, who writes:

> No, Mr. Golestan! Our miserable and low-literate people, among whom you have held up your nose and passed, don't want a work in the scales of Antonioni (at least not yet). If you make films for these people, you should know them first . . . *Khesht va Ayneh* shows in every part that you don't know them.[10]

What such critiques demonstrate is a strong resistance to the notion that art cinema, especially in its most stylized instances, can speak to pertinent questions that are assumed to be part of a national cinema's political mandate. Thus, although these are indeed problematic projections of what Iranians expected and wanted to see on screen, they nevertheless open out to more complex debates about the nature of political cinema. While the search for new cinematic forms was connected with the Pahlavi government's general position on fostering a place for Iran on the global cultural stage, it is also reflective of how this modernizing ideology operated at a remove from Iranian society. It is important that this place on the global stage reflect the Iranian monarch's *modernized* patronage of culture. The Pahlavi support of art—evidenced especially by Empress Farah Diba's position in the international art scene—operated on the basic premise that Iran was continuing a rich, centuries-long tradition of art and culture.[11] Agencies such as the MCA and National Iranian Radio and Television (NIRT) were established to oversee the organization of the arts. The MCA included literary and performance arts in addition to cinema, while the NIRT produced short and feature-length films (for both television and cinema). Alongside these large umbrella organizations there were a few independent studios. The most important for the establishment of a political cinema in Iran was that of Ebrahim Golestan, the prominent writer, translator, and intellectual who used funds earned making newsreel films for the Anglo-Iranian Oil Company to fund his eponymous Film Workshop.[12] The structure of Golestan's studio was radically different from the larger production studios, particularly his approach to film crews. He often hired people trained or active in distinct fields to work in radically new fields at his studio, where he would provide the training for this shift. This produced a rich filmography for the new wave, one that bore the intermedial traces of its creators' diverse backgrounds. One of the strongest examples of this cross-pollination is the acclaimed poet Forough Farrokhzad, who was trained as an editor at the Golestan Film Workshop and later directed her own films. Farrokhzad's poetry practice is legible in her experimental use of montage in the film *Khaneh siah ast/The House Is Black* (1962), which I discuss in the final section of this essay.

Documentary Cinema

One rich area of cultural output during the 1960s and 1970s was in documentary film productions. We can see documentary film production in Iran as encompassing several forms. In the early 1960s, almost as many as fifty documentary films were shot annually in Iran. This output matches that of feature filmmaking, which had increased exponentially since the 1940s.[13] The production of documentary cinema in Iran developed in earnest only from 1950 onward. The majority of documentaries (apart from newsreels) were travelogues or films on agriculture and education projects. The MCA and the NIRT were crucial in supporting the development of these expository documentaries that examined diverse elements of Iranian culture, such as sculpture, stained glass, music, dance, and even the prized domestic commodity, caviar. Adjacent to this were documentaries that many have described as "poetic." These documentaries have been characterized as poetic in large part due to the literary language they employ in voice-over. At the onset of the 1960s, we see a prime example of poetic documentary in Ebrahim Golestan's *Yek Atash/A Fire* (1961), a film that poignantly narrates a fire of the oil fields in southern Iran. Indeed, Golestan would go on to make several of these poetic documentaries, including *Javaherat-e Saltanati/The Crown Jewels* (1965), which embedded, under the auspices of a heritage film, a severe critique of the Pahlavi regime's governance of Iran.[14] The poetic documentaries produced by Golestan are a sharp departure from his earlier work in producing newsreel documentaries for the Anglo-Iranian Oil Company. Golestan's work as filmmaker is significant for its elaboration of this poetic form, but his contributions to articulating alternative forms of Iranian cinema extend beyond that of his role as director. As I have already discussed, in his role as head and sponsor of his own film studio, Golestan provided infrastructure for key new wave films as well as the careers of several important figures in the history of Iranian countercinema. Thus, he serves as a kind of figurehead for a significant section of Iranian documentary filmmaking. Finally, we can consider a third category of documentary filmmaking, and that is the activist documentaries as made by Kamran Shirdel and others.

Kamran Shirdel's filmography occupies a singular position in the history of Iranian cinema. Unlike the documentaries of Farrokhzad and Golestan, which relied on experiments with modern, poetic language, Shirdel's work uses more direct contrapuntal strategies reminiscent of films such as Fernando Solanas and Octavio Getino's *La Hora de los Hornos/The Hour of the Furnaces* (1968). However, while Shirdel is in conversation with the militant documentaries of Third Cinema, his work also alludes to Iran's poetic documentary practice. Because his cinema calls on spectators to make these intertextual connections, his work is a particularly apt introduction to radical documentary cinema in Pahlavi Iran. Shirdel is most well known for his feature film *Oun shab ke baran oumad/The Night It Rained . . . or the Epic of a Gorgan Village Boy*, made between 1967 and 1974, a satire on the concept of documentary truth. Like many new wave filmmakers, he trained abroad, first studying architecture at Rome University, then working as a dubber at Dariush Film Studio in Rome, and finally studying filmmaking at the Centro Sperimentale Cinematographica, where his teachers included Pier Paolo Pasolini. He returned to Iran in 1965 and immediately began making documentaries for the Ministry of Culture and Arts. The MCA oversaw the development of a form of documentary that Hamid Naficy describes as "statist" for its cultivation of an official style.[15] This style is characterized by a set of conventions such as a slow pace with linear narration that avoided sudden transitions, shifting from the general (through a long shot) to the particular (through a close-up), and voice-overs employing people speaking with "good" Persian accents as opposed to minority dialects. In his own films, the subject of the current discussion, Shirdel tackles subjects that directly challenge the vision of a modernized democracy that the regime of Mohammad Reza Shah attempted to display to the West. Films like *Tehran paytakht-e Iran ast/Tehran Is the Capital of Iran* (1966–81) and *Nedamatgah/Women's Prison* (1965) address the disparities between official representations of Iran and the lived experience of poverty and violence for many Iranians. For their exposure of what the state desperately tried to conceal and deny and the manner in which this exposure implicated the state, Shirdel's films were banned, confiscated, or reduced to limited screenings.

One of Shirdel's first films, *Ghaleh*, translated as *Women's Quarter* or *Fortress: The Red Light District*, is an examination of the lives of sex workers living in Tehran's sex district. Due to its treatment of its subject and its critique of the state, *Ghaleh* suffered from explicit censorship and confiscation. Like Shirdel's other documentary shorts, it was made between 1967 and 1980. This long period of time attests to the disruptions that the MCA imposed on the film's release. The film was sponsored by the Women's Organization of Iran, led by Princess Ashraf Pahlavi—the twin sister of the Shah. But the film directly critiques this organization and its failure to improve the lives of women. It uses a contrapuntal style that juxtaposes the state's narrative of modernization as it is taught in the school established for the women alongside interviews with the women sex workers themselves. Through this juxtaposition, the film offers a harsh critique of the official ideology of the state—particularly in the midst of the White Revolution—which caused it to be censored. The focus on women sex workers' rights directly challenged the state's self-constructed image of a modern, emancipated society. The reality that the film exposed should be seen in conjunction with the feminist movement of the time.[16] Not only was filming disrupted in 1966, but SAVAK, the Shah's secret police, confiscated Shirdel's footage and materials. It was only in 1980, following the 1979 Revolution that ousted the Shah, that the negatives and soundtrack were found in the Ministry of Culture and Art's film lab. Like the story of many other prerevolutionary

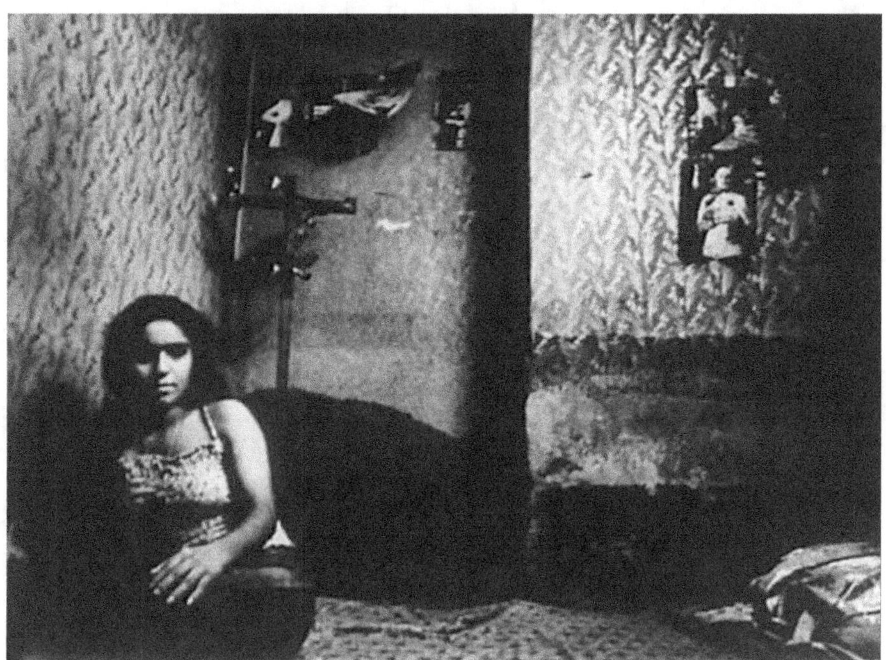

Women's Quarter (Kamran Shirdel, 1966–80).

films, rumor has it that a sympathetic technician safeguarded the material. Shirdel then edited this recovered footage with photographs taken by Kaveh Golestan—son of new wave filmmaker Ebrahim Golestan—during the shoot of the film.

In *Women's Quarter*, as with Shirdel's other short films of this time, the subjects of the documentary provide the voice-over. Their voices comprise a heterogeneity of accent, age, education, and tone, thus forming a stark contrast with the official style of the state documentaries as well as with the poetic documentaries, which employ poetic language with a refined, formal, and learned style of speaking. The shift between the classroom scenes and Golestan's photographs of the women in their small rooms and other makeshift living quarters draws our attention to the absurdity of the pedagogical call for an engaged and educated citizenry, while many of the testimonies of women implicate the police and other representatives of the state in practices of sex trafficking. The film is on the one hand an expository treatment of the lives of sex workers in Iran's capital and on the other hand a kind of ethnographic project that seems to understand itself as a vehicle through which the most marginalized voices speak. But the film also has strong pedagogical overtones that interpellate its educated, elite audience by forging a direct link between the institutional structures that facilitated their own advancement in Iranian society and the lack of access to those same institutional protections for much of Tehran's population. The practices and formulations operating in *Ghaleh* and many other new wave films have been deemed didactic and as a result have been almost discredited by contemporary historiography. This treatment has been underscored by an implicit link between the reception and exposure of Iranian cinema and its aesthetic value, an attitude that has steered research away from this lesser known era. I want to venture that because the more radical new wave films are really risk-taking experiments, there is a kind of contingency to their status within historiographical accounts. But as the example of *Women's Quarter* demonstrates, this contingency also characterizes the material conditions of the film's production. The risk-taking quality of new wave works can be considered within what Jonathan Buchsbaum has described as the inherently speculative nature of the project of Third Cinema as written in Solanas and Getino's groundbreaking essay.[17] Although it did not receive the attention it deserved during the time of its production, Shirdel's work has enjoyed a new following in recent years, due to exhibitions such as *Modern Iran*, which took place in 2013 at the Asia Society in New York. The work of Shirdel, along with that of filmmakers like Farrokhzad and Rahnema also paved the way for a documentary film movement in the 1970s known as Cinemaye Azad Iran, or the Free Cinema of Iran.[18]

Feature Films

If there is one film widely known and associated with prerevolutionary Iranian cinema, it is Dariush Mehrjui's *Gav/The Cow* (1968). It has been widely cited by critics and scholars as the founding film of the Iranian New Wave. When it was released in the year 1348 of the Iranian calendar, film critic Jalal Omid announced the "Year Zero" of Iranian cinema.[19] Although it is a singular film, it heralds what is broadly understood as the Iranian New Wave—a number of feature-length films bearing the influence of realist movements, various international new wave, and—perhaps most significantly—the influence of the socially committed literature that flourished in Iran during the mid-twentieth century. *The Cow* is emblematic of these patterns both in its aesthetics and politics. Yet *The Cow* must also be understood as part of a larger group of new

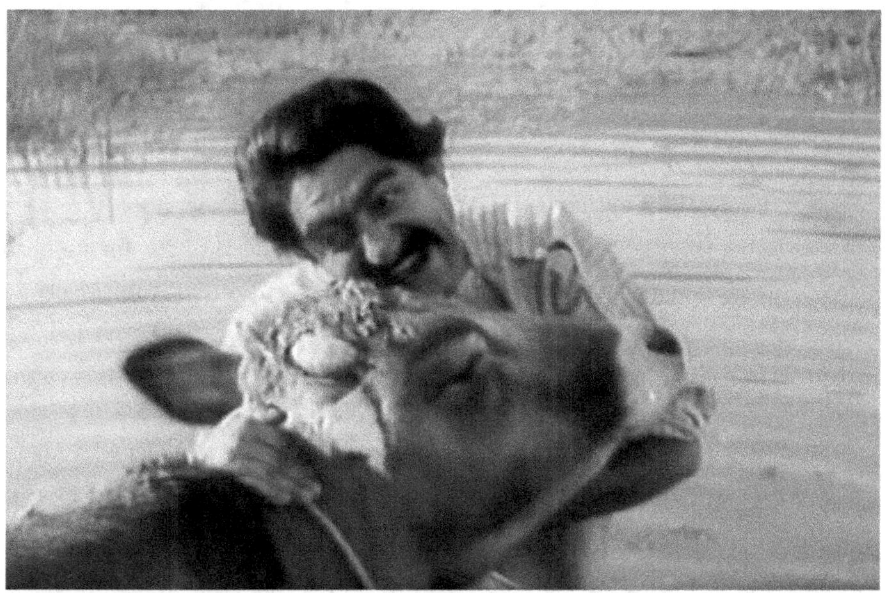

The Cow (Dariush Mehrjui, 1968).

wave films that examined the deterioration of collective forms of solidarity in the face of economic and political crisis from the 1950s to the 1970s.

As film scholars have widely discussed, the development of cinema in Iran must be understood in tandem with the widespread change brought on by increased modernization, beginning in the late nineteenth century.[20] These changes, which included increased literacy, modern infrastructure, and a strengthened economy, arguably created the condition of possibility for a socially committed literature that pointed to the paradoxes inherent in the modernization associated with the Pahlavi dynasty. The influence of contemporary literature on Iranian cinema is not novel to the period of the 1960s and 1970s. Much of early Iranian cinema used the rich history of Persian literature as its source material, seen in early films such as *Khosrow and Shirin*, *Leyli and Majnun*, and others such as *Dash Akol*, *Prince Ehtejab*, and *Tall Shadows of the Wind*.[21] However, in the period following World War II, it is possible to see a rich, symbiotic relationship between new voices in contemporary literature and the newly emergent notion of a political cinema. As Mohammad Reza Shah's tightening over dissent became more extreme in the 1950s and 1960s, the literati responded with an outpouring of texts that critiqued many elements of life under dictatorial rule. These texts, written by authors such as

Simin Daneshvar, Gholam-Hossein Sa'edi, Sadegh Chubak, and others, often used allegorical form to dramatize the struggles of everyday Iranians under Pahlavi rule.[22] Sa'edi is one of the most important for the history of Iranian cinema, for he wrote *The Cow*, as well as *Dayereh Mina/The Cycle* (dir. Dariush Mehrjui, 1975). Both of these works can be understood as socially committed, simple stories (the loss of a village's sole cow and the need to pay for medical care, respectively) that unfold to allow a complex critique of the society in which they take place. At every turn, these narratives show the Pahlavi vision of Iran as modern, progressive, and emancipated as an Iran known only to the urban elite.

The Cow follows the story of Masht Hassan, a farmer whose life revolves around his cow, the only source of his joy and livelihood. The cow is the sole source of milk for the village where Masht Hassan lives. One day, the cow is mysteriously killed, setting off a chain of events that conclude with Masht Hassan embodying the spirit of the cow. One of the most striking elements of the film is the way that it stages the intimate relationship between human and nonhuman. The film has also been credited with prompting the rebirth of Iranian cinema after the 1979 Revolution.[23] This particular historical link belies some of the negative critical reactions to the film at the time of its release. Most of these comments focused on the negative portrayal of the villagers in the film, echoing the Pahlavi regime's desire to present a modernized Iran to the world. The film has also been read as an examination of the limits of recognizability that confer acceptance within a particular community.[24]

In this vein, *The Cow* belongs to a group of feature films that are preoccupied with the politics of Iranian society in the 1960s and 1970s. In Nasser Taghvai's *Aramesh dar Hozur-e Digaran/Tranquility in the Presence of Others* (1973), which like *The Cow* is based on a story written by Sa'edi, the tension between tradition and modernity are allegorized through the encounter between a retired colonel who returns to the city to live with his unwed daughters. He suffers mentally and physically from the strains of modern life, which are exacerbated by his daughters' vibrant social life. Although the colonel is represented as the odd figure who cannot be reconciled into modern, hip Tehran society, all the characters in the film suffer from some form of social anxiety. The film was screened at the Shiraz Arts Festival but banned for several years, due to this bleak depiction of Iranian society, which, as Naficy argues, contradicted the "state-sanctioned utopianism."[25] One of the earliest new wave feature films, *Khesht va Ayneh/Brick and Mirror* (dir. Ebrahim Golestan, 1965) examines this social anxiety primarily through the affect of paranoia. The film, which is markedly influenced by existentialist philosophy, also presents a cynical view of Iranian society under the Shah, suggesting that ordinary citizens cannot trust each other in the climate of suspicion and fear that the regime promoted. While the feature-length films discussed here do not employ radical formalism, they draw from contemporaneous film movements that align art cinema with a critique of existing regimes of representation as well as an analysis of politics. As such, they represent the most moderate strain of new wave films and their influence on postrevolutionary Iranian cinema, particularly films made after 2000, suggests the longevity of this form in the national context.

A Feminist Cinema

In addition to feature-length films exploring questions of community and the nation-state, the Iranian New Wave also had a smaller contingent of radical filmmakers whose main goals were formal experimentation or what I earlier called the politics of form. These filmmakers included Fereydoun Rahnema, Parviz Kimiavi, and Ahmad Faroughi. These filmmakers made works that employed strategies of the Brechtian alienation effect and often borrowed from experiments in form familiar from European new waves. In what follows I will focus on the work of two feminist filmmakers—Forough Farrokhzad and Marva Nabili—in order to examine some of the key insights into the formal politics of cinema generated by the Iranian New Wave. Their work suggests that the Iranian New Wave, both in the early 1960s as well as at the end of the Pahlavi period, was highly attuned to the important relationship between aesthetics and politics.

Forough Farrokhzad was one of the most important poets working in modern Persian literature. She is widely known for her works *The Captive* (1955), *Rebellion* (1960), and *Another Birth* (1965), which are part of a contemporary movement carrying on the new modern verse known as *shehr-e no* (New Poetry).[26] Farrokhzad's poetry was considered groundbreaking for its use of the authorial voice, its sense of rhythm, and the subject matter of the poems. Instead of cloaking controversial subject matter in formal language, or

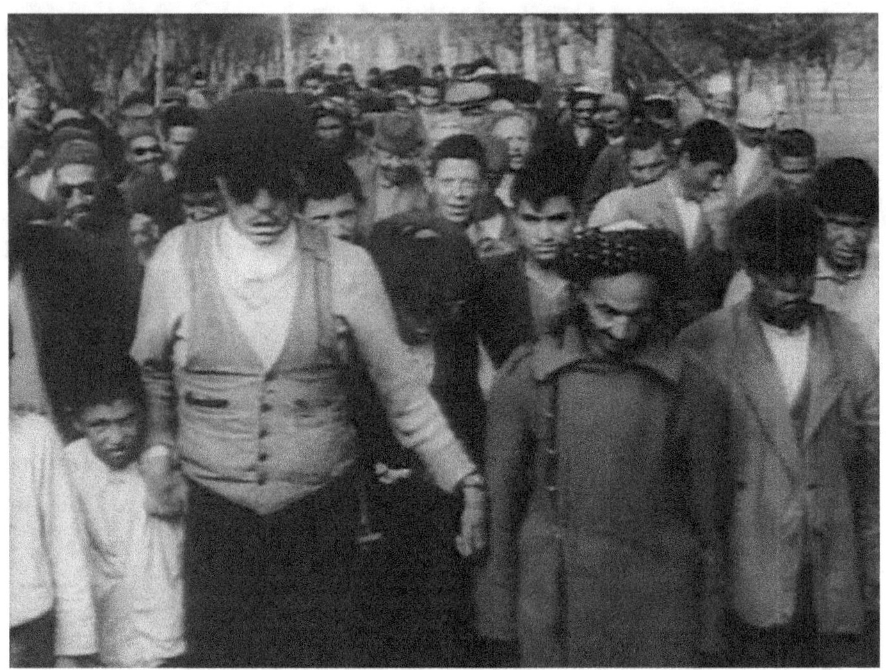

The House Is Black (Forough Farrokhzad, 1962).

avoiding it altogether, Farrokhzad directly addressed her emotive and sensorial experiences as a woman.[27] Farrokhzad worked first as an editor and then filmmaker at Golestan's studio, where she edited many films, including *A Fire*, and made her own film, *Khaneh siah ast/The House Is Black* (1962). The film, which takes place in a leper colony in northwestern Iran, is considered by many to be one of the most important films in the history of Iranian cinema. It is possessed of an experimental style that features a vivid dissonance between image and sound. This dissonance is staged through an encounter between the filmmaker and the subjects of the film—the people who live in the leper colony.[28] Although the film has been primarily characterized by critics for its humanist qualities, I venture that it rejects the notion of humanizing lepers and instead offers a more radical notion of collectivity.[29] For example, there are many scenes in which Farrokhzad upends conventional uses of point of view and, through voice-over, creates an alliance between herself and the members of the colony, producing a projection of a collectivity that does not yet exist in the available notions of a "public."

Marva Nabili can be considered, alongside Forough Farrokhzad, as one of the more experimental filmmakers of the Iranian New Wave. Having worked as a producer and editor for the NIRT, Nabili shot one feature film, *Khakh-e sar be morh/The Sealed Soil* (1977) in Iran before leaving for permanent exile in the United States. In *The Sealed Soil*, Nabili challenges the limits of the new wave's formalism by employing a distanced look. The film is a double narrative about a young woman's independence and her rural village's struggle to maintain autonomy in the face of encroachment by a large agricultural corporation. In *The Sealed Soil*, the camera is fixed for the entirety of the film, and cinematography consists mainly of long shots that preclude proximity between the viewer and the subjects of the film. As an example of 1970s feminist filmmaking, the film must be considered in tandem with feminist film theory and specifically its analysis of woman as spectacle.[30] Through this formal resistance to ideological uses of the camera, *The Sealed Soil* inaugurates the "modest" or distanced look that most scholars attribute to later, postrevolutionary Iranian cinema. Nabili challenges how women have appeared in prerevolutionary Iranian cinema (especially in *film farsi*), thus inaugurating a feminist film poetics/politics in the Iranian New Wave.[31] The example of feminist experiments with film form in 1970s Iran suggest that the critique of cinema and ideology must be read as part of a broader political culture, one that includes the religious-nationalist rejection of cinema, but is not limited to it. Furthermore, Nabili's work suggests that although the new wave was dominated by male filmmakers, it was also a movement that featured close thinking about the relationship of cinema to the gendered politics of looking.

The films of Farrokhzad and Nabili, though overlooked by most scholars of Iranian cinema, also function to place the Iranian New Wave of the 1960s and 1970s in an international context. *The House Is Black* won the top prize at the Oberhausen International Short Film Festival in 1962 and it traveled to several other festivals around the world. *The Sealed Soil*, although it was finished in exile in the United States, circulated as a text of Iranian radical politics during the height of the anti-Shah activities of the late 1970s. *The Sealed Soil* and its circulation at international film festivals as a *feminist* film did the work of expanding the social and political concerns of the revolutionary action beyond solely a Marxist or an Islamic framework. The formal politics of *The Sealed Soil* belong to an international history of women's countercinema, as well as to genealogies of political cinema around the globe.[32] This history of exhibition, for both films, also provides strong evidence for the ways in which the Iranian New Wave films circulated during the 1960s and 1970s.

Conclusion

There is a myriad of ways in which cinema was part of the political struggle against dictatorship and imperialism during the Pahlavi era. Much work remains to be done on this period of Iranian film history, which has been overshadowed by the success of postrevolutionary Iranian art cinema. At the same time, the notion that the Iranian Revolution did not turn out the way leftist intellectuals and artists had hoped has caused some new wave films to be read dismissively as didactic experiments that did not work. This "failure" of the Revolution to materialize as a Marxist revolution, I argue, should be rethought in generative terms. New directions in Iranian history, such as Behrooz Ghamari-Tabrizi's *Foucault in Iran: Enlightenment after the Islamic Revolution* (2016), suggest that the possibility posited by the activities and energy of the Revolution is in and of itself worthy of maintaining. Through an examination of the diversity of what might be deemed "political cinema" in 1960s and 1970s Iran, I have attempted to show the complex modes through which Iranian filmmakers sought to register resistance to the dictatorial rule of the Pahlavi regime and especially to its capitulation to imperialist power. Although the Iranian New Wave was interrupted and indeed terminated by the religious-nationalist turn of the Iranian Revolution, it dared to put forth an ambitious new set of politics, a politics that was reflected in the formal strategies of the movement. New work in the area of film aesthetics and politics would shed light on the artistic, intellectual, and political legacies of these films, not only in Iran but also as part of a conversation on the global 1960s.

Notes

1. I explore these questions in greater detail in my forthcoming manuscript on the aesthetics and politics of Iranian art cinema during the 1960s and 1970s.
2. On the Cinema Rex fire, see Hamid Naficy, *A Social History of Iranian Cinema*, vol. 3, *The Islamicate Period, 1978–1984* (Durham, NC: Duke University Press, 2012), 15–22.
3. For the roots of this shift to a modern political sphere, see Afshin Marashi,

Nationalizing Iran: Culture, Power, and the State, 1870–1940 (Seattle: University of Washington Press, 2008).

4. See Ervand Abrahamian, *The Coup: 1953, the CIA, and the Roots of Modern U.S.-Iranian Relations* (New York: New Press, 2013).
5. Nikki Keddie, "Royal Dictatorship: 1953–1977," in her *Modern Iran: Roots and Results of Revolution* (New Haven, CT: Yale University Press, 2003), 132–69.
6. Ali M. Ansari, "The Myth of the White Revolution: Mohammad Reza Shah, 'Modernization,' and the Consolidation of Power," *Middle Eastern Studies* 37, no. 3 (2001): 2.
7. Hamid Naficy, *A Social History of Iranian Cinema*, vol. 2, *Industrializing Years, 1941–1978* (Durham, NC: Duke University Press, 2011), 328.
8. See Naficy, *Social History*, vol. 2.
9. There are reexaminations of *film farsi* in recent scholarship. See Pedram Partovi, *Popular Iranian Cinema before the Revolution: Family and Nation in Fīlmfārsī* (London: Routledge, 2017). For an example of nativist discourse during this time, see Jalal al-e Ahmad, *Occidentosis: A Plague from the West*, trans. R. Campbell (Berkeley, CA: Mizan, 1984).
10. Parviz Jahed, "The Forerunners of the New Wave Cinema in Iran," in *Directory of World Cinema: Iran*, ed. Parviz Jahed (London: Intellect, 2012), 89.
11. This attempt to create a lineage along the lines of the production and support of art paralleled Mohammad Reza Shah's desire to thread an ahistorical line of continuity from his own family's reign back to the empire of Cyrus the Great (r. 559–530 BC). For a compelling discussion of this, see Tallin Grigor, *Building Iran: Modernism, Architecture, and National Heritage under the Pahlavi Monarchs* (New York: Prestel, 2009).
12. For more on the Golestan Film Workshop, see Naficy, *Social History*, 2: 79.
13. See M. Ali Issari, *Cinema in Iran, 1900–1979* (Metuchen, NJ: Scarecrow Press, 1989).
14. See Mehrnaz Saeed-Vafa, "Ebrahim Golestan: Treasure of Pre-Revolutionary Iranian Cinema," *Rouge* 11 (2007). http://www.rouge.com.au/11/golestan.html.
15. See Naficy, *Social History*, vol. 2.
16. For a discussion of feminist movements in 1970s Iran, as well as interventions from Western liberal feminism, see Nima Naghibi, *Rethinking Global Sisterhood: Western Feminism and Iran* (Minneapolis: University of Minnesota Press, 2007).
17. Jonathan Buchsbaum, "One, Two . . . Third Cinemas," *Third Text* 25, no. 1

(2011): 13–28.

18. Very little research exists on this movement. See Naficy, *Social History*, vol. 2, and Issari, *Cinema in Iran*.
19. Jalal Omid, *Tārīkh-i sīnimā-yi Īrān, 1279–1357* (Tehran: Intishārāt-i Rawzanah, 1995), 275.
20. See Hamid Dabashi, "On Modernity and the Making of a National Cinema," in *Close-Up: Iranian Cinema Past, Present, and Future* (London: Verso, 2000), 12–21, and Hamid Naficy, "Introduction: National Cinema, Modernity, and Iranian National Identity" in *A Social History of Iranian Cinema*, vol. 1, *The Artisanal Era, 1897–1941* (Durham, NC: Duke University Press, 2011), 1-25.
21. Hamid Naficy, "Iranian Writers, the Iranian Cinema, and the Case of Dash Akol," *Iranian Studies* 18 (1985): 231–51.
22. This literary movement can also be understood in tandem with nativist discourses, particularly Al-e Ahmad's theory of Gharbzadegi (often translated as "Westoxification" or "Occidentosis." See Al-e Ahmad, *Occidentosis*).
23. The film has also been credited with prompting the rebirth of Iranian cinema after the 1979 Revolution, particularly due to its positive reception by the Ayatollah Khomeini. For a discussion of Khomeini's view on film and technology, see Negar Mottahedeh, *Displaced Allegories: Post-Revolutionary Iranian Cinema* (Durham, NC: Duke University Press, 2008).
24. Richard Gabri, "Recognizing the Unrecognizable in Dariush Mehrjui's *Gav*," *Cinema Journal* 54, no. 2 (2015): 49–71.
25. Naficy, *Social History*, 2: 371.
26. For a discussion of the New Poetry movement, see Ahmad Karimi-Hakkak, ed., *An Anthology of Modern Persian Poetry* (Boulder, CO: Westview Press, 1978).
27. For an overview of Farrokhzad's poetry, see Michael Hillman, *A Lonely Woman: Forugh Farrokhzad and Her Poetry* (Washington, DC: Three Continents, 1987).
28. For an extensive analysis of the film, see Sara Saljoughi, "A New Form for a New People: Forough Farrokhzad's *The House Is Black*," *Camera Obscura* 32, no. 1 (94) (2017): 1–31.
29. See Jonathan Rosenbaum, "Radical Humanism and the Coexistence of Film and Poetry in *The House Is Black*," in *Goodbye Cinema, Hello Cinephilia: Film Culture in Transition*, ed. Jonathan Rosenbaum (Chicago: University of Chicago Press, 2010), 260–65; Hamid Dabashi, *Masters and Masterpieces*

of Iranian Cinema (Washington, DC: Mage, 2007); and Nasrin Rahimieh, "Capturing the Abject of the Nation in *The House Is Black*," in *Forugh Farrokhzad, Poet of Modern Iran: Iconic Woman and Feminine Pioneer of New Persian Poetry*, ed. Dominic Parviz Brookshaw and Nasrin Rahimieh (London: I. B. Tauris, 2010), 125–60.

30. See especially, Laura Mulvey, "Visual Pleasure and Narrative Cinema," *Screen* 16, no. 3 (1975): 6–18.
31. For an elaboration of this argument, see Sara Saljoughi, "A Cinema of Refusal: *The Sealed Soil* and the Political Aesthetics of the Iranian New Wave," *Feminist Media Histories* 3, no. 1 (2017): 81–102.
32. Saljoughi, "Cinema of Refusal."

Contributors

Morgan Adamson is Assistant Professor of Media and Cultural Studies at Macalester College. Her research interests include documentary and avant-garde cinema, film and media theory, and critical political economy. Her book, *Enduring Images: A Future History of New Left Cinema* (2018), examines collectively produced documentaries of the 1960s and 1970s in light of the cultural and economic transformations of that era. She has been published in *South Atlantic Quarterly*, *Film Philosophy*, and the *Minnesota Review*.

Laurence Coderre is Assistant Professor of East Asian Studies at New York University. Her research focuses on the literature, film, music, and material culture of the Mao and post-Mao periods. Her first book manuscript considers media, materiality, and the commodity of the Chinese Cultural Revolution (1966–76). Her work has been published in the *Journal of Chinese Cinemas* and *Modern Chinese Literature and Culture*.

Rita de Grandis is Professor of Spanish at the University of British Columbia. Her research focuses on Latin American leftist utopias and their representations. Her book *Cultural Recycling and Revolutionary Memory: The Polemical Practice of José Pablo Feinmann* (2006) won the Best Book Prize of the Canadian Association of Hispanists in 2007. Her writing has been published in the *Canadian Journal of Latin American and Caribbean Studies, Latin American Literary Review*, and *Studies in Latin American Popular Culture*.

David Desser is Professor Emeritus of Cinema Studies at the University of Illinois at Urbana-Champaign. His research focuses on Japanese and Asian cinema and Jewish cinema. He is the author of *The Samurai Films of Akira Kurosawa* (1983); *Eros Plus Massacre: An Introduction to the Japanese New Wave Cinema* (1988); and *Ozu's Tokyo Story* (1997); and editor of *Reframing Japanese Cinema: Authorship, Genre, History* (1992); and *Cinematic Landscapes: Observations on the Visual Arts and Cinema of China and Japan* (2000). His writing has been published in *Film Criticism, Film Quarterly, Post Script, Quarterly Review of Film and Video*, and *Screen*.

Victor Fan is Senior Lecturer in the Department of Film Studies at King's College London. His research focuses on Chinese cinema and media, contemporary Hollywood, and comparative studies in world film theories. His publications include *Cinema Approaching Reality: Locating Chinese Film Theory* (2015). His articles have been published in *Camera Obscura, Journal of Chinese Cinemas, Screen*, and *Film History*.

Allyson Nadia Field is Associate Professor of Cinema and Media Studies at the University of Chicago. She is author of *Uplift Cinema: The Emergence of African American Film and the Possibility of Black Modernity* (2015) and coeditor with Jan-Christopher Horak and Jacqueline Najuma Stewart of *L.A. Rebellion: Creating a New Black Cinema* (2015). Since 2009 she has served as co-curator of the L.A. Rebellion Preservation Project of the UCLA Film and Television Archive. Her essays have been published in *Cinema Journal*, *Framework*, and the *Journal of Popular Film and Television.*

Christina Gerhardt is Associate Professor of German at the University of Hawaiʻi at Mānoa. She has been awarded grants by the Fulbright Commission, the DAAD, and the NEH and held visiting appointments at Harvard University, Columbia University, the Free University in Berlin, and the University of California at Berkeley, where she taught previously. She is author of *Screening the Red Army Faction: Historical and Cultural Memory* (2018); coeditor with Marco Abel of *Celluloid Revolt: German Screen Cultures and the Long Sixties* (2019); and editor of *1968 and West German Cinema*, a special issue of *The Sixties* 10 (2017). Her writing has been published in *Cineaste*, *Film Criticism*, *Film Quarterly*, *German Studies Review*, *New German Critique*, *Mosaic*, *Quarterly Review of Film and Video,* and *The Sixties: A Journal of History, Politics and Culture.*

Rocco Giansante is a PhD candidate at the Hebrew University. His research interests include the Portuguese Cinema Novo, Israeli cinema, postpolitical Italian cinema, and contemporary live art performances. He also works as a filmmaker and lighting designer.

Sarah Hamblin is Assistant Professor of English and Cinema Studies at the University of Massachusetts, Boston. Her research focuses on global art cinema, emphasizing the relationships among aesthetics, affect, and radical politics. Her first book manuscript is *Screening the Impossible: The Global Politics of Form and Feeling in Second Wave Revolutionary Cinema*. Her writing has been published in *Cinema Journal*, *Black Camera*, *Film and History*, and *Studies in Popular Culture.*

Peter Hames is Visiting Professor of Film Studies at Staffordshire University, United Kingdom. His books as author and editor include *The Czechoslovak New Wave* (1985/2005), *The Cinema of Jan Švankmajer: Dark Alchemy* (1995/2008), *The Cinema of Central Europe* (2004), *Czech and Slovak Cinema: Theme and Tradition* (2010), *Cinemas in Transition in Central and Eastern Europe after 1989* (with Catherine Portuges, 2013), and *Best of Slovak Film, 1921–91* (2013). He has most recently contributed to *Fairy-Tale Films beyond Disney* (2015), *Marx at the Movies: Revisiting History, Theory, and Practice* (2014), *Screening Neighbours: Eastern*

European Cinema and Postcolonial Theory (2014), and *Beyond the Border: Polish Cinema in a Transnational Context* (2014).

Pablo La Parra-Pérez is a PhD candidate at New York University in the Department of Spanish and Portuguese. His dissertation, "Displaced Cinema: Militant Film Culture and Political Dissidence in Spain (1967–1982)," examines resistance in cinema under Franco and during the transition to democracy. His writing has been published in the *Journal of Spanish Cultural Studies* and *Sociologias.*

Man-tat Terence Leung is Lecturer in Film and Cultural Studies at Hong Kong Polytechnic University. He is currently finishing his first monograph, titled *The Dialectics of Two Refusals: French May '68 and Its Chinese Nexus in Western Cinematic Imaginaries* (under review). His articles on various subjects, including Kieslowski's cinema and Godard-Gorin's militant films, have been published in *Partial Answers*, and edited volumes, such as *Intimate Relationships in Cinema, Literature, and Visual Culture* (2017).

Paula Rabinowitz is Professor Emerita of Cinema and American materialist feminist cultural studies. She focuses on contemporary and modernist American women's art and literature. Her work explores hidden histories within working-class, pulp, and popular cultures. Her books include *Labor and Desire: Women's Revolutionary Fiction in Depression America*; *They Must Be Represented: The Politics of Documentary*; *Black & White & Noir*; and *American Pulp: How Paperbacks Brought Modernism to Main Street.*

Mauro Resmini is Assistant Professor of Film Studies and Italian at the University of Maryland, College Park. His research is situated at the intersection of film and media studies (with a specific focus on Italian cinema) and critical theory. He has published on transmedial narratives (*The Italianist*), contemporary French cinema (*Camera Obscura*), and Italian political cinema (in the edited collection *The Essay Film: Dialogue, Politics, Utopia*, 2016). He is currently working on a book project that explores the encounter between political cinema and radical political theory in Italy between 1968 and 1989.

Lily Saint is Assistant Professor of English at Wesleyan. Her research explores the nexus of ethics and cultural practice in the Global South. She is author of *Black Cultural Life in South Africa: Reception, Apartheid and Ethics* (2018) and co-editor of *Genre in Africa*, a special issue of the *Cambridge Journal of Postcolonial Literary Inquiry* 4, no. 2 (2017). Her writing has been published in *Postcolonial Studies*, *Journal of African Cinemas*, *Safundi*, and *Critical Quarterly*, and in the collection, *Print, Text, and Book Cultures in South Africa.*

Sara Saljoughi is Assistant Professor of English and Cinema Studies at the University of Toronto. Her research focuses on political cinema, film theory (especially aesthetics and politics), Iran and the Middle East, and postcolonial studies. Her first book manuscript, *Burning Visions: The Counter-Cinema of the Iranian New Wave*, examines the aesthetics and politics of art cinema in Iran during the 1960s and 1970s. Her writing has been published in *Camera Obscura*, *Feminist Media Histories*, *Iranian Studies*, *Film Criticism*, and *Film International*.

Robert Stam is Professor of Cinema Studies at New York University. He has received fellowships from the Fulbright Commission, the Guggenheim, the Rockefeller and the Woodrow Wilson Foundation. He has published widely on film history and theory. He is author of *Francois Truffaut and Friends: Modernism, Sexuality, and Film Adaptation* (Rutgers, 2006); *Literature through Film: Realism, Magic and the Art of Adaptation* (Blackwell, 2005); *Literature and Film: A Guide to the Theory and Practice of Adaptation* (Blackwell, 2005); *Companion to Literature and Film* (Blackwell, 2004); *Film Theory: An Introduction* (Blackwell, 2000); *Tropical Multiculturalism: A Comparative History of Race in Brazilian Cinema and Culture* (Duke, 1997); and *Brazilian Cinema* (Associated University Presses, 1982). He is coauthor with Leo Goldsmith and Richard Porton of *Keywords in Subversive Film/Media Aesthetics* (Wiley-Blackwell, 2015) and with Ella Shohat of *Multiculturalism, Postcoloniality, and Transnational Media* (Rutgers, 2000) and *Unthinking Eurocentrism: Multiculturalism and the Media* (Routledge, 1994). He is coeditor (with Toby Miller) of *A Companion to Film Theory* (Blackwell, 1999) and *Film and Theory: An Anthology* (Blackwell, 2000).

Graeme Stout is Senior Lecturer and Film Studies Coordinator at the University of Minnesota, where he earned his doctorate in comparative literature. His teaching and research focus on the nature, deployment, and transformation of power in the modern age and the relationship of aesthetic form to social consciousness. His current book project studies the cultural legacy of terrorism in Italy and Germany from the late 1960s to the present day.

J. M. Tyree is Visiting Professor of Cinema at the Virginia Commonwealth University. He is the author of *BFI Film Classics: Salesman* and coauthor of *BFI Film Classics: The Big Lebowski* and of *Our Secret Life in the Movies*. He is a contributing editor at *Film Quarterly*. His writing has been published in *Film Quarterly*, *Lapham's Quarterly*, and *Sight and Sound*.

Index

Adorno, 131, 192, 196, 323
The Adversary (Ray), 15, 289–309
"Aesthetics of Hunger" (Glauber Rocha), 8, 38, 39
affect, 38, 44, 45, 47, 48, 49, 51, 54, 55, 66, 110, 147, 153, 154, 156, 159, 194, 203, 397, 406
Africa Addio (1966), protests against, 101, 113
After the Call to Action (Lumbreras), 363–384
Akerman, Chantal, 263
Algeria, 9, 25, 26, 27, 28–30, 38, 43–60, 63, 64, 67, 70, 71, 100, 235, 251, 255, 258
alienation, 13, 23, 28, 31, 37, 40, 61, 66, 68, 71, 92, 94, 108, 202, 211, 223, 237, 281, 305, 313, 315, 322, 386, 397
allegory, 185, 194, 195, 196, 396, 402
Althusser, Louis, 190, 196, 221–222, 225, 226, 235, 236, 237, 239, 292, 331
American Indian Movement, 26. *See also* indigenous
Anderson, Lindsay, 14, 50, 90, 93, 94, 183–197
Anger, Kenneth, 241–271
Angola, 27, 70, 279, 280
anthology films, 14, 33, 199–215
antiauthoritarian, 23, 26, 63, 64, 70, 148, 206, 211, 212, 365, 372
anticolonial, 1, 2, 3, 6, 7, 9, 10, 11, 23, 24, 25, 26, 27, 28, 29, 43, 44, 45, 49, 61, 63, 97, 119, 124, 126, 188, 251, 256, 275, 277, 292, 302, 329, 334, 346, 348, 349, 386, 387
anti-imperial, 1, 6, 7, 11, 24, 26, 37, 56, 128, 129, 146, 156, 235, 255, 256, 275, 277, 279, 280, 283, 292, 293, 296, 346, 348, 349, 387
antinuclear, 157
Antonioni, 79, 84, 196, 389
apparatus theory, 29, 34, 189, 190, 192, 196, 226, 244, 248, 317, 318, 322, 331, 334, 335, 336, 338, 340, 355
Apu trilogy (Ray), 7, 293, 295
Argentina, 9, 10, 13, 31, 36, 37, 117–143
Army Film Unit (Czechoslovakia), 80, 92
art cinema, 4, 17, 19, 36, 175, 213, 243, 252, 275, 289, 292, 308, 345, 369, 389, 397, 400, 406, 408
Art Theatre Guild (ATG), 170–182
assemblies (e.g., workers'), 16, 81, 367, 373, 374
audience participation, 13, 122, 147, 155, 184, 194
auteur cinema (Second Cinema), 34, 38, 69, 122, 128, 129, 137, 147, 166, 215, 219, 220, 377, 383
authoritarianism, 8, 12, 13, 24, 26, 33, 34, 39, 61, 63, 64, 66, 72, 148, 297, 337, 385, 388, 395

autogestion, 293, 296, 297, 306, 308, 380, 383
avant-garde cinema, 6, 18, 19, 34–35, 39, 40, 41, 80, 85, 92, 94, 96, 100, 108, 117, 118, 119, 121, 122, 124, 128, 130, 131–134, 135, 136, 137, 141, 142, 143, 154, 155, 167, 170, 174, 180, 181, 248, 259, 264, 267, 270, 290, 292, 307, 405

Badiou, Alain, 204, 206, 210, 213, 236, 304, 309
Barthes, Roland, 31, 36, 245, 264, 269, 314
Battle of Algiers (Pontecorvo), 7, 9, 12, 28–30, 40, 41, 43–60, 251, 255–256, 258, 266, 267, 269
The Battlefront for the Liberation of Japan—Summer in Sanrizuka (Ogawa Pro), 13, 145–164, 168, 179
Bellocchio, Marco, 14, 199–215
Bengali Independence Movement, 293
Benjamin, Walter, 34, 137, 245, 250, 377
Bergman, Ingmar, 84, 315, 321, 325
Bertolucci, Bernardo, 14, 199–215, 238
Beyer, Frank, 79, 99
Birri, Fernando, 129, 135, 139–140
black militancy, 149, 151
Black Panther: Off the Pig! (San Francisco Newsreel), 154
Black Panthers (Varda), 32, 33, 257
Black Panthers, 9, 26, 30, 154, 155, 242, 253, 257, 324
black power, 149, 282, 346
black radicals, 282, 348
Blood of the Condor (Sanjiné), 8
Boal, Augusto, 28, 40, 41
Bolivarian tradition, 125
Bolivia, 8
Brakhage, Stan, 241–271
Brazil, 2, 5, 8, 10, 11, 18, 23–42, 98, 129, 408
Brecht, Bertolt, 5, 36–38, 40, 41, 47, 108, 121, 122, 128, 130, 166, 178, 208, 211, 239, 313, 315, 397
British New Wave (also known as British "Free Cinema" and Angry Young Men), 2, 11, 18, 85, 90, 183–190
Brown, H. Rap, 149, 151
Burn! (Pontecorvo), 45, 55, 365

Cabbage (Wiley), 260
Cabral, Amílcar, 25
Cahiers du Cinéma, 34, 36, 46, 53, 58, 59, 73, 89, 93, 94, 237, 246, 337, 338, 339, 343, 344, 378, 381
Calcutta trilogy (Ray), 14, 289–309
Camera Obscura, 93, 94, 263, 402, 405, 407, 408
Cannes film festival, 31, 78, 89, 165–166, 234, 248; May 1968 shutdown of, 31, 165–166, 234
Cantonese (and Cantonese cinema), 335, 339, 340, 341, 343
Canyon Cinema, 243, 268, 269, 271
capitalism, 17, 31, 67, 101, 126, 139, 146, 154, 156, 157, 184, 188, 190, 191, 193, 202, 211, 213, 214, 220, 229, 238, 250, 260–262, 268, 290, 294, 297, 321, 330, 331, 338, 342, 353
carework, 374

censorship, 28, 31, 33, 39, 49, 56, 81, 93, 245, 246, 249, 256, 260, 262, 268, 392, 397
Centro Sperimentale di Cinematografia Roma (Experimental Cinematography Center), 129, 391, 365
Césaire, Aimé, 25, 27, 40, 41
Change of Life (Paulo Rocha), 13, 61–75
China, 7, 14, 16, 24, 26, 220, 235, 329, 331, 332, 333, 334, 335, 336, 339, 342, 345–362
Chinese cinema, 16, 336–340, 341, 342, 345–362. *See also* Cantonese cinema, Mandarin cinema, Shanghai cinema
Chinese Communist Party (CCP), 331–335, 345–362
La Chinoise (Godard), 32, 108, 172, 226–227, 351
Chytilová, Věra, 77–94
CIA-assisted coups, 8
ciné-tracts, 32, 34
Cineaste, 34, 40, 41, 161, 163, 239, 244, 307, 379, 383, 406
Cinegiornali Liberi (Free Newreels, Italy), 368–369, 379, 383
Cinegiornali Liberi del Proletariato (Free Proletarian Newsreels), 369
Cinema Novo (Brazilian New Wave), 2, 5, 11, 18, 30, 33, 37
Cinema Novo (Portuguese New Wave), 7, 11, 13, 61–75, 406
cinéma vérité, 15, 84, 85, 86, 99, 100, 158, 178, 248, 249, 254, 258, 326
Civil Rights Movement, 26
Clark, Larry, 275, 282–283, 288
Clarke, Shirley, 248–260, 264, 265, 268, 269, 271
class, 10, 11, 18, 23, 33, 34, 39, 40, 44, 49, 62, 64, 65, 70, 84, 91, 120, 138, 146, 190, 200, 202, 211, 219, 221–225, 238, 245, 262, 274, 277, 279–281, 289–309, 324, 330, 334–335, 339, 345–362, 363–384, 407
close-up, 48, 104, 108, 127, 158, 159, 187, 260, 301, 337, 370, 392
Cold War, 6, 7, 78, 98, 176–177, 330, 331, 332, 342, 359–360, 361
Colectivo de Cine de Clase (CCC, Class Cinema Collective, Spain), 363–384
collective, 3, 5, 11, 13, 14, 16, 20, 32, 33, 34, 35, 37, 39, 47, 51, 52, 69, 96, 105, 107, 119–143, 145–164, 169, 179, 181, 188, 189, 199–215, 219–240, 243, 244, 250, 251, 255, 256, 257, 262, 273–275, 279, 280, 297, 300, 363–384, 395, 398, 405
Collettivo Cinema Militante (CCMT, Militant Cinema Collective, Turin), 140, 370, 380, 381
colonialism, 8, 9, 13, 24, 25, 27, 28–30, 33, 40, 41, 49, 63, 64, 70, 72, 74, 125, 171, 177, 187, 195, 278, 330, 333, 336, 342, 346; internal, 26, 146
Columbia Revolt (New York Newsreel), 13, 33, 145–155, 158, 179, 257
comedy, 45, 63–67, 70
common(s), 145, 147, 151, 152, 160, 161, 163
commune, 153, 208
communism, 24, 55, 80, 82–83, 87, 91, 238, 268, 293, 296, 330, 336, 337, 351, 365, 371
Communist Party. *See communist party*

for specific country
Communist Party of Argentina, 120, 138
Communist Party of India (CPI), 294, 296
Congo, Republic of, 100–101, 112, 187
control, societies of, 183–197
coproductions, 87, 93, 199
countercinema, 6, 15, 220, 223–224, 237, 275, 283, 385, 386, 391, 397–400
counterinformation, 132–133
Cow (Mehrjui), 386, 394–397
Cuba, 8, 10, 26, 34, 36, 40, 41, 93, 124, 139, 140, 235
Cuban Institute of Cinematic Art and Industry (ICAIC), 124, 140
Cuban Revolution, 37, 38, 119, 125
Cultural Revolution, China, 14, 16, 156, 200, 234, 238, 240, 329, 334, 345–362, 405
Czechoslovak New Wave, 2, 11, 13, 17, 18, 77–94, 406

Dadaism, 35, 87, 93, 94, 120, 122, 137
Daisies (Chytilová), 77–94
Death by Hanging (Oshima), 14, 165–182
Debord, Guy, 31, 250, 251, 292
Deleuze, Gilles, 188–189, 193, 195, 196, 344
Deren, Maya, 254, 259, 263
deutsche film- und fernsehakademie berlin (dffb), German Film and Television Academy Berlin, 13, 95–116
dialectics, 2, 15, 18, 35, 36 40, 41, 82, 126, 130, 131, 155, 202, 211, 220, 224, 233, 234, 247, 254, 266, 270, 287, 298, 306, 307, 335, 339, 344, 352, 358, 377, 392, 407
dialogue, 48, 50, 71, 84, 85, 86, 103, 184, 205, 221, 223, 365, 366
diaspora (diasporic cinema, diasporic filmmakers), 5, 27, 180, 181, 279
dictatorship, 7, 8, 11–12, 26, 32, 33, 36, 39, 54, 65, 98, 119, 124, 128, 132, 133, 138, 139, 140, 234, 352, 363, 364, 376, 400, 401
didactic, 121, 140, 142, 194, 212, 219, 225, 228, 239, 319, 363, 394, 400
direct cinema, 15, 99, 311–327, 369
direct democracy, 371
documentary, 2, 9, 15, 17, 19, 20, 29, 33, 37, 43, 59, 65, 71, 79, 80, 84, 85, 86, 91, 96, 103, 129–130, 135, 140, 143, 145–164, 168, 171, 175, 229, 235, 239–240, 241–271, 284, 311–327, 380, 383, 386, 390–394, 405, 407
Drew, Robert, 99, 311
Dziga Vertov Group (DVG, Groupe Dziga Vertov), 8, 14, 219–240, 275

---

eastern Europe, 24, 77–94, 98, 227, 348, 406
Egypt, 100, 108, 145, 388
Eisenstein, Sergei, 8, 35, 36, 52, 84, 99–100, 108, 130–131, 135, 235
El Volti (Spanish communist distribution company), 369, 379, 381
England, 34, 101, 184–189, 264, 269
Entranced Earth/Terra em Transe

(Glauber Rocha), 7–8, 33, 38
environment, 157, 194
essay film, 11, 121, 124, 126, 127, 147, 160, 407
Esteban, Manuel, 371, 379, 381, 382
ethnic studies (establishment of Departments of, at San Francisco State, Cornell), 151
European art cinema, 213, 243, 252, 275, 308
Everybody or Nobody (Lumbreras), 363–384
Everything's Fine (Godard-Gorin), 231
experimental cinema, 15, 35, 87, 92, 123, 128, 133, 137, 170, 183, 184, 193, 234, 243–271, 381, 386, 390, 398, 399
extraterritorial space, 329–344
extreme close-up, 189, 202

---

factory films, 11, 16, 32, 71, 84, 85, 146, 190–191, 193, 236, 363–384
FAMU (Filmová a televizní fakulta, Akademie múzických umění; Film and TV School of the Academy of Performing Arts in Prague also referred to as the Prague Film School), 77–94
Fanon, Frantz, 25, 27–30, 38, 41, 56, 59, 119, 121, 123, 125, 126, 128, 139, 199, 255, 279, 292, 302, 303, 309
Far from Vietnam (Ivens, et al.), 11, 31, 214
farmers, 28, 65, 156–159, 168, 169, 180, 181, 228, 231, 387, 396, 399
Farocki, Harun, 96–116, 234, 366, 378, 382
Farrokhzad, Forough, 386, 390, 391, 394, 397–400, 402, 403
Fellini, Federico, 79, 84, 365
feminism, 3, 4, 13, 15, 17, 19, 23, 28, 111, 225, 241–271, 374, 392–393, 397–400, 401
feminist filmmaking, 4, 13, 15, 17, 19, 86, 92, 94, 97–98, 111, 114, 241–271, 316, 363–384, 392–393, 397–400, 403
Film Comment, 88, 180, 181, 238, 326
Film Culture, 246, 259, 264–265, 268, 269, 271
film distribution, 8, 9, 39, 79, 87, 92, 146, 154, 155, 175, 224, 241–271, 275, 365, 369
film farsi (Persian language film), 388–389, 399, 401
film festivals, 3, 4, 9, 62, 78, 86, 92, 95, 99, 122, 174, 241–271, 275, 345, 346, 365, 385, 399. *See also* Cannes
film journals, 241–271. *See also* Cahiers du Cinéma, Cineaste, Film Comment, Film Culture, Film Quarterly, Jump Cut
Filmmaker's Coop, 243
Film Quarterly, 40, 41, 56, 88–89, 138, 143, 161, 163, 180, 181, 265, 267, 268, 269, 270, 271, 380, 383, 405, 406, 408
film schools. *See specific film school*
Firestone, Shulamith, 254, 255, 258, 266, 270
First World, 6, 7, 9, 15, 25, 26, 27, 30, 37, 140, 274, 276, 277, 286, 330, 348,

349, 351
Fofi, Goffredo, 370
"For an Imperfect Cinema" (Espinosa), 8–9, 19
Forest of Pressure (Ogawa Pro), 154–164
Foucault, Michel, 188, 239, 314, 400
found footage, 31, 104, 105, 242, 284
France, 1–3, 9–11, 23–42, 45, 47, 62, 63, 64, 67, 70, 88, 93, 98, 101, 119, 135, 155, 168, 169, 199–215, 219, 221, 228, 229, 234, 236, 239, 246, 264, 292, 348, 351, 380
Franco, Francisco, 7, 8, 11, 16, 363, 364, 365, 366, 367, 373, 407
Free Speech Movement, 149, 150
freeze frame, 230, 283, 305
Freire, Paulo, 28, 40, 41
French Communist Party (Parti communiste français, PCF), 23, 222, 236, 237, 347, 379
French Maoism, 228, 231, 348, 359, 361
French Marxist-Leninist Communist Party (Parti communiste marxist-léniniste français, PCMLF), 239
French New Wave, 2, 5, 9, 10, 11, 12, 13, 14, 17, 30, 61–70, 74, 75, 77, 85, 97, 107, 108, 220, 324
Fuses (Schneemann), 260, 264, 268

gangster film, 266
García Espinosa, Julio, 8–9, 19, 38
gender, 28, 34, 150–151, 157, 224, 308, 363–384, 399
genre, 5, 55, 129, 132, 193, 201, 245, 253, 266, 354, 357, 374, 405, 407. *See also* anthology, comedy, documentary, essay, gangster, melodrama, opera film, spaghetti western, testimonial
Gerima, Haile, 273–288
German Film and Television Academy Berlin (deutsche film- und fernsehakademie berlin, dffb), 13, 95–116
Germany, 7, 13, 19, 30, 36, 86, 95–116, 212, 215, 360, 362, 408
Getino, Octavio, 6, 8, 9, 13, 36, 37, 38, 41, 98, 117–143, 154, 155, 162, 164, 275, 278, 283, 287, 391, 394
Gimme Shelter (Maysles Films), 311, 318, 319, 321, 324
Global North. *See* First World
Global South. *See* Third World
Godard, Jean-Luc, 2, 8, 14, 17, 18, 24, 31, 32, 35, 36, 62, 79, 84, 89, 90, 93, 108, 130, 135, 172, 199–215, 219–240, 257, 258, 263, 287, 292, 315, 321, 324, 351, 381, 382, 407
Golestan, Ebrahim, 389–391, 393, 397, 398, 401
Gorin, Jean-Pierre, 8, 14–15, 56, 219–240, 407
Gramsci, Antonio, 138, 359, 361
Great Britain, 166, 330, 332, 333
The Green Years (Paulo Rocha), 13, 61–75
Gregoretti, Ugo, 369, 370, 375
Grey Gardens (Maysles Films), 311–327
Groupe Medvedkine, 219, 235
Grupo Cine Liberación (Liberation Cinema Group), 98, 117–143
Grupo de Madrid (GM), 367, 372
Guerra, Ruy, 36, 166

Guevara, Ernesto "Che," 25, 120, 124, 125, 128, 200, 253, 292, 296
Guinea-Bissau, 27
Gutiérrez Alea, Tomás, 35–36, 40, 41

---

hand-held camera, 29, 104, 105, 159, 257, 322
happening, 13, 52, 86, 107–108, 117–143, 246, 247, 253, 262
Haskell, Molly, 243, 263
Hirsch, Storm de, 259, 268, 269
Hirzman, Leon, 35
Holland, Agnieszka, 80
Hollywood (First Cinema), 36, 37, 39, 78, 108, 128, 165, 235, 237, 243, 244, 252, 254, 255, 264, 265, 266, 267, 269, 271, 278, 281, 283, 313, 318, 325, 341, 343, 355, 388, 405
Hong Kong, 14, 15–16, 329–344, 345
Hong Kong cinema, 329–344
horizontality, 372–376
Hour of the Furnaces (Solanas and Getino), 8, 13, 117–143, 391
House Is Black (Farrokhzad), 390, 398–399, 402, 403
Hungarian uprising, 23
Hungary, 10, 100

I Am Curious (Yellow) (Sjöman), 116
IDHEC (Institute des hautes études cinématographies, Institute for Advanced CinematographicStudies), 13, 61, 62, 79, 98
If...(Anderson), 14, 90, 183–197
Il Manifesto group (Italy), 365
imperialism, 8, 9, 26, 27, 33, 70, 72, 101, 126, 146, 149, 156, 157, 162, 163, 177, 188, 190, 195, 257, 258, 260, 277, 280, 286, 346, 348, 400
independence struggles, 7, 28
India, 31, 36, 97, 101, 145, 332
Indian Parallel Cinema, 11, 31, 289–309
indigenous, 8, 26, 27, 57, 59, 256, 276
individualism (bourgeois), 202, 297
Institute des hautes études cinématographies (IDHEC, Institute for Advanced Cinematographic Studies). *See* IDHEC
Institute for Film Research and Experiences (Madrid), 365
inter-titles, 32, 103, 232
Iran, 16, 98, 100–102, 113, 385–403
Iranian New Wave, 6, 11, 14, 16–17, 385–403
Italian Communist Party (Partito Comunista Italiano, PCI), 59, 235, 236, 365, 369
Italian Neorealism. *See* Neorealism (Italian)
Italy, 16, 31, 32, 34, 44, 45, 55, 63, 86, 88, 118, 123, 138, 140, 147, 183–197, 199–215, 228, 229, 235, 363–384, 407, 408
Ivens, Joris, 11, 32, 135, 229–230, 239–240

Japan, 6, 10, 13–14, 23, 62, 69, 145–164, 165–182, 330, 331, 332, 333, 340, 342, 350, 405
Japanese Communist Party, 154
Japanese New Wave, 6, 11, 24, 62, 145–164, 165–182

Japanese Red Army, 175
Jeanette Rankin Brigade (Newsreel), 252
Jeanne Dielman, 23 quai du Commerce, 1080 Bruxelles (Akerman), 263
Jeiso Collective, 13, 154–164. *See also* Ogawa Pro
La Jetée (Marker), 99, 171
Le Joli Moi de Mai (Marker), 32
Jordá, Joaquín, 376–377, 380, 383
jump cut, 11, 105, 108, 220, 304, 305
Jump Cut (journal), 18, 19, 34, 114, 236, 240

Kiarostami, Abbas, 387, 388
King, Martin Luther, Jr., 25, 26, 149, 242
Kipling, Rudyard, 187
Klein, William, 32
Kluge, Alexander, 36, 212, 215
Knaudt, Ulrich, 95–116
Korea, 7, 14, 165–182, 350
Kristeva, Julia, 214
Kuomintang (KMT or Nationalist Party), 331, 332, 335

L.A. Rebellion, 8, 11, 15, 19, 273–288, 406
Lacan, Jacques, 166, 199, 204, 205, 208, 211, 214, 215, 243, 331
Laos, 229–230
Larkin, Alile Sharon, 273–288
Leacock, Richard, 99, 311
Leipzig Film Festival, 365
leitmotif, 191–192
Lelouche, Claude, 32
Lenin (also Leninism or Leninist), 195, 196, 221–222, 239, 352
Linares, Andrés, 375, 381, 383
Lisa, Mariano, 363, 366, 367, 368, 370, 371, 372, 373, 378, 383
Living Theater, The, 199–215
Lizzani, Carlo, 14, 199–215
Loach, Ken, 90
long lenses, 29, 367
long shot, 105, 392, 399
long take, 11, 172, 203, 221
Losey, Joseph, 35, 36
Love and Anger (Lizzani, Bertolucci, Pasolini, Godard, Bellocchio), 14, 199–215
Loy, Nanni, 365
Lumbreras, Helena, 16, 363–384
Lumumba, Patrice, 25, 100, 101, 112

Makavejev, Dušan, 36, 166
Malcolm X, 25
Mandarin (and Mandarin cinema), 335, 337, 338, 339, 340, 341
Mangini, Sandra, 365
manifestos, 10–11, 28, 30, 35, 38, 44, 95, 110, 117, 132, 142, 213, 249, 254, 255, 266, 269, 365
Maoism, 14–15, 24, 32, 34, 219–240, 292, 293, 309, 345–362, 375
Marcuse, Herbert, 292, 306
Marighela, Carlos, 32
Marker, Chris, 2, 11, 18, 20, 32, 35, 99, 117, 171, 219, 235, 380, 383
Marxism, 3, 12, 23, 34, 82, 133, 135, 157, 161, 163, 199, 224, 225, 234, 237, 261, 289, 291, 292, 299, 314, 315, 321, 323, 324, 326, 329, 331, 348, 353, 355, 400

Marxism-Leninism, 5, 24, 220, 224, 225, 228, 230, 243, 294
Masculin féminin (Godard), 24, 172, 220
masculinity, 183–190, 192, 195, 243, 246, 255, 257, 299
mass media, 24, 29, 132–133, 183–195, 317, 321, 324
May '68, 2, 3, 10, 15, 17, 19, 23–43, 47, 48, 60, 119, 135, 178, 185, 214, 220–240, 264, 270, 345, 347, 379, 380, 383, 407
Maysles Films, 14, 15, 99, 311–327
Medium Cool (Wexler), 32–33, 243, 256, 258, 262, 265, 270
Meet Marlon Brando (Maysles Films), 311, 317–318, 321, 324
Mehrjui, Dariush, 386, 394–397, 402
Mekas, Jonas, 99, 241–271
melodrama, 193, 345
Mencken, Marie, 244, 259, 261
Metcalfe, Jr., Ralph, 150
Mexico, 24, 30, 98, 145, 147, 228, 242
militant cinema, 5, 7, 14, 15, 16, 117–143, 145–164, 363–384, 391
"Militant Cinema: An Internal Category of Third Cinema," 117, 127, 391
militarism, 24, 26, 33, 70, 156, 167, 175
Ministry of Culture and Arts (MCA, Iran), 388, 390, 391, 392
Mirzoeff, Nicholas, 367, 379, 383
mise-en-scène, 294, 337, 358, 359, 361, 375
misogyny, 150–151, 157–158, 186–187, 200, 202, 204, 206, 225–227, 257, 262
Missa Luba, 186–187
modernism, 1, 2, 3, 4, 17, 18, 34–35, 69, 134, 241, 286, 291, 292, 295, 306, 307, 308, 314, 315, 321, 323, 324, 326, 341, 401, 407, 408
montage, 35, 37, 48, 85, 87, 97, 105, 107, 129–130, 131, 132, 134, 140, 212, 233, 390
Morricone, Ennio, 12, 43–60, 192
Mossadegh, Mohammad, 113, 387
Mozambique, 27, 74
music, 12, 14, 19, 37, 43–60, 87, 88, 131, 148, 176, 183–197, 317, 323, 356, 360, 362, 390, 405

Nabili, Marva, 386, 397, 399–400
narrative (e.g., classical, continuity), 3, 9, 10, 14, 15, 17, 34, 39, 48, 49, 57, 60, 61, 62, 84, 86, 87, 89, 91, 100, 101, 108, 129, 175, 184, 185, 188, 189, 192, 194, 195, 200, 223, 224, 227, 229, 232, 233, 237, 241, 243, 248, 257, 263, 267, 274, 276, 279, 281, 283–285, 291, 294, 295, 305, 306, 313, 315, 318, 337, 346, 350, 351, 357, 358, 372, 388, 389, 392, 396, 399, 403, 407
National Iranian Radio and Television (NIRT), 390, 399
Naxalism, 289–309
Nehru, Jawaharlal, 289, 290, 293
Nelson, Gunvor, 243, 244, 259–260, 264, 268, 271
neocolonialism, 26, 27, 28, 39, 119, 125, 126, 136, 278
neoliberalism, 231, 234, 364
Neorealism (Italian), 5, 9, 11, 12, 30, 36, 37, 38, 54, 63, 84, 97, 100, 129, 199,

275, 369, 386
New American Cinema, 31, 100, 241–271
New German Cinema, 30, 95, 96, 111
New Hollywood, 244, 325
New Indian Cinema, 31
New Left, 23, 101, 112, 145–164, 236, 243, 244, 253, 261, 262, 266, 267, 405
Newsreel(s), 9, 13, 33, 145–164, 170, 200, 210, 243, 244, 252, 255–258, 266, 390, 391
Nicolas, Bernard, 273–288
Nigeria, 145
Night It Rained . . . or the Epic of a Gorgan Village Boy (Shirdel), 391
Nkrumah, Kwame, 25, 112
Non-Aligned Movement, 8, 88
nonprofessional actors, 9, 11, 62, 84, 86

---

occupations (e.g., of factories), 29, 145–164, 169, 364, 366, 367, 369
offscreen space, 85, 108–109, 115, 249
Ogawa Pro, 13, 146, 154–164
On the Docks (Xie Tieli and Xie Jin), 16, 345–362
opera film, 345–362
Oshima, Nagisa, 14, 36, 165–182
OSPAAAL (Organization of Solidarity of the People of Asia, Africa and Latin America), 8, 139

Pahlavi, Mohammad Reza Shah, 16, 101, 385–389, 391, 392, 395, 396, 397, 400, 401
pan-Africanism, 280
Parallel Cinema (India), 11, 289
Pasolini, Pier Paolo, 14, 43, 52, 183–197, 199–215, 391
patriarchy, 371, 373
Pennebaker, D. A., 99, 311, 321, 325
The People and Their Guns (Ivens), 229–230
phonograph, 57, 60, 183–197
photography, 32, 68, 102, 106, 132, 134, 137, 141, 171, 175–176, 200, 245, 248–249, 260–261, 264, 265, 269, 272, 281, 317, 393
Phrase-Image, 230, 232, 233, 234
Pierrot le fou (Godard), 172
police violence, 9, 33, 159, 281, 282, 293, 334, 367
political cinema, 1, 2, 5, 6, 7, 8, 9, 10, 11, 12, 15, 16, 18, 43, 96, 106, 107, 110, 129, 137, 194, 200, 219, 221, 231, 234, 386, 389, 390, 395, 400, 406, 407, 408
Pontecorvo, Gillo, 7, 9, 12, 28, 29, 43–60, 251, 255, 365
Portugal, 7, 8, 11, 13, 61–75
Portuguese Cinema Novo. *See* Cinema Novo (Portugal)
poverty, 33, 67, 71, 129, 130, 171, 392
Prague Spring, 24, 78, 81, 89, 91, 242
prisons, 24, 63, 69, 137, 138, 172, 173, 175, 176, 177, 238, 258, 279, 283–285, 367, 392
"Problems of Form and Content in Revolutionary Cinema" (Sanjinés), 8, 19
Protti, Daniele, 368, 379, 383
psychoanalytic theory, 3, 12, 166, 203, 213, 243, 331

public and private spheres, 5, 192, 212, 215, 243, 246–247, 241–271, 335, 398
Puerto Rican rights, 152

Qing, Jiang, 346, 353

---

racism, 24, 26, 27, 28, 33, 57, 145–154, 170–178, 277, 281, 330
Ray, Satyajit, 7, 14, 15, 289–309
realism, 1, 2, 4, 5, 15, 16, 18, 19, 84, 85, 86, 87–88, 90, 130, 155, 166, 175, 183, 184, 196, 197, 290, 311, 312, 313, 321, 322, 324, 325, 326, 338, 346, 354, 355, 357, 358, 375, 389, 394, 408
reenactment, 9, 374, 375
refusal, 23, 51, 90, 207, 214, 262, 280, 283, 293, 296, 297, 298, 312, 320, 370, 374, 376, 403, 407
Resnais, Alain, 32, 36, 73, 79, 84, 130, 135
Rich, Adrienne, 261, 263, 268
Rivera, Lluís, 378
Rocha, Glauber, 7–8, 28, 33, 35, 36, 38, 39, 40, 41, 84, 135, 166
Rocha, Paulo, 13, 61–75
Ross, Kristin, 10, 19, 47, 57, 60, 147, 161, 163–164, 235, 363, 366, 368, 379, 380, 383

---

sabotage, 349–350, 378
Sa'edi, Gholam-Hossein, 396
Said, Edward, 50, 314, 323, 324, 325, 326, 327
Salazar, António, 7, 8, 11, 13, 61, 63, 64, 65, 66, 72
Sales, Bill, 150
Salesman (Maysles Films), 311, 318, 319, 321, 324, 325, 408
Sander, Helke, 95–116
San Francisco State on Strike (San Francisco Newsreel), 151
Sanjiné, Jorge, 8, 19
Sao Tomé, 27
Sartre, Jean-Paul, 25, 40, 41, 82, 117, 121–122, 230, 239
Schmeerguntz (Nelson and Wiley), 243, 251, 259, 260–261, 264, 268, 269
Schneemann, Carolee, 244, 246–247, 258, 259, 260, 261, 264, 265, 268, 270, 271
Sealed Soil (Nabili), 399, 403
Second World, 7
self-liberation wars, 1, 28, 61, 63, 97, 101, 106, 139
self-management, 221, 230, 364
self-reflexivity, 16, 219, 230, 286, 313, 315, 317, 318, 319, 325, 345, 347, 354, 355
semiotics, 3, 12, 243
Sen, Mrinal, 36, 289
Senghor, Léopold Sédar, 25, 40, 41
separation of labor (e.g., manual and intellectual), 146, 157–158, 184, 195, 231, 374
sexuality, 34, 64, 183, 186, 187, 189, 191, 204, 245, 260, 262, 392–393, 408
Shanghai cinema (1930s), 335, 337, 338, 339, 341
Shinsuke, Ogawa, 154, 162, 163
Shirdel, Kamran, 386, 391–394

Singapore, 342
Sino-Japanese War, 332
Sino-Soviet split, 220, 227–228, 238, 348, 355
Situationist International, 28, 31, 211
SLON (Société pour le lancement des oeuvres nouvelles, Society for the Creation of New Works), 11, 32, 219
Slovak cinema, 77–94, 406
socialism, 24, 81, 87, 126, 139, 141, 221, 278, 290, 291, 331, 350, 355
socialist realism, 17, 38, 80, 85, 195, 356, 357
social reproduction, 374
Société pour le lancement des oeuvres nouvelles (Society for the Creation of New Works). *See* SLON
Solanas, Fernando, 6, 8, 9, 13, 36, 37, 38, 41, 98, 117–143, 154, 155, 162, 164, 275, 278, 283, 287, 391, 394
Solanas, Valeria, 249
Soler, Llorenç, 365, 366, 369, 378, 379, 380, 382, 383
Solinas, Franco, 29, 46, 47, 48, 54, 55, 56, 59, 60, 365, 367
sound, 12–13, 14, 32, 43–60, 88, 103, 104, 105, 130, 131, 148, 153, 156, 158, 170, 183–195, 202, 208, 220, 221, 225, 228, 229, 230, 238, 241, 282, 287, 317, 322, 339, 342, 356, 392, 398
South Africa, 45, 47, 48, 49, 98, 407
Soviet cinema, 37, 84, 100, 117, 233
Soviet Communist Party, 23, 81, 238
Soviet Union, 7, 13, 23, 35, 98, 100, 117, 220, 228, 260, 347, 348
spaghetti western, 44–60, 221, 266
Spain, 7, 8, 9, 11, 14, 16, 124, 126, 140, 228, 363–384, 407
Spanish Communist Party, 371, 372
spectacle, 31, 37, 39, 122, 128, 194, 207, 211, 242, 250, 251, 388, 399
Stalinism, 23, 24, 78, 80, 81, 226–234
Stark, Trevor, 235, 370, 380, 383
Strand, Chick, 264, 268, 270
strikes, 8, 10, 11, 20, 33, 48, 99, 130, 151, 153, 169, 221, 229, 235, 329, 334, 364, 366, 367, 372, 374, 375
student activism, 3, 13, 24, 33
Student Afro-American Society (SAS), 149–150
super 8 mm, 372
surrealism, 14, 18, 24, 34, 35, 36, 38, 93, 99, 118, 175
surveillance, 206, 207, 250, 284, 367

Taiwan, 6, 10, 19, 337, 342
technology, 191, 192, 194, 202, 206, 347, 355, 386, 402
television, 103, 114, 168, 170, 171, 185, 189, 202, 244, 245, 256, 257, 262, 317, 342, 365, 369, 379, 384, 390
Teorema (Pasolini), 14, 183, 184, 190–195, 196, 197
Tercer Cine (Argentina), 31, 41, 117–143
testimonial, 125, 129, 132, 134
Thailand, 24, 145
theater, 16, 28, 35, 36, 37, 80, 93, 99, 122, 170, 178, 208, 250, 262
Third Cinema, 2, 6, 8, 9, 12, 15, 18, 37, 41, 117–143, 154, 155, 162, 164, 221, 273–288, 292, 378, 382–383, 391, 394, 401–402

Third World, 6, 8, 9, 11, 12, 16, 19, 24, 25, 26, 27, 28, 30, 36, 37, 38, 101, 111, 113, 117–143, 126, 131, 133, 221, 256, 266, 271, 273–278, 281, 287, 288, 291, 292, 307, 346–348, 354, 360, 362
Third World Newsreel, 151, 243
Three Resurrected Drunkards (Oshima Nagisa), 14, 165–182
Toshio, Matsumoto, 155–156
Touré, Sékou, 25
"Towards a Third Cinema" (Solanas and Getino), 6, 8, 9, 41, 121, 123, 127, 137, 138, 143, 154, 155, 162, 164, 278, 283, 287, 394
tracking shot, 11, 104, 189, 231, 234, 285
Tricontinental, 8, 10, 26, 30, 37, 41, 125, 137, 139, 140, 143, 292
Tronti, Mario, 147, 161
Truffaut, 2, 31, 63, 73, 89, 108, 252, 408
Tucumán arde (exhibition), 117–143
Turkey, 145

---

unions, 9, 81, 101, 133, 136–137, 167, 221–223, 225–226, 236, 237, 302, 332, 334, 343, 364, 367, 373
United Kingdom, 56, 80, 88, 90, 93, 103, 184–189
United States, 1, 4, 7, 9, 23–42, 88, 91, 92, 98, 101, 103, 125, 135, 136, 145, 146, 149, 151, 154, 155, 159, 160, 161, 165, 167, 168, 169, 180, 181, 229, 239, 241–271, 275, 277, 278, 282, 283, 312, 316, 318, 332, 333, 342, 346, 399
Unitelefilm (production and distribution company of the Italian CP), 365
Untimely Happening ("El Happening inoportuno," Argentina), 117–143
urban/rural binary, 64–66, 68–69

Vallejo, Gerardo, 98, 117–143
Varda, Agnès, 32, 257, 264
Vertov, Dziga, 8, 35, 40, 41, 99–100, 108, 135, 235
VGIK (Vsesoyuznyi gosudarstvennyi institut kinematografii, All-Union State Cinema Institute in Moscow), 79, 98
Vietnam War, 1, 7, 24, 25, 26, 33, 39, 70, 101, 105, 106, 107, 118, 149, 156, 159, 168, 169, 175–176, 200, 241–271, 282, 283, 292
voice-over narration, 29, 32, 104, 148, 158, 171, 220, 221, 224, 227, 230, 236, 372, 392, 393, 398
Vsesoyuznyi gosudarstvennyi institut kinematografii (All-Union State Cinema Institute in Moscow). *See* VGIK

Warsaw Pact, Soviet invasion of Czechoslovakia, 78, 89
Watts Rebellion, 276, 282
Weekend (Godard), 32
western, 44–60, 221, 266, 283
West Germany, 13, 24, 86, 95–116, 212, 360, 362
Wexler, Haskell, 32–33, 35, 36, 256–257
What's Happening? The Beatles in the USA (Maysles Films), 311, 316–317, 324

white supremacy, 25, 26, 149
Wiley, Dorothy, 243, 259–260, 261, 264, 268, 271
Wilson, Cicero, 150
Wilson, Harold, 185
Wind from the East (Godard-Gorin), 14, 219–240, 359, 362
Winter Soldier (De Antonio), 33
The Woman's Film (San Francisco Newsreel), 244
Women Make Movies, 243
Women's Quarter (or *Fortress: The Red Light District*, Shirdel), 392–394
workers, 3, 5, 9, 10, 11, 13, 14, 16, 23, 31, 32, 33, 48, 65, 71, 81, 84, 85, 91, 120, 133–134, 141, 146, 151, 161, 166, 168, 190–191, 193, 221–240, 289–309, 329, 331, 332, 334, 336, 339, 349, 350, 355, 356, 358, 363–384, 392–394

Young Lords, 26
Yugoslavia, 10, 98, 221, 230
Yugoslav School (of filmmaking), 80

Zavattini, Cesare, 36, 368–369, 370, 375, 379, 380, 383
Zengakuren, 156, 167–168
Zenkyōtō, 169
Zhou Enlai, 329, 334
zoom, 29, 104, 127, 370
Zwerin, Charlotte, 318

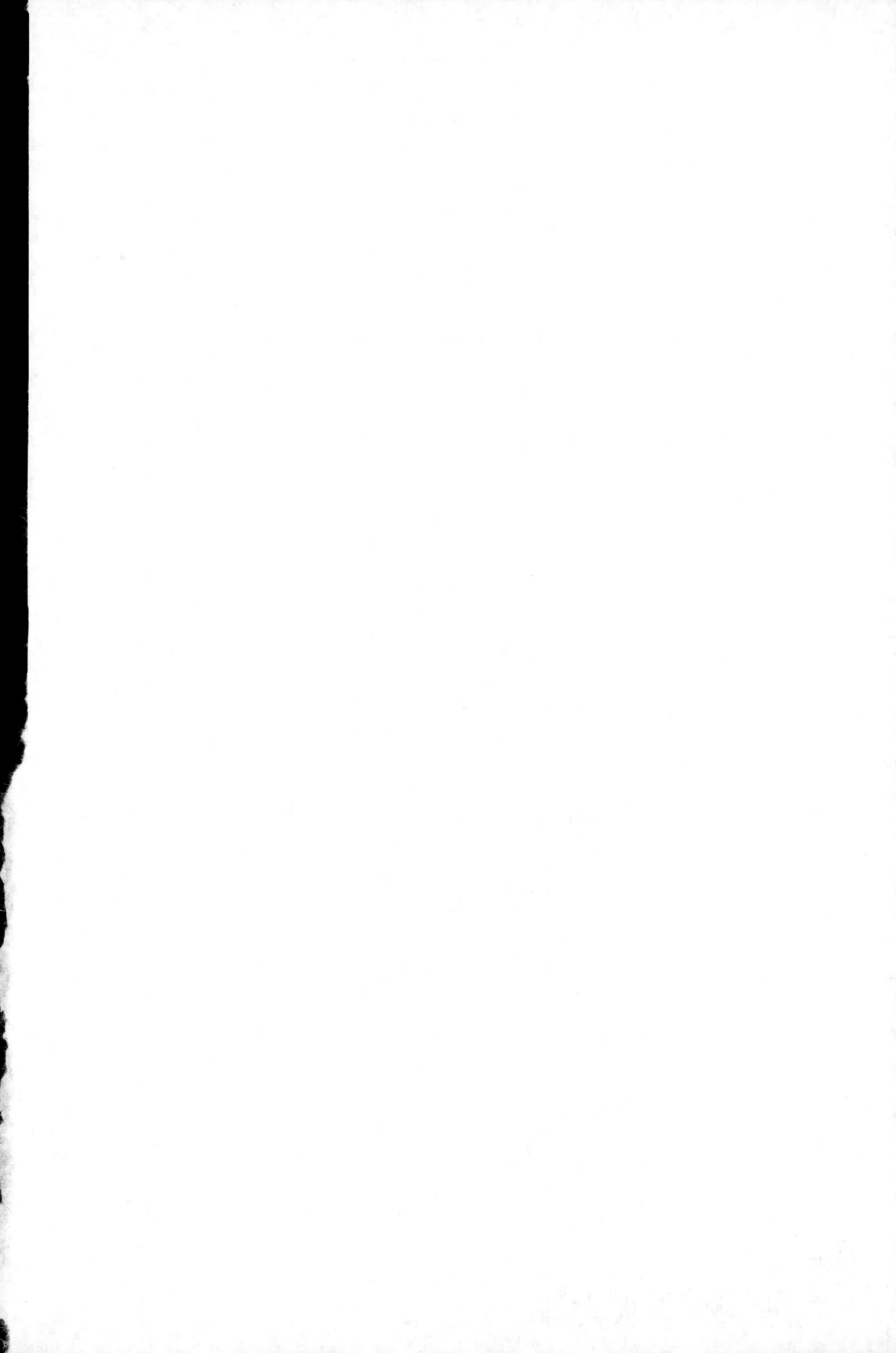

www.ingramcontent.com/pod-product-compliance
Lightning Source LLC
LaVergne TN
LVHW020430080826
844660LV00034B/1379

* 9 7 8 0 8 1 4 3 4 2 9 3 0 *